Protestant Missionaries and Humanitarianism in the DRC

Protestant Missionaries and Humanitarianism in the DRC

The Politics of Aid in Cold War Africa

Jeremy Rich

JAMES CURREY

James Currey
is an imprint of Boydell & Brewer Ltd
PO Box 9, Woodbridge
Suffolk IP12 3DF (GB)
www.jamescurrey.com
and of
Boydell & Brewer Inc.
668 Mt Hope Avenue
Rochester, NY 14620-2731 (US)
www.boydellandbrewer.com

British Library Cataloguing in Publication Data
A catalogue record for this book is available from the British Library

ISBN 978-1-84701-258-6 (James Currey cloth)

This publication is printed on acid-free paper

Printed and bound in Great Britain by
TJ International Ltd, Padstow, Cornwall

Contents

Illustrations

Map

Photographs

Acknowledgements

I struggled for nearly a decade to write a book about Protestant aid workers in the Congo. Such work incurs a great deal of intellectual debts. First, I sincerely wish to thank the former Congo Protestant Relief Agency volunteers who spoke with me about their experiences. Many times, I called them out of nowhere, just hoping they would not mistake me for some wayward telemarketer. Their generosity will forever rest in my heart. Family members of deceased CPRA members spent time looking through old letters and stirring up memories a half century old. I hope this book will honour the work of their loved ones who have passed away.

Without the patience and support of archivists, this book never would have been written. I sincerely thank the archivists who assisted me. In the United States, the personnel of the following archives helped: the Presbyterian Historical Society in Philadelphia, the Disciples of Christ Historical Society (now in Bethany, West Virginia), the United Nations Archives in New York, the National Archives and Records Administration in College Park (Maryland), the Mennonite Central Committee in Akron (Pennsylvania), the Mennonite Church USA (now Goshen, Indiana), and the American Baptist Historical Society (Atlanta, Georgia). A generous research grant from the Association for the Study of the Middle East and Africa in 2017 allowed me to consult three archives in Geneva, the humanitarian capital of the world. I extend my gratitude to the archivists at the International Committee of the Red Cross, the World Council of Churches, and the United Nations High Commission for Refugees. I also relied on a number of people to photograph materials. Joshua Hertzler, an undergraduate at Goshen College, photocopied materials at the Mennonite Historical Society. Drexel University student Deniz Ozturk photographed some records at the Presbyterian Historical Society. My former Middle Tennessee State student Rosalie Howell met the love of her life and moved to Peoria, which just happened to be close to materials on Archie Graber I needed for this book. Thank you for photographing holdings at the Congo Inland Mission archives then stored in Metamora, Illinois.

Many colleagues have watched this book slowly form from a vague interest in Protestants in Congo to the finished project. This project began while I taught at Middle Tennessee State University and slowly sputtered along during my years at Marywood University. I acknowledge the financial support I received from Marywood University to conduct research and to attend conferences. My colleagues never failed to at least feign interest in this project. In Murfreesboro, I particularly thank Pippa Holloway, Robert Hunt, Susan Myers-Shirk, David Rowe, and Amy Sayward. My Marywood colleagues past and present who supported this project include Samantha Christiansen, Adam Shprintzen, Alexander Vari, and my former dean Fran Zauhar.

My colleagues in African studies and in history have encouraged the progress of this work. Individual chapters between 2012 and 2017 were presented at the meetings of the African Studies Association, the European Conference on African Studies, the New York African Studies Association, the Association for the Study of the Middle East and Africa, the Study of the History of American Foreign Relations, the Greater New York African History Workshop, and the Refugees in African History workshop held in Burlington, Vermont. Thanks to all the people who shared panels and time with me over the years. The following scholars might well forget the insights they shared with me, but I didn't! Some notable individuals include in no particular order John Cinnamon, Benjamin Lawrance, Marissa Moorman, Michelle Moyd, Meredith Terretta, and Christian Williams. Wendy Urban-Mead deserves some sort of award for hearing about this book for so long. Alas, there is no tangible benefit for such a prize. The growing numbers of scholars of the DRC particularly welcomed me, despite being on unfamiliar territory. Nicole Eggers, Ch.-Didier Gondola, David Gordon, Bob Harms, Nancy Rose Hunt, Emery Kalema, Curtis Keim, Miles Larmer, Gillian Mattisse, Pedro Monaville, Charles Tshimanga, and Tom Turner all deserve thanks for their suggestions at various stages. All mistakes certainly are my own, no matter how long this list of friends may be.

I thank James Currey Publishers for reaching out to me in Basel at the European Conference on African Studies in 2017 to consider publishing this book. I had not planned to shop my manuscript there. Forcing me to put together a prospectus gave me confidence the book could finally be completed. My editor Jaqueline Mitchell and the production staff at Boydell and Brewer have been thoroughly professional in their dealings with me. Mennonite Central Committee archivist Frank Peachey allowed me to use photographs in MCC records for the book. Scholars unfamiliar with the Anabaptist tradition really ought to go to these archives. There is a treasure trove of materials on 20th-century humanitarian history there.

My family is the foundation for all that I do, or so I try to convince others. My wife Chantal put up with an awful lot as this manuscript stumbled along the course of a decade. My children, Beatrice and Lucien, made their way from diapers to middle school in the time it took to finish this manuscript. As Congolese and as Americans, my children's heritage connects to the bond between North America and the Congo that this book examines. Even if my children may ultimately find my writing to be as tedious as I may be in person, I wrote this book for them.

Abbreviations

ABHSA	American Baptist Historical Society Archives
AIMMR	Africa Inter-Mennonite Mission Records
AMBM	American Mennonite Brethren Mission
ANC	Armée National Congolais
APL	Armée Populaire de la Libération
ASSK	Autonomous State of South Kasai
BMS	Baptist Missionary Society
CEDECO	Centre for Community Development
CIM	Congo Inland Mission
CNL	Conseil National de la Libération (popularly known as Simba)
CPC	Congo Protestant Council
CPRA	Congo Protestant Relief Agency
CWS	Church World Service
ECC	Église du Christ au Congo
FNLA	Frente Nacional de Libertação de Angola
HEKS	Hilfswerk der evangelischen Kirchen Schweiz
ICRC	International Committee of the Red Cross
IME	Institut Médical Evangélique
LRCS	League of Red Cross Societies
MCC	Mennonite Central Committee
MCCA	Mennonite Central Committee Archives
OMP	Orie Miller Papers, Mennonite Historical Society
PHS	Presbyterian Historical Society
PVO	private voluntary organisations
SARA	Servigo de Assistencia aos Refugiados de Angola
UCC	United Church of Canada
UCCA	United Church of Canada Archives
UN	United Nations
UNHCR	United Nations High Commission for Refugees

UNHCRA	United Nations High Commission for Refugees Archives
WCC	World Council of Churches
WCCA	World Council of Churches Archives

Introduction

Clashes for power in the Democratic Republic of Congo in the 1960s brought about a humanitarian crisis. Yet in the rich and growing scholarship on the tumultuous path from Congolese independence in 1960 to the early years of Mobutu Sese Seko's dictatorship at the end of the decade, the simple fact that hundreds of thousands of Congolese had to flee from violence is rarely deemed worthy of much attention. The intricate manoeuverings of diplomats, policy makers on rival sides of the Cold War, UN officials, and major Congolese politicians such as Patrice Lumumba and Moise Tshombe have taken centre stage in the historical literature. Likewise, scholars of humanitarian agencies and operations in the Cold War have kept silent about the Congo's civil wars after independence. I challenge this long-standing focus on elite political intrigues by exploring how and why North American and European aid programmes intervened in the DRC. This book rectifies the lack of attention on how the wars of the 1960s impacted on the lives of civilians and how the DRC had again become a site of international humanitarian action.

To begin, this study seeks to unravel this silence about suffering and humanitarianism. Haitian historian Michel-Ralph Trouillot has observed, 'The unearthing of silences, and the historian's subsequent emphasis on the retrospective significance of hitherto neglected events, requires not only extra labor at the archives – but also a project linked to an interpretation.'[1] Certainly, humanitarian responses to political crises in DRC are very well known in other periods, especially the Congo Reform Association's exposés of the rapacious rule of Leopold II in the late nineteeth century and international humanitarian aid for victims of the great Congo wars from 1998 to 2006. International concern about abuses against civilians in both of these eras often depicted most Congolese as passive victims of European imperialism, elite Congolese politicians, and the demands of international capitalism. By contrast, Congolese suffering and humanitarian action in the 1960s offers a new perspective on well-worn stories of international Cold War struggles, the collapse of Belgian colonialism, the martyrdom of Patrice Lumumba, and

---

1 M.-R. Trouillot, *Silencing the Past: Power and the Production of History* (Boston: Beacon Press, 1995), 60.

Mobutu's seizure of power in November 1965. Starvation, a marked decline in public health, and the mass displacement of civilians did not fit with narratives of heroic nation building or Cold War ideological struggles.

This silencing of the Congolese humanitarian crisis after independence stands in contrast to Western press coverage from this period. In early 1961, Western reporters came, briefly, in droves to an unfamiliar location: the ill-fated Autonomous State of South Kasai, a short-lived secessionist government in the Democratic Republic of Congo. Hundreds of thousands of Luba people had fled other parts of the Congo to South Kasai in the face of violence.[2] Congolese politicians encouraged popular resentment of Luba people for their alleged favoured status under Belgian rule. In the northern Kasai and Katanga regions, neighbours of Luba families avenged themselves by razing Luba homes and killing Luba people. Albert Kalonji, an agricultural specialist who had become the leader of the fledgling South Kasai government, called on Luba people to move to South Kasai. Journalists managed to take hundreds of photographs documenting African suffering. Well before better-known African humanitarian emergencies such as the Nigerian Civil War from 1967 to 1970 and the Ethiopian famines of the 1980s, readers throughout the world could see images of malnourished children in South Kasai. Emaciated women begged for help. Starving children barely hung on to life. Such depoliticised objects of pity elicited sympathy, just as international organisations like Oxfam and the World Council of Churches had hoped.

The United Nations launched a fundraising campaign for relieving the South Kasai famine at the end of 1960, in part because its unprecedented civilian and military intervention in the Congo lacked the financial means to obtain supplies. The response from Canada, Western Europe, and the US was astounding. In the small Dutch town of Zaltbommel in late January 1961, people gathered money and 3.5 tons of food 'with the bells of all churches ringing'.[3] Canadians demanded their parliamentary representa-

---

2   The South Kasai humanitarian emergency is discussed at length in chapter 2. For a brief overview of the literature on violence and famine in South Kasai from the 1950s to 1964, see M. Kalanda, *Baluba et Lulua, une ethnie à la recherche d'un nouvel équilibre* (Brussels: Remarques Congolaises, 1959); R. Lemarchand, *Political Awakening in the Congo: The Politics of Fragmentation* (Berkeley: University of California Press, 1964), 206–09; C. Young, *Politics in the Congo* (Princeton: Princeton University Press, 1965), 263–5; M.B. Lushiku Lumana, *Les Baluba du Kasaï et la crise congolaise (1959–1965)* (Lubumbashi: [no publisher], 1985); M.-B. Libata, "Regroupement des Balubas et ses conséquences géopolitiques dans la périphérie de Luluabourg (1891–1960)," *Annales Aequatoria* 8 (1987), 99–129.

3   Survey Relief Work in the Netherlands for Congo, 1 February 1961, Folder Congo 1958–1962, Box 425.3.272, Africa Documents, WCCA.

tives do something for the Luba of the Kasai. Danish and Norwegian church organisations purchased dried fish to send to Mbuji-Mayi (then Bakwanga), the capital of Kalonji's semi-independent regime. This press campaign thus marked the beginning of a long string of marketing campaigns for relieving African pain that have lasted for over half a century. From the vantage point of the early 21st century, it is impossible to miss the continuities between the humanitarian crisis of the Congo in the early 1960s and current perceptions of Congolese people as needy victims of irrational violence. Pictures of suffering Congolese children and women circulated widely during the Congolese civil wars that dragged on from 1996 to 2006, after a long hiatus during most of the authoritarian reign of Mobutu Sese Seko (1965–1997). Scholars such as Claude Kabemba and Cherie Ndiako Rivers have also observed how foreign governments and aid agencies have deployed images of casualties of warfare to present the Congo as a place desperately in need of foreign rescuers up to the present day.[4]

The end of the Cold War helps explain why the DRC's civil wars did not galvanise popular opinion elsewhere after 1989 as had the crises of the 1960s. During the African Cold War of the 1960s, Western attention focused on the future of the Congo as a vital part of the global conflict between Communism and capitalism. The Congo was a testing ground for liberal internationalism and the viability of African governments after the end of colonial rule. It is true that aid agencies and the United Nations continued to provide food and shelter to Congolese internally displaced people and foreign refugees from the early 1990s well into the early 21st century. But, this later humanitarian crisis has not generated the same level of international concern as during the Cold War, particularly in regards to well-publicised aid initiatives. For example, a new revolt against the central government erupted in northern Kasai in 2016. Tens of thousands of people fled and UN officials warned of the threat of starvation, although such news elicited only a feeble response compared with the Western outpouring of aid in 1961.[5]

4   C. Kabemba, "The Democratic Republic of Congo: The Land of Humanitarian Interventions," in B. Everill and J. Kaplan, (eds) *The History and Practice of Humanitarian Intervention and Aid in Africa* (New York: Palgrave Macmillan, 2013), 140–57; C.R. Ndaliko, *Necessary Noise: Music, Film, and Charitable Imperialism in the East of Congo* (New York: Oxford University Press, 2016).

5   J. David, "WFP's Immediate Response Account – Saving Lives in the Kasai Region of DRC," *World Food Program Insight*, 8 March 2018, Available at: insight.wfp.org/wfps-immediate-response-account-saving-lives-in-the-kasai-region-of-drc-b029bd-b4e5af?ga=2.200457256.743967345.1559868501-300330291.1559868501 (Accessed 25 October 2019).

1. CPRA relief project manager Archie Graber on truck carrying food in the Autonomous State of South Kasai, 1961. Graber's Mennonite missionary background allowed him to effectively negotiate with rebel leaders and government officials alike. (MCCA)

While the Western media highlighted secular United Nations relief efforts, journalists generally gave little credit to the Canadian and US Protestants who had led the way in bringing food aid to South Kasai. The United Nations wanted to emphasise what historian Keith David Watenpaugh has described as modern humanitarianism: a 'permanent, transnational, neutral, and secular regime' for addressing the causes of human suffering.[6] Yet a linear evolution from religious to secular humanitarianism is undermined by the 1960s Congolese humanitarian experience, in which secular and religious aid both operated. Archie Graber, an experienced Mennonite missionary, led the first Western programme to furnish humanitarian aid to starving Luba people, beginning in October 1960. Rather than being supplanted by secular technical aid specialists, Graber and other missionaries gave out supplies in the name of their Protestant faith. The Congo Protestant Relief Agency (CPRA), a loosely organised aid programme put together by missionaries and US Protestant organisations such as the Church World Service (CWS), hired Graber

6   K.D. Watenpaugh, *Bread From Stones: The Middle East and the Making of Modern Humanitarianism* (Berkeley: University of California Press, 2015), 5.

to oversee relief in the South Kasai region. It attracted support from North American and European Protestants who felt their efforts were sincere acts of charity unsullied by politics. Yet Graber's trucks carried large amounts of food donated by the US government under its Public Law 480 food programme.

One might well argue a photograph of an elderly white man handing out food to starving children exemplifies practically every cliché of European and North American altruism. Likewise, how surprising is it to learn that a supposedly apolitical humanitarian programme depended on the US government during the Cold War? Yet, it is a colossal error to simply toss aside the CPRA as just another implicitly racist and demeaning example of Western charity working to further US influence in Africa. The humanitarian playing field of the Congo in the 1960s was as chaotic and varied as the local and national conflicts for power in the country. This book is an examination of how the CPRA represented the possibilities of how missionaries and aid workers reimagined relationships between Western countries in a newly decolonised Africa. Even with the ethnocentrism that underlay the work of Archie Graber and other CPRA personnel, Protestant humanitarian aid workers believed sincerely their work could overcome the brutal legacy of colonialism and the damage wrought by Congolese armed conflicts. The CPRA marked an experimental phase in humanitarian aid, in which the boundaries between Congolese and Western aid organisations were fluid.

Graber's work itself demonstrates the improvisational nature of Protestant humanitarian aid in the Congo in the 1960s. While he certainly benefitted from his position as a respected white pastor, he was also a tremendous diplomat. He negotiated with the South Kasai rebel government and the official Congolese government along with the United Nations, Luba displaced people, roving deserters from the Congolese army, the US embassy, and various North American mission boards. The old Belgian colonial order that provided security for missionaries had collapsed in the wake of Congolese independence. Graber's efforts put in him in the firing lines of skirmishes between South Kasai, United Nations peacekeepers, and armed militias hostile to Luba people. To paint him and the CPRA as merely tools of US foreign policy would be to ignore the complexity of humanitarian aid and the volatile political battles in the Congo.

Argument of the book

This book explores the work and organisation of the CPRA, the aid organisation that formed as a result of the choice of British and North American Protestant missionaries to return to the DRC despite the mass evacuations ordered by the US State Department in July 1960. From 1960 until the early 1970s, the CPRA ran relief campaigns to assist Congolese and Angolan refugees, shipped food throughout the DRC, recruited North American medical volunteers to staff Congolese hospitals, and established agricultural development projects. The CPRA worked to try to heal the wounds of independence: abandoned hospitals, people driven from their homes by Congolese civil wars and Portuguese repression, and fields left abandoned after fighting. For all of the courage CPRA volunteers showed in caring for refugees and their patients, the CPRA deserves more than a hagiography, a footnote of benevolence to the grim record of Western efforts to establish a government hostile to Communism and friendly to international capital in the DRC in the 1960s. Instead, this study probes how Protestant aid programmes expose a great deal about the impact of decolonisation and Cold War conflict on both Congolese and North American stakeholders, from bureaucrats in New York City offices to women struggling to survive ruptured placentas in rural Congolese towns.

North American and British Protestants used humanitarian relief to promote a vision of a stable, Christian, anti-Communist Congo and a renewed transnational vision of global Christianity that defied the legacy of colonialism during the onset of African independence. This particular brand of humanitarian action had numerous blind spots. CPRA workers often considered Congolese and foreign refugees first as objects of aid rather than active partners, rarely questioned US foreign policy, and ultimately decided to accept Mobutu's authoritarian regime as preferable to continued civil war or a successful leftist revolution. Protestant humanitarian aid in the Congo served the agenda of the US government. At the same time, the CPRA has its own institutional history in which missionaries, aid workers, and Congolese stakeholders negotiated with each other over setting policy and determining how aid would be provided. Government actors, whether Western or Congolese, were not central to these developments.

The CPRA owed its existence to the rapid internationalisation of Congolese political struggles. The Belgian, US, and Soviet governments along with the massive United Nations presence set off a burst of activity by state and private aid organisations in the first year of Congolese independence. While UN civilian officers delivered logistical and technical aid, private voluntary organisations (PVOs) donated personnel, food supplies, and technical expertise. As Congolese factions and foreign governments vied for power, the DRC government had little ability to control and monitor the activities of PVOs. This situation appears to be significantly different from most other African countries, whose governments were better able to enforce their own authority on foreign aid organisations. The CPRA could insert itself into a range of humanitarian issues involving refugees and health in part because the Congolese government was ill-equipped to supervise refugees and staff hospitals.

The CPRA's formation at Congolese independence through the early 1970s marked a watershed period in humanitarianism in Africa during the Cold War. The end of colonial rule in most of the continent posed challenges to Western aid organisations. The US government and its European allies recognised the potential of PVOs to help exert influence in African states without being open displays of Western intervention. French officials, for example, had high hopes for scientific research programmes to reinforce prestige for France.[7] Yet aid agencies and personnel did not just follow the dictates of governments; they operated as autonomous agents seeking to promote social and economic progress in the Congo, even if Congolese and international politics placed limits on what they could or could not do.

To see the CPRA only as a tool of the US government would be to neglect the sincerity of CPRA staff in their efforts to develop new ideals of Protestant charity. CPRA staff tried to place their work in the context of internationalist humanitarian ideals and a Christianity not dependent on colonial hierarchies of power, rather than making anti-Communism the central inspiration of their work. The CPRA relied on a somewhat incoherent mélange that wove together confidence in Western technical superiority, apolitical neutrality, paternalism towards Africans, optimism about African progress, and angst over the devastating results of colonial rule. Even as the CPRA's motivates and actions reflected the international tensions within ecumenical North American Protestantism at mid-century, it also inspired volunteers to provide food and medical care to Congolese. The CPRA's amorphous ideas and ad hoc structure allowed the organisation to negotiate effectively with Congolese and Western governments and an array of foreign private supporters.

The CPRA relied on a diverse group of volunteers whose background and experiences varied considerably, with little effort to try to promote a cohesive professional identity. Over 80 medical professionals from North America, Norway, and Great Britain received CPRA support from 1960 until 1971. Most of these individuals were not former or aspiring missionaries, but rather felt called to serve the Congolese people despite having very little knowledge of Africa. The CPRA also relied on veteran missionaries who directed relief programmes effectively for long periods of time because of their expansive knowledge of African languages and cultural beliefs. Alongside these different aid workers, a small group of CWS personnel kept track of food shipments

---

7 J.L. Pearson, *The Colonial Politics of Global Health: France and the United Nations in Postwar Africa* (Cambridge, MA: Harvard University Press, 2018).

and facilitated the CPRA's links to various mission boards and donors. With such an eclectic cast of participants and the lack of a clear chain of command, individual CPRA members could have wildly divergent experiences and views. Some felt quite comfortable accepting the privileges most white missionaries took for granted in the colonial era. Others wanted to free Africans from the colonial hierarchies that so demeaned them. The common denominator all CPRA staff shared was that the tumult of independence had overthrown the colonial state's alliance with missionaries. Aid workers often found themselves anxiously vulnerable to the unpredictable turns of Congolese politics.

The CPRA's unclear mandate represents the ambiguity of humanitarian action in Africa in the 1960s. The allegedly universal order of human rights that emerged more fully after the Second World War did not fully extend to the Congo. Secular humanitarian organisations such as the International Committee of the Red Cross (ICRC) contended that independent African states lacked the maturity to follow the Geneva Conventions and respect humanitarian ideals. The United Nations High Commission for Refugees (UNHCR) did not apply the 1951 UN Convention on Refugees or other international conventions to the Congo. The DRC thus was imagined as an exotic, violent place where allegedly universal humanitarian norms did not apply.[8] CPRA staff, whose Christian mandate of charity did not reference human rights, felt more at ease in the DRC than secular humanitarian organisations, whose personnel felt more bound to follow international protocols. With the advent of the Organisation of African Unity's Refugee Convention in 1967 and the Nigerian government's success against the Biafran revolt, international humanitarian organisations became more clearly governed by bureaucratic and secular norms than in the Congo crises. While international humanitarian organisations continued to use imagery of depoliticised African pain, by the 1970s humanitarian work in Africa increasingly resembled secular, modern humanitarianism elsewhere.

Angolans and Congolese who received support from the CPRA were not simply passive victims to be saved by Western largesse. They sought with varying success to control CPRA programmes. Some rural communities guarded volunteer doctors from attack by rebels and government troops,

---

8   J. Rich, "Manufacturing Sovereignty and Manipulating Humanitarianism: The Diplomatic Resolution of the Congolese Mercenary Crisis, 1967–1968," *Journal of African History* 60:2 (2019), 277–96. For a similar discussion of how Red Cross staff's emphasis on cultural difference undermined recourse to universal human rights conventions, see Y. Pingle, "Humanitarianism, Race and Denial: The International Committee of the Red Cross and Kenya's Mau Mau Rebellion, 1952–1960," *History Workshop Journal* 84 (2017), 89–107.

even as Congolese soldiers used CPRA food relief to entice rebels to surrender. By 1966, Congolese Protestant ministers had begun to enforce their authority over the CPRA. Unlike most aid organisations involved in the DRC, the CPRA transformed from being entirely under expatriate control to becoming a part of a single Congolese church, the Église du Christ au Congo (ECC).[9] Congolese took over the leading role in Protestant churches formerly controlled by European and North American missionaries. National development and an end to foreign domination – the ostensible goals of Mobutu's government – led Congolese Protestants to make more demands on North American donors. Western Protestant NGOs and mission boards no longer promoted emergency measures such as food distribution, partially out of fear of continued dependence and partially because of declining financial resources. The Biafran secession also drew international attention and resources away from the DRC. The onset of a more clearly defined bureaucratic model of development within the CPRA eroded the previous ambiguity of the organisation's loose structure that split authority between its offices in New York and Kinshasa. Just as dissident nationalisms and Pan-Africanist ideals briefly competed before ultimately losing out to the model of the nation state in the first years of African independence, so too did the CPRA's autonomous position give way to a more clearly demarcated, national model of Congolese development.

The significance of Protestant humanitarian aid in the DRC in the 1960s

A study of the CPRA offers significant contributions to the already extensive historiography of the DRC in the 1960s and early 1970s. As a Cold War battleground, US officials and church aid agencies sought to combat nationalist rebels and the threat of Communist victory via relief as well as arms. Tales of heroic and selfless missionary doctors will hardly surprise anyone familiar with the history of the DRC, and they helped justify American intervention in the country. While the machinations of US policy makers in the Congo is well known, neither missionaries nor humanitarian aid have attracted the attention of the scores of academic scholars who have written about the US role in the DRC in the 1960s.[10] Stephen Weissman's 1974

9   On the establishment of the ECC and the Africanisation of Protestant church leadership in the DRC, see P. Kabongo-Mbaya, *L'Église du Christ au Zaïre: Formation et adaptation d'un protestantisme en situation de dictature* (Paris: Karthala, 1992).

10   For a brief overview, see Young, *Politics in the Congo*; M. Kalb, *The Congo Cables: The Cold War in Africa from Eisenhower to Kennedy* (New York: Macmillan, 1982);

overview of US foreign policy in the Congo barely mentioned missionaries at all, save for their lack of influence on US government actions.[11] Kevin Dunn's study of US constructions of the DRC also ignores the role of Protestant mission staff.[12] Philip Dow's study of US evangelical missionaries denotes how they backed Tshombe and how they propagated the image of a Congo beset by the threat of Communism.[13] However, Dow's work does not encompass the diversity of missionary views on the DRC, nor the crucial role Protestants played in relief efforts. In some ways, CPRA personnel acted in similar fashion to the model of large organisations such as the Ford Foundation, which promoted orderly capitalist development and technical support against the perceived threat of Communism as was common in the 1950s and 1960s.[14]

Likewise, historians of 20th-century humanitarianism rarely reference the DRC in the 1960s, despite the fact that the Congolese crisis was among the first humanitarian international interventions in Africa after independence,

---

R. Mahoney, *JFK: Ordeal in Africa* (New York: Oxford University Press, 1983); D. Gibbs, *The Political Economy of Third World Intervention: Mines, Money, and US Policy in the Congo Crisis* (Chicago: University of Chicago Press, 1991); S. Kelly, *America's Tyrant: The CIA and Mobutu of Zaire* (Lanham, MD: University Press of America, 1993); O. Westad, *The Global Cold War: Third World Interventions and the Making of Our Times* (New York: Cambridge University Press, 2005), 136–43; J. Kent, *America, the UN, and Decolonisation: Cold War Conflict in the Congo* (New York: Routledge, 2010); P. Muehlenbeck, *Betting on the Africans: John F. Kennedy's Courting of African Nationalist Leaders* (New York: Oxford University Press, 2012); G. Bechtolsheimer, "Breakfast with Mobutu: The United States and the Cold War, 1966–1981." (PhD thesis, London School of Economics, 2012); L. Namikas, *Battleground Africa: Cold War in the Congo, 1960–1965* (Stanford: Stanford University Press, 2013); W. Mountz, "Americanizing Africanisation: The Congo Crisis, 1960–1967" (PhD thesis, University of Missouri, 2014).

11 S. Weissman, *American Foreign Policy in the Congo, 1960–1964.* (Ithaca: Cornell University Press, 1974), 69, 109, 172, 293.

12 K. Dunn, *Imagining the Congo: The International Relations of Identity* (New York: Palgrave, 2003).

13 P. Dow, "Accidental Diplomats: The Influence of American Evangelical Missionaries on US Relations with the Congo during the Early Cold War Period," in B. Sewell and M. Ryan (eds) *Foreign Policy at the Periphery: The Shifting Margins of US International Relations since World War II* (Lexington: University Press of Kentucky, 2016), 172–205.

14 G. Hess, "Waging the Cold War in the Third World: The Foundations and the Challenges of Development," in L. Friedman, and M. McGarvie (eds), *Charity, Philanthropy, and Civility in American History* (New York: Cambridge University Press, 2003), 319–40.

seven years before Biafra.[15] Teresa Tomas Rangil's essay on UN humanitarian aid in DRC during the early 1960s is a very rare exception to the generally neglected view of the Congo crises as a humanitarian problem.[16] Given how Andrew Zimmerman estimated that the DRC received roughly $1.1 billion in foreign aid from 1960 to 1990, this case deserves much more attention from scholars seeking to examine the failures and the consequences of foreign aid.[17] Few observers have seen missionaries or church-affiliated relief programmes as influential in any sense, other than as a pretext for US-backed military interventions against the leftist Simba rebels who killed nearly 300 missionaries in 1964 and 1965. Yet the CPRA proved to be a major distributor of aid to Angolan, Congolese, and Sudanese refugees in this turbulent era, as well as a source of technical support for agriculture.

In the broader literature, any consideration of humanitarian programmes challenges the more familiar narratives of political developments. Patrice Lumumba, so significant that no less than four biographies have been published in the last twenty years on his brief rise and fall, was not in power long enough to have any lasting impact on relief programmes that only came together after his arrest at the orders of army officer and future dictator Joseph-Désiré Mobutu in September 1960.[18] The destruction that struck much of the Kasai

---

15 On humanitarian aid and the Cold War in the 1960s, see V. Ruttan, *United States Development Assistance Policy: The Domestic Politics of Foreign Economic Aid* (Baltimore: Johns Hopkins University Press, 1996); S. Butterfield, *US Development Aid – An Historic First* (Westport: Praeger, 2004); R. McCleary, *Global Compassion: Private Voluntary Organisations and U.S. Foreign Policy since 1939* (New York: Oxford University Press, 2009), 83–122; M. Barnett, *Empire of Humanity: A History of Humanitarianism* (Ithaca: Cornel University Press, 2011); P. Gatrell, *Free World?: The Campaign to Save the World's Refugees, 1956–1963* (New York: Cambridge University Press, 2011). On the Cold War, a rare example of how US Protestants became anxious about the Communist threat in the DRC is P. Settje, *Faith and War: How Christians Debated the Cold and Vietnam Wars* (New York: New York University Press, 2011), 63–7.

16 T. Rangil, "The UN and Economic Policy Design and Implementation during the Congo Crisis, 1960–1964," Unpublished paper presented at the Work Bank Workshop, Using History to Inform Development Policy: The Role of Archives, October 2012.

17 R. Zimmerman, *Dollars, Diplomacy, and Dependency: Dilemmas of US Economic Aid* (Boulder: Lynne Rienner, 1993), 117–20.

18 L.D. Witte, *The Murder of Lumumba* (London: Verso, 2001); G. Nzongola-Ntalaja, *Patrice Lumumba* (Athens, OH: Ohio University Press, 2014); E. Gerard and G. Kuklick, *Death in the Congo: Murdering Patrice Lumumba* (Cambridge, MA: Harvard University Press, 2015); L. Zeilig, *Lumumba: Africa's Lost Leader* (London: Haus, 2015).

province in 1960 and 1961, largely an under-studied sideshow in the current historical literature, forced over half a million people to take sanctuary in the short-lived Autonomous State of South Kasai (ASSK).[19] Lumumba was not a hero for people living in this region. Government troops sent on his orders in August 1960 massacred civilians in South Kasai's capital, Mbuji-Mayi. A study of the CPRA's activities allows for a reframing of Congolese competition for authority which does not emerge in dominant narratives in the current historiography. Much as Severine Autesserre has observed of the civil wars of the DRC in later decades, local and regional conflicts often fuelled the violence, not always clearly linked to the Cold War dynamics that are often used to explain the crises of the 1960s.[20]

The CPRA is part of a neglected but crucial period in the long genealogy of foreign aid in post-colonial DRC. Some parts of the CPRA story are quite familiar in the larger sweep of foreign assistance. The CPRA and other private programmes could intervene in the DRC because Congolese political contenders focused much more on using military force and controlling territory than on maintaining medical care and promoting economic development. The sense that it was necessary to furnish aid drove humanitarian agencies to intervene in the DRC. And, as armed conflicts dragged on, donors began to exhibit symptoms of a condition quite familiar in the DRC in later decades: fatigue. By 1965, personnel of the United Nations High Commission for Refugees and the International Committee of the Red Cross had become jaded about the prospects for effective humanitarian action in the country. The CPRA soldiered on, regardless of whether its donors cut back their assistance. Just as Congolese NGOs shaped themselves in new ways to attract donor support, so too did CPRA projects shift over time to try to solicit declining funds once earlier donors tired of emergencies. Even as Mobutu rode the economic boom of the late 1960s, the foundation of dependence remained despite the new mantra of self-sufficiency taken up by donors and Congolese NGOs alike.

The Congolese state's reliance on foreign assistance has been a cornerstone of the political order since 1960. Lumumba's failed efforts to turn to the Soviet bloc for support, Mobutu's squandering of financial support from the US and Western countries, and Joseph Kabila's continued reliance on international NGOs, China, and Western countries all illustrate

---

19 I refer to South Kasai and the ASSK interchangibly, as was the practice in the early 1960s.

20 S. Autesserre, *The Trouble with the Congo: Local Violence and the Failure of International Peacebuilding* (New York: Cambridge University Press, 2010).

the DRC's dependence on other governments and foreign aid agencies. However, the CPRA case exemplifies how international NGOs did not always simply follow the lead of Western governments. Claude Kabemba and Cherie Ndaliko have both critiqued humanitarian aid as a front for Western economic interests. Ndaliko has gone so far as to argue Congolese activists and musicians have to negotiate with 'charitable imperialism', in which foreign expatriates in the UN and various NGOs use their financial leverage to impose their agenda and their rhetoric on Congolese people.[21] Without denying the validity of Congolese frustrations about the privilege and the power of foreign humanitarian organisations today, I assert that the CPRA case shows how private humanitarian organisations in the 1960s had less control over Congolese political leaders than they would after the 1990s. Furthermore, aid was not merely a matter of the World Bank and bilateral agreements between the Congolese state and Western allies. How Congolese NGOs negotiated with international organisations had its own internal dynamics which were not under the control of state authorities.

Protestant aid to the DRC also reflects the limits of placing humanitarianism easily into a framework of Western domination. Social theorist James Scott has argued that mid-20th-century 'high modernist' regimes imposed social classification and planning with little regard for the concerns of local communities. One cannot apply this model to the humanitarian aid activities which operated the DRC in the 1960s, where the limits of both state power and humanitarian agencies were quite apparent.[22] Anthropologist Joël Glasman has argued (correctly in my view) that Scott's model does not correspond well with how humanitarian organisations actually operated in Africa.[23] Rather, he proposes that the UNHCR's limited resources and influence made its efforts to reorder refugees less imposing than those of authoritarian governments.[24] If the UNHCR is to be considered a weak institution, the CPRA was even less able to act as an organisation that could force itself on Congolese refugees. Dependent on a range of mission boards, outside donors, Congolese politicians, and Congolese churches, the CPRA's small group of aid workers in the field had to rely on collaboration with Western governments, the United

---

21 Ndaliko, *Necessary Noise*, 26–7.

22 J. Scott, *Seeing Like a State: How Certain Schemes to Improve the Human Condition Have Failed* (New Haven: Yale University Press, 1998).

23 J. Glasman, "Seeing Like a Refugee Agency: Short History of UNHCR Classifications in Central Africa (1961–2015)," *Journal of Refugee Studies* 30:2 (2017), 354–5.

24 Ibid., 355.

Nations, and a range of Congolese stakeholders. A common theme of my informants was their sense of powerlessness and isolation in rural hospitals, entirely dependent on Congolese co-workers and the erratic actions of Congolese officials and soldiers. This is not to suggest that racist and ethnocentric views were somehow absent among US, Canadian, and British aid workers. However, their ability to control Africans was certainly limited.

This book also grapples with the efforts of missionaries to redefine their roles in independent Africa after the end of colonialism. Though I draw on the impressive work of David Hollinger and Melani McAlister in examining the impact of missionary work on ecumenical and evangelical Protestantism in the US, the CPRA's work complicates both Hollinger's and McAlister's perspectives. McAlister's discussion of US evangelicals in the DRC rightly notes the racialised fears of African violence among missionaries, but misses how liberal and evangelical Protestants also saw new opportunities for evangelisation and collaboration with Congolese after colonialism.[25] Ecumenical Protestants in the 1960s did increasingly question the missionary enterprise in favour of seeking a common humanity not confined to Christianity, as Hollinger notes, but the CPRA case shows how British and North American Protestant missions and individual members still intertwined in the 1960s missionary evangelisation and internationalist humanitarianism in the aftermath of Congolese decolonisation.[26] Furthermore, the plethora of missionary and Congolese Protestant churches makes it hard to easily distinguish aid workers' perspectives based on the evangelical/ecumenical divide. Some evangelicals embraced the end of colonial rule, while some Protestant aid workers were just as anxious about accepting orders from Africans as evangelical missionaries.

Missionaries in the DRC in the 1960s also found themselves at the intersection of changes within their denominations, their supporting donors, and Congolese Protestant churches. Expatriates still controlled practically all the Protestant missions in the Congo in 1960. Most missions had ceded authority to Congolese churches by 1970, although some denominations such as the Conservative Baptists became deeply divided in the process of becoming independent of missionary control.[27] Congolese pastors such as

---

25   M. McAlister, *Kingdom of God Has No Borders: A Global History of American Evangelicals* (New York: Oxford University Press, 2018), 30–52.

26   D. Hollinger, *Protestants Abroad: How Missionaries Tried to Change the World but Changed America* (Princeton: Princeton University Press, 2017).

27   Individual denominational histories expose a continuum of experiences, from the relatively smooth transition of the Disciples of Christ to the sharp battles within the Conservative Baptists and the Christian and Missionary Alliance. For some

Methodist Pierre Shaumba and Jean Bokeleale of the Disciples of Christ pressured expatriates to allow Congolese to become the leaders of mission-founded churches. While most denomination mission boards acceded to these requests, mission boards were less willing to immediately surrender control over property and finances.

This book examines a topic often ignored in the Africanisation of mission-founded churches after the end of colonial rule: material aid and support. Redefining mission was not merely a question of theology. Much like debates between African veterans and the French state over benefits, Congolese churches and missions shared a common vocabulary of moral debts with foreign donors and mission boards, even if African and North American perspectives on how funds and material aid should satisfy these debts remained contentious. I draw here from Gregory Mann's discussion of the ways in which 'the language of mutual obligation and interdependence is and always has been fraught with misunderstandings, malentendus, and false confidence in which one group or another believes that it is finally being heard and understood.'[28] Likewise, Britt Halvorson's study of Malagasy-US Lutheran missionary cooperation denotes how missionaries viewed themselves as breaking away from old hierarchies of colonialism.[29] The decline of missionary authority played out throughout Africa after the end of colonisation, the chaos of DRC politics of the early 1960s, fears of a Communist revolution, and multiple evacuations by missionaries became important strands in the tangled connections between Congolese churches and foreign donors. After the end of the worst of the revolts against central Congolese authority by 1967, donors eager to move on to other crises became ensnared by Congolese reminders of the bitter legacy of political violence. Congolese churches embarked on their own cultural nationalist projects running parallel with Mobutu's ambitious projects of making a new Congolese national identity

---

examples of histories of individual mission churches, see D. Nelson, *Christian Missionizing and Social Transformation: A History of Conflict and Change in Eastern Zaire* (New York: Praeger, 1992); M. Kasongo, *History of the Methodist Church in the Central Congo* (Lanham, MD: University Press of America, 1998); B. Munongo, "Aspects du protestantisme dans le Congo-Zaïre indépendant (1960–1990)," (PhD thesis, Université de Lille III, 2000); E. Wild-Wood, *Migration and Christian Identity in Congo (DRC).* Leiden: Brill, 2008; D. Garrard, "The Protestant Church in Congo: The Mobutu Years and Their Impact," *Journal of Religion in Africa* 43:2 (2013), 131–66.

28   G. Mann, *Native Sons: West African Veterans and France in the Twentieth Century* (Durham, NC: Duke University Press, 2006), 5.

29   B. Halvorson, *Conversionary Sites: Transforming Medical and Global Christianity from Madagascar to Minnesota* (University Park: Pennsylvania State University Press, 2018).

and his schemes for economic growth. Mission boards and donors wrestled with their relationship to CPRA as they found their own nation building plans to bring stability to the DRC now had to contend with rival Congolese models for how the organisation should be run.

To trace the political and cultural networks of missionary humanitarian aid in the DRC, I use approaches drawn from previous work on decolonisation and early post-colonial Africa, even as I connect this literature to studies on Cold War networks. CPRA staff often presented their role as part of a project to prevent the DRC from falling into general anarchy. This approach also served to reconcile, or at least to paper over, tensions among missionaries over racial divides in the US and Cold War politics.[30] By healing the wounds of colonial repression and the violence of independence – abandoned hospitals, starving refugees, economic recession – CPRA staff sought to ensure a Christian Congo would emerge allied to Western countries. Some CPRA staff eschewed Cold War rhetoric by highlighting suffering and downplaying its political causes. Others argued that if Protestants in Western countries did not help the Congolese create a stable society, then Communists would have a better chance of seizing power. Though the rise of Mobutu Sese Seko's dictatorship eased these fears of complete collapse by the late 1960s, these apocalyptic views help explain how CPRA staff and mission boards did not challenge the new authoritarian order.

The CPRA story is one of nation building, a particularly powerful metaphor for development and emergency in the 1960s. Though much of the research on nation building focuses on bilateral aid between governments, the CPRA case is an example of how NGOs could imagine their own role in national reconstruction.[31] While some followed the Mennonite Central Committee's

---

30   M. McAlister, "The Body in Crisis: Congo and the Transformations of Evangelical Internationalism, 1960–1965," in A. Preston and D. Rossinow (eds), *Outside In: The Transnational Circuitry of US History* (New York: Oxford University Press, 2016), 123–52.

31   For some works on modernisation and nation-building in the Cold War era, see D. Engerman, N. Gilman, M. Haeffele, and M. Latham (eds), *Staging Growth: Modernisation, Development, and the Global Cold War* (Amherst: University of Massachusetts Press, 2003); N. Gilman, *Mandearins of the Future: Modernisation Theory in Cold War America* (Baltimore: Johns Hopkins University Press, 2007); D. Ekbladh, *The Great American Mission: Modernisation and the Construction of an American World Order* (Princeton: Princeton University Press, 2009); M. Latham, *The Right Kind of Revolution: Modernisation, Development, and U.S. Foreign Policy From the Cold War to the Present* (Ithaca: Cornell University Press, 2011); A. McVety, *Enlightened Aid: U.S. Development as Foreign Policy in Ethiopia* (New York: Oxford University Press, 2012).

model of what Philip Fountain has described as 'quietist techno-politics' in promoting development with limited engagement with authoritarian states, other CPRA staff actively collaborated with the Congolese government.[32] Missionaries and aid workers could alternatively position themselves as apolitical dispensers of help, Cold War activists battling Communist-inspired revolts, or even as participants in Congolese efforts to overcome the remnants of colonialism. Individual aid workers sometimes worked close to US government efforts to help form a stable government. Others made individual journeys to understand Congolese beliefs or to correct the ethnocentrism of career missionaries. The vague mandate of the CPRA created much room for variation.

Another contribution of this book is to examine the afterlives of humanitarian interventions for aid workers and in the places they had worked. In the DRC, projects designed to provide emergency aid became remade into church-run economic programmes by the early 1970s. Ironically, the goal of promoting self-sufficiency touted by CPRA staff in the 1960s sometimes became a means by which Congolese aid programmes continued to rely on foreign financial support a decade later. Elsewhere, elderly Congolese medical staff lamented the departure of CPRA medical staff and their supplies. Aid workers themselves carried their own experiences home. Relatively few aid workers kept close contact with Congolese that they had known, but their careers often took new turns because of their time in the DRC. This debris of humanitarian intervention became material for later North American narratives about the Congo. One notable example came thanks to Wendell Kingsolver, a Kentucky physician and CPRA medical volunteer who brought along his daughter Barbara in 1962. She went on to write *The Poisonwood Bible*, one of the most popular novels by a US author about the Congo.[33]

Plus ça change?: Comparing humanitarian action in the Congo in the 1960s with the early 21st century

The appearance of a still perpetually dysfunctional country haunted by pain ignores the profound differences between humanitarian aid in the Congo in the 1960s and in later decades. Western Protestant missionaries in the decade after Congolese independence directly managed relief programmes. Secular

---

32 P. Fountain and L. Meitzner-Yoder, "Quietist Techno-Politics: Agricultural Development and Mennonite Mission in Indonesia," in C. Scheer, P. Fountain, and R.M. Feener (eds), *The Mission of Development: Religion and Techno-Politics in Asia* (Leiden: Brill, 2018), 213–42.

33 B. Kingsolver, *The Poisonwood Bible* (New York: HarperCollins, 1998).

international humanitarian organisations might be still entangled with white saviours helping destitute Africans from the 1990s onward, but none rely on foreign missionaries nearly as much as their predecessors did at Congolese independence. Ecumenical North American Protestant churches took centre stage in humanitarian aid in the 1960s. Over half a century later, large British and North American Protestant churches have ceded their prominence to more evangelical counterparts in missionary work. Furthermore, the international and national contexts of the Congolese crises were substantially different from the 1960s. Then, US officials and missionaries feared the Congo would become a Communist base to promote revolutions across Africa. Unlike the 21st century, Congolese suffering became international news since the DRC was a focal point of US and Soviet interests. Finally, the unprecedented United Nations intervention in the DRC in 1960 made the alleviation of Congolese pain one criterion to judge international cooperation in resolving the violent aftermath of decolonisation.

Between the formation of the Congo Protestant relief agency and the early 1970s, the international framework of humanitarianism and ecumenical Protestant activism changed tremendously. North American and British Protestant aid workers showed few qualms in their partnership with the US government or the Congolese government, yet still imagined themselves to be acting impartially. Christian aid workers in South Vietnam, by contrast, wrestled more openly with reconciling their alleged neutrality as they questioned their own role in supporting the US military. In Biafra, other aid personnel were divided over the role of apolitical humanitarianism: Bernard Kouchner and other French Red Cross doctors rejected the ICRC's anxieties over taking sides in the war with Nigeria. Major US Protestant churches such as the United Methodist Church and the Disciples of Christ, torn by the Vietnam war and the cultural divides of the 1960s, became less engaged with foreign aid and questioned the colonial and racist underpinnings of the missionary enterprise.

As for the DRC, the religious and political landscape had also undergone transformation between the beginning of the 1960s and the end of the decade. Mobutu Sese Seko's authoritarian regime crushed his political enemies in three years after he seized power in November 1965. While regional famines and epidemics caused hardship in the Congo in the late 1960s and 1970s, the Congo was no longer in the grips of a humanitarian emergency deemed worthy of international intervention. Congolese Protestant leaders argued that they themselves should control relief programmes as well as their churches, rather than missionaries. North American donor agencies felt conflicted about these demands. US staff members struggled to accept the ideal of African control.

Western mission boards and aid agencies had far more financial resources than their Congolese counterparts. Should Congolese alone control how these funds were to be spent? Relief programmes created in the wake of the hardship of the first years after independence increasingly became designed to promote self-sufficient economic development.

Scholarship on African development in the early years after colonial rule has asserted the primacy of newly independent states in domesticating foreign NGOs. Priya Lal, Gregory Mann, and Michael Jennings among others have noted how governments often used the recourse of African sovereignty to keep foreign aid organisations in line.[34] Declining economic fortunes, the spread of the universal human rights model, and the increased power of the World Bank and the International Monetary Fund (IMF) weakened the ability of African states to impose their authority on NGOs. The DRC, by contrast, significantly differed from this pattern. The internationalisation of the struggle for power in the DRC and the fractured state of Congolese politics ensured that Congolese political leaders in the early 1960s had little ability to monitor and make demands on civil society NGOs like the CPRA. CPRA staff could thus firmly support Angolan rebel movements, distance themselves from the Congolese state, or alternatively align with the Congolese army. The DRC's government only managed to assert its power over church-affiliated NGOs in the late 1960s and early 1970s, later than in some other African independent states. Mobutu's botched nationalisation of foreign businesses, the economic recessions of the 1970s, and the onset of structural adjustment ensured humanitarian and developmental NGOs could again increasingly act autonomously from state control by the early 1990s. This resurgence of NGOs at the end of the 20th century, in contrast to the 1960s, relied on a framework of universal human rights and professionalism rather than on transnational Christian hopes for a newly decolonised Africa.

A study of humanitarian relief in the first decade of Congolese history brings out familiar themes in the longer historical experience of the country. Kai Koddenbrock's ethnography of Western aid workers in Kivu province includes insights that correspond all too well to the CPRA. The 'failed state effect', by which aid workers compare governance in the DRC against a

---

34 M. Jennings, *Surrogates of the State: NGOs, Development and Ujamaa in Tanzania* (Bloomfield, CT: Kumarian, 2008); G. Mann, *From Empires to NGOs in the West African Sahel: The Road to Nongovernmentality* (New York: Cambridge University Press, 2014); P. Lal, "Decolonisation and the Gendered Politics of Developmental Labor in Southeastern Africa," in S. Macekura and E. Manela (eds), *The Development Century: A Global History* (New York: Cambridge University Press, 2018), 181–6.

'universal standard of statehood', served to justify humanitarian intervention in the 1960s just as much as it did half a century later.[35] Another thread that ties humanitarian interventions of the early years of the DRC with later practices was a celebration of manoeuvering around DRC officials.[36] Paternalist and racist depictions of Congolese emerged time and again in how aid workers described their work, in similar fashion to other international humanitarian organisations such as the ICRC. And, as Cherie Ndaliko forcefully demonstrates in the early 21st century, North American aid workers rarely took into consideration how Western interference helped maintain corrupt regimes and left out local perspectives in their deliberations. This was perhaps even more pronounced for the CPRA, where personnel made no public effort to question the role of the US government in exacerbating tensions among Congolese.

Though some continuities exist between the agendas and practices of humanitarian organisations since the 1990s with the early years of the CPRA, there are also major differences, particularly in terms of the relationship between CPRA staff with Congolese churches. For all of their ethnocentrism, CPRA staff were far more concerned about breaking from what they perceived to be the racism and paternalism of Belgian colonialism than their counterparts after the 1980s. A newly independent Congo might have been viewed through the rhetoric of crisis that skewed understandings of Congolese agency, as Nancy Rose Hunt has argued.[37] But, the end of colonialism allowed CPRA staff to imagine themselves as part of a transnational Christian community that could engage in nation building alongside Congolese. This optimism about Congolese partners gave increasing weight to Congolese church leaders' demands to control how and where the funds of foreign donors were to be used in the late 1960s. Foreign missionaries and Congolese pastors shared a common vocabulary based on overcoming the legacy of colonialism, even if they increasingly disagreed on what the new roles of missions, donor agencies, and Congolese churches should be. By the 1990s, the deployment of colonialism as a point of debate and of common purpose was no longer nearly as influential.

Methods and sources

One of the great methodological challenges of this book has been in reconstructing Congolese responses to CPRA programmes. This study relies mostly on archival records and the perspectives of North American aid

35 K. Koddenbrock, *The Practice of Humanitartian Intervention: Aid Workers and Institutions in the Democratic Republic of Congo* (New York: Routledge, 2016), 34–8.

36 Ibid., 33.

37 N. Hunt, *A Nervous State: Violence, Remedies, and Reverie in Colonial Congo* (Durham, NC: Duke University Press, 2016), 2–3.

workers. Unfortunately, CPRA staff often left the Congolese contributions to their work on the margins of their correspondence. Veteran missionaries serving as project directors wrote extensively on people receiving aid in their correspondence, not their Congolese assistants. Missionaries tried to impose a sense of Christian, paternal order in their reports of refugee camps and medical work. While this worked to elicit the sympathy of donors, there was less room for more ambiguous situations where CPRA staff struggled with Congolese and Angolan stakeholders. Compared with missionaries and professional aid workers, CPRA medical volunteers from the US and Canada produced much less writing for public consumption. I tracked down 28 volunteers and surviving family members. Most of the surviving volunteers were over 75 years old by the time I interviewed them. Their memories varied as much as their backgrounds and the span of their time in the CPRA. Some families of volunteers remembered watching slides taken in the DRC after their return, while still others accompanied their mothers and fathers in the Congo. Their own stories tended to reify differences between the DRC with the safety and order of the US and Canada. Even so, these accounts included a great deal about how Congolese soldiers, nurses, and patients tried to negotiate with aid workers.

Above all else, the greatest problem for this study arises from what I was unable to do: conduct fieldwork in the DRC. Part of the difficulty lay in simple finances. It is admittedly dubious for a historian in the US to whine about a lack of money considering the subject matter of this book. Yet for scholars at institutions where research funding is a low priority, fieldwork is a challenging expense. Congolese politics also played a crucial factor. After US Secretary of State John Kerry criticised Congolese president Joseph Kabila's arrest of young human rights activists in early 2016, Kabila's diplomatic staff responded by not issuing visas to some Americans for nearly a year.[38] My plans of tracking down medical assistants of CPRA doctors thus came undone. Joseph Kabila's decision to postpone presidential elections at the end of 2016 led to further protests and government repression over the course of 2017 and 2018, again blocking me from going to the DRC. My inability to conduct research in the Congo also meant I was not able to examine the archives of the L'Église du Christ au Congo and the CPRA in Kinshasa, which are, as of 2020, in a catastrophic state of disarray.[39] Another logistical problem came with the scope of the CPRA. Protestant aid workers worked throughout most of the country. To trace

---

38 X. Monnier, "Au Congo-Kinshasa, la guerre des visas aura bien lieu," *Le Monde*, 8 July 2016 2016. Available at: www.lemonde.fr/afrique/article/2016/07/08/au-congo-kinshasa-la-guerre-des-visas-aura-bien-lieu_4966630_3212.html (Accessed 25 October 2018).

39 Personal communication, Anicka Fast, 29 October 2018.

CPRA's actions in each province would have required a tremendous amount of resources. The hundreds of thousands of Angolan refugees that the CPRA tried to help largely returned home decades ago. In Kasai province, a regional revolt against the central government beginning in 2016 made returning to the sites of CPRA-supported refugee camps a dangerous proposition.

Congolese perspectives on aid thus emerge only intermittently in this book, much as I had hoped otherwise. I do turn to secondary literature to try to contextualise the limited sources on African engagement with the CPRA. Emery Kalema's masterly dissertation on the cultural meanings and historical memories of Pierre Mulele's revolt in the Kwilu region from 1963 to 1967 has deeply shaped my own understandings of the context in which aid workers operated.[40] Up to now, Kalema's seminal work is the only one that places civilians in the 1960s at the forefront of analysis of the Simba revolt and its aftermath. A number of Congolese since the 1970s have turned their attention to the short-lived Autonomous State of South Kasai, where CPRA established its first successful relief effort from 1960 until its collapse in 1962. On Angolan refugees, the work of Inge Brinkman, Joanna Tague, Kate Burlingham and others have helped to reveal the political views of missionaries and at least the leadership of the FNLA, the rebel group that claimed to represent the true government in exile of Angolans in the DRC.[41] Admittedly, the experiences of ordinary civilians in the maelstrom of the 1960s in the DRC have been neglected for far too long in academic research. It is striking that journalist David van Reybrouck's relatively recent survey of Congolese history managed to represent more perspectives from individuals outside of the political elite than other scholarship by historians on the DRC in the 1960s.[42] Reuben Loffman's work on the experiences of generations of people living in southeastern DRC with colonial and post-colonial modalities of development has informed my own work here.[43]

---

40   E. Kalema, "Violence and Memory: The Mulele 'Rebellion' in Post-Colonial D.R. Congo," (PhD thesis, University of the Witwatersrand, 2017).

41   I. Brinkman, "Refugees on Routes: Congo/Zaire and the War in Northern Angola (1961–1974), in B. Heintze and A.V. Oppen (eds), *Angola on the Move: Transport Routes, Communications, and History* (Frankfurt: Verlag Otto Lembeck, 2008), 198–220; K. Burlingham, "In the Image of God: A Global History of the North American Congregational Mission in Angola, 1879–1975," (PhD thesis, University of Rutgers – New Brunswick, 2011).

42   D. Van Reybrouck, *The Epic History of A People*, translated by S. Garrett (New York: HarperCollins, 2014).

43   R. Loffman, "An Obscured Revolution: USAID, the North Shaba Project, and the Zaïrian Administration, 1976–1986," *African Studies* 48:3 (2014), 425–44; R.

Readers may also take note of the partial use of US diplomatic records stored in the US National Archives and at various presidential libraries. This choice began as a logistical problem in getting to these archives, but it eventually became a deliberate decision. So much of the historiography of the Congo crises of the 1960s rests on state archives that it is little wonder that formal political actors should be the main subjects of interest. Here I concur with Brenda Gayle Plummer's trenchant remark: 'Receptivity to an array of sources is important because national archives can subtly dictate a methodology that privileges intergovernment binary relations and occludes the circulation of ideas and activities that occur outside the state framework.'[44] I did consult some US State Department records as well as previously unused US Aid for International Development (USAID) archival material. However, this book primarily turns to mission board archives, those of other NGOs such as the ICRC, and the CPRA's own materials as a means of recovering not only the experiences and goals of CPRA workers but of the Angolans and Congolese they assisted. These records have been almost entirely ignored by historians outside of research on individual denominations and organisations. I draw from the well-developed diplomatic historical work on the DRC, even as this book shows how humanitarian aid programmes and missionary records broaden our understanding of the human cost of the Congo crises and demonstrate how Congolese stakeholders made their own demands on aid workers.

The CPRA depended on a range of donors and church-affiliated organisations across North America and Europe. I also turned to donor records scattered in two continents. Just as it is commonplace for diplomatic historians to consult materials in multiple countries, researchers of humanitarian programmes need to take a similar approach. These archives, particularly those of the Mennonite Central Committee, the World Council of Churches, and the United Nations High Commission on Refugees, have also never received the attention they deserved from historians of the DRC in the immediate period following independence. This approach also allowed me a better understanding of how donors related and debated with each other about how aid should be provided to the DRC. Some of these quarrels between donors expressed anxieties about Congolese administrative capacity that resonate with humanitarian work in the DRC since the 1990s. Still other debates regarding the CPRA reflected tensions between evangelical

---

Loffman, "Belgian Rule and its Afterlives: Colonialism, Developmentalism, and Mobutism in the Tanganyika District, Katanga, 1885–1985," *International Labor and Working Class History* 92 (2017), 47–68.

44 B.G. Plummer, *In Search of Power: African Americans in the Age of Decolonisation, 1956–1974* (New York: Cambridge University Press, 2013), 13–14.

mission boards which were distrustful of other church organisations they feared had become too politically liberal.

I employ several sets of institutional, PVO, and mission board archives. The most reliable and influential donor to the CPRA was the CWS. This organisation was the relief and development agency of the National Council of Christian Churches, a coalition of the most prominent Protestant churches in the US. The CWS even lent a secretary and office space in its headquarters in New York City. The CWS's Africa department staff, particularly Theodore Tucker and Jan S.F. van Hoogstraten, had CWS staff members serve as technical assistants to the CPRA. These records are especially important to understanding the CPRA and its shifting relationships to donors, particularly as CWS staff increasingly disparaged the expensive development programmes of Congolese Protestant church leaders. With the exception of a few works, scholars have yet to engage with how the CWS laboured to place US Protestants into the development of newly independent nations in the 1960s.[45]

Another source of information came from the United Nations. The correspondence of their mission in the DRC from 1960 and 1964 is preserved at the UN archives in New York City, while organisations such as UNICEF and the UN High Commission for Refugees maintain their archives in Geneva. UN relief efforts sometimes worked alongside the CPRA. On other occasions, UN officials closed their emergency aid programmes down much earlier than the Protestant organisation. In still other cases, local stakeholders had more confidence in the CPRA than the United Nations.

I also draw evidence from denominational and interdenominational archives, including the Mennonite Congo Inland Mission, the Disciples of Christ, the American Baptist Mission, the Mennonite Central Committee, the World Council of Churches, and the ICRC. To continue a familiar refrain, historians have only scratched the surface of these sources in regards to the DRC after 1960. While this list may seem lengthy, many more archives related to aid and missionaries in the DRC have yet to be examined at all, particularly Catholic PVOs such as Catholic Relief Services and a range of large and small Protestant archives largely located in the US and Canada. Thus, this study is hardly the last word on humanitarian aid to the DRC in the 1960s, even if it is a significant contribution to this neglected topic.

---

45 R. Stenning, *Church World Service: Fifty Years of Help and Hope* (New York: Friendship Press, 1996); J. Gill, *Embattled Ecumenism: The National Conference of Christian Churches, the Vietnam War, and the Trials of the Protestant Left* (DeKalb, IL: Northern Illinois University Press, 2011).

Organisation of the book

Chapter 1 furnishes an overview of major political developments in the DRC from 1960 to 1965 as well as the formation of the CPRA. This chapter also examines the evolution of emergency aid in the DRC from the CPRA, the ICRC, and other international organisations. Most humanitarian organisations had originally only planned to operate relief in the DRC for a year at most. Once it became clear that armed Congolese political conflicts would last for much longer than a few months, donors agreed to keep supporting the CPRA. The CPRA only had a small number of administrative staff to hold together the logistics of sending personnel, money, and supplies to various projects in the DRC. In keeping with the growing role of Congolese pastors in mission-founded churches, the CPRA agreed to accept Presbyterian pastor Samuel Bukasa as its director by the end of 1965.

The next three chapters examine different aspects of the CPRA's relief work in relation to the challenges of promoting national unity. The first CPRA relief programme for Luba Congolese refugees in Kasai province is the subject of chapter 2. CPRA staff, particularly Mennonite missionary Archie Graber, managed to skillfully negotiate with the South Kasai secessionist government, the Congolese government, and the United Nations as they tried to alleviate starvation among refugees. Since the CPRA and most Westerners framed the refugee crisis on decolonisation, the secessionist government failed to use the highly publicised famine as a means of gaining legitimacy against the central government. The South Kasai government's hopes of founding a national identity on refugees failed, in part because organisations like the CPRA did not endorse the secessionist government.

While the CPRA tried not to take sides in the political conflict in the Kasai, the organisation took a clearly partisan role in assisting Angolan refugees who fled Portuguese military repression, beginning in 1961. How the CPRA provided the rebel FNLA organisation with aid and ways to place Angolan refugees under its legal jurisdiction is the subject of chapter 3. While other aid organisations had backed away from the FNLA by 1962, CPRA volunteer David Grenfell had a close relationship with its leader, Holden Roberto. Decolonisation was the cry with which the CPRA rallied around Roberto's organisation, even as other donors and volunteer aid workers criticised Roberto. CPRA recordkeeping and ration distribution were building blocks for the FNLA project of making refugees into subjects of FNLA authority.

In chapter 4, I discuss how CPRA relief work became a tool of the Congolese military to defeat the Simba leftist revolutionaries of the Armée Populaire de la Libération (APL) from 1964 to 1967. APL attacks on missionaries as well as fears that the APL would establish a Communist government fueled

CPRA emergency aid to civilians suffering from hunger and fleeing from fighting. Though individual CPRA workers despised the ruthlessness of the Congolese military against civilians, the organisation did not openly protest against the brutality of the repression. Evangelical CPRA staff believed their relief would help remake the DRC into a Protestant nation that could recover from the horror of the APL. Mennonite CPRA members privately condemned the Congolese army, but also relied on the army's support.

Besides refugee work, the CPRA ran Operation Doctor, a recruitment programme for medical professions to work in the DRC. This project ran from October 1960 until the last CPRA medical volunteer left the DRC a decade later. Chapter 5 explores the administration and organisation of this programme. As the Congolese government lacked the means and the will in the early 1960s to train medical doctors, the CPRA offered Canadian and US doctors and nurses the opportunity to serve at Protestant hospitals from one month to two years. CPRA staff in the US wrestled with selecting candidates who could work in mission settings. Due to the Simba revolts and growing discontent from donor agencies about the prolonged political crisis in the DRC, Operation Doctor drastically curtailed its work from 1965 until it ended in 1970. Aid agencies increasingly preferred programmes that trained Congolese to become medical professionals rather than rely on expatriates.

Chapter 6 is an overview of the experiences of CPRA medical volunteers from 1960 until 1966. These volunteers included retired missionary doctors who had lived in the Congo along with physicians with only a hazy knowledge of Africa. For the majority of medical professionals sent to rural hospitals, they quickly discovered that local communities viewed them as important assets, regardless of their general lack of familiarity with tropical medicine and their very limited supplies. Some doctors received protection from local people when threatened by Congolese army soldiers. In particular, Congolese patients sought CPRA doctors' expertise in childbirth. Still other doctors served in the capital. Buford Washington, an African-American doctor from Philadelphia, even became the personal physician of Congolese president Joseph Kasa-Vubu. Though some shared the paternalistic outlook of the Belgian doctors they often replaced, others trained Congolese medical assistants so that work could go on even after Western-trained volunteer physicians had left. Many volunteers felt they could not accomplish very much, but they also believed by training competent medical assistants that they were building a new Congolese nation.

Chapter 7 considers the shift from emergency aid to economic development in the late 1960s and early 1970s. Congolese pastors demanded that donor organisations and mission boards accept that Africans were in charge of the CPRA. Chapter 7 examines the strains between Congolese church authorities and the Church World Service over the operation of the CPRA. CWS staff increasingly balked at the CPRA's dependence on donors and the willingness of Congolese pastors to exchange donor contributions in dollars on the black market into Congolese currency. The unification of all Protestant churches in the DRC into a single giant church, endorsed by the Congolese government, also created tensions between the CPRA and some mission boards. Ultimately, the CWS had severely cut its support for the CPRA by 1973, but other donors then stepped into the breach.

The final chapter concentrates on a single CPRA project, the Centre for Community Development (CEDECO), to better understand the transition from emergency aid to development. CEDECO originally was a training programme for Angolan refugees to become craftsmen and skilled farmers in 1965. It later opened up to Congolese living in Bas-Congo province. In keeping with Mobutu Sese Seko's cultural nationalist policies, the CPRA had placed Africans in charge of CEDECO by 1971. UK and Canadian technical experts clashed with Africans over the administration of CEDECO, even as the project attempted to promote small-scale, low-cost programmes favourable to rural farmers. Though this programme survived through the early 1990s and successfully promoted the interests of rural farmers, it also serves as a testimony to the difficulties of collaborations between foreign expatriates and Africans during the early years of Mobutu's dictatorship.

This book closes in the early 1970s for several reasons. By 1968, the worst of the refugee and food crises of the 1960s had come to an end. As the justification for emergency relief declined, the CPRA and other aid organisations shifted their attention to economic development. As the Congolese economy deteriorated, many Congolese Protestant development projects suffered. The heroic era of emergency relief had become eclipsed as Congolese churches and donors promoted expansive developmental projects. The loose structure of the CPRA became firmly bureaucratized under the control of the L'Église du Christ au Congo. The global recession that began in 1973 severely disrupted the Congolese economy and the ability of donors to raise money at the same time. Mobutu Sese Seko's appropriation of foreign businesses made him and his entourage wealthy at the expense of the country's economy. New anxieties over how to produce development in a country burdened by a collapsing economy, rampant corruption, and an authoritarian regime supplanted the redemptive call of alleviating Congolese suffering in the name of Christian charity.

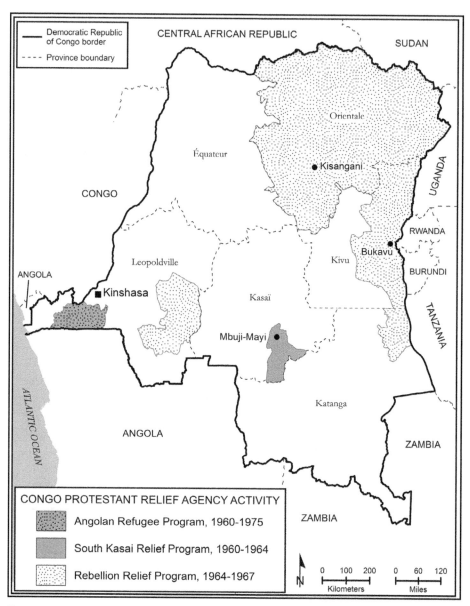

Democratic Republic of Congo in the 1960s

1

The CPRA, Protestant Missions, and the Congo Crises, 1960–1965

The Congo Protestant Relief Agency's work depended on a wide array of international donors. From the standpoint of the donor institutions who supplied the CPRA with the funds and the materiel that kept it running, Protestant aid constituted one provider to deal with the humanitarian challenges of the DRC. US officials recognised full well the political implications of famines, unemployment, refugees, and internally displaced peoples. The US Agency for International Development (USAID) harnessed the CPRA to distribute food supplies authorised by the Public Law 480 Food for Peace Programme. The United Nations also considered the CPRA as an ally in its efforts to promote a stable Congolese society. Christian international organisations such as the World Council of Churches sponsored the CPRA to ally themselves with Congolese Protestants in the aftermath of decolonisation. Congolese authorities, whose commitment to social programmes wavered at best, turned to Protestant aid to make up for their own lack of resources. Finally, the impoverished Congolese churches that ostensibly presided over the CPRA had their own pressing need for resources.

Each one of these donors placed their own agendas on the CPRA. Some sponsors had a steady set of guidelines for Protestant aid. USAID required the CPRA to monitor and account for how US government food donations were transported and distributed. Though US officials watched over CPRA food distribution, they had little interest in the internal dynamics of how expatriates managed and organised the CPRA. The World Council of Churches (WCC) also asked for financial information, but its vision of a transnational partnership between Christians in the Global North and South also impacted the CPRA. WCC staff sometimes felt the US and Canadian expatriates did not listen enough to Congolese church leaders, who had very little control over the CPRA until 1965. The United Nations civilian operations in the Congo made common cause with the CPRA at certain moments, but spent less time tracking supplies than USAID and had no interest in the CPRA's organisation. Even if all of the CPRA's sponsors considered the Congo to be a humanitarian disaster in the 1960s, their negotiations and impositions on Protestant aid varied.

The CPRA also answered to foreign mission boards as well as Congolese leaders of churches originally founded by missionaries. In 1960, North Americans still controlled the vast majority of Protestant churches. The upheavals of independence made many Protestants question how missionaries could separate themselves from the racist legacy of colonialism. By participating in the construction of a new Congo, missionaries saw new opportunities for evangelisation. They also viewed themselves as partners to Congolese church leaders. Their opinions went hand in hand with a sense Congolese still required the tutelage of their North American partners.

This chapter begins with a summary of how political conflicts set in motion a series of hardships for Congolese people. Claude Kabemba and Kevin Dunn among others certainly are correct in the ways international press coverage portrayed the social dilemmas of the newly independent Congolese nation as desperately in need of Western saviours.[1] This point should not allow us to forget how often scholars have ignored the famines, violence, and dislocation civilians endured in the civil wars of the 1960s. I then turn to the organisation of the CPRA, which reflected the ad hoc and experimental nature of aid and mission work in the early 1960s in the DRC. Finally, the varied donors of the CPRA and their related, but not identical, engagement with Protestant aid come under discussion, particularly the US government and the World Council of Churches.

The Congo crises as a humanitarian emergency

The Congolese political crises from 1960 to 1967 left a heavy toll on civilians. Almost a full year before independence day on 30 June 1960, Lulua chiefs in Kasai province had called for the forcible expulsion of Luba clan members whose families had migrated from the southern Kasai province into the city of Kananga and the surrounding region. By the spring of 1960, Lulua militas had razed numerous Luba villages and driven tens of thousands of Luba people south towards Mbuji-Mayi. In the copper-rich southern province of Katanga, Moïse Tshombe's CONAKAT (Confédération des associations tribales du Katanga) political party had rallied southern Katangese communities to attack Luba migrants from the Kasai region as well as Luba clans in the northern part of Katanga. Nande, Hunde, and other communities in Kivu province launched attacks on Kinyarwanda-speakers who they deemed

---

1   Dunn, *Imagining*; Kabemba, "Humanitarian Interventions."

to be foreigners, even though some Kinyarwanda families had lived in Congolese territory well before the establishment of colonial rule.[2]

Prime minister Patrice Lumumba's rivalry with Tshombe led to a three-year struggle between the Armée Nationale Congolaise (ANC) with the Katangese army. With the backing of the Belgian mining conglomerate Union Minière du Haut Katanga and the overwhelming support of Belgian settlers, Tshombe announced in July 1960 that Katanga would become an independent country. Tshombe's forces slaughtered Luba civilians in northern Katanga for their refusal to recognise the secession, while Luba militias attacked civilians and Katangese soldiers.[3] Lumumba convinced the United Nations to provide military forces to keep his country together. UN peacekeepers from India, Ethiopia, Sweden, Nigeria, and elsewhere engaged in a series of intermittent military campaigns against Tshombe's government. After a series of convoluted negotiations and clashes, UN forces finally routed the Katangese army in the beginning of 1963.

Lumumba himself became a victim of the competition for power in the Congo. Lumumba's charismatic personality and willingness to seek Soviet support in his struggle with Katanga alarmed US President Dwight Eisenhower along with the British and Belgian governments. Joseph Kasavubu, president of the DRC and leader of the ABAKO (Alliance des Bakongo) party, which was popular only in Bas-Congo province, tried to have Lumumba dismissed on 10 September 1960. Ambitious military officer Joseph-Désiré Mobutu had Lumumba jailed and set up a new government stocked with anti-Communist and pro-Western Congolese officials. Lumumba's political supporters formed a new government in Kisangani, the largest city in eastern Congo. The former prime minister managed to escape his detention in December 1960, but was recaptured by ANC forces. Mobutu, Belgian military advisers, and most likely US and British intelligence then had Lumumba sent to Moise Tshombe, who ordered his execution in February 1961.

---

2   On the attacks on Rwandan refugees in the early 1960s in DRC, see A.K. Onoma, *Anti-Refugee Violence and African Politics* (New York: Cambridge University Press, 2013), 200–36.

3   For some of the many works dealing with violence between the Katangese state and Luba communities, see C.C. O'Brien, *To Katanga and Back: A UN Case History* (London: Hutchinson and Co, 1962); J. Gérard-Libois, *The Katangese Secession* (Madison: University of Wisconsin Press, 1966); S. Vinckel, "Violence and Everyday Interactions between Katangese and Kasaians: Memory and Elections in Two Katangese Cities," *Africa* 85:1 (2015), 78–102; E. Kennes and M. Larmer, *The Katangese Gendarmes and War in Central Africa: Fighting Their Way Home* (Bloomington, IN: Indiana University Press, 2016).

After Mobutu and Kasavubu agreed under US pressure to install Cyrille Adoula as prime minister in 1961, violence continued to wrack the DRC. Conflicts emerged from local and regional divisions. For example, southern Kasai was engulfed by warfare. Albert Kalonji, a former ally of Lumumba, chose instead to form the Autonomous State of South Kasai (ASSK) to defend Luba-speakers from the depredations of Lulua militas and the ANC. Lumumba had ordered the ANC to neutralise Kalonji's government in August 1960. Using Soviet-supplied trucks, Congolese national forces rampaged through southern Kasai before Lumumba's arrest and local resistance drove them into Lulua territory by late September 1960. By the end of 1960, over half a million refugees had poured into Kalonji's territory. The Belgian diamond company Forminière funded mercenaries and arms to the ASSK army, which then attacked the Kanyok ethnic community for not surrendering their authority to Kalonji. In the diamond mining town of Tshikapa in government-controlled territory, Luba militas clashed with Pende and Tchokwe groups. UN peacekeeping forces held rival Congolese groups at bay at times, but even UN forces sometimes faced attacks. A mutiny by ASSK troops against Kalonji backed by ANC forces put an end to the ASSK in October 1962, but Congolese regional leaders battled each other over control of the new provincial government, setting off a new round of fighting in the first half of 1963.

Even as southern Kasai finally settled down by the beginning of 1964, a new round of revolts commenced. A loose coalition of leftist political leaders in exile in the Republic of Congo (Brazzaville) formed the Conseil National de la Libération (CNL) in late 1963. The CNL included Pierre Mulele, Lumumba's former minister of education, who spent some months receiving training in Communist China. Mulele returned to his home province of Kwilu in western DRC and launched a guerilla war against the government. In eastern DRC, the CNL recruited large numbers of supporters to fight against the pro-Western government. While Mulele's forces failed to break out of Kwilu, eastern rebels seized major cities such as Kisangani and Kindu over the course of the middle of 1964. The US government, eager to find a strongman to effectively defeat the rebels, backed Moïse Tshombe's decision to return to the DRC. The US government hired anti-Communist Cuban pilots and South African, Belgian, French, and other European mercenaries to try to crush the rebellion. Belgian paratroopers flown by US Air Forces planes recaptured Kisangani from the rebels. ANC and mercenary forces fought CNL rebels from 1964 until early 1967, as rebel units continued to fight in rural areas of the Orientale province.

Civilians suffered greatly during the 1964–7 revolts. Rebels killed those suspected of loyalty to mission churches and the government. At least 7000 Congolese civilians alone were believed to have executed during the rebel occupation. ANC forces often attacked civilians suspected of backing the CNL. Government troops stole and killed most of the chickens and livestock of rural Kwilu villages from 1964 to 1966. Fighting so disrupted farming among many Orientale farmers that famine took hold by 1965 in much of the province. Kwashiorkor, an illness caused by protein deficiencies, killed children in much of eastern Congo and in the western province of Kwilu. Perhaps hundreds of thousands of Congolese fled their homes. Medical care was very limited in rebel-held areas.

Alongside the Congolese displaced by the Congolese civil wars, hundreds of thousands of foreign refugees entered the DRC in the 1960s.[4] The Sudanese government tried to force southern Sudanese to conform to its Arabisation and Islamisation campaigns in the early 1960s, prompting some southern Sudanese to form the Anya-Nya rebel movement. Over 10,000 Sudanese fled into Orientale province. Further east, the 1962 Rwandan revolution forced tens of thousands of Tutsi people to resettle in Congolese territory. By far, the largest group of refugees came from the Portuguese colony of Angola. The União dos Povos de Angola (UPA) Angolan political party commenced a guerilla war in northern Angola in March 1961. The Portuguese government struck back by killing thousands of civilians during their military campaign against the UPA. Over 300,000 Angolans had escaped their homeland by the end of 1962, mainly settling in the Bas-Congo province that bordered on the northern Angolan heartland of the UPA and its successor organisation, the FNLA (Frente Nacional de Libertação de Angola). While many Angolan refugees belonged to the BisiKongo ethnic community predominating in Bas-Congo province, some Congolese resented the Angolans as competitors for scare jobs and resources.

Even in regions not directly affected by warfare, the political crises of the 1960s left their mark on daily life. ANC soldiers, undisciplined and poorly paid, regularly demanded bribes from villagers and in roadblocks across the country. Most Belgian medical personnel left the DRC in 1960, leaving rural

---

4   A short summary of foreign refugees in the DRC in the 1960s can be found in E. Burstin, "The Congo," in H.C. Brooks and Y. el-Ayouty (eds) *An African Dilemma: Refugees South of the Sahara* (Westport, CT: Negro Universities Press, 1970), 183–8; J. Grenfell, "Refugees in the Republic of Zaire (Congo-Kinshasa)," in L. Holborn (ed.), *Refugees: A Problem of Our Time – The Work of the United Nations High Commissioner for Refugees, Vol. 2* (Metuchen, NJ: Scarecrow Press, 1975), 1045–115.

hospitals critically understaffed and without access to most medicines. Although the League of Red Cross Societies and the World Health Organisation (WHO) sent teams of doctors to the DRC after independence, the need for physicians was far greater than either organisation could satisfy. A smallpox epidemic ravaged parts of the DRC in 1961 and 1962, in part because of the lack of doctors.[5]

In the parlance of humanitarian aid in the late 20th century, the DRC had become a complex humanitarian emergency, but neither the DRC government nor international aid organisations were prepared to handle the enormity of the situation. The Congolese state, fractured by its civil wars and the cupidity of its leadership, did not invest in social services and emergency aid. Regular army units, mutinous soldiers, and rebels alike robbed, murdered, and assaulted civilians with impunity. The DRC fell quite short of the standard of Nkrumah's Ghana or many other states seeking to establish an African version of the developmentalist model of social services and state-supported industries already in place in European countries, Egypt, India, and elsewhere. The United Nations mission in the DRC (UNOC) began to send in supplies and civilian officers to oversee aid in 1960. Despite the ability of the UNOC to deliver food and supplies, its resources and personnel still could not meet demand for help.

For the US government, social upheaval constituted a serious threat to its Cold War aim of establishing a reliable, anti-Communist Congolese state. Food aid became one notable aspect of the multipronged US efforts to alleviate civilian unrest through the PL 480 programme, originally created in 1954 and redubbed the Food for Peace programme under President Kennedy.[6] Aimed originally at school children, unemployed people, and others designated as needy by USAID, food consisted mainly of milk, rolled wheat, bulgur, beans, and oil.[7] As one USAID officer stationed in

5   D. Flauhault, J. Geerts, R. Lasserre, and A. Van der Heyden, "Quelques aspects épidémiologiques et cliniques de l'épidémie de variole à Léopoldville (septembre 1961 – mai 1962)," *Bulletin of the World Health Organisation* 29:1 (1963), 117–25.

6   R. Stanley, *Food For Peace: Hope and Reality of U.S. Food Aid* (New York: Gordon and Breach, 1973), 25–9. For a general overview of US foreign policy and food aid, see B. Riley, *The Political History of American Food Aid: An Uneasy Benevolence* (New York: Oxford University Press, 2017).

7   "Title III – Congo," (unpublished manuscript, no date [1966]), Folder FPC 6 VolAgs Programming CY 1967, Box 3, USAID Program Files 1961–1967, Record Group 286 Records of the US Agency for International Development, NARA II.

2. Congolese unload CPRA food from US Air Force plane, possibly Bukavu, c. 1964–1966. The US government used the CPRA to distribute US government surplus food to civilians to help reinforce the weak Congolese government. (NARA II)

the Congo put it, 'We were trying to make a nation out of a huge country … We provided a lot of relief assistance. We did help people, we prevented them from starving, we helped them medically. What this did to help build up a nation I have my doubts,' he concluded.[8] Congolese officials recognised how much they depended on this assistance. Cyrille Adoula, the Congolese prime minister, assured President Kennedy in 1963: 'Even though some propaganda circles may attempt to distort the nature of American aid and make it appear that the US is trying to establish its rule over the Congo, the people understand that the assistance comes from

8   Association for Diplomatic Studies and Training, "Democratic Republic of the Congo (Zaire) Country Reader" (2018), 246, 254. Available at: adst.org/wpcontent/uploads/2018/02/Democratic-Republic-of-the-Congo-Zaire.pdf (Accessed 27 October 2019).

the American people."[9] It is in this context that British, US, and Canadian Protestants developed aid programmes.

Protestant missions in the DRC

At independence, over 2,500 Protestant missionaries from over 50 separate denominations lived in the DRC.[10] US Protestants like the American Baptist Foreign Missionary Society and the Disciples of Christ had over one hundred missionaries, while some small fundamentalist denominations only had a handful of expatriates. Protestant missions had operated in the DRC from the first years of colonial rule in the late 19th century to independence. The small group of missionaries from the Baptist Missionary Society (BMS) had begun to work in the western Bas-Congo region by 1881 and quickly formed missions along the Congo and other rivers. The BMS solicited other Protestant missions from the US, Great Britain, and Canada to come to the DRC with the approval of Leopold II's government.[11] To avoid conflict between Prot-

---

9   "430. Memorandum of Conversation," *Foreign Relations of the United States*, Vol. XX, Congo Crisis, 879.

10 J. Crawford, *Protestant Missions in Congo, 1878–1969* (Kinshasa: Librarie Evangelique du Congo, 1969), 15.

11 On the growth of Protestant missions in the colonial era, see Braeckman, *Histoire du protestantisme*; Markowitz, *Cross and Sword*; Kabongo-Mbaya, *Église*, 47–110; Munongo, "Aspects du protestantisme dans le Congo-Zaïre indépendant (1960-1990)." (PhD thesis, Université de Lille III, 2000), 57–85. Individual denominations also produced a lengthy number of institutional histories. They include A. Reid, *Congo Drumbeat: History of the First Half Century in the Establishment of the Methodist Church among the Atetela of Central Congo* (New York: World Outlook Press, 1964); N. Oldberg, "A History of the Zaire Mission of the Evangelical Free Church, 1922–1975," (MA thesis, Trinity Evangelical Divinity School, 1977); A. Makumunwa Kiantandu, "A Study of the Contribution of American Presbyterians to the Formation of the Church of Christ in Zaire, with Special Reference to Indigenisation, 1891–1960," (ThD thesis, Union Theological Seminary in Virginia, 1978); D. Kirkwood, *Mission in Mid-Continent, Zaire: One Hundred Years of American Baptist Commitment in Zaire, 1884–1984* (Valley Forge, PA: International Ministries ABC/USA, 1984); B. Stanley, *The History of the Baptist Missionary Society 1792–1992* (Edinburgh: T. and T. Clark, 1992), 336–68; J. Bertsche, *CIM/AIMM: A Story of Vision, Commitment, and Grace* (Elkhart, IN: Fairway Press, 1998); P. Williams, "The Disciples of Christ Congo Mission (DCCM), 1897–1932: A Missionary Community in Colonial Central Africa," (PhD thesis, University of Chicago Divinity School, 2000) 2000; R. Hollinger-Janzen, N. Myers, and J. Bertsche (eds), *The Jesus Tribe: Grace Stories from Congo's Mennonites 1912–2012: A Project of Africa Inter-Mennonite Mission* (Elkhart: Institute of Mennonite Studies,

estant denominations, mission boards agreed to divide up evangelisation in the DRC into individual fields. For example, the Disciples of Christ mission received much of southern Équateur province. New Protestant denominations kept entering the DRC, as mission boards who had established themselves in earlier decades gave up parts of their original mission field to newcomers.

Some Protestant missionaries had taken the lead in criticising abuses by Leopold II's government at the turn of the 20th century. Leopold II's regime coerced Congolese to collect ivory and rubber for concessionary companies. European administrators and African chiefs and soldiers in the employ of the colonial government punished Congolese, from burning and raiding villages to chopping off hands of family members who had not gathered enough rubber. These missionaries ecame more quiescent towards colonial authorities after Leopold II cynically sold his African colony to the Belgian government in 1908. African-American Presbyterian pastor William Sheppard exemplified the crusading critics of the violence of Leopold II's administration, even as some Protestant mission boards tried to avoid confrontations with the colonial state for fear Leopold II would expel them from the colony.[12]

Theology, national and regional origins, finances, and political views divided Protestant missionaries in the DRC. Some large missions belonged to what were known in North America as 'mainline' Protestant churches. I will occasionally use this term 'mainline' as shorthand. In the mid-20th century, several large deniminations comprised together a majority of Protestants in the United States.[13] They included four churches that had missions in the DRC: the American Baptists, the Presbyterian Church USA, the United Methodist Church, and the Disciples of Christ. These large institutions cooperated with each other on relief and political action, despite having little agreement on numerous theological issues, to the point these churches claimed to represent the majority or 'mainline' of US Protestants. In the

---

2012). This list hardly exhausts the number of individual denominational histories of evangelisation in the DRC, particularly those written during the colonial era.

12   D. Lagergren, *Mission and State in the Congo: A Study of the Relations between Protestant Missions and the Congo Independent State Authorities with Special Reference to the Equator District 1885–1903* (Uppsala: Studia Missionalia Upsaliensia, 1970); S. Shaloff, *Reform in Leopold's Congo* (Richmond, VA: John Knox Press, 1970); P. Kennedy, *Black Livingstone: A True Tale of Adventure in the Nineteenth-Century Congo* (New York: Viking, 2002); D. Pavlakis, *British Humanitarianism and the Congo Reform Movement, 1896–1913* (New York: Routledge, 2015).

13   For a good overview of the mainline Protestant tradition in the USA, see J. Lantzer, *Mainline Christianity: The Past and Future of America's Majority Faith* (New York: New York University Press, 2012).

first half of the 20th century, newer evangelical and Pentecostal churches had critiqued mainline Protestants for allegedly straying from literal interpretations of the Bible, being too willing to downplay Christian beliefs to gain acceptance with leftist and moderate secular groups as well as members of other religious traditions outside of Protestantism, and for downplaying orthodox Christian beliefs such as eternal damnation. Missionaries from mainline churches undermine a simple split between mainline and evangelical Protestants, since many of them could be defined as evangelicals based on their theology. More importantly for this study, missionaries tended to avoid sharp disputes over theology in DRC in comparison to their much more public disputes in Europe and North America.

Although categorisation between mainline and evangelical Protestants is much harder to make the more one considers individual theological perspectives, there was a clear gulf between the well-finaced and large missions of the American Baptists, the Disciples of Christ, the Southern Presbyterians, and the United Methodist church with much smaller missions identifying as evangelical. Only two self-idenified evangelical churches had a significantly large mission presence in the DRC: the Christian and Missionary Alliance in the western coastal province of Bas-Congo and the Africa Inland Mission operating in northeastern Congo. Over 20 smaller missions idenfiying as evangelical ran much smaller missions, primarily in parts of eastern DRC.

To make matters even more complicated, a number of missions in DRC belonged to churches from Canada, the UK, and several European countries or represented churches whose theology and political views did not neatly coincide with the US categories of evangelical and mainline. The UK-based BMS belonged to the Dissenting movement outside of the dominant Anglican tradition in the UK. The BMS stood out from the larger North American mission field particularly for its national origins and as the first Protestant mission to evangelise in the DRC in the late 19th century. Smaller Swedish, Norwegian, and Belgian Protestant churches cooperated with the big North American missions as well. Finally, the Congo Inland Mission and its more evenaglically oriented Mennonite Brethren counterpart represented the Anabaptist movement in DRC. Because of their commitment to pacficism and outlier theological positions, Anabaptists tended to be on the margins of North American Protestant movements. In colonial Congo, however, they cooperated relatively easily with mainline and evangelical Protestants.

Despite these dissimilarities, these various missions generally cooperated with each other and shared common anxieties working in a Belgian African colony. In 1934, delegates of a group of missions formed the Congo Protestant Council, a loose group designed to further cooperation between missions.

These alliances came together in part because of the dominant role of Roman Catholicism in the Congo. The colonial government favoured Roman Catholic missionaries, deemed to be far more loyal to Belgium than Protestants. Some Protestant missionaries took great pride in how Congolese respected them more than the Belgians, but it would be a mistake to assume this meant most Protestant missionaries viewed Congolese as their equals. Protestants at odds with the state about their perceived second-class status did not go so far as to undermine European rule. Very few missionaries rejected colonialism or white supremacy outright.[14] Most Protestant missions from North America and Great Britain had only begun to transfer leadership over to Congolese shortly before independence in 1960.[15]

Between 1956 and 1960, Protestants had to adjust as Belgian dominance foundered. Despite the Nazi occupation of Belgium during the Second World War and the rise of anti-colonial nationalist movements in Africa in the early 1950s, colonial administrators and most Belgian politicians believed they could control the Congo for many decades to come. A disparate group of Congolese intellectuals and politicians challenged the colonial order. Many of them had direct connections to Protestant missions. Patrice Lumumba, a postal clerk who had attended a Methodist school in the east-central town of Wembo Nyama, became the leader of the Mouvement National Congolais (MNC). Even as Lumumba denounced colonialism and racism in the name of a united, centralised DRC, his rival Moïse Tshombe called for a federalist Congo that would grant his copper-rich home province of Katanga a great deal of autonomy from the central government. Tshombe, a favourite of Methodist missionaries, thoroughly opposed Communism. Lumumba, by contrast, accepted support from Belgian Communists and eventually the Soviet Union. In Bas-Congo province, Joseph Kasavubu led the ABAKO party that favoured the BisiKongo ethnic community. Though Kasavubu was raised a Catholic, he had a good rapport with Protestant missionaries by 1960.

The DRC's prolonged political crises in the 1960s posed serious challenges for Protestant missionaries as well as Congolese civilians. Given that over 50 different Protestant mission boards operated in the DRC at the end of colonial rule, missionary responses to the Congo crises differed a great deal. One response at independence, particularly among older pastors and medical

---

14 For a summary of tensions between Catholic and Protestant missionaries after 1908, see Markowitz, *Cross and Sword*, 38–75; Kabongo-Mbaya, *Église*, 21–46; J. Rogers, "Ye Are All One: Missionaries in the Congo and the Dynamics of Race and Gender, 1890–1925," (PhD thesis, Ohio Union Institute and University, 2006).

15 Kabongo-Mbaya, *Église*, passim.

missionaries, was disgust. Titus Johnson, a physician who had worked in the DRC for three decades, depicted the mutiny of July 1960 as part of 'a storm of outrage against all white people and its purpose was to get rid of them in the cruelest way possible.'[16] Johnson, filled with horror at being threatened repeatedly by drunk Congolese soldiers, harped on about how the Congolese army had raped white women, destroyed white-owned homes, and wreaked havoc until European United Nations staff had begun to restore order.[17] Carroll Stegall, a Presbyterian missionary since 1910, returned briefly from retirement in late 1960 to assist the CPRA. After returning to missions he had once directed over 40 years beforehand, he ruefully described abandoned buildings and unkept gardens at his former mission station at Luebo. 'I felt more at home among the graves in the cemetery,' Stegall wrote in despair.[18] Former Presbyterian missionary Daniel Juengst contended that many missionaries could not accept the collapse of colonial domination: 'The frame of mind in the missionary remaining in the field after [the 1960] evacuation has been characterised by frustration, uncertainty, pessimism, and in the best moments, a determination to work in whatever way for as long as possible.'[19] Still other missionaries faced challenges for control of their churches. Congolese Conservative Baptists in the eastern Kivu province split between supporters of missionaries and other who rejected missionary authority.[20]

Some narratives of Congolese independence might have been drenched in Afro-pessimism, yet not all missionaries shared this sense of discouragement. The end of Belgian rule meant the dethroning of Roman Catholicism in the DRC from its privileged place as a cornerstone of colonial authority. Roman Catholic missionaries outnumbered Protestants and denounced their Protestants competitors.[21] An independent Congolese government was an opportunity for Protestants to freely evangelise. Pierre Shaumba, a Congolese Methodist pastor, took pride as Belgian authorities agreed at the

16 T. Johnson and M. Larson, *When Congo Bursts at Its Seams* (Chicago: Moody Bible Institute, 1961), 11.

17 Ibid., 13, 15–17, 29, 35–8.

18 Carroll Stegall diary, 'Dad's Last Trip 1961,' 8, Folder 7 Carroll Richard Stegall Diary, Box 2, Record Group 454, Carroll Stegall papers, Presbyterian Historical Society, Philadelphia, Pennsylvania.

19 D. Juengst, "Cultural Dynamics at Luebo: An Ethnography of Religious Agents of Change in Zaire," (PhD thesis, University of Florida, 1975), 152–3.

20 Nelson, *Christian Missionizing*.

21 A. Bita Lihun Nzunfu, *Missions catholiques et protestantes face au colonialisme et aux aspirations du people autotchone à l'autonomie et à l'indépendance politique au Congo Belge (1908–1960)* (Rome: Gregorian Pontifical University, 2013), 397–415.

last minute to include Protestants in the official independence ceremonies in Kinshasa on 30 June 1960. The Methodist credited prayer for this miracle in which 'Roman Catholics and Protestants are on equal footing', but his threat that there might be trouble in the African neighbourhoods if Protestants were neglected might have also explained the colonial government's change of heart.[22] Methodist missionary Alexander Reid credited Shaumba for saving 'Congo from being considered as under control of the Church of Rome' via a papal envoy supposedly tasked with ensuring Catholic domination of the new government – a particularly hyperbolic example of Protestant fears about Roman Catholic influence.[23]

Some mission board leaders considered independence to be a crucial time for missionaries to cast off the racist legacy of colonialism. Robert Nelson, the director of African and Jamaican missions for the Disciples of Christ, wrote: 'If the churches of the West are willing to accept in Christian partnership and love those whom they have sent the message of God's redeeming love through Christ, they may yet find in [the Congo] their truest allies.'[24] George Carpenter, an important figure in the Church World Service (CWS), denounced colonialism. The CWS was the relief relief agency of the National Council of Christian Churches (NCCC), a coalition of large US Protestant churches. 'To many Belgians the African adult was a grown-up child, incapable of mature judgement … More than one African remarked to me, "We can put up with low wages, with hardships, even with abuse, *if only we are treated like human beings*"', Carpenter noted.[25] Protestant missionaries, unsullied by close Catholic cooperation with racist Belgians, now had the chance to commit themselves to the Congolese people through cooperation with the Congolese government and Congolese churches.[26] Communists, Carpenter warned, were only taking advantage of the Belgians resisting independence: 'If [Belgian] leaders had not built up frustration and fear and distrust in the hearts of the Congolese, the seeds of Communist malice could not have

---

22 Pierre Shaumba, 23 July 1960, Folder Congo Emergency July 1960, Box 14, Record Group 8, CWS/PHS.

23 A. Reid, *The Roots of Lomomba: Mongo Land* (Hicksville, NY: Exposition Press, 1979), 102.

24 R. Nelson, *Congo Crisis and Christian Mission* (St. Louis, MO: Bethany Press, 1961), 104.

25 G. Carpenter, "Collapse in the Congo: The Price of Paternalism," *Christianity Today* (19 September 1960), 129.

26 Ibid., 132.

taken root and grown.'[27] Mennonite Central Committee members viewed the Congo crises in similar fashion. Elmer Neufeld, the director of MCC's Congo programme, observed how Congolese people recognised how heavily the US government had invested in Cyrille Adoula's government in 1963 and 1964. One Congolese informant told Neufeld, 'What is the United States trying to do, buy the Congo?'[28]

Organisers of a conference on the future of Protestant missions organised by the CWS in September 1960 solicited the opinions of a group of American Baptist and other Protestant pastors. These letters expressed self-doubt, shock, and humility in the face of Congolese independence. Missionaries castigated themselves. Norman Riddle recommended: 'Let's live with the people and not form a little American oasis in the midst of the undeveloped African culture.'[29] Another writer noted, 'We have for too long carried on a policy of paternalism on most of our stations ... We sometimes criticise the Belgian government for carrying on paternalism when we are just as guilty.'[30] Phyllis Benner declared, 'Only the Congolese have the right to say who should return to Congo, and when.'[31] Other writers still could include patronising comments, such as 'Africans are at their best around a fireplace ... They are born orators and equal to most any situation, but if whites are rather in the background, Africans gradually warm up and speak their minds earnestly' rather than trying to tell 'what they think (often erroneously) the white wants to here.'[32] Yet even older missionaries most likely to express such attitudes admitted they probably

27 Ibid., 132.

28 Elmer Neufeld to William Snyder, 10 March 1964, Folder Congo Office I 1964 111/128, Box 190, IX-6-3, MCCA.

29 Norman Riddle, 28 August 1960, Folder 20 Mission Conference on Future Program in the Congo Republic, Box 138 Post-War Baptist International Mission, ABHSA.

30 C. Gerald Weaver, 23 August 1960, Folder 20 Mission Conference on Future Program in the Congo Republic, Box 138 Post-War Baptist International Mission, American Baptist Foreign Mission Society, ABHSA.

31 Phyllis Brenner, 16 September 1960, Folder 20 Mission Conference on Future Program in the Congo Republic, Box 138 Post-War Baptist International Mission, American Baptist Foreign Mission Society, ABHSA.

32 M. Eldridge, 25 August 1960, Folder 20 Mission Conference on Future Program in the Congo Republic, Box 138 Post-War Baptist International Mission, American Baptist Foreign Mission Society, ABHSA.

should retire: 'The new Congo will have no roots in the past while all of us are firmly rooted in the past.'[33]

Not all missionaries were so reflective about colonialism's impact on themselves and on Congolese, but still recognised a need for action. The Africa Inland Mission and the Free Evangelical Church missions, for example, resolutely rejected the more politically and theological liberal leanings of the Disciples of Christ and the American Baptists.[34] But, conservative missionaries with few qualms about colonialism had their own concerns. They believed chaos and adversity in the Congo could transform this African nation into a new Red China – a particularly unsettling prospect given how Protestant missions had operated in Chinese territory before the revolution of 1949.[35] United Methodist bishop Newell S. Booth Sr, a prominent defender of Moïse Tshombe's Katangese secession, warned in 1963 that Congolese could hear Chinese broadcasts in Swahili denounce 'disturbances between the races' in the US.[36] Ensuring mission hospitals remained at work was of profound importance to evangelical missionaries. Missionary medical care was a crucial part of evangelisation in the colonial period. African Inland Mission pastor William Deans may have felt that Jesus could only transform people as 'social work will never do it', but even evangelicals wanted to keep the mission hospitals running after independence: 'Thrilling stories are told of the Christian doctors' tremendous influence for the Gospel in far-flung Congo communities … Thousands of souls have been won to Christ by the direct testimony of missionary doctors and nurses.'[37] Whether liberal or conservative on theology, North American and British missionaries endorsed humanitarian relief.

33 Ben Armstrong, 16 August 1960, Folder 20 Mission Conference on Future Program in the Congo Republic, Box 138 Post-War Baptist International Mission, American Baptist Foreign Mission Society, ABHSA.

34 For the perspective of a Free Evangelical Church missionary, see Johnson and Larson, *Congo Bursts*.

35 E. Parker, "The Congo: Another China?" *Christian Century* (2 September 1960), 1081–4. US officials such as US Ambassador to the United Nations Henry Cabot Lodge also made this comparison. See "Telegram from the Mission at the United Nations to the Department of State," 26 August 1960, *Foreign Relations of the United States, 1958–1960 Vol. XIV Africa*, 444–6.

36 Cited in N. Kotz, *Judgement Days: Lyndon Baines Johnson, Martin Luther King Jr., and the Laws that Changed America* (New York: Houghton Mifflin, 2005), 132.

37 W. Deans, *Muffled Drumbeats in the Congo* (Chicago: Moody Bible Institute, 1961), 52, 122.

An overview of the CPRA, 1960–1965

In July 1960, the idea of the CPRA was born in an unlikely place: an airport in the Ghanaian capital of Accra. There, about 75 evacuated missionaries met as they awaited their next flight to the US after leaving the Congo under the orders of the US Embassy.[38] Political events had literally thrown together missionaries from many denominations, heedless of theological and political divides. Though Protestant missionaries had anxiously awaited Congolese independence on 30 June 1960, few had counted on a sudden departure from the former Belgian colony. One reason for their exodus from their missions came from the disrespect of Belgian officers for the idea of a Congo free of European tutelage. Belgian camp commander Colonel Émile Janssens informed the Congolese soldiers under his command at the Thysville army base not far from Kinshasa, 'Before independence = after independence.'[39] His troops, appalled by the idea that Congolese independence would be merely colonial rule under a new guise, mutinied. They would only answer to Patrice Lumumba, a fiery critic of colonial abuses and now the new prime minister of the DRC. Some mutineers marched on the Congolese capital of Kinshasa. Still others attacked Belgian and other expatriates, especially after the Belgian government used the mutiny as a pretext to send more troops to the DRC.

Panic among US State Department officials at the idea that black troops might harm white expatriates also prepared the way for the retreat from the DRC. US President Dwight Eisenhower, US Secretary State John Foster Dulles, and lower ranking members of the US diplomatic corps in Kinshasa considered the mutiny to be proof of the inherent primitive and uncontrollable nature of Congolese people. US ambassador to the DRC Claire Timberlake pointed to the revolt had 'removed any lingering trace of the fiction that we are dealing with a civilised people or a responsible government in the Congo'.[40] The US embassy made arrangements for missionaries to flee the country immediately, although C. Vaughan Thompson, the head of the State Department's Africa Department, later denied the US embassy in Kinshasa had done more than

---

38 Robert Bontrager to John Frame, 18 January 1992, RBP. I sincerely thank Robert Bontrager for providing me copies of his CPRA correspondence two years before he passed away in 2014.

39 On the July 1960 mutiny, see L. Vanderstraeten, *Histoire d'une mutinerie: De la Force Publique à l'Armée nationale congolaise* (Brussels: Academie Royale de Belgique, 1993); I. Ndaywel è Nziem, *Histoire Générale du Congo: De l'héritage ancient à la République Démocratique* (Brussels: De Boeck et Larcier, 1998), 568–73.

40 Cited in D. Schmitz, *The United States and Right-Wing Dictatorships, 1965–1989* (New York: Cambridge University Press, 2006), 21.

recommend US citizens leave the country.[41] US Air Force helicopters and air-craft picked up missionaries across the vast territory of the DRC, although a few missionaries (all male) decided to stay. Racist fears of irrational Africans freed from the yoke of colonialism literally moved missionaries out of the Congo, just as the same anxiety led the US government to work for the elimination of Patrice Lumumba, a man who officials felt was a demagogue willing to implant Soviet influence in Central Africa.

Canadian and US missionaries generally held a common view that Con-golese were ill-prepared for the sudden transition to independence in 1960, but they did not all agree with the US embassy's decision to rush them out of the Congo to safety. They recognised an obvious fact that remains on the sidelines of the voluminous scholarly literature on Congolese inde-pendence and the battles for power in the DRC in the 1960s: the country faced a profound set of health challenges. Belgian state and private physi-cians left the DRC in droves in 1960. Protestant medical missionaries also took flight. The Belgian colonial government had done very little to train Congolese to become doctors, to the point that the first Congolese allowed into medical school enrolled only in 1959.[42] Belgian officials had set up an educational system designed to keep Congolese under the tutelage of colonial authority, not produce medical professionals. State and missionary hospitals throughout the newly independent country now had no trained medical staff beyond Congolese nurses. Although these skillful nurses later impressed US and Canadian Protestant medical volunteers, the missionaries thrown together in Accra feared for the survival of Western biomedicine at their former posts. The upheaval also allowed Congolese health practitioners to run independent private clinics free of state intervention, a fact never mentioned in missionary discussions of public health in the early 1960s.[43] For missionaries, Congolese lacked the training to immediately replace European and North American medicial professionals.

Besides the threat of the collapse of public health, North American and Brit-ish missionaries also pondered how Congolese Christians looked at their sudden departure. Several weeks after the airport meeting, a delegation of pastors led by

41 Theodore Tucker, "Republic of the Congo, Whereabouts of American Protestant Missionaries (as of July 23, 1960)," 25 July 1960, Folder Congo Emergency July 1960, Box 22, Record Group 8, CWS/PHS.

42 On the formation of Congolese physicians in the 1960s, see R. Fox and W. De Craemer , *The Emerging Physician: A Sociological Approach to the Development of a Congolese Medical Professional* (Stanford: Hoover Institution Press, 1968).

43 J. Janzen and W. Arkinstall, *The Quest for Therapy: Medical Pluralism in Local Zaire* (Berkeley: University of California Press, 1978), 53–7.

George Carpenter arrived in Kinshasa from the CWS. The CWS had acted as one of the most influential Protestant organisations in the US, representing the internationalist political views and liberal theological perspectives of what David Hollinger has labelled as 'ecumenical' Protestantism, in contrast to the conservative theology and political views among evangelical churches.[44] Carpenter, the Africa department direct for the CWS, met with Congolese president Joseph Kasa-Vubu, aid organisation staff, and US embassy officials. On 29 July 1960, he warned members of Protestant mission boards: 'George Vumi of ENVOL [a Belgian aid agency] tells us that the departure of missionaries at same time [sic] with the Belgians has raised questions among Africans: "Were they siding with the Belgians against us?" It is important to get back and <u>serve</u>.'[45] Protestant missionaries did not always see Congolese independence as supposed proof of African savagery, but instead as a new occasion to build a nation. They also did not want to disappoint the Congolese congregations they had worked with. Colonialism clearly benefited missionaries, but they wanted a place in Congolese society that did not rely on Belgian rule.

Robert Bontrager, the first head of the CPRA's Kinshasa office, on giving his reason for returning to the DRC, wrote: 'Was it right to leave behind our Congo brethren in their sorest hour of trial? Were we really ready to turn our backs on this hopeless situation?'[46] He and other missionaries decided to create a medical relief programme to staff missionary hospitals that now were bereft of trained physicians.[47] Eight people initially volunteered to staff the project. Four were physicians: American Baptist missionaries Carrie Stuart and Glen Tuttle and the Evangelical Covenant missionaries Warren and Gretchen Berggren. Mennonites Robert and Mable Bontrager agreed to manage the project from the interdenominational Protestant bookstore in Kinshasa. Carrie Stuart's husband Allan (a hospital administrator) and Glen Tuttle's wife completed the team willing to immediately return to the Congo. While many flights departed Accra for Kinshasa each day full of United Nations personnel just assigned to the DRC, Glen Tuttle only managed an open seat to fly to Léopoldville on 20 July. Robert Bontrager arrived a week later. He soon was joined by the remaining original members of the CPRA. In

44 D. Hollinger, *After Cloven Tongues of Fire: Protestant Liberalism in Modern American History* (Princeton: Princeton University Press, 2013).

45 George Carpenter to Theodore Tucker, 29 July 1960, Folder Congo Emergency July 1960, Box 22, Record Group 8, CWS/PHS.

46 Robert Bontrager, draft manuscript for Taylor University alumni magazine (Unpublished manuscript, October 1960), RBP.

47 The following is drawn from Robert Bontrager to John Frame, 18 January 1992, RBP.

late August 1960, William Rule joined the CPRA. A Presbyterian missionary doctor stationed in the northern Kasai prior to independence, Rule returned to Congo in October 1960 after having a medical furlough. He helped coordinate CPRA medical work.[48]

Just as the initial CPRA volunteers returned to DRC by the beginning of August to try to find a way to help, influential Protestant organisations conducted missions to the DRC to evaluate the possibility of assistance. The World Council of Churches in Geneva organised a visit to the DRC by George Carpenter, the prominent Nigerian doctor Sir Francis Ibiam, and the French Protestant pastor Pierre Benignus from 27 July to 1 August 1960. They blamed Belgian paternalism for preparing 'fertile soil for the seeds of malice', agreed with Congolese Protestants who felt Belgian military intervention threatened to destroy Congolese independence, and saw Protestants as vital for providing relief and exercising 'the ministry of reconciliation'.[49] Less than two weeks after Ibiam's team left the Congo, Mennonite Central Committee executive committee member Orie Miller also flew to Kinshasa.[50] Miller's report resonated with the World Council of Churches' mission. 'A whole social order [is] in psychological shock,' the MCC leader noted before asserting that independence constituted 'for the Church a time to intercede for the Congo – and to sense and follow the Spirit's leading'.[51] These visits prepared the way for the World Council of Churches, the Church World Service, and the Mennonite Central Committee to support the CPRA.

From its beginnings, a tension existed over whether the CPRA would be a temporary organisation to face humanitarian emergencies or become a permanent institution. The CPRA's constitution stated that the organisation would only exist until 31 December 1965.[52] CPRA officially became the relief section of the Congo Protestant Council (CPC). Originally formed in 1934 to promote coordination and unified negotiations among Protestant mission boards with the colonial government, practically all the top

---

48 W. Rule III, *Milestones in Mission* (Franklin, TN: Providence House, 1998), 138–9.

49 Francis Ibiam, Pierre Benignus, and George Carpenter, "The Congo Crisis" (Unpublished manuscript, no date [August 1960], Folder Congo 1958–1962, Box 425.3.272 Africa Documents Congo 1958–1962, WCCA.

50 The following is drawn from Orie Miller, Diary August 11 –25, 1960 to Congo Republic, Folder MCC Correspondence 1961 - Congo (Zaire) 1960–1961 108/138, Box 181, IX-6-3, MCCA.

51 Ibid.

52 Constitution of the CPRA in America, December 1960, Folder CPRA of America, Box 14, Record Group 8, CWS/PHS.

positions of the CPC were held by expatriate missionaries at independence. Representatives from most major Protestant missions had discussed issues such as state financial support for Protestant mission schools in the past. To try to limit the concurrence of separate mission board aid programmes, the CPC leadership backed the formation of the CPRA. Robert Bontrager would maintain an office for the CPRA in Kinshasa to manage medical relief and supplies, while a separate CPRA office in New York City would raise money by which missionaries engaged in Congo relief could organise their activities and receive funding, supplies, and new recruits.[53]

From 1960 until 1964, US and Canadian missionaries completely controlled the US and the Congolese sections of the CPRA. The CPRA Executive Committee in New York featured representatives from over a dozen mission boards active in the DRC, including mainline denominations such as the American Baptists and the Disciples of Christ and more conservative denominations such as the Free Evangelical Church. Wade Coggins, the director of the Evangelical Foreign Mission Association that brought together various evangelical, reformed, and fundamentalist mission boards, also joined.[54] The hope that the CPRA signaled a new era of Protestant cooperation continued to inspire donors for several years. As Mennonite Central Committee (MCC) director Orie Miller put it in 1962, 'What CPRA symbolises might become a new Sub Sahara Kingdom Witness frontier and through which Protestantism could speak more and more with a single voice.'[55]

In October 1960, the CPRA set up two projects. Operation Doctor recruited paid volunteers from North America and Europe to serve at clinics and hospitals originally run by missionaries prior to independence.[56] Glen Tuttle, the Beggrens, and Bontrager had already succeeded with the support of the CWS in obtaining more than US$500,000 worth of food and medical supplies from the US government and private donors channeled through CWS.[57] CPRA member Roland Metzger had already secured an informal alliance with

53 Notes – Congo Meeting, 8 September 1960, Folder Congo Emergency, September 1960 –1962, Box 14, Record Group 8, CWS/PHS; Minutes of Organisational Meeting of the Supporting Committee in the USA for the Congo Protestant Relief Agency of the Congo Protestant Council, 26 September 1960, Folder 75/6, Orie Miller Papers, MHS.

54 Ibid.

55 Orie Miller to Theodore Tucker, 6 June 1962, Folder CPRA 1960–1963, Box 14, Record Group 8, CWS/PHS.

56 Roland Metzger, Congo Protestant Relief Agency Information Sheet, October 1960, Folder 75/4, OMP.

57 Ibid.

the United Nations mission in DRC and the World Health Organisation in August 1960.[58] By October 1960, CPRA had received $520,000 in donations, primarily from the CWS, the MCC, the evangelical Interdenominational Foreign Mission Association, and the WCC.[59] The second CPRA project was to help internally displaced Luba people who had fled to the Autonomous State of South Kasai. Archie Graber, a Mennonite missionary in Kasai province since 1930, agreed to oversee the relief programme for Luba people. The CWS and the WCC together raised funds for the CPRA's work, even if CPC and CPRA staff worried publicising the WCC's presence would potentially alienate conservative evangelical mission boards.[60] Operation Doctor sent its initial volunteers in the field and Archie Graber's relief project started in earnest by December 1960.

The CPRA joined a rapidly growing number of NGOs, Western governments, and the United Nations in humanitarian relief in the DRC. The League of Red Cross Societies (LRCS) had recruited over 30 medical teams, even including from East Germany and Poland despite the anti-Communist views of the Congolese government. The World Health Organisation also sent physicians to the DRC, including a notable number of Haitians. André Cauwe, a Belgian priest, formed the Congolese chapter of Caritas in 1960. The US-based Catholic Relief Services also set up an aid campaign directed by Monsignor Roland Bordelon in 1961.[61] The UN's enormous mission featured civil technical advisors. In this chaotic proliferation of humanitarian interventions, the CPRA stood out in its ability to provide missionaries with extensive local knowledge.

The CPRA's ostensibly apolitical stance allowed it to keep friendly relationships with the main international stakeholders in the DRC, even as the organisation also depended on Washington. USAID and Department of State officials harnessed the CPRA to deliver large amounts of US surplus food until the end of the 1960s. Such partnerships were a cornerstone of relief and

---

58 George Carpenter to William Du Val, World Council of Churches, 25 August 1960, Folder Congo Emergency August 1960, Box 14, Record Group 8, CWS/PHS.

59 Roland Metzger, Congo Protestant Relief Agency Information Sheet, October 1960, Folder 75/4 Congo Protestant Relief Agency, OMP, MHS.

60 Robert Bontrager, Pierre Shaumba, R V. de Carle Thompson, and Colin Kapini to Leslie Cooke, 12 November 1960, RBP.

61 Roland Bordelon, "A Report of the Congo (Léopoldville) Office, Catholic Relief Services, 1961–1965" (Unpublished manuscript, 1966), Folder VolAgs Programming CY 1966 (formerly Title III), Box 4, USAID Program Files 1961–1967, Record Group 286, Records of the US Agency for International Development, NARA II.

development for US foreign policy during the Cold War.[62] Malcolm McVeigh, CPRA material aid director, made clear the CPRA's loyalties in his annual application for food from USAID in 1967: 'We must face the fact that if USAID would be withdrawn, the [CPRA] program as presently envisaged would cease to exist despite church aid.'[63] Listing off the successes of CPRA projects since 1960, he added, 'Our program is a force for stability ... The people as a whole appreciate what America has done to help the Congo recover its equilibrium.'[64]

The CPRA also adhered to the United Nations mission in the Congo. Other than sending a handful of volunteer doctors and helping to move Luba refugees out of the Katangese capital of Lubumbashi, the CPRA never engaged in any activities in Katanga. Even the Luba exodus from Lubumbashi only took place after the United Nations agreed to work with the CPRA. UN planes, food shipments, and personnel served to assist CPRA staff. Aid workers certainly knew their efforts improved the image of the US in the DRC. 'Missionaries as a category are an asset to the total American cause in the Congo,' wrote Ernest Lehman, the CPRA director in the Kinshasa office in 1961.[65] It is striking how little Congolese politicians appear in CPRA correspondence, although the Congolese ministry of health gave the CPRA a free hand in staffing hospitals.

One major difference between the CPRA and its secular partners in humanitarian aid was its commitment to stay in the DRC for a long time. Leslie Cooke, the head of the World Council of Churches' Department of Inter-Church aid, warned Robert Bontrager in December 1960 that organisations like the Red Cross and the World Health Organisation would eventually leave the scene. 'You will find that the one permanent element in the situation is that of the ministry of the Christian Church,' Cooke advised.[66] Though the WHO kept its personnel in the DRC for much of the 1960s, the United Nations mission began to close down in 1964. The

---

62 On religious aid agencies and US foreign policy in the 1960s, see McCleary, *Global Compassion*, 83–102.

63 Malcolm McVeigh, Estimation of Requirements FY 1969 CPRA, 30 March 1967, FPC 6 Congo Protestant Relief Agency (CPRA) FY 67, Box 4, USAID Program Files 1961–1967, Record Group 286, Records of the US Agency for International Development, NARA II.

64 Ibid.

65 Ernest Lehman to Orie Miller, 8 March 1961, Folder 105/138 Congo Office 1961, Box 181, IX-6-3, MCCA.

66 Leslie Cooke to Robert Bontrager, Box 425.3.272 Africa Documents Congo 1958–1962, WCCA.

LRCS assisted Angolan refugees beginning in April 1961, but cut off aid by February 1962 on the grounds that the newcomers had already become so dependent on foreign aid that they would not farm on their own.[67] A visiting LRCS official in August 1961 praised the Red Cross for avoiding 'the usual mistake of making refugees depend on relief' and contended 'the country is rich enough to provide food supplies … if a guiding hand is always present behind the Congolese administration.'[68]

Donors continued to support the CPRA after the South Kasai funding drive of 1960 and early 1961. The CWS agreed to furnish the CPRA with the bulk of its funding. From 1962 to 1964, CWS support comprised three quarters of the CPRA budget.[69] The Kasai famine prompted the United Nations, Oxfam, and the World Council of Churches in December 1960 to publicise the famine. US and European churches raised funds, donated food, and even sent chicks to the CPRA operation in the DRC. Although UNHCR staff avoided becoming entangled in the South Kasai crisis on the grounds that Luba displaced people did not qualify as refugees living in a different country, the UNHCR headquarters in Geneva received requests from concerned charities and the Swiss government about the need to save the starving Luba.[70] An institutional history of Oxfam credited the Kasai publicity campaign as a major success in raising money and putting pressure on the British government to step up assistance to Luba communities.[71]

With the resolution of the Kasai crisis by 1962 and the UN victory over the Katangese secession at the end of the same year, donors started to turn their attention away from the DRC. By late 1963, the CPRA had trouble maintaining its medical relief programme even as Congolese demand for

67 Robert Schaeffer to Henrik Beer, 21 November 1961, Folder 15/GEN/ANG [1] Angolan Refugees, Box 250, UNHCRA; Report on the Activities of the League's Delegation in the Congo, February 1962, Folder 51 15/78 Situation in the Congo, Box 272, UNHCRA.

68 Brief Summary of Mr R. Brown's Statement on His Congo Visit, 29 August 1961, Folder 51 15/78 Situation in the Congo, Box 272, UNHCRA.

69 Analysis of CPRA Checking Account July 1, 1962 – June 30, 1963, Analysis of CPRA Checking Account, July 1, 1963 – June 30, 1964, Folder CPRA, 1960–1963, Box 14, Record Group 8, CWS/PHS.

70 Gobius to Gilbert Jaeger, 16 January 1961; V. Tedesco to Gilbert Jaeger, 19 January 1961, Folder 51 15/78 Situation in the Congo, Box 272, UNHCRA; C. de Kemoularia to Ivan-Smith, 19 January 1961, Folder 51 15/78 Situation in the Congo, Box 272, UNHCRA.

71 M. Black, *A Cause for Our Times: Oxfam – The First Fifty Years* (Oxford: Oxfam, 2012), 67–70.

North American doctors, nurses, and technicians remained steady. CWS African Department director Jan S.F. Hoogstraten warned CPRA in September 1963 that CWS funding for Operation Doctor was going to be cut, and the Mennonite Central Committee could not fully replace this lost source of support.[72] James McCracken, the associate director of CWS, preferred that mission boards acted as the main sponsors of the programme since CWS was meant to fund temporary aid programmes rather than continuing aid projects.[73] The WCC did furnish $45,000 to Operation Doctor in 1964, so the programme could maintain its previous expenses.[74] The victories of Pierre Mulele's rebel movement in Kwilu province and the eastern Congolese revolutionary coalition in 1964 radically disrupted Operation Doctor and all of CPRA's relief efforts. The revolt created a gigantic population of refugees. The death of Paul Carlson at the hands of Simba rebels in November 1964, a former CPRA volunteer who had become a permanent medical missionary, probably made recruiting new doctors afterwards more difficult. MCC withdrew from recruiting physicians from Operation Doctor in 1965 out of concerns about whether Operation Doctor would have enough money to stay open.[75] As the end of 1965 neared, CWS staff and CPRA volunteers in New York debated whether or not they should close CPRA's US operations or if the organisation should continue. Wade Coggins from the Evangelical Foreign Missions Association argued that the CPRA should not become a permanent organisation.[76] However, a majority of CPRA's New York executive members decided to prolong their work to 1967.[77]

Other interdenominational Protestant aid programmes in the DRC vied with the CPRA for funding from donors, and new humanitarian challenges elsewhere diverted attention from the Congo. The Institut Médical Evangélique (IME), an interdenominational hospital founded by Protestant missionaries in the town of Kimpese in the western Bas-Congo province, had

72   Orie Miller to Robert Miller, 27 December 1963, Folder 75/5a Congo Protestant Relief Agency, OMP.

73   CPRA in America, Minutes of Meeting, 9 September 1963, Folder 75/7 Congo Protestant Relief Agency, OMP.

74   CPRA in America Executive Committee, Minutes of Meeting, 21 May 1964, Folder 75/7 Congo Protestant Relief Agency, OMP.

75   Elmer Neufeld to Robert Miller, 14 September 1964, Folder Congo Office I 1964 111/128, Box 190, IX-6-3, MCCA.

76   Wade Coggins to CPRA, 30 November 1965, Folder CPRA, 1960–1963, Box 14, Record Group 8, CWS/PHS.

77   Minutes, Executive Committee CPRA Meeting, 10 September 1965, Folder CPRA, 1960–1963, Box 14, Record Group 8, CWS/PHS.

reliable support from a wide range of North American and European mission boards. A number of former CPRA medical volunteers ended up joining the IME. The creation of the Université Libre du Congo, the country's first Protestant university, drew financial support from North American missionary organisations. Individual denominations also preferred to fund their own development and medical programmes rather than contribute to the CPRA. As the emergencies of the early 1960s were slowly resolved in the early years of Mobutu Seke Seko's rule in the late 1960s, the CPRA had a harder time attracting support. Outside of central Africa, the CWS had pressing concerns. The French withdrawal from Algeria opened up a major new field for the CWS in 1962. Later, the Biafran war of secession in 1967 and the Vietnam war took central stage for Protestant donors.

World Council of Churches and the management of the CPRA, 1960–1965

The CPRA in the 1960s relied on a handful of volunteers to manage operations. Besides several administrative personnel in the New York and Kinshasa offices, individual projects received a single manager, such as Archie Graber in South Kasai and David Grenfell with the Angolan refugees. Operation Doctor short-term volunteers were generally supported by individual mission boards from their recruitment to their service in the DRC. Some Mennonite medical volunteers, for example, actually never knew they were in the DRC through the auspices of the CPRA, since they only dealt with MCC staff.[78] Such circumstances meant that there was little oversight of CPRA projects beyond financial issues.

Few CPRA staff in the Congo stayed in the organisation for more than two years. As mission boards became more assured that their work would not end in the DRC, some chose increasingly to fund their own medical projects rather than join the CPRA. For example, William Rule served as medical director of the CPRA medical operation from November 1960 for six months, but then felt called to work at a Presbyterian hospital in northern Kasai. MCC staff member Ernest Lehman and Disciples of Christ pastor Robert Bowers each briefly directed CPRA's office in Kinshasa, but they each left the post for other duties in less than a year. Archie Graber and the Baptist Missionary Society pastor David Grenfell, the individuals who did more than anyone else to manage relief, both retired due to health reasons in 1967.

---

78 Telephone interview, Arnold Nickel, 19 January 2016.

Thus, managers in the field had wide latitude to operate without much guidance or set policies from the CWS. Such freedom meant in practice that project managers and individual doctors were left largely on their own to solve difficulties. The apparatus of audits and assessment, familiar parts of humanitarian and development work in later decades, simply did not exist in the CPRA in the 1960s. Since the CWS did not force CPRA volunteers to follow a particular political stance or theological position, volunteers could make decisions in their negotiations with the UN, the Congolese government, and rebel groups without first consulting their alleged supervisors. UN and League of Red Cross workers, by contrast, had to follow set protocols set by their superiors and their agencies. The CPRA's flexibility thus allowed volunteers to act in a partisan way if they chose to do so. At times, other aid agencies considered CPRA staff to be prone to potentially dangerous violations of humanitarian neutrality. As will be discussed in chapter 3, for example, CPRA project director David Grenfell's quite open admiration for Angolam rebels stood at odds with UNHCR and the Red Cross.

Although US volunteers and the US-based CWS dominated the CPRA in its first years, some friction emerged between the CWS and another important donor, the World Council of Churches. WCC staff promoted the rise of Congolese leaders within Protestant churches and the Congo Protestant Council (CPC). The WCC decided to work with the growing numbers of Congolese taking up leadership roles in the CPC, which at times placed the WCC in disagreement with the CWS. Pierre Regard, an advisor to the Congo Protestant Council's first Congolese chairman Pierre Shaumba, took issue with how the CWS and the US missions acted too independently from the CPC's Congolese members. '[The CPRA] was constituted by the CPC and for the service of [Congolese churches] requires that certain domains are reserved to the CPC ... It is out of the question to go back and consider the [CPRA] to be independent of the CPC itself.'[79] With the authorisation of Shaumba at the CPC, the WCC recruited in spring 1962 the Swiss Protestant minister Hans Schaffert to replace the departing Mennonite director of the CPRA in Kinshasa, Ernest Lehman. Schaffert's arrival as CPRA director signaled that Congolese on the CPC no longer wanted only North Americans to control the organisation. Schaffert, who had saved French Jews during the Second World War as a young pastor, remained the head of CPRA until 1968.[80]

---

79 Pierre Regard to Theodore Tucker, 16 August 1962, Folder Congo 1958–1962, Box 425.3.272, WCCA.

80 Biographical information on Schaffert is drawn from M. Wagner and M. Meisels, *The Righteous of Switzerland: Heroes of the Holocaust* (Jersey City: Ktav, 2000),

The decision of the Congo Protestant Council to appoint Schaffert infuriated the New York office of CPRA. A telegram issued to the CPRA office in Kinshasa made their objections clear: 'Surprised [by] proposed unilateral appointment [of] Schaffert ... Deplore [Schaffert's] lack of English ... Is [this] appointment final?'[81] Robert Bowers, the man Schaffert replaced as CPRA director in the Congo, complained the CPC had given no information about Schaffert to CPRA staff. Schaffert's arrival suggested the CPC would no longer leave the CPRA largely autonomous.[82] From Pierre Regard's vantage point on the WCC, Schaffert was needed precisely to ensure the CPC would ultimately direct the CPRA in an organised way rather than continue the CPRA's ad hoc management style.[83]

Schaffert proved to be very anxious to serve the increasingly Congolese-run Congo Protestant Council rather than merely act in the interests of the CPRA US branch. As a sign of his loyalty, he moved CPRA's offices from a bookstore under US missionary management to the CPC building.[84] Schaffert demonstrated his concern about CPRA's autonomy in a discussion of warehouse space. The rented facilities where CPRA had stored its increasing amount of food, medicine, and supplies could no longer adequately serve its needs by 1963. Schaffert requested money to buy a new warehouse in May 1963. True to the multinational nature of CPRA, Schaffert solicited money from the CWS, the United Church of Canada, Oxfam, the WCC, the Swiss Protestant HEKS aid agency, and the German Protestant Brot für die Welt aid organisation.[85] The CWS agreed on the conditions that other agencies paid as well for the warehouse and that the warehouse would then be sold off once CPRA was disbanded. This last point shows how the original idea that CPRA was only a temporary project was still held by some donor agencies as late as 1963, even though CPRA would ultimately last for over five decades.

137–40; M. Kalt, *Tiermondismus in der Schweiz der 1960er und 1970er Jahre* (New York: Peter Lang, 2010), 245–6.

81   CPRA New York Executive Committee, 10 November 1962, CPRA News Sheet No. 19, May 1962, Folder 75/5 Congo Protestant Relief Agency, OMP.

82   Robert Bowers to Theodore Tucker, 28 July 1962, Folder CPRA, 1960 1963, Box 14, Record Group 8, CWS/PHS.

83   Pierre Regard to Leslie Cooke, 7 May 1962, Folder Congo 1958–1962, Box 425.3.272, WCCA.

84   Elmer Neufeld to Robert Miller, Mennonite Central Committee, no date (May or June 1963), Folder 75/5a Congo Protestant Relief Agency, OMP.

85   Church World Service for Discussion and Action in COPAF, 5 June 1963, Folder 75/5a Congo Protestant Relief Agency, OMP.

When the CWS and its partner the Mennonite Central Committee backed the warehouse, MCC member Elmer Neufeld expressed concerns regarding Schaffert's approach. According to Neufeld, Schaffert complained that other US staff members of CPRA bypassed his authority to communicate directly with CPRA's US branch. Schaffert found CWS' requirement that their partial funding of the warehouse would also include new offices for CPRA to be an infringement on CPRA's independence.[86] Furthermore, the WCC chose not to fund the project, which thus broke another CWS stipulation that CWS would only provide money if other agencies contributed. Neufeld warned that CWS' demands could be interpreted negatively by Swiss and other aid workers within CPRA, and that they could tell the Congolese leaders of the CPC that US agencies wanted to dictate how CPRA operated rather than respect it as an independent Congolese institution.[87] This last comment reveals how CPRA was no longer merely an all-American agency, but rather one in which members distanced themselves at times from US churches. The Swiss pastor argued a Congolese national should ultimately replace him as CPRA director and supported CPC efforts to operate without the tutelage of missionaries. Jim Paton, a young CWS staff remember who supervised the logistics of CWS material aid transport, nearly transferred out of the country in 1963 because of Schaffert's unwillingness to respect USAID regulations as well as the Swiss pastor's abrasive personality.[88]

An unexpected consequence of the friendly cooperation between mission boards and various Congolese Protestant churches was how the CPRA could furnish evidence for the cause of a single giant Protestant church for the entire DRC. Pierre Shaumba argued that the CPC should become a united single church of all Congolese Protestants, regardless of their individual denomination. Though church union movements gained traction in the 1960s in several countries such as Kenya, hardly any succeeded in unification in the way that would occur among Congolese Protestant churches. The political catastrophes of the DRC inspired Congolese Protestant leaders to try to reconcile denominational differences in the name of national unity and an authentic Congolese faith. This feeling matched the concerns of Mobutu Sese Seko as his government promoted a common Congolese ideology based on an imagined foundation of Bantu cultural unity The CWS and the WCC endorsed this sense of cultural nationalism to overcome the legacy of colonialism. The CPRA exemplified mission-founded

---

86   Elmer Neufeld to Robert Miller, Mennonite Central Committee, no date (May or June 1963), Folder 75/5a Congo Protestant Relief Agency, OMP.

87   Ibid.

88   Interview, Jim Paton, 14 August 2018.

churches' sense of cooperation and effectively served to heal the wounds of political division. Yet Congolese churches had precious few resources to put into the CPRA. The Congolese political struggles and internal disputes about church leadership plagued newly independent Congolese Protestant churches. Church union had very practical consequences for the CPRA only after 1967, but the seeds for the Africanisation of Protestant humanitarian and development projects had already been planted.

Conclusion

Battles for power in the Congo set off a series of humanitarian catastrophes in the early 1960s. Local, national, and international conflicts brought about the displacement of large numbers of people. Indiscriminate killings of civilians became commonplace. Famines took hold in the southern Kasai and areas held by leftist rebels. While the US government and its Western allies cynically justified interventions in the Congo as a means of ending suffering, there is no debate that the social disruptions of the civil wars took a substantial toll. It is within this context that secular and religious PVOs (private voluntary organisations) joined the United Nations and Western governments in establishing aid programmes in the Congo.

The CPRA embodied a number of major trends in humanitarian work in Africa and missionary thought in the wake of decolonisation. Protestant mission boards, interdenominational associations, and CPRA staff themselves considered Congolese independence to be a major opportunity. Nation building allowed Protestants to claim an equal place in Congolese society denied to them under Belgian rule. Protestant missionaries together feared the threat of Communist infiltration in the DRC. Humanitarian aid thus allowed US, Canadian, and European Protestants to participate peacefully in the crusade against Communism without having to endorse every US government policy related to the Congo. The DRC was one of many fields where Protestant missionaries and relief agencies could imagine recasting older colonial relationships of African dependency on Western leaders, even if the CPRA in reality was still run by expatriates until 1965. These transnational aspirations later influenced Congolese Protestant leaders when determining how donor funds were used. Compared to the US diplomats' and development workers' often narrow and condescending views of Africans, described by Larry Grubbs and others, the optimism of North American and European Protestants involved in the DRC is noteworthy.[89]

---

89   L. Grubbs, *Secular Missionaries: American and African Development in the 1960s* (Amherst: University of Massachusetts, 2009).

The inchoate management of the CPRA also matches with the experimental nature of humanitarian work in Africa in the 1960s. Personnel in the UNHCR, the League of Red Cross Societies, and the International Committee of the Red Cross regularly judged African politicians and African societies by a universal standard set by the model of Western countries.[90] Though members of these organisations had some criticisms of colonisation, they tended to be more pessimistic about newly independent African countries than Protestant aid workers. The reliance of the United Nations High Commission for Refugees (UNHCR) on ad hoc management of refugees without applying universal standards of determining the rights and eligibility of African refugees also corresponds with the very loose structure of the CPRA. Development and assistance projects run by a single Western government or the United Nations did not have the flexibility of the CPRA, but they also could rely on steady financial support in the way the CPRA could not.

With the dominance of formal state actors in the scholarly literature of the DRC in the 1960s, it would be easy enough to treat the CPRA and Protestant missionary aid as appendages of US foreign policy. There is no doubt the goals of the CPRA and its donors often dovetailed with Washington's determination to establish a steady ally in Kinshasa. Philip Dow's contention that US evangelical missionaries were 'accidental diplomats' who served the US government is correct.[91] Yet one needs to go beyond the constricting frame of church–state relations to properly grasp the actions and organisation of Protestant humanitarian aid in the DRC. CPRA staff and its patrons had their own aspirations in promoting transnational networks of charity and Christian witness. The next chapters illustrate the complexity of negotiations between the CPRA, the Congolese state, donors, and other players on the DRC stage in refugee work.

90 M.-L. Desgrandchamps, "Organising the Unpredictable: The Nigeria–Biafra War and its Impact on the ICRC," *International Review of the Red Cross* 94:888 (2012), 1409–52.

91 Dow, "Accidental Diplomats."

2

The CPRA and Luba Refugees in South Kasai, 1960–1962

On 30 June 1961, Congo Protestant Relief Agency aid worker Archie Graber wrote to his missionary colleagues: 'Today Congo celebrates her first year of independence. For millions this means a year of haunted memories, a year of hunger and starvation, a year of destruction ... It was the African who demanded independence at once, when they were not prepared for it, yet as an African proverb puts it, "If your child sets your house on fire, do you throw him in the fire?"'[1] Graber's paternalism was hardly noteworthy among the North American and European aid workers who entered the Congo after the onset of armed political struggles in July 1960. Graber's story was celebrated by Mennonite missionary journalist Levi Keidel, but Graber and the CPRA have never been incorporated into the larger historiography of the DRC.[2]

Graber worked in the southern region of the Kasai province, a territory wracked by fighting beginning in 1959. Over the course of the 1950s, the northern Kasai became embroiled in a competition between Lulua clans, who claimed to be the original inhabitants of the region, and Luba people, whose families had originated in southern Kasai. Luba ethnic identity had become linked to educational aspirations and migrant labour. Colonial officials favoured Lulua claims to land and political supremacy and urged Luba migrants to move to southern Kasai, much as Moïse Tshombe's CONAKAT political party in the copper-rich southern province of Katanga stigmatised Luba people as interlopers who threatened to usurp communities already established in the region.[3] Lulua militias in northern Kasai and Tshombe's government in Kasai drove Luba people into southern Kasai, to the point hundreds of thousands

1   Archie Graber to Friends in the Homeland, 30 June 1961, Folder 7 Archie and Irma (Beilter) Graber, 1959–1961, Box 70, Gerber to Graber, 1936–1986, Africa Inter-Mennonite Mission Records, Mennonite Church USA Archives, Goshen, Indiana [AIMMR].

2   L. Keidel, *War to Be One* (Grand Rapids, MI: Zondervan, 1977).

3   Young, *Politics in the Congo*, 492–6; Gérard-Libois, *Katanga Secession*, 12–17; E. Kabongo Malu, *Épurations ethniques en RD Congo (1991–1995): La question Luba-Kasaï* (Paris: L'Harmattan, 1995).

of refugees had flooded into southern Kasai by August 1960. Albert Kalonji and Joseph Ngalula, two Luba politicians, worked with other Luba leaders to form an autonomous regime, the État Autonome du Sud-Kasaï ASSK), that refused to fully accept the authority of the central Congolese government based in Kinshasa (then Léopoldville). Even as the United Nations and the central Congolese government tried to pressure the ASSK to accept the authority of the Congolese state, ASSK leaders tried to harness the horrific condition of starving Luba refugees to obtain international support.

The United Nations, the US government, the ASSK, the Congolese state, and armed local groups all sought to manipulate CPRA aid for their own ends. The ASSK regime had a generally hostile relationship with the United Nations, yet UN and ASSK personnel endorsed Graber's relief efforts. Even as the UN tended not to publicly mention the service of the CPRA, the World Council of Churches celebrated the CPRA as an example of how Western Christians had a duty to aid newly independent Congolese people. The UN and the World Council of Churches (WCC) portrayed the Kasai conflict as a tragic result of decolonisation that required international humanitarian action. Meanwhile, the ASSK sought to present itself as the defender of Luba refugees against the central government and tried to force (with little success) the CPRA to obey its commands.

In this case, the CPRA followed the traditional humanitarian commitment to political neutrality modelled by the Red Cross: Graber steered clear of the ASSK's efforts to use the CPRA. The ostensibly neutral orientation of the CPRA allowed the organisation to negotiate with a wide range of individuals and institutions that were at odds with one another. Graber's deep understanding of Luba cultural practices, his fluency in the Tshiluba language, and his good relationships with international donors made him an effective meditator. So did his Mennonite beliefs, which stressed cooperation and peacemaking.

CPRA records also point out the limitations of humanitarian aid records for recovering the agency of refugees and Congolese workers. CPRA workers had daily interactions with Luba refugees, yet their writings left out a great deal on how refugees may have tried to make demands on the CPRA. Archie Graber presented refugees as subjects of pity more than active participants in the aid process. Young US volunteers, by contrast, spent more time on their frustrations with refugees and the trauma of witnessing violence and famine. How Luba people acted as partners in relief can be hard to discern from CPRA writings. Yet the tactics of displaced people do occasionally feature in CPRA sources, especially those written and remembered by other volunteers in the project besides Graber. Rather than being passive recipients of missionary aid, Luba refugees made demands on CPRA staff.

The origins of the Luba/Lulua struggles and the formation of the autonomous state of South Kasai

Rival claims on land and political rights made through assertions of ethnic identity led to warfare in Kasai province. When colonial troops invaded the Kasai region in the late 19th century, a fissure developed between Luba-speaking communities that accepted state authority and embraced missionary education and other Luba-speakers who did not.[4] Missionaries and colonial officials along with Luba intellectuals developed a sense of Luba ethnic identity in the early decades of the 20th century.[5] Luba identity became associated with mission education, white collar labour, and trade. Luba clerks and skilled laborers found work throughout the Belgian Congo. Colonial officials domesticated Luba political leadership by defeating leaders who refused to bend to the Belgian government and by redefining the position of chief to depend on the colonial state. Luba who migrated from northern Kasai, the old heartland of Luba-speaking kingdoms, became differentiated from Lulua, Luba-speakers who stayed in rural areas and preferred farming to positions that required mobility and Western education.

As Luba migrants established themselves in urban centres in the northern Kasai, Lulua chiefs increasingly made claims to land rights against urban Luba-speaking people.[6] Further reforms by colonial officials helped to set the stage for violent conflict in the 1950s.[7] The Belgian government agreed

---

4 For a more detailed discussion of European expansion into the Kasai, see N. Luadia-Luadia, "Les Luluwa et le commerce Luso-Africain (1870–1895)," *Etudes d'histoire africaine* 7 (1974), 55–104; D. Martens, "A History of European Penetration and African Reaction in the Kasai Region of Zaire, 1880–1908," (PhD thesis, Simon Fraser University, 1980); Achim von Poppen, *Terms of Trade and Trust: the History and Contexts of Pre-Colonial Market Production around the Upper Zambezi and Kasai* (Hamburg: LIT, 1993); J. Fabian, *Out of Our Minds: Reason and Madness in the Exploration of Central Africa* (Berkeley: University of California Press, 2000); B. Mwamba Mputu, *Le Congo-Kasai (1865–1950): De l'exploration allemande à la consécration de Luluabourg* (Paris: L'Harmattan, 2011).

5 The following is drawn from B. Jewsiewicki, "The Formation of the Political Culture of Ethnicity in the Belgian Congo, 1920–1959," in L. Vail, (ed.), *The Creation of Tribalism in Southern Africa* (Berkeley: University of California Press, 1991), 320–49.

6 A recent synthesis of Luba clan migrations in the Kasai is in J. Omasombo Tshonda (ed.), *Kasaï-Oriental. Un noeud gordien dans l'espace congolais* (Tervuren: Musée Royal de l'Afrique Centrale, 2014), 45–67.

7 For discussion of the growing competition along ethnic lines in the 1940s and 1950s, see Kalanda, *Baluba*; Lemarchand, *Political Awakening*, 206–9; Young, *Politics in the Congo*, 263–5; Lushiku Lumana, *Baluba*; Libata, "Regroupement."

to municipal elections in 1957. Although Luba people made up a majority of voters in Kananga, Lulua chiefs complained that the city truly belonged to Lulua people. Kalamba Mangole, the state-appointed chief of the Lulua, demanded Luba leave his domains in northern Kasai in 1959.[8] Furthermore, he received the backing of colonial officials. When the Belgian government called for the expulsion of Luba people from northern Kasai, the rift between Lulua and Luba widened further.

On 13 October 1959, Lulua militias had begun to attack Luba in the northern Kasai city of Kananga. Luba and Lulua militias launched attacks against one another throughout the Kasai. Many Luba fled southward. Even as Congolese politicians negotiated a framework for independence in January 1960 at the Round Table accords in Brussels, Lulua militias intensified their violent efforts to expel Luba from the northern Kasai.

Luba communities also organised themselves in Kasai province. One of the first politicians to exploit this changing sense of Luba solidarity was Albert Kalonji, a young agricultural expert.[9] Kalonji was an early member of the Mouvement National Congolais (MNC) political party, but fell out with the MNC's most popular leader, Patrice Lumumba. Kalonji headed a rival wing of the MNC party and drew support from other Luba intellectuals, most notably Joseph Ngalula.[10] By independence on 30 June 1960, Kalonji and Ngalula had returned to the southern Kasai region. The coming of independence led to more violence. Thousands of Luba continued to flee south. They were soon joined by Luba fleeing from Katanga, South Kasai's southern neighbour. Moïse Tshombe's CONAKAT party in Katanga had originally formed to contest Luba and other migrants into the province, and the Katangan state battled Luba communities unwilling to endorse the new government's break from the rest of the DRC.

The violence only grew worse when Congolese army units mutinied in July 1960 in Kananga. Lulua groups joined with the Congolese army in attacking Luba civilians and Kalonji's troops. Kalonji himself fled to the secessionist province of Katanga as the Congolese army and Lulua militias wreaked havoc on Luba communities.[11] Luba people fled for their lives,

8   Lushiku Lumana, *Baluba*, 75; Omasombo Tshonda, *Kasaï-Oriental*, 175–6.

9   On Kalonji, see A. Kalonji, *Congo 1960: La secession du sud-Kasaï. La verité du Mulopwe* (Paris: L'Harmattan, 2005); Omasombo Tshonda, *Kasaï-Oriental*, 196–208, 235–9.

10   Lemarchand, *Political Awakening*, 197.

11   Lushiku Lumana, *Les Baluba du Kasaï*, 87–91; Omasombo Tshonda, *Kasaï-Oriental*, 180–1.

leaving behind their possessions strewn on the streets of Kananga as they headed south. Patrice Lumumba and Congolese president Joseph Kasavubu briefly visited Kananga on 11 July, and agreed to allow Belgian troops to protect Europeans fleeing the city. Their brief intervention did little to halt to murder of Luba civilians.

On 8 August 1960, Kalonji proclaimed the southern half of Kasai province to be the Autonomous State of South Kasai. While Moïse Tshombe declared that the Katanga province had formally seceded from the rest of the DR Congo in July 1960, Kalonji initially refused to go so far. The Forminière diamond mining country bankrolled Kalonji's fledgling government much as the Union Minière du Haut-Katanga firm was a pillar of Moïse Tshombe's regime in Katanga.[12] Lumumba refused to recognise the ASSK as legitimate. Congolese government troops flown from Kisangani worsened the situation beginning on 26 August.[13] They pillaged Mbuji-Mayi and much of rural Kasai. Lulua towns did not fare much better, as government soldiers also pillaged Lulua settlements in northern Kasai.[14] The unrestrained violence of these forces as well as the use of Soviet aid turned UN secretary general Dag Hammarskjöld and other UN officials against Lumumba.[15]

By October 1960, the number of Luba refugees in southern Kasai had probably surpassed 100,000 people. The ASSK government, even with financial support from Forminière, lacked the resources to provide much help for the newcomers. ASSK president Albert Kalonji hired mercenaries and bought arms for his fledgling army, draining his precarious financial resources.[16] The disruptions of the early months of 1960 had not allowed many farmers to prepare fields, let alone cope with the giant influx of newcomers. A UN-mediated truce led ANC officers to pull out of the ASSK back towards Kananga in September, but it was already clear that the late autumn harvest could not possibly be enough to feed displaced people.

12 Omasombo Tshonda, *Kasaï-Oriental*, 185–6.

13 On this offense and the toll on civilians, see Lushiku Lumana, *Les Baluba du Kasaï*, 108–111; Omasombo Tshonda, *Kasaï-Orientale*, 188.

14 Archie Graber to Co-workers in the homeland, 16 October 1960, Folder 1960–1961, Folder 7 Archie and Irma (Beilter) Graber, 1959–1961, Box 70, Gerber to Graber, 1936–1986, AIMMR.

15 On this offensive and its grisly results for civilians, see Keidel, *War*, 133–4; Eric Packham, *Freedom or Anarchy?* (Happauge, NY: Nova Science, 1996), 54.

16 On the mercenaries, see M. Borri, *Nous…ces affreux* (Paris: Galic, 1962).

The CPRA intervention in South Kasai,
August–December 1960

The fledgling CPRA, first formed in July 1960, chose to intervene in the Kasai largely because of the longtime presence of the Mennonite Congo Inland Mission (CIM). CIM missionaries, horrified by the pitiful plight of the displaced Luba, reached out to the CPRA. The Mennonite Central Committee had good ties with the CIM and had been one of the first donors to support the CPRA. Mennonite Central Committee executive board member Orie Miller toured Mennonite missions in southern Kasai in late August 1960. As he flew into Kananga, Miller saw burned Luba villages and dozens of cars abandoned hastily by Belgians just a month before.[17] Kalonji and the ASSK minister of health informed Miller they had no money or medicine to treat Luba displaced people. These sights seemed to confirm the gloom of aid workers such as International Red Cross delegate Geoffrey Senn, who 'had a ... pessimistic picture ... of the Congo going to jungle and original tribalism again'.[18]

Unlike Senn's morose view of decolonisation, Miller expressed the hopes of other Mennonite missionaries and CPRA staff that relief work constituted a way for North American Christian missions to claim a new place for Protestants in an independent Congo.[19] 'The church motherlands must certainly brother now, and find anew and work this church here. We ... feel a [CPRA] relief project here in Baluba refugee land is an immediate other [need],' he noted to Mennonite mission board directors.[20] Miller helped organise a meeting in New York of representatives of the newly-formed CPRA Executive Committee that endorsed Graber as the head of CPRA relief in South Kasai. Archie Graber, a Mennonite Congo Inland Mission (CIM) missionary in the DRC since 1930, agreed to cut short his furlough in the US to take charge of the new relief programme.

17 Orie Miller, Diary August 11-25, 1960 to Congo to Republic for Congo Inland Mission, American Mennonite Brethren Mission, Mennonite Central Committee, 21–23 August 1960 entries, Congo 1960-1 Folder 104/138, Box 181, IX-06-3, MCCA.

18 Ibid.

19 For a general discussion of Western pessimism on Congolese decolonisation, see Dunn, *Imagining*, 87–97.

20 Orie Miller, Diary August 11-2, 1960 to Congo to Republic for Congo Inland Mission, American Mennonite Brethren Mission, Mennonite Central Committee, 21–23 August 1960 entries, Congo 1960-1 Folder 104/138, Box 98, IX-6-3, MCCA.

Graber was well placed to run the CPRA programme. While Methodist missionaries strongly endorsed Moïse Tshombe's secessionist government in Katanga, pacifist Mennonite missionaries like Graber refused to endorse either Kalonji's rebellious ASSK or the DRC government. The CPRA thus could act as a broker between political opponents. CPRA head administrators in the US gave Graber a carte blanche to operate. The UN mission in the Congo's civilian operations, stretched across the DRC and with limited resources, relied on NGOs like the CPRA as partners and as sources of local knowledge. Finally, Graber's three decades of living in the Kasai gave him a network of contacts, fluency in Tshiluba, and familiarity with local cultural practices.

Graber's first weeks in CPRA demonstrate how the rupturing political situation in the DRC impeded relief shipments. He first arrived in Luanda on 1 September 1960, where dubious Portuguese officials demanded to know why Graber wanted so many supplies to be shipped to the South Kasai.[21] After Graber convinced the Portuguese government to allow CPRA supplies to be sent to South Kasai via Angola, he flew to Kinshasa. The showdown between Patrice Lumumba and Joseph Kasavubu for power on 10–11 September slowed Graber down.[22] Graber only managed to reach the ASSK capital of Mbuji-Mayi on 1 October 1960, a full month after arriving in the DRC.

Graber grappled with the logistical challenges of trying to bring supplies to Mbuji-Mayi. Sending CPRA supplies through the balkanised political landscape in the DRC was an arduous task. Material sent by ship had to go first to the Congolese port of Matadi or by plane to Kinshasa. A railroad connected the Congolese capital to Mwene Ditu, a railroad depot that served as a hub for transport by truck to the ASSK capital city 98 kilometers away. ASSK forces battled ANC mutineers in the area between the ASSK and Mwene Ditu. One skirmish nearly killed Graber when he tried to unload food in late October 1960.[23] Another problem for transporting supplies was that railway workers pilfered food destined for South Kasai.[24] Though deteriorating roads and violence made the trip from Mwene Ditu to Mbuji-Mayi difficult, the

---

21 Archie Graber to Vernon Sprunger, 1 September 1960, Folder 7 Archie and Irma (Beilter) Graber, 1959–1961, Box 70, Gerber to Graber, 1936–1986, AIMMR; Keidel, *War*, 141 2.

22 Archie Graber to Vernon Sprunger, 11 September 1960 Folder 7 Archie and Irma (Beilter) Graber, 1959–1961, Box 70, Gerber to Graber, 1936–1986, AIMMR; Archie Graber to Vernon Sprunger, 28 September 1960, Folder 7 Archie and Irma (Beilter) Graber, 1959–1961, Box 70, Gerber to Graber, 1936–1986, AIMMR.

23 *Congo Protestant Relief Agency News Sheet* 7 (29 November 1960), Folder 75/4 Congo Protestant Relief Agency, OMP.

24 Ibid.

northern route between Kananga and Mbuji-Mayi was even more hazardous, since it went directly through areas where Lulua and Congolese army units fought Kalonji's forces.

After two months in Africa, Graber finally managed to bring the first CPRA food shipment to Mbuji-Mayi on 3 November 1960.[25] Graber relied on Abe Suderman and Allen Horst, two Mennonite Central Committee Pax volunteers who had avoided the US military draft by volunteering for alternative service, to assist him with distributing food. The ICRC delegation to the DRC sent in medical teams and authorised relief aid into the ASSK. By late November, Graber coordinated his efforts with UN civilian officials and ICRC representatives.[26] As fighting struck villages less than 30 kilometres from Graber's base of operations at Mbuji-Mayi, Graber coordinated shipments of powdered milk, corn, and rice.[27]

The CPRA's relief programme had close ties with the United Nations and acted as a neutral party between the UN and the ASSK. United Nations troops had been sent in September as peacekeeping forces between Kalonji's regime and government forces based in Kananga. Many Luba people distrusted Ghanaian UN troops because of Kwame Nkrumah's support for Lumumba, who Kalonji's supports viewed as responsible for the ANC's atrocities in August 1960. Graber's missionary colleague Glenn Rocke noted in December 1960, 'Bakwanga government [ASSK] does not have enough trucks to deliver food – UN want to help with theirs – but there is great suspicion of UN forces in this country because of the apparent friendship between Ghana's Nkrumah and Lumumba ... [Archie Graber and Presbyterian missionary Day Carper] was to go along [with UN trucks] and kinda break the ice [with Luba people]'.[28] Garber regularly had CPRA supplies sent by UN aircraft and asked UN officials to help with logistical matters, such as ensuring supplies help up at customs at the Angolan–Congolese border would be released to go to Mwene Ditu.[29]

---

25 Archie Graber to Co-workers, 30 November 1960, Folder 7 Archie and Irma (Beilter) Graber, 1959–1961, Box 70, Gerber to Graber, 1936–1986, AIMMR.

26 Ibid.

27 *Congo Protestant Relief Agency News Sheet* 7 (29 November 1960), Folder 75/4 Congo Protestant Relief Agency, OMP; Keidel, *War*, 143–8.

28 Glenn Rocke to Ina Rocke, 25 December 1960, Glenn Rocke Letters from Bakwanga, 1960–1961, Rocke family archives, Sellersville, PA [henceforth GRL]. I thank Glenn's son Darrel Rocke for allowing me access to these records.

29 Archie Graber to Vernon Sprunger, 1 October 1960, Folder 7 Archie and Irma (Beilter) Graber, 1959–1961, Box 70, Gerber to Graber, 1936–1986, AIMMR.

The ASSK, the United Nations, and the CPRA relief mission, December 1960–October 1962

The ASSK tried with limited success to harness the CPRA for building up its own legitimacy among refugees. ASSK president Albert Kalonji, faced with mounting demands for scarce amounts of food from refugees, kept sending Graber letters in September 1960 reaffirming his endorsement of CPRA relief.[30] The remaining Forminière staff in Mbuji-Mayi provided Graber with warehouse space and a house to stay in, just as the company also helped to buy Kalonji's government relief supplies and weapons. American Presbyterian missionaries in Kananga and nearby missions also furnished Graber with money, food supplies, and a plane.[31]

The ASSK used access to relief to help quell resistance from Kanyok communities who rejected Kalonji's authority. Members of the Kanyok ethnic group had long taken pride in rejecting Luba royal authorities in the pre-colonial period and they refused to acknowledge Kalonji as their leader.[32] They lived between Kalonji's centre of power and the vital Mwene Ditu railway station. ASSK mercenaries and troops capitalised on CPRA aid. John Roberts, a young British adventurer who became an officer in the ASSK army, tried to convince members of the Kanyok ethnic community to give their allegiance to Kalonji in October 1960. He persuaded some Kanyok insurgents to surrender to the ASSK by promising, 'Through the American missionaries … I will obtain seed for crops from the U.S.A. I am aiming to get 200 tons of rice from U.S.A. to feed the starving refugees.'[33] Ordinary ASSK soldiers also exploited their role in distributing CPRA food. A CPRA inspector observed in one town in August 1961, 'I saw at least one thousand refugees milling about, hoping to pick up grains that had broken through bags. The government had lines of soldiers around the area beating off the people with wooden clubs. Once in a while a soldier would throw a stick of dried fish as to the dogs, and then all the soldiers would laugh at the scrambling.'[34]

30　Keidel, *War*, 143.

31　Archie Graber to Co-workers in the homeland, 16 October 1960, Folder 7 Archie and Irma (Beilter) Graber, 1959–1961, Box 70, Gerber to Graber, 1936–1986, AIMMR.

32　Kanyok resistance to the South Kasai state has yet to attract researchers. For brief references, see R. Higgins, *United Nations Peacekeeping, 1946–1967: Documents and Commentary*, vol. 3 (Oxford: Oxford University Press, 1980), 312–13.

33　J. Roberts, *My Congo Adventure* (London: Jarrods, 1963), 129.

34　Keidel, *War*, 194–5.

Although the ASSK relied on the CPRA as a major source of support for refugees, it did not mean Kalonji or his officials viewed Graber as an equal partner. At times, Kalonji's commissioner general of refugees, Hilaire Ngoyi, criticised CPRA policies. The commissioner general gave a series of demands to the CPRA on 4 February 1961. The CPRA name was to be taken off all trucks distributing aid and henceforth all aid distribution was to be credited to the United Nations.[35] Graber viewed this as a plot by Roman Catholics.[36] Since the Belgian colonial government favoured Catholic missionaries dating back to the Leopoldian era, it is little wonder Graber viewed the commissioner general as a merely Catholic pawn.[37]

However, the ASSK's orders were hardly religious in nature. Ngoyi mandated that CPRA drivers should be Congolese rather than American on the grounds that unemployment in South Kasai was a major problem.[38] This is one of the first examples of a Congolese official questioning why foreigners involved in humanitarian aid should hold jobs that plenty of local people could already do. Kalonji's government tried unsuccessfully to bill CPRA $600,000 for transport costs and then forced CPRA to accept his government's administration of relief.[39] His regime would only pay relief workers it had appointed. Graber responded by keeping his own staff; CPRA funds maintained their salaries.[40] Graber did not directly respond to these demands other than to switch to distributing tents, Bibles, and religious tracts for a month. By late March 1961, Kalonji and Ngoyi relented.[41]

CPRA camps for refugees became drawn into the byzantine struggles between Kalonji, Lulua militias, and the Congolese government. Lulua groups continued to drive Luba villagers into South Kasai from Kananga over the course of 1961 and early 1962, and starving refugees often died

35   Archie Graber to Vernon Sprunger, 22 February 1961, Folder 7 Archie and Irma (Beilter) Graber, 1959–1961, Box 70, Gerber to Graber, 1936–1986, AIMMR.

36   Ibid.

37   On Protestant complaints about the power and the influence of Catholic missions in the DRC, see Markowitz, *Cross and Sword: The Political Role of Christian Missions in the Belgian Congo, 1908–1960* (Stanford: Hoover Institution Press, 1973).

38   Archie Graber to Vernon Sprunger, 22 February 1961, Folder 7 Archie and Irma (Beilter) Graber, 1959–1961, Box 70, Gerber to Graber, 1936–1986, AIMMR.

39   Keidel, War, 171, 178–9.

40   Ibid., 161.

41   Archie Graber to Vernon Sprunger, 1 April 1961, Folder 7 Archie and Irma (Beilter) Graber, 1959–1961, Box 70, Gerber to Graber, 1936–1986, AIMMR.

on route.[42] Tens of thousands of Luba people required shelter and food. Graber complained that the Compagnie du Chemin de Fer du Bas-Congo au Katanga (BCK) railroad company refused to send anything to the ASSK without a special licence from the Congolese government, which could take months to obtain once the central government blocked supplies from Kinshasa.[43] Graber had to bring supplies in from the railroad town of Mwena Ditu located 90 miles from the CPRA camp at Mbuji-Mayi. When CPRA obtained trucks to bring food from Mwena Ditu to the camps, Kalonji's soldiers demanded money and a new watch from Graber to allow convoys to enter Mbuji-Mayi.[44]

The United Nations and the ASSK both tried to raise international support for assistance in collaboration with the CPRA. From November 1960 until March 1961, the UN launched an international publicity campaign to raise funds for relief to southern Kasai. Western journalists and diplomats flew to Mbuji-Mayi in late December 1960 at the behest of the UN mission in Congo to witness the need for immediate action to aid starving refugees. Kalonji tried to convince these visitors that his regime was the saviour of Luba people. The visits may have revealed the depth of refugee suffering, but it did not do much to improve Kalonji's reputation with potential donors. UN military commander Rajeshwar Dayal remembered, 'The "Prime Minister" [Joseph Ngalula] kept up an incessant conversation about how much [Kalonji] had done for the starving Baluba (he belonged to their tribe) but when we reached the refugee area, our hearts sank. The sight that met our eyes was one of utter desolation. Thousands upon thousands of refugees, sick and emaciated, were crouching under trees or cowering in the rain in the most elementary shelter … Our United Nations doctors were doing a magnificent job and the Indian nursing sisters, the first to volunteer, were like ministering angels.'[45] To add to the awkwardness, Kalonji's government provided an official Christmas Eve dinner featuring a sumptuous meal for UN officials, CPRA staff, and Red Cross doctors.[46] The dubiousness of holding

---

42 *Congo Protestant Relief Agency News Sheet* 15 (August 1961), Folder 75/5 Congo Protestant Relief Agency, OMP.

43 *Congo Protestant Relief Agency News Sheet* 14 (July 1961), Folder 75/5 Congo Protestant Relief Agency, OMP; Keidel, *War*, 188.

44 Archie Graber, 10 June 1962, Folder 75/5 Congo Protestant Relief Agency, OMP.

45 R. Dayal, *Mission for Hammarskjold: The Congo Crisis* (Princeton: Princeton University Press, 1976), 166.

46 Archie Graber to Loved Ones, 25 December 1960, Folder 7 Archie and Irma (Beilter) Graber, 1959–1961, Box 70, Gerber to Graber, 1936–1986, AIMMR.

a lavish party for a group of expatriates with thousands of starving people outside escaped the ASSK government.

Humanitarian aid for refugees did more to elicit sympathy for international intervention than improve the image of the ASSK. Western reporters depicted the hardships of refugees as examples of the horrors of decolonisation. A *Life* magazine article title summed up the conclusions of reporters: 'Harvest of Anarchy in the Congo'. The first page featured a photograph of a Swiss aid worker with a UN armband and a Red Cross symbol holding a 'dying Luba child, too weak to cry'.[47] US Air Force planes bringing food and World Health Organisation (WHO) doctors ready to inspect starving children expressed Western benevolence. Horst Fass, a German photographer later known for his iconic images of the Vietnam war, captured scenes of desperation in Luba settlements, with dozens of black arms outstretched to receive plates of food.[48] A Red Cross film crew in 1960 presented the Kasai crisis in the context of 'hate boiling over'.[49] In keeping with Liisa Malkki's critique of the depoliticised presentation of need, these articles and reporters rarely addressed the roots of conflict beyond ethnic divisions.[50] The UN's self-representation as an apolitical, well-informed humanitarian presence in the DRC won out over Kalonji's claim that the ASSK was protecting Luba people from being eradicated.

CPRA aid workers barely garnered mention in Western press coverage. Ironically, reporters had endless opportunities to see CPRA workers on the job. 'Big article from some London paper by men who were here for Christmas – went on food delivery on our truck and Archie were [the] only ones – all reporter said was that Catholic sister was giving children UN milk which was Archie Graber's milk,' Glenn Rocke complained.[51] Rocke noted how a *Life* reporter kept taking pictures of him at work, although they did not make it into the article.[52] Why did the UN and reporters downplay the CPRA so much? Given the US's partisan role in the DRC, it would certainly have made

47 "Harvest of Anarchy in the Congo," *Life* (17 February 1961), 22.

48 H. Fass, "Congo Miabi Famine," Associated Press (26 January 1961), Accessible at: www.apimages.com/metadata/Index/Watchf-AP-I-COG-APHSL32122-Congo-Miabi-Famine/70dc8cd9fb4041c2bc0046d74728fa72/12/0 (accessed 27 October 2019).

49 International Committee of the Red Cross, *SOS Congo* (1960), Available at: avarchives.icrc.org/Film/5534 (Accessed 27 October 2019).

50 L. Malkki, *The Need to Help: The Domestic Arts of International Humanitarianism* (Durham, NC: Duke University Press, 2015), 77–105.

51 Glenn Rocke to Ina Rocke, 15 January 1961, GRL.

52 Glenn Rocke to Ina Rocke, no date [December 1960], GRL.

sense for the UN to want to distance itself in its publicity from Americans, even though the CPRA was hardly just a tool of Washington. The ostensibly universal humanitarian ideals of the Red Cross and the UN might have been sullied by highlighting Protestant missionaries. Regardless, the CPRA stayed on well after the Kasai story left the front pages of Western newspapers.

The publicity campaign inspired an outpouring of aid from organisations such as Oxfam and the World Council of Churches that certainly aided the CPRA. These organisations played on ideals of heroic missionaries and appalling suffering. A World Council of Churches press release described how Graber, on an 'errand of signal mercy' amidst Luba and Lulua fighting each other was 'the one man capable of getting help started because he was equally trusted by both the tribesmen and United Nations officials'.[53] Oxfam featured a starving Luba child in its campaign.[54] These generic images of white saviours and dying innocents did convince many US, Canadian, Swiss, Dutch, and other Europeans to act. Canadians asked their parliamentary representatives to send fish, even as Dutch secondary school students worked odd jobs to buy milk.[55]

Despite the UN's success in obtaining aid for South Kasai, the ASSK increasingly became hostile to the UN in ways that undermined the CPRA's work. The ASSK leader had plotted with Joseph-Désiré Mobutu and other top central Congolese government leaders to have Lumumba brought to Mbuji-Mayi to be killed, although Mobutu and his Belgian and other Western advisors ultimately had Lumumba sent to his death in Katanga instead.[56] Though he missed out on having his old rival killed in South Kasai, Kalonji did order six of Patrice Lumumba's top officials shot on 12 February 1961 as punishment for the ANC's massacre of civilians in Mbuji-Mayi during the previous year.[57]

The UN criticised Kalonji's government, and local hostility to Ghanaian UN forces intensified. 'Much tension here because of the killing of the 6 prisoners. The only two women that were working for the U.N. here were ordered

---

53   Geoffrey Murray, Churches Feed the Hungry in Strife-Torn Congo, World Council of Churches press release, 17 January 1961, Folder Congo 1958–1962, 425.3.2.272 Africa Documents, WCCA.

54   Black, *Cause for Our Times*, 67–70.

55   On Dutch responses to the WCC appeal, see Survey of Relief Action in the Netherlands for Congo, 1 February 1961, Folder Congo 1958–1962, 425.3.2.272 Africa Documents, WCCA. On Canada, see Spooner, 2010, 128–30.

56   Witte, *Lumumba*, 82–5.

57   *193* Ibid., 153.

to leave at once for [Kinshasa] ... Talks by president Kalonji, prime minister Ngalula, and other VIP's speaking against the United Nations,' Graber wrote on 23 February 1961.[58] Tensions between Kalonji's state and the UN mission, especially Ghanaian forces, became more pronounced over the next few months. By early May 1961, the UN-sponsored Austrian Red Cross mission in Mbuji-Mayi was closed.[59] UN civil staff moved out of Mbuji-Mayi. While the UN kept shipping food to Mwene Ditu via rail, UN civil staff left transporting supplies by road from Mwene Ditu to Mbuji-Mayi to the CPRA and the ASSK.[60] Despite these logistical problems, humanitarian supplies helped to hold off a return of the widespread hunger from August to December 1960 and the opening months of 1961.

The CPRA acted as a mediator between the UN and the ASSK in the beginning months of 1962 to help Luba refugees leave Lubumbashi, the capital of Katanga. In September 1961, the UN mission opened up a refugee camp for Luba people in Katanga, primarily from urban centres rather than the northern rural areas of Katanga where the Balubakat political party's forces fought against Tshombe's rule.[61] Although Irish UN officer Conor Cruise O'Brien felt the massive rush into the camp was more out of a rejection of the Katanga secession than out of fear of Katangese retaliation, it is striking that people stayed in the camp when malnutrition, disease, and despair were the order of the day.[62] Militias formed within the camp that robbed and attacked people in Lubumbashi, while Katangese soldiers and civilians sometimes fired on the camp.

Kalonji and the UN turned to the CPRA to help organise the removal of the Luba refugees to further their own interests. Luba militias and juvenile gangs in the camp raided surrounding neighborhoods in Lubumbashi.[63] Furthermore, providing supplies and trying to maintain security in the camp posed

58 Archie Graber to Co-workers, 1 March 1961, Folder 7 Archie and Irma (Beilter) Graber, 1959–1961, Box 70, Gerber to Graber, 1936–1986, AIMMR.

59 E. Schmidl, *Blau Helme – Rotes Kreuz: Das österreichische UN-Sanitätskontingent im Kongo, 1960–1963* (Vienna: Studien Verlag, 1995).

60 Archie Graber to Vernon Sprunger, 15 July 1961, Folder 7 Archie and Irma (Beilter) Graber, 1959–1961, Box 70, Gerber to Graber, 1936–1986, AIMMR.

61 While the camp itself has not been the object of study in its own right, some of sources include O'Brien, *Katanga*, 238–44; A. Tullberg, "We are in the Congo Now: Sweden and the Trinity of Peacekeeping during the Congo Crisis 1960–1964" (PhD thesis, Lund University, 2012), 206–19.

62 O'Brien, *Katanga*, 238–44.

63 Georg Hoffmann, 9 November 1961, Folder Réfugiés Balubas à Elisabethville 05/10/1961 – 27/02/1963, B AG 234 229-002, ACICR.

3. Starving child, South Kasai, 1961. The CPRA and its donors disseminated images of hungry victims to elicit charitable donations in 1960 and 1961. Inspired by these photographs, North American and European readers raised money, pressured their elected officials, and supported UN and CPRA operations. (MCCA)

a financial burden for the UN mission. The ASSK was ready to give sanctuary to the refugees from Katanga. A British officer in a Nigerian UN peacekeeper unit told CPRA volunteer Caleb Stegall in early 1961 that Kalonji had offered to pay the UN a million US dollars to have the Luba refugees in Lubumbashi flown to Mbuji-Mayi.[64] Kalonji's motives probably came from his dwindling popularity as much as out of altruism. Kalonji had dismissed his partner Joseph Ngalula from the government in 1961, then spent several months in prison in Kinshasa. After escaping from prison and returning to Mbuji-Mayi, Kalonji acted increasingly as an absolute monarch who favoured members of his own clan over others.[65] International Committee of the Red Cross (ICRC) delegate Geoffrey Senn, noting how tens of thousands of new arrivals from Katanga would stretch the ASSK's thin resources even further, speculated that the ASSK was seeking more 'manpower and importance' rather than actually helping displaced people.[66]

Graber toured the Lubumbashi camp at the invitation of the United Nations mission in March 1962. 'The past ten days I saw mud, filth, misery, sickness … the worst I have yet seen in 31 years in Congo,' observed Graber.[67] Unlike any of the UN civilian staff or the Red Cross teams, Graber could communicate directly in Tshiluba with refugees and had the social and political connections in South Kasai to engineer a resettlement plan. Graber had already served as a bridge between Luba people with international aid programmes. For example, he had mediated a tense stand-off between a group of displaced people and UN staff who had come to a rural location in a helicopter. The refugees became frightened, having never seen a helicopter before, and started to threaten the UN team. After Graber had settled refugee concerns about a possible attack, he advised UN staff to abandon further helicopter deliveries.[68] Such knowledge prepared the way for the mammoth undertaking of bringing tens of thousands of Luba refugees from Lubumbashi to Mbuji-Mayi.

64 Caleb Stegall, Dad's Last Congo Trip, (unpublished manuscript, 1961), page 29, Box 2, Folder 7, Caleb Stegall Papers, Record Group 454, PHS.

65 On Kalonji's increasingly authoritarian policies, see Lushiku Lumana, *Les Baluba du Kasaï*, 119–24.

66 Geoffrey Senn, Observations concerning the repatriation of Baluba refugees in the Elisabethville camp to their homeland of South Kasai, 8 April 1962, Folder Réfugiés Balubas à Elisabethville 05/10/1961 – 27/02/1963, B AG 234 229-002, ACICR.

67 Archie Graber to Vernon Sprunger, 15 April 1962, Folder 8 Archie and Irma (Beilter) Graber, 1962–1965, Box 70, Gerber to Graber, 1936–1986, AIMMR.

68 Archie Graber to Co-workers, 1 February 1961 Folder 7 Archie and Irma (Beilter) Graber, 1959–1961, Box 70, Gerber to Graber, 1936–1986, AIMMR.

Graber also negotiating with UN staff, village chiefs, and displaced people to expedite the safe arrival of displaced people to the South Kasai. First, he convinced local leaders to accept newcomers. 'One large village accepted to take as many as 10,000 [and] another village said they would take 4000 [and] other smaller villages will take less,' Graber reported.[69] How these agreements came together is not clear from correspondence related to the CPRA, but accounts from survivors of the Lubumbashi camp describe crowds of people in Mbuji-Mayi and surrounding towns celebrating the arrival of people coming from Katanga.[70] Besides ensuring that these refugees could find new homes, Graber also worked with UN personnel to supervise the evacuation. The final plans demonstrated yet again the transport problems that beset Kasai.[71] The UN balked at flying the refugees directly from Lubumbashi to Mbuji-Mayi due to the exorbitant cost. Graber and UN staff eventually decided to use armoured trains to transport refugees from Katanga to the Kamina UN military base. UN planes then moved the displaced people to Mbuji-Mayi.[72] A group of roughly 1,500 displaced individuals belonging to the Songye ethnic community arrived from the camp to Kamina. However, they balked at going to Mbuji-Mayi out of fear of attacks by Luba people. Graber convinced this group to go along with the final leg of the trip to the ASSK.[73]

Kalonji's support for the CPRA remained strong from the Lubumbashi resettlement until the final collapse of his government. On 29 September 1962, the president of South Kasai held a meeting with Graber. Kalonji rained praise on the CPRA: 'He has observed that the Protestants on his staff are superior to the Catholics … He would like us to send more people to help in the educational, economic, and social needs. Many of the Baluba who have come to [Mbuji-Mayi] are intellectual and able people, but there is no work for them, and he fears discontent.'[74] Mennonite Central Committee (MCC) executive board member Orie Miller, who accompanied Graber,

69 Archie Graber to Vernon Sprunger, 15 April 1962, Folder 8 Archie and Irma (Beilter) Graber, 1962–1965, Box 70, Gerber to Graber, 1936–1986, AIMMR.

70 M. Mbikay, *Entre le rêve et le souvenir* (Bloomington, IN: Lulu, 2013), 219–37.

71 Archie Graber to Vernon Sprunger, 8 May 1962, Folder 8 Archie and Irma (Beilter) Graber, 1962–1965, Box 70, Gerber to Graber, 1936–1986, AIMMR.

72 Ibid.

73 Archie Graber to Vernon Sprunger, 14 July 1962 Folder 8 Archie and Irma (Beilter) Graber, 1962–1965, Box 70, Gerber to Graber, 1936–1986, AIMMR.

74 *Congo Protestant Relief Agency Newsletter* 32 (30 October 1962), Folder 8 Archie and Irma (Beilter) Graber, 1962–1965, Box 70, Gerber to Graber, 1936–1986, AIMMR.

added: '[Kalonji] is interested in the American people understanding him and his motives – feels he has been misinterpreted by the world.'[75] Kalonji's last efforts to harness the CPRA to build legitimacy at home and in the US never came to pass. The next day in Mbuji-Mayi, the visiting MCC delegation heard gunfire and learned that central government ANC troops had arrived in the city. ASSK soldiers gave up without much of a fight. Although Kalonji slipped away without being captured yet again, the central government put an end to the ASSK permanently and officially dissolved Kalonji's regime on 8 October 1962.

It is remarkable that one of Kalonji's last acts in office was to try to request more aid from the CPRA. The ASSK's desperate search for legitimacy abroad made the CPRA particularly valuable. No matter how many photographs of starving children in the Kasai plastered Western newspapers, the ASSK failed to obtain more than humanitarian assistance. The CPRA, rather than take a partisan approach in the way Catholic and Methodist missionaries did for Katanga, remained resolutely neutral. Graber's Mennonite faith highlighted peaceful negotiation and eschewed close alliances with any government. This approach resulted in a steady flow of food and supplies from international donors and the UN by depoliticising the root causes of the humanitarian emergency. If the central government and the UN mission had considered the CPRA to be too close to the ASSK, then the CPRA programme would not have been nearly as successful.

Outside the lines: the limits of CPRA records for recovering refugee agency

For all the wealth of information that CPRA correspondence provides about the ASSK and the United Nations, Graber's letters contain silences regarding Congolese. African aid workers rarely drew much attention in Graber's writings, but they do appear on the margins. Young men oversaw the distribution of food in the village of Bwa Kashile in December 1960.[76] Elsewhere, an 'intelligent young Congolese girl' distributed milk to 200 people.[77] This work was clearly risky. Some ANC soldiers nearly killed one Congolese CPRA employee in the town of Miabi on the grounds that he had supposedly stolen

---

75   William T. Snyder Diary, 29 September 1962 entry, 11 September to 31 October 1962, Folder Snyder William T. Commissioner Trip to Congo, Folder 109/23, Box 186, IX-6-3.102, MCCA.

76   *Congo Protestant Relief Agency News Sheet* 8 (10 January 1961), Folder 75/5 Congo Protestant Relief Agency, OMP.

77   Ibid.

rice in late December 1960.[78] In 1963, Graber recalled a faithful driver who died in fighting between Kalonji partisans and central government supporters.[79] Again, names and specific details of these workers remain largely absent. Such a silencing of the Congolese role in feeding, housing, and caring for other Congolese often makes Graber appear to be the entire CPRA famine programme in Kasai.

Graber's detached, measured tone played down conflicts with refugees and the discouragement of negotiating with the ASSK. Crisscrossing the battleground between south Kasai and Lulua militas north of Mbuji-Mayi around Lake Munkamba, Graber saw the misery of civilians constantly. His references were usually terse, such as this example from April 1961: '10 miles from Lake Munkamba on the Lulua side we passed two villages that were burned down to the ground 4 days ago. These were Bena Konshi. Some had chosen to follow Mukenga Lulua and others Kalonji Baluba.'[80] Other members of the small CPRA staff were far less willing to keep their qualms silent, at least in their diaries. Allen Horst's journal offers a very different perspective on how Congolese people interacted with CPRA aid workers. Horst belonged to the Mennonite Pax youth programme, designed to provide Mennonites an alternative to service in the US military.[81] MCC staff reassigned Horst to the DRC in early September 1960. After a MCC staff member asked Horst if he wanted to go, Horst wrote in his diary, 'I figured he was pulling my leg so I said, "Sure thing" … Boy, I don't know about the whole deal…No sweat Allen, you can always say "Hi" to the folks back home in two years if you don't get punctured with twenty Congo spears and fifteen poison darts.'[82] This tone – with its mixture of comedy and discourses of primitive Congo – shaped much of Horst's daily accounts of his work with Archie Graber.

For a historian, one advantage of Horst's testimony compared to Graber's work was his willingness to complain about other people. Horst expressed frustration and bewilderment in his diary and in a 2018 interview. 'These crazy

78 *Congo Protestant Relief Agency News Sheet* 10 (19 January 1961), Folder 75/4 Congo Protestant Relief Agency, OMP.

79 Archie Graber to Co-workers, 10 May 1963, Folder 8 Archie and Irma (Beilter) Graber, 1962–1965, Box 70, Gerber to Graber, 1936–1986, AIMMR.

80 Archie Graber to Co-workers, 15 April 1961 Folder 7 Archie and Irma (Beilter) Graber, 1959–1961, Box 70, Gerber to Graber, 1936–1986, AIMMR.

81 C. Redekop, *The Pax Story: Service in the Name of Christ, 1951–1976* (Telford, PA: Pandora Press, 2001).

82 Allen Horst Diary, 12 September 1960 entry, Pax Collection, 1944–2005, HM1/927, Mennonite Church USA Archives, Elkhart, Indiana (henceforth AHD).

soldiers,' he wrote on 23 October 1960 just after arriving in Mbuji-Mayi, '[One] had some other dumb bunny carrying his sub-machine gun for him. He waved the thing around like a water pistol ... Jeepers, if I don't end up with a handful of lead in me, I'll consider myself fortunate!'[83] On the same day, he passed a market: 'Holy mackerel, I couldn't tell if they were selling rotten goat meat or flies ... I am enjoying the opportunity of seeing people of such a different culture.'[84] Like a fair number of other MCC youth volunteers, Horst tended to consider his experience as evidence of Western superiority rather than a means of building empathy with other peoples.

Fear, an emotion entirely absent in Graber's writing, was a constant theme in Horst's and fellow volunteer Abe Suderman's recollections of the ASSK. Graber decided to prepare his two assistants for their work on their first supply run in a novel way. The missionary had Horst and Suderman leave their truck after driving a short while. They then walked over a sandbank on the side of the road. Horst remembered in 2018, 'Guess what we saw and smelled? Dead people ... Dead meat. What kind of meat? There's a skull sticking out of the dirt over there. Over there next to him is a guy with his legs sticking out. There's a part of a guy that the dogs have eaten ... To wind up there looking at those dead people and skeletons, that was scary.'[85] Still traumatised by his experiences to the point he could not bring himself to write about them, Abe Suderman's disjointed account placed inexplicable violence in the foreground.[86] Corpses lined a road, the victims of ANC troops who slaughtered them in retaliation for the assassination of one of their officers by a Belgian mercenary. After dogs and then driver ants went to work, only bones lay behind. A soldier in the middle of the road aimed a rifle at Suderman one day, and Suderman thought he was going to die.

Horst and Suderman's fears also reflected racialised anxieties. Horst's first trip out of Mubji-Mayi on 6 November 1960 exposed how Congolese CPRA workers and soldiers negotiated with CPRA North American staff. En route to Mwene Ditu to pick up food supplies, Horst was alarmed by the terrible state of the road and the fact he didn't have enough diesel to finish the trip back to Mbuji-Mayi.[87] Soldiers repeatedly stopped the truck. When one Congolese CPRA driver tried to argue with some troops at a roadblock, the soldiers forced him to get out. 'I thought they were going to shoot

83   Allen Horst Diary, 23 October 1960 entry, AHD.

84   Ibid.

85   Telephone interview, Allen Horst, 13 June 2018.

86   Telephone interview, Abe Suderman, 17 December 2016.

87   The following is taken from Allen Horst Diary, 6 November 1960 entry, AHD.

him right there! Boy, my knees were shaking. [MCC Pax volunteer] Abe [Suderman] finally interceded in his broken Tshiluba and they let us go,' Horst recounted.[88] On another truck drive at night, Horst skidded into an ASSK military convoy and struck a jeep. He panicked, but then felt relief at the sight of a white mercenary officer: 'He knew I was just some white guy who didn't know what he was doing.'[89] This event alone demonstrates how soldiers treated Congolese CPRA staff differently than Graber or white aid workers – without white privilege, Congolese aid workers were more vulnerable to threats.

Displaced people emerge as both victims and as hassles in their own right in Horst's account. At the town of Miabi, Horst and Suderman picked up an old man who died at Horst's feet in their car. On arriving in one town, Horst saw 'little children with their ribs sticking out like toothpicks' and wondered, 'When we unloaded with food, the Congolese would hardly help us; don't know if they were weak from hunger or just not excited about manual labor.'[90] Other refugees did not passively accept aid. When Graber decided to give food to hospital patients before other people in Miabi, some refugees nearly rioted. 'We had a good fence between us and the refugees to keep from getting swamped … It's really hard to understand and feel sorry for people who act like that when you try to help them,' lamented the young American.[91] Other refugees demanded three times the agreed-upon wages after unloading and sorting crates of food.[92] After Horst and another CPRA worker searched the workers, they found dried fish and other food stolen from the UN shipment.[93] Horst quickly learned to share Graber's pessimism about decolonisation: 'I feel sorry for the poorer people that became victims of this whole independence thing.'[94] Yet Horst's diary also shows how Congolese fought to control how they worked and how they received aid, rather than simply being ignorant pawns. Other refugees sometimes told other CPRA workers they needed to be paid to haul water to distribution sites.[95]

88 Interview, Allen Horst, 13 June 2018.

89 Ibid.

90 Allen Horst Diary, 6 November 1960 entry, AHD.

91 Allen Horst Diary, 20 November 1960 entry, AHD.

92 Allen Horst Diary, 8 January 1961 entry, AHD.

93 Ibid.

94 Ibid.

95 Glenn Rocke to Ina Rocke, no date [January 1961], GRL.

Mennonite missionary and CPRA volunteer Glenn Rocke's letters to his family provided a more compassionate description of refugees than Horst, even as he also included more details on the daily tasks of relief work. Unlike Horst, Rocke used food distribution as an opportunity to evangelise: 'At each place I told them that this food was coming from the Christian people in America ... Christian have given because they love the Lord and they want the people of Congo to know and love the Lord too.'[96] Driving and distributing food brought Rocke together with old friends, including one Congolese woman who had lost 50 pounds from hunger since he had last seen her before independence.[97]

Interspersed between itineraries of distribution sites and the daily listing of tasks emerge more painful, less ordered moments. 'While riding with Archie so many people were trying to get as us as they do every 100 meters ... Archie stopped and explained that our cars are just for hauling food and sick people and that they would understand why we do not pick them up ... after talking for five or ten minutes the Africans' only deduction was that we are very bad people who have no love for them,' Rocke wrote in January 1961.[98] On one of Graber's many trips, his truck was stopped: 'Men and women had joined hands and made a double line across the road.' The group gave Graber a list of individual refugees in the village and asked him to come back with food.[99]

Narratives produced by CPRA volunteers thus often edited out both Congolese perspectives and potential dangers to aid workers themselves. Graber's emphasis on Christian reconciliation and his own authoritative voice left out the disordered moments of terror and insecurity that haunted younger volunteers. No matter if CPRA staff considered Congolese with either dread or pity, Congolese perspectives on their negotiations with the CPRA only can be made out fitfully. Younger volunteers with very little fluency in Tshiluba and French had difficulty communicating with Congolese, while experienced missionaries chose to leave out of their narratives how refugees might not always follow orders as well as the crucial role of Congolese aid workers themselves.

96 Glenn Rocke to Ina Rocke, 30 December 1960, GRL.

97 Glenn Rocke to Ina Rocke, 5 December 1960, GRL.

98 Glenn Rocke to Ina Rocke, no date [January 1961], GRL.

99 *Congo Protestant Relief Agency News Sheet* 8 (10 January 1961), Folder 75/4 Congo Protestant Relief Agency, OMP.

Conclusion

One way to sum up the CPRA and Archie Graber's role would be to celebrate humanitarian action. Jim Bertsche, a fellow Mennonite missionary, lauded him decades later. Describing how Luba chiefs came to say their farewells when Graber left the Kasai in 1964, Bertsche wrote: "'You are our savior!' they said, and insisted that if he had not come and entered into the danger and suffering of their refugee days, they all would have died.'[100] Without denying the crucial efforts of the CPRA under Graber's capable leadership in preventing death by starvation, this chapter has examined the political context of CPRA's relief programme. Protestant missionaries viewed Congolese independence as both a tragedy and a new opportunity to reach Africans hit hard by the violence of the Congo crises. At least in southern Kasai, Graber's CPRA relief project managed to stay neutral in political disputes. The CPRA was thus able to negotiate effectively with the ASSK, the United Nations, and the Congolese central government. Missionary relief was not merely a way to save lives in southern Kasai. It became a resource valuable to major stakeholders in the political conflicts in the region. For the United Nations, aid in the Kasai was a welcome public example of benevolence as it faced criticism from the right for attacking Katanga and from the left for being close partners with the US and its Congolese political partners. The CPRA was vital for the ASSK's legitimacy in the Kasai and in the international community. The flexibility of Graber's Mennonite background and his refusal to take a partisan position allowed him to talk to all the key figures in the Kasai famine crisis.

Generic tropes of white saviours and suffering Africans effectively mobilised support for aid to southern Kasai in late 1960 and early 1961 in Western countries, effectively erasing the specific agenda and history of the CPRA in the process. North American Protestant missionaries sought to make a place for themselves in an independent Congo by binding the wounds of independence through charity. However, Western press coverage made no room for the CPRA's story to be heard. Instead, the UN took credit for humanitarian aid. Likewise, the ASSK's self-representation as a heroic defender of Luba refugees from Lulua raiders and the Congolese military was muted. If the specific actors in Kasai aid received little attention, refugees themselves were defined only by their suffering in publicity surrounding the famine.

The CPRA case also illuminates the limits of using written and even oral sources made by humanitarian aid workers in recovering the agency of refugees themselves. Graber's correspondence highlighted individual examples of suffering, the achievements of charity, and logistical obstacles to food

100 Hollinger-Janzen, Myers, and Bertsche, *Jesus Tribe*, 117.

distribution. He spent little time on discussing refugees' negotiations to obtain food and make demands on the CPRA. Younger CPRA volunteers lacked both Graber's linguistic and cultural expertise and their supervisor's self-control in editing their own accounts. Allan Horst's diary exposes refugees willing to go on strike and set the terms of aid. However, the daily details of how Congolese distributed CPRA food in villages and the dynamics of violence are left out.

What significance does this chapter hold for the larger history of humanitarianism? The actions and dynamics of faith-based organisations in the era of African decolonisation are still not well understood, but the CPRA case indicates how missionaries adjusted to new political conditions after the end of European rule. The ASSK does provide an interesting counterpart to the much better-known role of humanitarian organisations in the Biafran war of secession. Foreign missionaries and members of aid organisations lobbied for Biafran independence.[101] The Biafran government effectively used images of famine to gain international sympathy. By contrast, Albert Kalonji's regime failed to gain the allegiance of the CPRA as an advocate. Instead, the CPRA worked with the United Nations and maintained a traditionally apolitical position in keeping with both Mennonite pacifism and secular NGOs like the Red Cross. Perhaps the most notable value for the Kasai case was how it served as an early precedent for state reliance on humanitarian aid later on in the DRC. The ASSK and the central government in the Kasai depended on the CPRA and other foreign organisations such as Caritas and Catholic Relief Service to furnish aid, rather than themselves providing much relief. Even after the end of the humanitarian crisis of the ASSK by 1964, state officials continued to leave promoting economic development to expatriate-led NGOs for decades to come.

---

101 E. Staunton, "The Case of Biafra: Ireland and the Nigerian Civil War," Irish Historical Studies 31:124 (1999), 513–35; K. Waters, "Influencing the Message: The Role of Catholic Missionaries in Media Coverage of the Nigerian Civil War," Catholic Historical Review 90:4 (2004), 697–718; A. Oko Omaka, *The Biafran Humanitarian Crisis: International Human Rights and Joint Church Aid* (Lanham, MD: Rowman and Littlefield, 2016); A. Moses and L. Heerten, *Postcolonial Conflict and the Question of Genocide: The Nigeria-Biafra War, 1967–1970* (New York: Routledge, 2017).

3

The CPRA and Angolan Refugees in the DRC, 1961–1967

In June 1961, Canadian pastor James Ormiston visited Angolan refugee settlements in the Bas-Congo province of the Democratic Republic of Congo. Three months earlier, rebel forces of the UPA (União dos Povos de Angola) had launched a surprise attack on Portuguese settlers in northern Angola. The Portuguese colonial government led a counter-offensive. Mission-educated intellectuals and poor farmers alike became the victims of the brutal crackdown by Portuguese settlers and solders. 'I have had to face the fact that the Portuguese really are slitting children's throats and chopping the hands and feet and heads off people. It is a chilling realisation that so-called civilised people can sink so far down their own offal of self-pride and self-pity,' Ormiston wrote to the United Church of Canada (UCC) mission board secretary.[1] Ultimately, several hundred thousand Angolans fled to the Democratic Republic of Congo between 1961 and 1965.

This chapter focuses on the political dimensions of CPRA aid in its support of the UPA, later known as the FNLA (Frente Nacional de Libertação de Angola) from 1961 until 1967, when CPRA staff member David Grenfell retired. Grenfell committed himself to collaborating with FNLA leader Holden Roberto. Despite the ostensibly apolitical nature of the CPRA, Grenfell's meticulous monitoring of refugee movements from Angola to the DRC reinforced FNLA's control of Angolan people. The British missionary made Angolans legible as citizens of FNLA's government in exile through a complicated system of ration cards. In addition, he and other CPRA staff regulated how FNLA officials and soldiers gave out permits to refugees seeking to escape Angola. The CPRA also procured food and supplies for refugees under FNLA's administration. CPRA advocacy for FNLA extended to public relations abroad as Grenfell supplied favourable information about Roberto and his movement to international donor organisations and mission boards.

1 James Ormiston to Floyd Honey, 27 June 1961, Folder 6 United Church of Canada Board of Overseas Missions, Congo 1961 Correspondence: Congo Protestant Relief, Box 1 UCC Board of World Mission Associate Secretary for Zaire, Accession no. 83.031C, UCCA.

Organisations such as the CWS (Church World Service) and the UCC funded relief for Angolan refugees. However, not all aid workers supported Grenfell's approval of Roberto. Ian Gilchrist, a Canadian doctor who worked directly for the FNLA rather than the CPRA, became embittered with the FNLA elite to the point Roberto tried to have Gilchrist arrested in June 1965. Other CPRA staff smuggled Gilchrist out of the DRC, even as Grenfell remained sympathetic to Roberto.

The CPRA's aid to Angolans offers insights into the history of the Angolan rebel movement based in the DRC. CPRA narratives provide details on the violence of Portuguese counter-insurgency. Grenfell's impressive record-keeping also allows for a better understanding of refugees, FNLA troops, and individuals who straddled the physical and ideological borders as they crossed from the Congo to Angola and back again. General histories of the Angolan war for independence have up to now neglected the CPRA, despite the wealth of material in CPRA correspondence on refugee experiences and the FNLA leadership.[2] This discussion builds on Inge Brinkman's examination of refugees and mobility in the Angolan civil war, although CPRA sources provide details on efforts and worries around stabilizing refugee movement in the DRC not raised by Brinkman.[3] This chapter also draws from Joanna Tague's work on George Houser's advocacy and limited US government assistance for Angolan refugees.[4] While her approach considers Houser's lobbying for FNLA with the US government, this chapter considers the role of missionary aid on the ground in the DRC. CPRA staff also became embroiled in disputes between Holden Roberto and dissidents who denounced how he favoured his BisiKongo ethnic group over other Angolans. This is particularly illuminating given how CPRA records expose fault lines within FNLA in

2   For some major works on the war for Angolan independence, see J. Marcum, *The Angolan Revolution. Volume II: Exile Politics and Guerilla Warfare, 1962–1976* (Cambridge, MA: Massachusetts Institute of Technology Press, 1978); F.W. Heimer, *Decolonisation Conflict in Angola, 1974–1976* (Geneva: Institut Universitaires de Hautes Études Internationales, 1979); J.J. Gann, *Counterinsurgency in Africa: The Portuguese Way of War, 1961–1974* (Westport: Greenwood, 1997; J.M. Mabeko Tali, *Dissidências e poder de estado: O MPLA perante si próprio (1962–1977)*, 2 vols. (Luanda: Editorial Nzila, 2001).

3   I. Brinkman, "Refugees on Routes"; I. Brinkman, *A War for the People: Civilians, Mobility, and Legitimacy in South-east Angola during the MPLA's War for Independence* (Cologne: Rüdiger Köppe Verlag, 2005).

4   J. Tague, "American Humanitarianism and Portugal's African Empire: Institutional and Governmental Interests in Assisting Angolan Refugees in Congo, 1961–1974," *Portuguese Journal of Social Science* 14:3 (2015), 343–59.

the mid-1960s, just as FNLA encountered increasing competition from the Marxists of the MPLA (Movimento Popular de Libertação de Angola).

Much as in the better-known case of humanitarian organisations in Biafra, CPRA staff broke with the impartiality of organisations like the Red Cross by openly denouncing Portuguese colonialism. When the Red Cross withdrew from Angolan refugee assistance in 1962, the CPRA became an even more important source of aid to Angolans in the DRC. CPRA staff saw themselves as participants in the struggle against white supremacy in southern Africa. They joined other Protestant missionaries in promoting the cause of Angolan independence that drew aid from Scandinavian, Canadian and US Protestants, the US and Congolese governments, and the Soviet bloc.[5] Cold War politics in the DRC did influence the CPRA's programmes in 1964 and 1965, when the US-backed ascension to power of Moïse Tshombe as the Congolese prime minister posed challenges to the CPRA. Although the Angolan refugee cause itself was not entirely split by Cold War divisions, Tshombe's willingness to seek a rapprochement with the Portuguese weakened Angolan rebels.

While the complexities of the Angolan refugee situation were to some degree different from cases where Cold War politics had a more direct role in humanitarian programmes for refugees, some aspects of aid to Angolans resembled other examples of humanitarian refugee assistance in the 1960s. Firoze Manji and Carl O'Coill have contended in a polemical article that missionaries transitioned from being advocates of colonialism to becoming 'missionaries of development'.[6] Missionaries, in their view, replaced their previous endorsement of white supremacy with a new rhetoric free of 'racial signifiers' that proved to be 'little more than a superficial reformulation of old colonial prejudices'.[7] The CPRA actually captured this moment of transition in the decolonisation period, since its expatriate staff consisted of former long-time missionaries in Angola or short-term new missionary volunteers. Though missionaries such as Grenfell could be paternalistic at times, Manji and O'Coill's blanket condemnations fail to capture how CPRA staff could see themselves as participants in promoting an independent Angola. The personalised style of leadership and the anxieties about refugee dependence on foreign aid found in other refugee aid programmes in the 1960s also

---

5   P. Byam, "New Wine in a Very Old Bottle: Canadian Protestant Missionaries as Facilitators of Development in Central Angola, 1886–1961" (PhD thesis, University of Ottawa, 1997); Burlingham, "Image of God," 149–75.

6   F. Manji and C. O'Coill, "The Missionary Position: NGOs and Development in Africa," *International Affairs* 78:3 (2002), 568–72.

7   Ibid., 572, 575.

characterise the CPRA. Donor organisations made little effort to try to evaluate individual aid directors like David Grenfell, who contended that refugees would require much supervision to ensure they did not become dependent on outside aid for over a year. Grenfell and other aid workers rejected the idea of creating separate camps, on the grounds that Congolese people allowed refugees to establish their own settlements and fields.

Sources on the CPRA aid programme for Angolans reflect the outsized role of individual leaders and the array of networks that sustained the programme. Rather than rely on formal government correspondence in keeping with most work on Congolese histories, this chapter relies instead on mission board archives that supported the CPRA. My use of David Grenfell's monthly reports on CPRA relief draw from various Canadian and US mission board and donor archives, as he sent his reports to his diverse range of supporters. Grenfell's nephew Jim donated his uncle's diaries and personal papers to Oxford University's Baptist Missionary Society holdings in 2015. Much like Archie Graber took a crucial role in shaping how Protestant donors viewed the South Kasai crisis, Grenfell's densely detailed reports influenced how Protestant churches and aid agencies understood the Angolan revolution in the early 1960s.

This chapter begins by analysing the initial CPRA aid programme to Angolans in 1961 and 1962, when the programme scrambled to assist the onrush of Angolan refugees. The next section considers how David Grenfell then instituted a programme of assisting new refugees for a year. His paternalistic policies towards refugees led him to develop detailed records on thousands of refugees. Refugees chafed at times against Grenfell's methods of distributing food. At the same time, they did rely on CPRA staff for medical care, help with employment, and schools. The last section analyses how CPRA personnel worked with the Congolese government and the FNLA. Grenfell had a very close relationship with FNLA leader Holden Roberto and sent information on FNLA internal politics and the Congolese government along to other CPRA members of staff.

Unlike Archie Graber's relative distance from any state actors, Grenfell's open partnership with the FNLA reached the point that the CPRA effectively acted to make Angolan refugees into FNLA subjects through rations and identification papers. Grenfell's reports dramatically exposed the human cost of Portuguese repression to churches in North America and Britain. Thanks to Grenfell's friendship with Roberto, these reports also provide a unique glimpse of Roberto's efforts to use diplomacy inside and outside the DRC to strengthen his position against the Portuguese and his Marxist rivals in the MPLA. Canadian missionaries shared Grenfell's commitment to Angolan refugees and generally the FNLA, even as some Canadians ultimately broke with Roberto's authoritarian policies. These partnerships stand in stark contrast to other agencies such as the UN High Commission for Refugees and the International Committee of the Red Cross, which viewed the FNLA as an obstacle to repatriating refugees to Angola. While these other organisations eliminated food assistance to Angolans within a year on the grounds that relief made Angolans unwilling to work for themselves, the CPRA under Grenfell's lead committed itself to the FNLA as the legitimate government of Angola.

The CPRA and the Angolan refugee crisis, 1961–1962

The CPRA joined the United Nations mission in Congo, the Catholic aid organisation Caritas, and the Red Cross in a scramble to furnish aid to the ever-growing numbers of Angolans crossing into the DRC in early 1961. Although the United Nations could furnish food and medical supplies, UN staff sought out the International Coalition of the Red Cross (ICRC), the CPRA, and the international Catholic aid agency Caritas to distribute food and other supplies to the swelling Angolan refugee population in Bas-Congo province. In a loose agreement in May 1961, the CPRA agreed to aid refugees in the Moerbeke-Kimpangu region, leaving other entry points for Angolans to the ICRC and Caritas.[8] Decolonisation may have disappointed some missionaries, but for CPRA staff, independence and even the Angolan crisis appeared as new opportunities to evangelise: 'The manner in which this refugee service has become an open door for us ... can be used in such a significant way here and later perhaps in Angola – all these would convince one of remarkable Divine leading and enablement.'[9]

The handful of full-time CPRA staff in the Congo were fortunate that experienced Protestant missionaries from Angola willingly joined the relief effort. Baptist Missionary Society pastors from Great Britain worked among BisiKongo communities in Bas-Congo and Angola. Canadian Baptists and UCC missionaries had worked in central and southern Angola. UCC pastor James Ormiston, forced out of Angola by the Portuguese government, flew to Bas-Congo to assess the situation for the United Church of Canada on May 1961. He noted how United Nations staff had a great deal of supplies, to the

8   Ernest Lehmann to Roland Metzger, 18 May 1961, Folder 6 United Church of Canada Board of Overseas Missions Congo 1961 Congo Protestant Relief Agency, Box 1, Accession no. 83.031C, UCCA.

9   Ernest Lehmann to Roland Metzger, 7 June 1961, Folder 6 United Church of Canada Board of Overseas Missions Congo 1961 Congo Protestant Relief Agency, Box 1, Accession no. 83.031C, UCCA.

point CPRA volunteers were distributing 65 tons of food per week from the UN in late June 1961 alone.[10] UN and ICRC staff relied on the knowledge and local connections of CPRA volunteers in 1961 and 1962.

Ormiston and other CPRA staff made no pretense that they opposed the Portuguese colonial government. Refugees reported to Ormiston about the 'special concern that the Portuguese have had to find and liquidate the teachers, nurses, carpenters, pastors … the intelligencia [sic]. These are the people we have spent a lot of time and money assisting and … [we] should do all we can to get them out of the way of the secret police [Polícia Internacional e de Defesa do Estado].'[11] Indiscriminate bombing by Portuguese planes on refugees close to the Congolese frontier left behind infants mutilated by shrapnel and numerous severe burn wounds from napalm.[12] Soldiers cut the hands, feet, and head off one Angolan village chief who allowed a traveller from Congo to stay a night in his town.[13]

Refugees who managed to reach the Congo told of the devastation of the Portuguese military campaigns against the rebels. Invariably, they lost loved ones in the initial Portuguese military campaigns of 1961 as well as through the hardships of hiding in rural areas. David Grenfell's bi-weekly reports from 1962 to 1966 feature hundreds of terse summaries of these deaths. One typical report noted that refugees recalled 83 dead killed by mines, bullets, decapitation, 'a sword', and illness.[14] Grenfell included the names of individual informants and in many cases identified individuals who had died. While a

---

10   James Ormiston, On the Spot in Congo (unpublished manuscript, no date [1961], Folder 9 United Church of Canada Board of Overseas Missions Congo 1961 Ormiston Reports on Angolan Refugees, Box 1, Accession no. 83. 031C, UCCA.

11   James Ormiston to Floyd Honey and Roy Webster, 8 June 1961, Folder 6 United Church of Canada Board of Overseas Missions Congo 1961 Congo Protestant Relief Agency, Box 1, Accession no. 83. 031C, UCCA.

12   James Ormiston, Angola Report 2, 14 June 1961, Folder 9 United Church of Canada Board of Overseas Missions Congo 1961 Ormiston Reports on Angolan Refugees, Box 1, Accession no. 83. 031C, UCCA; James Ormiston, Angola Report 3, 25 June 1961, Folder 9 United Church of Canada Board of Overseas Missions Congo 1961 Ormiston Reports on Angolan Refugees, Box 1, Accession no. 83. 031C, UCCA.

13   James Ormiston, Angola Report 3, 25 June 1961, Folder 9 United Church of Canada Board of Overseas Missions Congo 1961 Ormiston Reports on Angolan Refugees, Box 1, Accession no. 83. 031C, UCCA.

14   David Grenfell, Notes No. 4 1964, Folder 40 United Church of Canada Board of World Mission Congo 1964 Baptist Mission News Notes D. Grenfell, Box 2, Accession no. 83. 031C, UCCA.

detailed analysis of these reports deserves a book in its own right, the results were clear enough. Tens of thousands of sick, malnourished, and traumatised Angolans entered the Congo in the second half of 1961.

The United Nations High Commission for Refugees (UNHCR) and the League of Red Cross Societies agreed to set up emergency ration distribution centres by the summer of 1961 with the cooperation of the CPRA, but this assistance did not last for long. Red Cross officials decided to withdraw food aid from the Angola refugee emergency, on the grounds that refugees had access to plenty of land in Bas-Congo and that they could be self-sufficient after a single harvest.[15] Part of the official rationale for this withdrawal came from demands for resources to aid victims of another African humanitarian crisis: Algerian refugees in Morocco and Tunisia.[16] Unbeknownst to the CPRA, the Red Cross and UNHCR delegates distrusted Roberto and considered the CPRA to be too partial to the rebels.

League of Red Cross Society and UNHCR correspondence presented Angolan refugees as unwilling to work, unpopular with Congolese looking for jobs, and too stubborn to agree to resettle in land far from the Angolan border.[17] These views led Red Cross officials to complain about the CPRA and to condemn the FNLA. In January 1963, a UNHCR representative told his superiors, 'In my opinion, the Protestant mission of Kibentele has a tendency to appear to be a political and commercial center.'[18] Another UNHCR official complained Angolans refused to work because they could count on food from 'religious missions' and that Angolan nationals encouraged people to resist resettlement plans promoted by the Catholic relief agency Caritas Congo.[19] UNHCR staff rejected a request for funding to build a reception centre for refugees partially on the grounds it would attract more Angolans to flee the Congo in 1963.[20] Geoffrey Senn, an

---

15 Grenfell, "Refugees," 1051–4.

16 Ibid., 1052.

17 V.A. Temnomeroff to High Commissioner for Refugees in Geneva, 20 November 1961, Folder 15/GEN/ANG [1] Angolan Refugees, F11, S1, Box 250, UNHCRA; Henrik Beer to R.T. Schaeffer, 21 November 1961, Folder 15/GEN/ANG [1] Angolan Refugees, F11, S1, Box 250, Fonds 11, UNHCRA.

18 Cable, UNHCR Léopoldville to UNHCR, 24 January 1963, Folder 15/GEN/ANG [3] Angolan Refugees, F11, S1, Box 250, Fonds 11, UNHCRA.

19 Note as basis for discussion for to-day's meeting on refugees from Angola to the Congo, no date [January 1963], Folder 15/GEN/ANG [3] Angolan Refugees, F11, S1, Box 250, Fonds 11, UNHCRA.

20 F.J. Homann-Herimberg to Thomas Jamieson, 7 May 1963, Folder 15/GEN/ANG [4] Angolan Refugees, F11, S1, Box 250, Fonds 11, UNHCRA.

4. A small group of the over 100,000 Angolans who fled Portuguese repression to enter the Bas-Congo province in 1961. CPRA aid workers interviewed newcomers and learned of the many refugees killed by Portuguese troops or natural hazards en route for sanctuary in the Congo. (WCCA/John Taylor B5715-25)

International Red Cross delegate, denounced Roberto's government: 'The FNLA are, as far [as] value and efficiency are concerned, a farce; and with regard to human lives and outlook and ethics, a tragedy.'[21] By 1970, neither the International Red Cross nor UNCHR agreed to intervene to help Angolan refugees in Bas-Congo on 'political grounds,' since the FNLA effectively controlled the Angolan community.[22]

The Portuguese government also condemned US aid to Angolans through aid organisations, even as US officials downplayed their assistance to Angolan exiles. In October 1962, Portuguese foreign minister Franco Nogueira sparred with US diplomats over US policies in Africa. US diplomats wanted to ensure the US Navy had access to the strategically important Portuguese-controlled Azores islands. Nogueira fumed, 'the Red Cross was ready

21 G.C. Senn, Note for the ICRC, 5 September 1965, B AG 234 013-001.01 Généralités 12.4.1961 – 1.8.1975, ACICR.

22 U. Bédert, Rapport concernant la mission de M. U. Bédert à Kinshasa du 30 novembre à 11 décembre 1970, 22 December 1970, B AG 225 229-008 Condition de detention dans la République démocratique du Congo, ACICR.

to let the Angolan refugees in the Congo go back to Angola but U.S. groups intervened at this moment with assistance to the refugees which encouraged them to remain in the Congo'.[23] This statement ignored the fact League of Red Cross and UNHCR officials had known since the summer of 1961 of Portuguese atrocities against civilians.[24] Impoverished Angolan refugees refused blankets donated by the Portuguese Red Cross in June 1961, leading one UNHCR official to assure his superiors that refugees preferred exile over a return to Portuguese domination.[25] While the CPRA never directly entered the discussion, US representatives declared they did not directly assist refugees.[26] The Portuguese government correctly guessed that the US government funnelled aid to Angolans via the CPRA and Catholic Relief Services. Nogueira, for example, denounced 'the American' aid agencies as anti-Portuguese to UNHCR staff in early 1963.[27]

CPRA staff, unaware of Portuguese pressure and the mixed views held by personnel in other aid agencies, felt that the Red Cross had inexplicably abandoned the Angolans. David Grenfell decried how bad the situation had become in January 1962: 'Much to our distress, the International Red Cross decided to suspend operation; even though we pointed out there was not yet time for the people to have collected their first harvest from the seeds coming to them … This created a fantastic situation, with thousands of people coming to us for food and help, and we had nothing to give them.'[28] Red Cross and UNHCR staff had wrongly believed that new refugees would stop entering the DRC. A new Portuguese military campaign to flush out Angolans still hiding in northern Angolan forests sent no fewer than over 16,000 refugees into Bas-Congo from 4 June to 7 June 1962 alone.[29] With

---

23 United States Government, Department of State, "348. Memorandum of Conversation," 24 October 1962, *Foreign Relations of the United States. Volume XIII, Western Europe and Canada, 1961–1963*, 946–52.

24 J.D.R. Kelly, "Report on Refugees in Angola," Folder 15/9/GEN/ANG, Box 250, Fonds UNHCR 11 Records of the Central Registry Series 1 Classified Subject Files, 1951–1970 13/7/GEN – 15/9/GEN/ANG, UNHCRA.

25 Ibid.

26 United States Government, Department of State, "348. Memorandum of Conversation," 24 October 1962.

27 V.A.M. Beerman to UNHCR High Commissioner, 12 February 1963, Folder 15/GEN/ANG[3], F11, S1, Box 250, UNHCRA.

28 Grenfell, "Refugees," 1055.

29 David Grenfell to Friends, June 1962, Folder 16 United Church of Canada Board of World Mission Congo 1962 Reports on Angolan Refugee Situation, Box 1, Accession no. 83. 031C, UCCA.

no funds coming in to help start schools or provide clothing, Angolan refugees faced increasingly difficult conditions.[30]

The most crucial CPRA staff member was David Grenfell, who took the lead organising a system by which new refugees could be registered to receive aid for a year. Grenfell had spent more than two decades in Angola as a Baptist Missionary Society missionary before being forced out by the Portuguese in July 1961.[31] Four months later, he volunteered to work with the BMS missionaries in Bas-Congo to distribute aid under the aegis of the CPRA. He interviewed a member of each family that entered the DRC via Kibentele, a town on the border with Angola that served as a major entrance point into the DRC. Determined to ensure that refugees did not try to come back and forth across the border to prolong their access to rations, Grenfell and his CPRA colleagues kept detailed records on individual refugees.

Grenfell and the surveillance of refugee aid, 1961–1967

On 14 August 1963, an Angolan refugee named Luvualu Bale agreed to an interview with David Grenfell as a new refugee seeking a ration card. Bale claimed to come from the town of Coma in the northern Angolan province of Uige and showed Grenfell a tax receipt from May 1963 as proof he had entered the Congo for the first time. The missionary began to doubt this story once he read the receipt – it had been paid in Maquela, a different district from where Coma was located. Bale also lacked a permit from FNLA soldiers to enter the DRC and claimed to have entered the DRC through a forest region rather than through an official FNLA clandestine checkpoint. When Grenfell demanded Bale explain the receipt locale, the refugee answered he had fled into Maquela and then pretended to be from this district when officials conducted a census. Bale added he had been a soldier prior to being discharged in 1958, when he moved to the Angolan capital of Luanda. Grenfell then asked Bale about political trouble in Luanda in February 1961 – something Grenfell knew quite a bit about, since he had still been in Angola. Bale denied any violence took place in the capital, which to Grenfell meant Bale had not really lived in Luanda. Grenfell granted Bale a ration card, but people outside of Grenfell's office began to accuse Bale of being a Portuguese agent. 'When the others had gone, [Bale] stayed behind and I said to him [in Kikongo], "Look, if you ARE in the pay of

30 David Grenfell to Friends, August 1962, Folder 16 United Church of Canada Board of World Mission Congo 1962 Reports on Angolan Refugee Situation, Box 1, Accession no. 83.031C, UCCA.

31 Stanley, *Baptist Missionary Society*, 453.

the Portuguese, you had better think again"; all he said in reply was "*Ingeta*" (yes). He has settled in a town very close to the mission.'[32]

This encounter illuminates Grenfell's role as an aid worker on the frontiers of the Angolan war for independence. First, Grenfell saw himself as the arbitrator of what separated 'real' new refugees from fraudulent ones. Besides the missionary's long experience in Angola, Grenfell had also heard thousands of refugee testimonies by the time he spoke with Bale. His local knowledge about refugee routes and experiences thus placed Bale at a disadvantage, especially as he had not acquired FNLA-approved identification to enter the Congo. Grenfell thus participated in FNLA efforts to produce Angolan national subjects through bureaucratic practices tied to the distribution of food, clothing, and medical care. Grenfell's interrogation shows how CPRA was firmly allied with Angolan revolutionaries. Finally, if Bale was indeed an operative of the Portuguese colonial state, his presence demonstrates how colonial authorities sought to monitor (and evade) CPRA and FNLA surveillance and regulation of Angolan refugees in the DRC.

Grenfell's personal archive on Angolan refugees in Bas-Congo came from his position as a humanitarian aid worker who worked hand in hand with the FNLA. Though the missionary never officially joined Holden Roberto's organisation, he acted as a conduit for relief aid from European and North American donors to refugees under the jurisdiction of the Angolan exile government. CPRA's tiny administrative staff gave carte blanche to missionaries to oversee individual projects, without much effort to try to rein in the political leanings of project managers such as Grenfell. Furthermore, other BMS and Canadian missionaries shared Grenfell's horror at the ruthlessness of the Portuguese colonial regime.

Grenfell played a key role in successfully bringing in aid from donors. He and other CPRA staff had little trouble finding a range of donors to support their project. USAID food shipments distributed through CWS were a mainstay of the refugees. Dutch, French, British, Swiss, and Congolese teachers all taught in camp schools partially funded by CPRA.[33] David Grenfell even praised a Czech donation of white cloth – the only example of aid from a

---

32 David Grenfell, Notes No. 19 (1963), Folder 31 United Church of Canada Board of World Mission Congo 1963 Baptist Mission News Notes D. Grenfell, Box 2, Accession no. 83.031C, UCCA.

33 Report of the Secondary Education Project for Angolan Refugees – Sona Bata 1966–1967, Folder Zaire 1966–1967, Box 22 Africa Department, Record Group 8, CWS/PHS.

Soviet bloc country accepted by the CPRA.[34] As in Mozambique, the struggle of African liberation against Portuguese oppression created an extensive alliance in the international aid community to aid Angolan refugees.[35] Yet his strong support for the Angolan exile community did not limit CPRA's access to foreign funds and supplies.

Grenfell backed Holden Roberto's leadership, though he also considered himself true to the humanitarian ideal of impartiality. He listened to members of minor political parties willing to compromise with the Portuguese. As he informed a member of the short-lived UPRONA party that called for peaceful negotiations with Portugal, 'I am a pastor not a politician. I love the Angola people and that is why I am here. I have friends in every political party … I can help more Angolans by not joining any political party … Most of the supplies I get for this work, but not all, comes from Christian people who are not interested in politics but only that of helping suffering people.'[36] Despite such sentiments, Grenfell also worked extremely closely with FNLA.

His cooperation with FNLA was especially evident in his main task for the CPRA: the supervision of rations to refugees. He supervised a weekly distribution that had no less than six different lines.[37] The first line consisted of people who already had ration cards who then could pick up oil, dried milk, and soup powder. New arrivals seeking ration cards who had been provisionally approved for rations, clothes, and tools a week before formed the second group. If people from the second line passed Grenfell's review of their papers, they then went behind the main mission house to receive clothes. After that, they moved on to another line where they received a free hoe. The next group consisted of brand new refugees who needed to show their FNLA permits to Grenfell or other CPRA staff members, who then gave those whom they deemed to be legitimate new arrivals a piece of cardboard they could exchange for an official ration card seven days later. Another line was of people switching their cardboard for an official ration card.

34 David Grenfell to Reginald Heifferich, 11 January 1965, Folder Zaire 1965–1966, Box 22 Africa Department, Record Group 8, CWS/PHS.

35 On Mozambican refugees, see J. Tague, *Displaced Mozambicans in Postcolonial Tanzania: Refugee Power, Mobility, Education, and Rural Development* (New York: Routledge, 2019).

36 David Grenfell, Notes No. 30 1965, 19 November 1965, Folder Zaire 1965–1966, Box 22 Africa Department, Record Group 8, CWS/PHS.

37 David Grenfell, Notes No. 5 1964, 14 April 1964, Folder 40 United Church of Canada Board of World Mission Congo 1964 Baptist Mission News Notes D. Grenfell, Box 2, Accession no. 83.031C, UCCA.

This complex system of distributing rations served several purposes. First, Grenfell and CPRA staff wanted to ensure continued support from international donors such as the UN High Commission for Refugees and the US government. UNHCR representative François Chassaing complained in March 1963 that the CPRA was not adequately distinguishing between newly arrived refugees and Angolans who had been in the Congo for over a year, to the point Chassaing wondered if some refugees were reselling tools and seeds to Congolese rather than supporting themselves.[38] Three weeks after Chassaing's complaint, the UNHCR representative again observed Grenfell's ration distribution and reported the CPRA now had an effective system to spot 'fraudsters' ineligible for rations.[39] CWS staff member Jim Paton kept US officials advised on CPRA ration distribution. US embassy staff did not want to draw attention to how the CPRA gave out US government food surplus to Angolans for fear of further offending the Portuguese, but they also wanted to make sure US aid was not misused.[40]

The process led to problems. First was the long backlog of new arrivals. This complex system and the sheer number of applicants for new ration cards reached the point in April 1964 when Grenfell required new arrivals to wait up to three months before their identification passes would be reviewed and their eligibility for rations would be determined.[41] Other CPRA staff and volunteers interviewed refugees along with Grenfell. Then, Grenfell summarised their findings. Grenfell only deviated from this system once, when he relented with one family who begged for immediate help. Once the missionary approved them, the other 20 or so people who had entered the Congo with the family immediately demanded that they receive their ration cards as well.[42] When faced with crowds of refugees, Grenfell at times could not find the time to question everyone.[43] Another difficulty was that refu-

---

38 François Chassaing to Franz-Josef Homann-Herimberg, 6 March 1963, Folder 15/GEN/ANG[3], F11, S1, Box 250, UNHCRA.

39 François Chassaing to Franz-Josef Homann-Herimberg, 28 March 1963, Folder 15/GEN/ANG[3], F11, S1, Box 250, UNHCRA.

40 Interview, James Paton, 14 August 2018.

41 David Grenfell, Notes No. 5 1964, 14 April 1964, Folder 40 United Church of Canada Board of World Mission Congo 1964 Baptist Mission News Notes D. Grenfell, Box 2, Accession no. 83.031C, UCCA.

42 David Grenfell, Notes No. 7 1964, 1 May 1964, Folder 40 United Church of Canada Board of World Mission Congo 1964 Baptist Mission News Notes D. Grenfell, Box 2, Accession no. 83.031C, UCCA.

43 David Grenfell, Notes No. 8 1964, 10 May 1964, Folder 40 United Church of Canada Board of World Mission Congo 1964 Baptist Mission News Notes D.

gees weren't always willing to accept Grenfell's discipline. On 30 April 1964, Grenfell wrote: 'Many of the women are very nervous, because they have never had much to do with white people. I spent a full hour with one old man who could only give three correct names out of 15 on the permit, and these did not include the name of his own wife. He would not listen to my questions, but launched into a long monologue that had nothing to do with what I asked.'[44]

Grenfell's vigilance about distributing supplies to refugees who had spent less than a year in the DRC led him to enforce a strict policy requiring ration cards. From November 1961 until his retirement in 1967, Grenfell supervised aid on behalf of CPRA for refugees that had just entered the DRC in Bas-Congo. Though Grenfell had decried the Red Cross decision to stop supplying assistance, he agreed with the ICRC that no separate refugee camps should be set up given that most newcomers belonged to the BisiKongo ethnic community that predominated in Bas-Congo. Perhaps more importantly, the idea that refugees might manipulate the permit and ration system irked Grenfell's moral sensibilities. In a typical remark from 1964, he wrote about a day spent reviewing FNLA travel permits: 'Inevitably, the "spivs" have begun to make their appearance, and so a great deal of time has to be given to examine the permit. The necessity to do this is going to cut sadly into our packed program ... By now we know most of the secretaries and commanders of the [UPA] posts [in Angola] by name, and with so many travelling permits, one can always compare signatures, permit numbers and dates, and routes taken, but it all takes time.'[45]

Ebbs and flows of refugee movements can be traced by using Grenfell's records from 1963 to 1966. The early months of 1964 marked a significant uptick in new refugees emerging from hiding places in northern Angola. Over 23,000 Angolans passed through the Kibentele centre alone between January and April 1964.[46] These numbers slowly declined over the course of 1964 and 1965. Only 8681 refugees passed through Kibentele for the entire year of 1966.[47]

Grenfell, Box 2, Accession no. 83.031C, UCCA.

44 David Grenfell, Notes No. 7 1964, 1 May 1964, Folder 40 United Church of Canada Board of World Mission Congo 1964 Baptist Mission News Notes D. Grenfell, Box 2, Accession no. 83.031C, UCCA.

45 David Grenfell, Notes No. 5 1964, 14 April 1964, Folder 40 United Church of Canada Board of World Mission Congo 1964 Baptist Mission News Notes D. Grenfell, Box 2, Accession no. 83.031C, UCCA.

46 David Grenfell, Notes No. 4 1964, Folder 40 United Church of Canada Board of World Mission Congo 1964 D. Grenfell Baptist Missionary Society, Box 2, Accession no. 83.031C, UCCA.

47 David Grenfell, Annual Report for 1966, 4 January 1967, Folder 72 United Church of Canada Board of World Mission Congo 1966 Notes: Grenfell, BMS,

For most refugees, competition and obtaining proper identification for aid constituted a major challenge. Grenfell and CPRA tried to limit food aid to refugees in their first year in the DRC, on the grounds that individuals and families could establish their own fields after twelve months. Much of Grenfell's correspondence focused on how refugees tried to get access to rations after they had been in the DRC for over a year. Some Angolans who had stayed longer than a year tried to join groups of new arrivals seeking their first ration cards. Still others dressed in rags when lining up for clothes distribution. In 1965, some individuals changed the numbers on their ration cards to take more food for themselves. Another common tactic was to forge FNLA permits to appear as though the owners had only recently escaped Angola. When Grenfell demanded in 1964 that individuals provide proof they had actually not entered the Congo without first obtaining official permits, some responded by bringing FNLA soldiers to Grenfell's mission. These soldiers carried long lists of individual names, and the missionary soon realised the soldiers were writing out permits and documentation for individuals who had already been living in exile long enough to no longer be eligible for CPRA assistance.

Grenfell zealously scrutinised identification papers, stories of refugee journeys into the Congo, and even the physical appearance of refugees. Though Grenfell denied he belonged to or even favoured FNLA, he acted as a quasi-official overseer of refugee identity and border controls. He regularly boasted in his reports of his knowledge of northern Angolan geography, individual FNLA officials still in Angola, fugitive accounts of how they received FNLA permission to leave Angola, and techniques to evade Grenfell's extensive controls over rational distribution. In a sense, Grenfell tried to 'see like a state' by ensuring the legibility of refugees as both subjects of FNLA and as marked individuals to be placed in CPRA record-keeping. This blending of humanitarian aid and political authority did not receive any criticism from other CPRA staff. Grenfell's monitoring extended to FNLA soldiers and agents themselves. A FNLA soldier became the target of Grenfell's suspicions in October 1963 after the guerilla had accompanied a refugee from Kuzi in Angola. 'The soldier presented a travelling permit that was an old one with new names written in. He also had a letter supposedly written by Garcia Lambourne, whom I know ... The letter asked for clothes. There have been reports of people receiving clothes and selling them on this side of the frontier,' Grenfell observed.[48]

Box 3, Accession no. 83.031C, UCCA.

48 David Grenfell, Notes 1963 No. 29, 7 November 1963, Folder 31 Baptist Mission News D. Grenfell, Box 2, Accession no. 83.031C, UCCA.

Local Congolese authorities and FNLA officials and soldiers assisted Grenfell's surveillance as well as the maintenance of order at his refugee reception centre. Daniel da Costa, a refugee who had written his own FNLA permit, became enraged on 1 November 1965 with Jim Grenfell when Grenfell refused to accept his documents as valid for rations.[49] Da Costa claimed he had just brought a group of new refugees from Angola, but Jim Grenfell responded that the group needed to show Congolese residency cards and health permits. Da Costa smashed a table and punched his first through a door window as he tried to avenge himself on the aid worker. Congolese police arrived, arrested da Costa, and brought the prisoner along with Jim Grenfell to Moerbecke to hear the case. The Congolese police chief sided with the missionary and reprimanded da Costa: 'You have done wrong in four ways. First of all, this permit is of no value at all, for there is no carimbo (official stamp) on it. Then, even when it was accepted, you refused to wait your turn. You then became violent and did damage to property. Last of all, and this amazes me, you have no respect whatsoever to people who are working to help such as you.'[50] A man drunk on palm wine wanted to fight Jim and David Grenfell when they turned him down twice for rations and clothes. FNLA soldiers who had led refugees to Kibentele from the frontier intervened. One soldier struck the angry man with a belt, and the Grenfells led him to the Kibentele clinic to dress the wound.[51] At the behest of Grenfell, FNLA troops also seized ration cards altered to grant permit holders much more food.[52]

Disciplining refugees required security. Fights often broke out among the hundreds of refugees in line for daily rations. In January 1965, one female refugee left a small saucepan with her things as she collected her rations. When she returned, she saw another woman in line had stolen the pan. After the first woman showed off the lid of her pan to African aid workers and the crowd, she attacked the thief. 'Immediately everyone began to cheer the contestants,' Grenfell noted, and the brawl dragged on despite Grenfell's failed effort to grab one of the 'hefty' women. The fight came to an end once the pan 'became a useless piece of crumpled metal' after the fighters had banged each other

49 David Grenfell, Notes No. 28/1965, 5 November 1965, Folder Zaire 1965–1966, Box 22 Africa Department, Record Group 8, CWS/PHS.

50 Ibid.

51 David Grenfell, Notes No. 6/65, 13 February 1965, Folder Zaire 1965–1966, Box 22 Africa Department, Record Group 8, CWS/PHS.

52 David Grenfell, Notes No. 18/65, 14 May 1965, Folder Zaire 1965–1966, Box 22 Africa Department, Record Group 8, CWS/PHS.

with it over and over.[53] FNLA representatives handed out permits to new arrivals once they crossed the border into the DRC, which then needed to be shown to CPRA workers at the camp. Some individuals who had stayed in the DRC for over a year somehow acquired other people's permits so that they could still receive rations, while others without permits who felt they deserved food resorted to screaming and even threatening aid workers with violence.[54]

CRPA administrators of the Angolan refugee centres also had to cope with the ambiguous relationship between Angolan exiles and the Congolese state. At the ration centres, local police kept order and arrested individuals who were disorderly or violent.[55] In September 1965, the Congolese government required all refugees to show Congolese residency cards to obtain food or supplies for the second time from CPRA camps, on the grounds that refugees emerging from the forests were often infected with sleeping sickness. CPRA staff supported this requirement, as it helped them detect cases of fraud.[56] Unlike ordinary refugees and low-ranking FNLA officials, Grenfell was very well-informed about elite exile politics thanks to his very close relationship with FNLA leader Holden Roberto. Grenfell's reports on his conversations with Roberto are a fascinating insight into how Roberto looked at Grenfell as well as into Roberto's relationship with the DRC government, the Organisation of African Unity, and aid workers who sided with Roberto's critics within the Angolan exile community.

Holden Roberto, the FNLA elite, and David Grenfell

Grenfell spoke regularly with Roberto and other members of the FNLA elite. He discussions with other missionaries occurred in 1964 and 1965, a pivotal time in the history of Roberto's FNLA organisation. By 1964, FNLA had begun to fall on hard times.[57] Their Communist rivals, the MPLA, had

53 David Grenfell, 1965 Report No. 4, 30 January 1965, Folder Zaire 1965–1966, Box 22 Africa Department, Record Group 8, CWS/PHS.

54 David Grenfell, Notes 1965 No. 16, 23 April 1965, Folder Zaire 1965–1966, Box 22 Africa Department, Record Group 8, CWS/PHS; David Grenfell, Notes 1965 No. 28, 11 November 1965, Folder Zaire 1965–1966, Box 22 Africa Department, Record Group 8, CWS/PHS.

55 David Grenfell, Notes 1965 No. 28, 5 November 1965, Folder Zaire 1965–1966, Box 22 Africa Department, Record Group 8, CWS/PHS.

56 David Grenfell, Notes 1965 No. 22, 24 September 1965, Folder Zaire 1965–1966, Box 22 Africa Department, Record Group 8, CWS/PHS.

57 For an overview of FNLA's difficulties in 1964 and 1965, see Marcum, *Angolan Revolution*, 133–6, 141–9.

established themselves in Congo-Brazzaville and received assistance from the Soviet bloc. Roberto disparaged the MPLA and the US government furnished him covert aid. FNLA forces could still launch attacks in northern Angola. Even so, the Portuguese military presence and the indiscriminate attacks of Portuguese troops made decisive military victories impossible. Another difficulty came from ethnic and regional divisions within FNLA. Critics of Roberto contended that he favoured members of his BisiKongo ethnic group over other exiles coming from central and southern Angola. The Organisation of African Union initially declared FNLA to its favoured choice to represent Angola over the MPLA, but some members of the OAU appeared to be losing interest in Roberto.[58]

Roberto and Grenfell continued their partnership into the mid-1960s. Certainly, Grenfell's refugee programmes bolstered the FNLA by documenting the movement and identities of Angolans who had fled to the DRC. The Baptist minister also acted as a defender of FNLA, particularly in regards to negative articles about Roberto's rebels in the British and Canadian press. After *The Guardian*, one of Great Britain's most influential left-wing newspapers, published an article in 1964 portraying FNLA as an organisation run aground by infighting and the Portuguese army, Grenfell assured his missionary and donor organisation readers that FNLA's troops were still in high spirits, still launching attacks in Angola against the colonial government.[59] '[FNLA soldiers] have spent months in the bush, walking hundreds of miles through thick tall grass ... They do not talk party politics, but they often mention independence. Roberto Holden is their man, and they have all complete confidence in him,' Grenfell reported in September 1964.[60] The missionary also objected to Canadian and British reporters who published stories favourable to the Portuguese. He also intervened on behalf of FNLA's health services – Servigo de Assistencia aos Refugiados de Angola (SARA) – to North American donor organisations. When the International Rescue Committee expressed concern over reports of possible theft of medical supplies by SARA

58 Ibid., 105, 133–6.

59 David Grenfell, Notes 1964 No. 11, 31 May 1964, Folder 40 United Church of Canada Board of World Mission Congo 1964 Baptist Mission News Notes D. Grenfell, Box 2, Accession no. 83. 031C, UCCA.

60 David Grenfell, Notes 1964 No. 25, 12 September 1964, Folder 40 United Church of Canada Board of World Mission Congo 1964 Baptist Mission News Notes D. Grenfell, Box 2, Accession no. 83. 031C, UCCA.

employees, Grenfell defended SARA and reported that SARA director Barros Necaca had investigated the matter.[61]

Roberto spoke to Grenfell in great detail of his anxieties over the Congolese government in 1965. Moïse Tshombe, the leader of the Katangese secession movement from 1960 until its collapse at the end of 1962, became the Congolese prime minister in June 1964 at the behest of the US government as leftist rebels in the loose coalition of the Armée Populaire de la Libération (APL, better known as Simbas) rapidly seized much of eastern DRC. Tshombe made what one missionary called a 'gala visit' to the Sona Bata secondary school for Angolan refugees run by the CPRA, but Roberto had little confidence in the Congolese leader.[62] The Angolan rebel leader believed Tshombe wanted to cut a deal with the Portuguese government in return for aid. Such a move would have been catastrophic for FNLA and Roberto, since FNLA's principal ally had been the DRC since 1961. FNLA also lost access to arms from countries who favoured the APL insurgency against Tshombe's pro-US government.[63]

In the byzantine world of Congolese politics in the mid-1960s, Grenfell had the unenviable task of sorting out rumours to guess the next moves of Tshombe and other Congolese power brokers. In February 1965, Congolese authorities at the Kinshasa airport refused to allow Roberto to leave to visit Zambian president Kenneth Kaunda.[64] However, Roberto called Congolese president Joseph Kasavubu, who contended the incident was an error by officials at the airport.[65] FNLA minister João Eduardo Pinnock claimed Congolese interior minister Godefroid Munongo had declared Roberto was plotting with Kaunda to aid 'the enemies of the Congo' (most likely rebel leaders) and that Munongo wanted to limit FNLA activity.[66] Grenfell expressed surprise that Muongo, a friend of Roberto, might be turning against him, adding, 'Holden may not like Tshombe, but he is fully aware that if his struggle against the Portuguese is to continue, he MUST keep in good relationship

61 David Grenfell to Gilbert Jonas, International Rescue Committee, 14 November 1965, Folder Zaire 1965–1966, Box 22 Africa Department, Record Group 8, CWS/PHS.

62 On the visit, see J. Keith, *The First Wars Are The Worst* (Mississauga, ON: Canadian Baptist Ministries, 1998), 63, 69.

63 David Grenfell, Annual Report for 1966, 4 January 1967, Folder 72 United Church of Canada Board of World Mission Congo 1966 Notes: Grenfell, BMS, Box 3, Box 3, Accession no. 83.031C, UCCA.

64 David Grenfell to Clifford Parsons, 15 February 1965, Folder Zaire 1965–1966, Box 22 Africa Department, Record Group 8, CWS/PHS.

65 Ibid.

66 Ibid.

with the Congo leaders.'[67] Such editorialising in letters reveals how Grenfell was hardly an apolitical observer of Angolan refugees.

Grenfell also became embroiled in a personal conflict between Roberto and Ian Gilchrist, a Canadian doctor who had joined SARA. Gilchrist was the son of Sid Gilchrist, a long-time missionary doctor in Angola who had become the fiercest foe of Portuguese colonial rule in all of Canada. [68] Ian Gilchrist and SARA received financial support from George Houser, the leader of the American Committee on Africa (ACOA), an organisation opposed to Portuguese colonial rule that was secretly receiving backing from the US Central Intelligence Service.[69] SARA's history has yet to be written, but Gilchrist's frustrations with the health service show the deteriorating conditions of FNLA by 1965. José Liahuca, an Angola doctor from central Angola, had originally directed the health service. He broke with Roberto in July 1964 on the grounds Roberto favoured BisiKongo from northern Angola over other ethnic groups.[70] After Liahuca escaped to Brazzaville to join the MPLA, Gilchrist felt SARA's organisation had declined.[71] The Canadian doctor became convinced Roberto's cronies were stealing CPRA food 'to feather their own nests'. Patients and workers complained about the lack of sustenance at the packed facility.[72] Grenfell himself 'was aghast' at seeing starving patients and workers at the FNLA hospital after Gilchrist showed him around.[73]

Just as Grenfell could defend Roberto to his transnational networks, Gilchrist expressed his concerns to his own connections: the United Church of Canada, the CWS, and Roberto himself. Floyd Honey, a UCC representative touring the DRC, wrote in January 1965, 'Ian Gilchrist is very depressed about the liberation movement. UPA is becoming increasingly racial and people who are not Bacongo [BisiKongo] are being fired from their jobs.'[74] Gilchrist warned Houser in early 1964 that Roberto had ignored FNLA official Jonas

---

67 Ibid.

68 G. Houser, *No One Can Stop The Rain: Glimpses of Africa's Liberation Struggle* (New York: Pilgrim Press, 1989), 162–3.

69 On Houser's advocacy for the FNLA, see Tague, "American Humanitarianism."

70 Houser, *No One*, 166.

71 Ibid., 167.

72 David Grenfell to Clifford Parsons, 15 March 1965, Folder Zaire 1965–1966, Box 22 Africa Department, Record Group 8, CWS/PHS.

73 Ibid.

74 T.E. Floyd Honey, Report of Visit to Congo, 13 January 1965, Folder 58 United Church of Canada Board of World Mission, Box 3 Congo 1965 Floyd Honey's Visit to Congo, Box 3, Accession no. 83. 031C, UCCA.

Savimbi when Savimbi studied in Switzerland and that the rift between the two Angolan nationalists continued to widen.[75] Theodore Tucker, the head of the African department of the CWS, heard similar complaints about Roberto from southern Angolan refugees.[76] Gilchrist had introduced a Canadian journalist writing for the United Church of Canada to Roberto. Grenfell hinted the reporter's negative view of the rebel leader came as a result of the Canadian CPRA doctor.[77] The Canadian doctor also warned that Tshombe had written a harsh letter to Roberto, even as the prime minister pretended to continue to support Angolan independence.[78]

Angolans critical of Roberto expressed their doubts in Kinshasa from April to June 1965, and Grenfell became increasingly concerned for Roberto. FNLA dissidents held a protest denouncing Roberto for his alleged role in ordering the death of João Bapitsta, a UPA military commander.[79] A dissident FNLA commander who claimed to have witnessed Baptista's death led the rally.[80] Grenfell had met in 1964 an Angolan BMS church secretary who had come from Bembe, the Angolan town where Baptista had been killed by Portuguese troops in a FNLA attack in February 1962. Some FNLA members claimed Roberto had commanded Baptista to launch a suicidal attack to dispose of a possible rival. Grenfell's Angolan contact claimed the attack failed because more Portuguese troops were stationed at Bembe than the inexperienced rebel unit had expected. Baptista had been mortally wounded and had to be left behind as the guerillas retreated.[81] Grenfell's informant added Kassanga was not present, despite Kassanga's claims he had seen how Baptista had been

75 Houser, *No One*, 166.

76 T.E. Floyd Honey, Report of Visit to Congo, 13–14 January 1965, Folder 58 United Church of Canada Board of World Mission, Box 3 Congo 1965 Floyd Honey's Visit to Congo, Box 3, Accession no. 83. 031C, UCCA.

77 David Grenfell to Clifford Parsons, 17 April 1965, Folder Zaire 1965–1966, Box 22 Africa Department, Record Group 8, CWS/PHS.

78 T.E. Floyd Honey, Report of Visit to Congo, 13 January 1965, Folder 58 United Church of Canada Board of World Mission, Box 3 Congo 1965 Floyd Honey's Visit to Congo, Box 3, Accession no. 83. 031C, UCCA.

79 David Grenfell to Clifford Parsons, 17 April 1965, Folder Zaire 1965–1966, Box 22 Africa Department, Record Group 8, CWS/PHS.

80 Ibid.

81 David Grenfell, Notes 1964 No. 13, 20 June 1964, Folder 40, United Church of Canada Board of World Mission Congo 1964 notes D. Grenfell, Baptist Missionary Society, Box 1, Accession no. 83. 031C, UCCA.

killed.[82] Ian Gilchrist later informed Grenfell that Munongo had initially authorised the event, but police came once Roberto complained.[83]

Roberto's relationship with Tshombe worsened in the late spring of 1965. Roberto told Grenfell that Tshombe was plotting a coup to replace Joseph Kasavubu as president of the DRC. Kasavubu somehow caught wind of the plot, called Tshombe for a meeting, and reprimanded the prime minister for placing his personal interests over the country.[84] When Grenfell then said to Roberto that Kasavubu never should have appointed Tshombe as prime minister, Roberto responded that it was a brilliant plan. Tshombe had supposedly schemed to join with the leftist APL rebels and had proposed to give the insurgents two million Congolese francs. In Roberto's eyes, Kasavubu had 'beat [the rebels] to the punch' by bringing Tshombe into the government.[85]

After a failed putsch by dissidents within FNLA against Roberto, loyalists to Roberto detained Gilchrist. According to F.J. Grenfell, David Grenfell's nephew, Gilchrist saw FNLA police using a SARA ambulance to arrest suspected supporters of the Taty and Kassinga revolt.[86] Gilchrist, irked to see a SARA ambulance used for political purposes, complained and went to the FNLA headquarters. There, Roberto supporters struck Gilchrist and accused him of helping to incite the rebellion. Roberto himself intervened and ordered the doctor to leave or otherwise face arrest. People threw stones at Gilchrist. CPRA staff in Kinshasa, particularly material aid director Malcolm McVeigh, arranged to bring Gilchrist to the home of the Canadian ambassador to the DRC.[87] Roberto had decided in the meantime to issue a summons to have Gilchrist detained for his alleged subversive activity.[88] The order came too late to have the volunteer doctor tried. McVeigh had hidden Gilchrist in a CPRA truck and smuggled him to the Kinshasa airport to board a flight to Canada on 27 June 1965.[89] These chaotic events show how CPRA workers unbeknownst to Grenfell had decided to intervene to protect another expatriate from becoming the subject of FNLA authority.

82 Ibid.

83 David Grenfell to Clifford Parsons, 8 May 1965, Folder Zaire 1965–1966, Box 22 Africa Department, Record Group 8, CWS/PHS.

84 Ibid.

85 Ibid.

86 F.J. Grenfell, 10 July 1965, Folder Zaire 1965–1966, Box 22 Africa Department, Record Group 8, CWS/PHS.

87 Ibid.

88 Ibid.

89 Interview, Malcolm McVeigh, Whiting, New Jersey, 12 October 2012.

Grenfell and Roberto had a conversation about Gilchrist after his escape. Roberto's version of events portrayed the Canadian volunteer as a meddler in FNLA affairs.[90] According to the FNLA leader, Gilchrist had tried to intervene on behalf of a SARA Angolan nurse believed to be a Taty supporter. After his detention, Roberto claimed he upbraided the doctor who kept quiet: 'How should I explain this to George Houser [of the ACOA], who had told [Gilchrist] to keep out of political matters? .... How can I pardon you?'[91] Roberto thus portrayed Gilchrist as a misguided younger client in need of parental intervention – an inversion of Grenfell's paternalist missionary attitudes. Now an aid worker was the subject of FNLA discipline. Roberto added Gilchrist was lucky to have left immediately, as Mobutu Sese Seko – then a general – wanted Gilchrist and two European expatriates arrested for their supposed role in the Taty/Kasinda plot.[92]

The Gilchrist affair did nothing to undermine CPRA support for Roberto and the FNLA, but the nature of Protestant relief had begun to change for several reasons by 1966. First, Grenfell decided to retire from active service in the DRC and returned home due to health problems in 1967. While his nephew Jim Grenfell stayed on, he provided less lengthy documentation than his uncle about daily life for refugees and did not seem to have as close a relationship with Roberto. Secondly, the numbers of new refugees dipped considerably from 1966 until the end of the decade. With very few newcomers, the need for maintaining an elaborate ration system declined as well. Though 5,412 rations were given out in one week in January 1967, these numbers decreased afterwards, in no small part because of effective Portuguese surveillance and military operations in the border region.[93] Jim Grenfell informed his sponsors at the United Church of Canada in November 1967, 'As you know, the direct aid in the form of food and clothing for refugees is no longer needed on anything like the scale of previous years. The numbers of new refugees arriving at Kibentele are very small these days'.[94] Finally, the closure of the CPRA office in New York and the declining role

90   David Grenfell to Clifford Parsons, 15 September 1965, Folder Zaire 1965–1966, Box 22 Africa Department, Record Group 8, CWS/PHS.

91   Ibid.

92   Ibid.

93   David Grenfell, Notes 2/67, 27 January 1967, Folder 95 Congo 1967 Board of World Mission Rev. D, Grenfell, Box 4, Associate Secretary for Zaire, Accession Number 83.031C, UCCA.

94   Jim Grenfell to Garth Legge, 1 November 1967, Folder 95 Congo 1967 Board of World Mission Rev. D, Grenfell, Box 4, Associate Secretary for Zaire, Accession Number 83.031C, UCCA.

of the Church World Service in the Congo after 1967, as discussed in chapter 7, meant fewer records on Angolan refugees were available.

Conclusion

The CPRA Angolan refugee programme from 1961 to 1967 marked a significant departure from the political neutrality of the Kasai CPRA project. Protestant missionaries, horrified by the indiscriminate violence of the Portuguese military against Angolan rebels in 1961, considered the UPA and later the FNLA to be the true government of the Angolan people. CPRA volunteers did not present the violence as an inevitable part of decolonisation. Nor did they shy away from upholding the FNLA government against Portuguese efforts to discredit the rebels. Although David Grenfell sometimes claimed to be merely an impartial missionary, his advocacy ensured a steady supply of financial support from the World Council of Churches, the Baptist Missionary Society, and North American churches. CPRA volunteers also ran schools and treated refugees at hospitals.

The FNLA took advantage of the CPRA's alliance. Holden Roberto, faced with his Marxist MPLA competition and stuck with an impoverished and divided Congolese government with few resources to support the Angolan struggle, could count on Grenfell to defend his image to Protestant donors. Ration cards for newly arrived refugees created a new opportunity to try to document individual refugees. By treating FNLA documents as legitimate, Grenfell acted to enforce the Angolan rebel organisation's identification system. Grenfell's work thus helped transform refugees into FNLA's subjects, with ration cards making Angolans legible to the FNLA and the Congolese government. His reports also documented what refugees endured in their travels to their Congo refuge: booby-trapped corpses, napalm, botched executions, and losing children to drowning and Portuguese bombs. By witnessing for Angolans fleeing colonial repression, Grenfell gave legitimacy to the Angolan struggle to churches on both sides of the Atlantic.

Such advocacy had its own blind spots. Roberto's favouritism towards BisiKongo people and his authoritarian rule over refugees did not trouble Grenfell. FNLA troops ensured order as Grenfell oversaw ration distribution without any objection on his part. The British missionary and relief worker presented Roberto's critics as naïve or even simply tools of the Portuguese. Ian Gilchrist's gradual turn against mismanagement in the FNLA's health section and his sympathy with southern Angolans eventually made him a target of Roberto's anger. Roberto's anxieties about the unreliability of the Congolese government and the very real threat of Portuguese infiltration into the FNLA also led him to turn on the Canadian doctor. Grenfell's unwillingness to condemn Roberto's actions is reminiscent of allies of other insurgencies, whether the FLN in Algeria or the Communists in South Vietnam.

The CPRA's lack of central direction thus allowed some staff to follow a more traditional apolitical orientation to alleviate harm regardless of the political circumstances even as Grenfell took up the cause of Angolan liberation. The following chapter on CPRA aid during the Simba revolts shows another choice for Protestant aid workers: uneasy collaboration with a repressive counter-insurgency. While Roberto and much of the FNLA elite were products of Protestant missions and defended missionary interests, the leftist Congolese rebels that briefly appeared ready to conquer the entire country in 1964 considered missionaries to be their ideological opponents. Roberto skillfully kept good relations with the CPRA, even as other aid agencies kept their distance from the FNLA. By contrast, the Conseil National de la Libération (CNL) in eastern Congo and Pierre Mulele's insurgents in Kwilu province killed missionaries and Congolese Christians. Though individual CPRA personnel became disgusted by the Congolese military, they continued to work with the government and presented their efforts as part of a generalised project against hunger and pain instead of a tool of the military to retain control over much of rural Congo.

4

The CPRA and the Simba Revolts, 1964–1967

The Armée National Congolaise (ANC), the armed forces of the US-backed Congolese government, led a successful campaign from 1964 to 1967 against a coalition of leftist rebels, the Conseil National de la Libération (CNL).[1] These revolutionaries, popularly known as Simba (lions in Kiswahili), intended to overthrow the pro-Western Congolese government in Kinshasa. Although the CNL's armed wing, the Armée Populaire de Libération (APL), managed to capture almost half of all Congolese territory by the summer of 1964, the US government took a decisive role in the APL's defeat. ANC forces, relying on expatriate mercenaries, captured most major cities in eastern DRC by December 1965.[2] Pierre Mulele's rebels in the western Kwilu province, cut off from rebels further east, became constricted by ANC forces.

Assessing the final collapse of the rebellion, US officials in 1968 credited humanitarian aid as a key factor. Rebel forces had little choice left but to give up by 1968. One reason was hunger. The Congolese arny cut off rebels from US food supplies sent through the CPRA and other agencies and made it very

---

1   On the CNL rebellion, see B. Verhaegen, *Rébellions au Congo*, 2 vols (Brussels: CRISP, 1969); C. Coquery-Vidrovitch, ed. *Rébellions-Révolutions au Zaïre, 1963–1965*, 2 vols (Paris: L'Harmattan, 1987); P. Gleijeses, *Conflicting Missions: Havana, Washington, and Africa, 1959–1976* (Chapel Hill: University of North Carolina Press, 2002), 77–159; B. Verhaegen, ed. *Mulele et la revolution populaire au Kwilu (République Démocratique du Congo)* (Paris: L'Harmattan, 2006); Bechtolsheimer, "Breakfast," 27–50; Namikas, *Battleground Africa*, 181–222; L.D. Witte, "The Suppression of the Congo Rebellions and the Rise of Mobutu, 1963–5." *International History Review* 39:1 (2016), 107–25.

2   On the Belgian intervention and the use of foreign mercenaries, see M. Hoare, *Congo Mercenary* (New York: Bantam, 1967); F. Vandewalle, *L'Ommegang: Odysée et reconquête de Stanleyville 1964* (Brussels: Le Livre Africain, 1970); P. Gleijeses, "Flee! The White Giants Are Coming!: The United States, the Mercenaries, and the Congo, 1964–65," *Diplomatic History* 18:2 (1994), 207–37; F. Villafaña, *Cold War in the Congo: The Confrontation of Cuban Military Forces, 1960–1967* (New Brunswick, NJ: Transaction, 2009); A. Hudson, *Congo Unravelled: Military Operations from Independence to the Mercenary Revolt, 1960–1968* (Solihull, UK: Helion, 2012).

difficult for rebels to maintain their fields. Robert McBride, the outgoing US ambassador to Congo, reported that Congolese soldiers had apprehended over 19,000 rebels in Kwilu after Mobutu's 1968 general amnesty to rebels.[3] Soldiers remained to give out food and medical supplies to rebels and civilians who left isolated forest areas still in rebel hands. Far to the east, general Étienne Tshinyama credited the surrender of several thousand rebels on the eastern Congolese border as being 'as a result of the [Congolese army]'s carrot-and-stick mop up strategy.'[4] Civilians and APL soldiers alike, at the mercy of Congolese troops for food and shelter, often died from hunger in detention camps.[5]

Researchers have long discussed the US government's covert assistance to explain the ANC's victory. Formal political and military history has taken centre stage, leaving out the humanitarian crisis that came in the wake of the revolt. The fighting led to famine and the killings of thousands of civilians by the rebels and the Congolese military. Western media coverage highlighted how rebels butchered European and North American prisoners, particularly missionaries.[6] What has been most painfully absent from the research on the rebellions is the suffering of Congolese civilians in the conflict. Emery Kalema's recent dissertation on the government repression of the Mulele revolts is a startling and vital exception to this rule.[7] Western observers dwelled on the brutality of rebels towards foreigners. The experiences of Congolese civilians caught in the crossfire received only cursory attention. Another weakness of the extensive literature on the DRC is the negligence of humanitarian organisations as both actors and as sources of evidence about the political turmoil of this period. The

3   Robert McBride to Department of State, 27 December 1968, Folder 23-9 THE CONGO 1/1/68, Box 2537 POL 23-9 THE CONGO 11/1/67 to POL 23-9 1/1/69, Record Group 59 Department of State Central Policy Files, 1967–1969, NARA II.

4   Robert McBride to Secretary of State, 21 November 1968, Folder 23-9 THE CONGO 1/1/68, Box 2537 POL 23-9 THE CONGO 11/1/67 to POL 23-9 1/1/69, Record Group 59 Department of State Central Policy Files, 1967–1969, NARA II.

5   Kalema, "Violence and Memory."

6   J. Kestergat, *Congo Congo* (Paris: Table Ronde, 1965); D. Reed, *111 Days in Stanleyville* (London: Collins, 1966); M. Hayes, *Captive of the Simbas* (New York: Harper and Row, 1966); M. Hoyt, *Captive in the Congo: A Consul's Return to the Heart of Darkness* (Annapolis, MD: Naval Institute Press, 2000). For a localised analysis of the various uses of violence by the APL in the city of Kindu, see Verhaegen, *Rebellions*, 598–623. For analysis of Western media coverage of the CNL and missionaries, see McAlister, "Body in Crisis."

7   Kalema, "Violence and Memory."

case of the CNL revolts indicates how humanitarian organisations, despite their repugnance for the Congolese military, ultimately helped the ANC to victory. International humanitarian organisations furnished food, clothes, medical supplies, transport, and tools to civilians in areas once occupied by rebels.

This chapter considers how the CPRA contributed to the government's victory through humanitarian aid. Though the CPRA presented itself as an apolitical organisation, it worked quite closely with the Congolese military and the US government from 1964 to 1967. Especially for pacifist Mennonites assigned to assist victims of violence in Kwilu province, the Congolese army's treatment of civilians forced CPRA staff to wrestle with the moral ambiguities of humanitarian assistance. Evangelical volunteers with the CPRA, by contrast, wholeheartedly endorsed their Congolese military partners. In both cases, the CPRA participated in an extensive relief project in which the US and Congolese governments coordinated their efforts with Catholic Relief Services, other international organisations, and the United Nations.

While the viciousness of rebel forces against civilians received extensive coverage in the Western press, the Congolese army's own cruelty remained obscure outside of internal diplomatic and humanitarian correspondence. Congolese government forces employed aid to control civilians and to entice rebels to surrender. Conversely, rebel forces had no access to international humanitarian aid from its supporters. The wanton destruction by government and rebel troops left civilians deprived of food and shelter. Some CPRA workers presented government victories as crucial for Congolese to recover from the rebel onslaughts, while Mennonites tended to frame their work as a way of reconciliation and a general critique of militarism. Humanitarian workers generally presented Congolese civilians as innocent victims grateful for Western benevolence. Occasionally, Congolese did question the intent and the methods of CPRA aid. Still others tried to profit from aid, from ANC forces to traders.

The case of CPRA relief in the Simba revolts fits well with Anthony Thompson's recent discussion of the challenges of decolonisation for the ICRC. Thompson observes, 'The distribution of relief and the giving or denying of aid were a way to achieve these ends [of defeating anti-colonial insurgencies]. Hence, decolonisation posed very starkly the question of whether humanitarians were able to set conditions about their presence in conflict zones when tied to interests very different to their own.'[8] Just as the British government in Kenya and the French government in Algeria tried to harness the International Committee of the Red Cross (ICRC) and aid organisations to efforts

---

8   A. Thompson, "Humanitarian Principles Put to the Test: Challenges to Humanitarian Action during Decolonisation," *International Review of the Red Cross* 97 (2016), 53.

to maintain colonial rule, the DRC government sought material aid and international support by allowing humanitarian organisations to work in territory controlled by the Congolese army.[9]

Another way humanitarian aid assisted the Congolese government came from press coverage of the violence. Humanitarian aid workers reported on the horrific consequences of the revolt on civilians. They tended publicly to downplay the role of the government on inflicting harm, even when they directly witnessed abuses by government forces. Instead, aid workers helped portray the hardships brought about by the civil war as mainly the result of the CNL. One of the manifold failures of the CNL was its inability to publicise the violence by the ANC for propaganda purposes, in part because of its hostile relationship with humanitarian organisations. The Congolese and US governments framed CPRA humanitarian work as a means of showing how the counterinsurgency saved civilians from the oppressive rule of the rebels. Unlike in South Vietnam or in Algeria, expatriate aid personnel almost never expressed empathy for the insurgents. The entire rebellion was generally viewed as the result of an overly speedy path to independence.

The case of the CNL revolts provides interesting comparisons with other humanitarian crises in the 1960s and 1970s. The Biafran government befriended aid agencies during the Nigerian civil war.[10] The North Vietnamese government and the FLN in Algeria had more success in winning the sympathy of Western foreign aid agencies in comparison with the inept diplomacy of Congolese rebels, who failed to win much sympathy outside of Communist regimes and some African countries.[11] Despite the intentions of international humanitarian organisations, the Congolese government benefited from relief in its war against the CNL insurgency.

9   N. Lanza, "Le Comité international de la Croix-Rouge et le soulèvement des Mau-Mau au Kenya, 1952–1959," *Relations Internationales* 133:1 (2008), 91–110; F. Klose, *Human Rights in the Shadow of Colonial Violence. The Wars of Independence in Kenya and Algeria*, Translated by D. Geyer (Philadelphia: University of Pennsylvania Press, 2012); J. Johnson, *The Battle for Algeria: Sovereignty, Health Care, and Humanitarianism* (Philadelphia: University of Pennsylvania Press, 2015).

10 Staunton, "Case of Biafra"; Waters, "Influencing the Message"; Oko Omaka, *Humanitarian Crisis*; Moses and Heerten, *Postcolonial Conflict*.

11 On Algeria, see Klose, *Human Rights*; Johnson, *Battle for Algeria*. On South Vietnam, see C. Kauffman, "Politics, Programs, and Protests: Catholic Relief Services in Vietnam, 1954–1975," Catholic Historical Review 91:2 (2005), 223–50; J. Kumin, "Orderly Departure from Vietnam: Cold War Anomaly or Humanitarian Innovation?" *Refugee Survey Quarterly* 27:1 (2008), 104–17; J. Elkind, *Aid Under Fire: Nation Building and the Vietnam War* (Lexington, KY: University Press of Kentucky, 2016).

US food aid, coordinated relief, and the revolt of 1964

In 1963, US diplomats and NGO staff felt that the worst of the Congolese humanitarian crises had finally come to an end. United Nations forces had defeated the Katangese secession and Moïse Tschombe fled into exile, just several months after Congolese troops put an end to South Kasai state. Roland Bordelon, the director of Catholic Relief Services operations in Congo, referred to late 1963 and early 1964 as a 'respite of peace followed by open rebellion'.[12] USAID had even decided to cut back in 1963 its scheduled amount of food for the future 1965 fiscal year, albeit largely as a punishment for the Congolese government's inability to pay for the inland transport of Food for Peace relief.[13]

Pierre Mulele's rebels attacks stepped up by the end of 1963 in Kwilu, sending thousands of civilians fleeing into the provincial capital of Kikwit. Others joined the rebels in camps in rural areas. Mennonite missionaries especially feared the rise of Mulele. Rebels razed American Mennonite Brethren Mission churches and schools and many Congolese Mennonites fled to cities or into remote rural areas.[14] Mennonite missionaries viewed the CNL as a tool of international Communism. Mennonite missionary and journalist Levi Keidel reported how some Mennonite missionaries heard APL rebels boast, 'We only want Russia here ... The Russians will give us everything. Our chiefs have shown us pictures of the things promised, when we have thrown all other white people out of the country!'[15]

By February 1964, the United Nations mission, USAID, and private NGOs joined together to coordinate assistance to Kikwit. A delegation that included CPRA director Hans Schaffert along with representatives from the ICRC, Catholic Relief Services, and the World Health Organisation

---

12 Roland Bordelon, "A Report of the Congo (Léopoldville) Office, Catholic Relief Services, 1961–1965" (Unpublished manuscript, 1966), 16, Folder VolAgs Programming CY 1966 (formerly Title III), Box 4, USAID Program Files Congo 1961–1967, Record Group 286, Records of the US Agency for International Development, NARA II.

13 "Title III – Congo," (unpublished manuscript, no date [1966]), Folder FPC 6 VolAgs Programming CY 1967, Box 3, USAID Program Files Congo 1961–1967, Record Group 286 Records of the US Agency for International Development, NARA II.

14 For examples of APL abuses of Mennonite missionaries and attacks on missions, see Levi Keidel, Kwilu Diary (unpublished essay, no date [1964]), Folder Congo IX-12 (#3), MCCA; Hollinger-Jenzen, Myers, and Bertsche, *Jesus Tribe*.

15 Levi Keidel, "Kwilu Diary" (unpublished essay, no date [1964]), Folder Congo IX-12 (#3), MCCA.

travelled to Kwliu province to plan food shipments.[16] Food shortages had begun to plague towns outside of Kikwit, to the point rebel prisoners were starving to death.[17] Congolese officials agreed to have government troops guard food sent by the US and the UN. Weeks later, rebels had made it very difficult for traders to bring manioc from the rural regions that supplied both Kikwit and Kinshasa.[18] A Belgian trader warned a US Agency for International Development (USAID) officer, 'a foot shortage [in Kikwit] could only benefit the terrorists' since Pende and Bumba people in the city generally sympathised with Mulele.[19]

The CPRA became part of American plans to buttress the Congolese government against the CNL. US funds paid for South African, Cuban, and European mercenaries to stiffen up ANC resistance to the rebels. Alongside these military initiatives, the US embassy authorised food shipments to territory recaptured from the rebels as well as cities threatened by APL advances. US Air Force C-130 Hercules plans transported food to major cities such as Bukavu from the middle of 1964 until 1966. While US and Congolese officials in some cases directly ran food distribution, they also brought in CPRA representatives to manage food delivery.[20] USAID staff member Eugene Moore claimed these operations bolstered confidence in the government. 'It was believed that support for [Mbandaka], of any sort, which came from the capital at Leopoldville would have a beneficial effect

16 A.C. Gilpin, Report on visit to Kikwit, 20 February 1964, Folder PFC 2 Title II, Kivu and Kwilu Food and Asst., FY 64-66, Box 1, USAID Program Files Congo 1961–1967, Record Group 286, Records of the US Agency for International Development, NARA II.

17 Eugene Moore, Food Situation in the Kwilu, 14 February 1964, Folder PFC 2 Title II, Kivu and Kwilu Food and Asst., FY 64-66, Box 1, USAID Program Files Congo 1961–1967, Record Group 286, Records of the US Agency for International Development, NARA II.

18 Eugene Moore to Vincent Brown, 3 March 1964, Folder PFC 2 Title II, Kivu and Kwilu Food and Asst., FY 64-66, Box 1, USAID Program Files Congo 1961–1967, Record Group 286, Records of the US Agency for International Development, NARA II.

19 Ibid.

20 Eugene Moore, Civic Impact Program, Folder FPC 6 VolAgs, Programming CYs 1961, 1962, 1963, 1964 (formerly Title III), 27 January 1965, Box 1, USAID Program Files Congo 1961–1967, Record Group 286, Records of the US Agency for International Development, NARA II.

on the population,' Moore noted as he described how CPRA representatives accompanied a flight carrying five tons of food in September 1964.[21]

Congolese government victories opened up new fields for the CPRA and other NGOs to give out US government food. Belgian paratroopers took Kisangani (then Stanleyville) from the APL in November 1964. The day after Kisangani was once again under government control, the US government hired a barge to carry food from Kinshasa to Kisangani along the Congo River. The shipment arrived two months later.[22] CPRA material aid worker Jim Paton flew to Kisangani on 15 December 1964 to develop a plan to distribute the roughly 100 tons of food slowly making its way towards the city. He found the centre of the city to be eerily deserted: 'You could hear your footsteps.'[23]

USAID worked with various religious aid programmes to better organise food shipments. In part, this was to avoid embarrassing moments when Congolese politicians promised civilians aid than the US embassy had never approved. On a tour of Bukavu in April 1965, a Congolese national government representative assured the public in Bukavu that a gigantic shipment of 200 tons of food was on its way from Kinshasa even though the US consul in the city had never heard about it.[24] The CPRA formed a committee in 1965 with USAID, Catholic Relief Services, Caritas, and the UN to solve obstacles to distribution.[25] Thanks to these discussions, the CPRA divided its efforts in 1965 among three major zones. The first was Kwilu province. Government forces there treated rural communities as rebel sympathisers, killing and maiming people with impunity. They systematically seized livestock to consume or simply to slaughter as punishment for the rebellion. Such abuses remained silent in communications between USAID and the CPRA. Orientale province also became a major area for CPRA relief. Much of rural Orientale remained in the hands of APL forces through early 1967. The last area was Kivu province in the Great Lakes region.

The value of food relief to polish the image of US involvement in the DRC worked in several ways. Placing NGOs in the forefront of aid allowed the US

21 Ibid.

22 Ibid.

23 Interview, Jim Paton, 14 August 2018.

24 US Consul Matherton to US Embassy Léopoldville, 12 April 1965, Folder FPC 2 Kivu and Kwilu Food and Asst. FY 64–66, Box 1, USAID Program Files Congo 1961–1967, Record Group 286, Records of the US Agency for International Development, NARA II.

25 See Folder FPC 2 Disaster Relief Inter-Agency Committee, Box 1, USAID Program Files Congo 1961–1967, Record Group 286, Records of the US Agency for International Development, NARA II.

government to present itself as a benevolent supporter of humanitarian aid. At times, this effort to keep the US role behind the scenes could be perceived as diminishing the value of relief. To underline this point, the US consul in Bukavu asked his colleagues in the US Information Service in 1967 to publicise food aid: 'Usually our friends in Protestant and Catholic Relief Services get most of the credit ... This time, however, we want the emphasis put on the fact that is the Government and people of the US which sends this stuff, free of charge.'[26] USAID packing prominently featured the words, 'Gift of the People of the United States of America'. Such phrases occasionally left Congolese wondering if the aid came unconditionally. An anonymous newspaper article condemned the sale of what should have been free US food in some markets in a way that questioned the sincerity of US assistance: 'Since the famine threatened to exterminate the Congolese people, Uncle Sam, generous as always, has transported food to us ... marked "not to be sold" ... One wonders if these words are only meant to be free propaganda.'[27] The complaint of misuse of food came with a recognition that aid was indeed designed to persuade Congolese to trust the US.

The pacifist's dilemma: Mennonite relief and counterinsurgency in Kwilu, 1965–1966

Mennonites took the lead within the CPRA's Kwilu programme, though their views on the Congolese government varied significantly. On the one hand, Mennonite Brethren missionaries had confidence in the US government's policies. Archie Graber, who had expected to retire after the CPRA closed down its Kasai project in early 1964, agreed to direct CPRA's relief and rehabilitation plans in Kwilu. The Mennonite Central Committee also furnished food and youth volunteers to assist in relief. Elmer Neufeld, director of Mennonite Central Committee (MCC) activity in the DRC from 1962 to 1965, wanted MCC to distinguish itself from US foreign policy objectives. 'I also feel uneasy about the [Mennonite Brethren] tendency here to identify very closely with US Government political and military interests,' Neufeld wrote in February

---

26 James Farber to Don Foresta, 13 April 1967, Folder FPC 6 VolAgs Programming CY 1967, Box 3, USAID Program Files Congo 1961–1967, Record Group 286 Records of the US Agency for International Development, NARA II.

27 "La limite de la verité à ne pas vendre ou échanger," *L'Étoile du Congo* (19 November 1965), in Folder FPC 6 Congo Protestant Relief Agency FY 1965, Box 4, USAID Program Files Congo 1961–1967, Record Group 286 Records of the US Agency for International Development, NARA II.

1965.[28] Bridging differences between Congolese and North American Mennonites made Neufeld particularly interested in Kwilu. Neufeld blamed the revolt on the oppressiveness and economic failures of the Congolese state, but also believed that the government could gain popular support: 'If the central government can arrest the Kwilu disturbances and at the same time work toward basic economic and political reform, then there is hope for the future.'[29] MCC thus could help by setting an example of peaceful development for the state to follow. In keeping with Neufeld's Anabaptist ethos of peacebuilding, he viewed the relief project as a way of bringing together missionaries, MCC, and Congolese churches in a common altruistic goal.

Direct CPRA/MCC aid to the Kwilu commenced in June 1965 under the auspices of the CPRA. By this point, famine had taken hold in much of rural Kwilu. Congolese troops controlled the provincial capital of Kikwit. Rebels occupied much of the countryside for much of the year. People from outside Kikwit fled to the city.[30] Malcolm McVeigh, a CPRA staff member, noted with shock in February 1966 that he had never seen so much severe malnutrition before.[31] While hunger and disease took their toll in refugee lives in Kikwit, at least some limited amount of medical care and food was available in the city. People in rural areas had less access to relief. Rebels confiscated local livestock and ANC troops slaughtered animals to punish villages suspected of backing the insurgents.[32]

The Congolese military set parameters for the CPRA/MCC humanitarian programme. ANC roadblocks and moving patrols did not allow Mennonite relief to enter areas unless the territory was considered free of rebel activity. Alvin Dahl recalled how the CPRA had to wait for military approval before relief distribution could begin.[33] Congolese troops also accompanied MCC trucks to ensure rebel forces would not confiscate the vehicles. Troops also

---

28 Elmer Neufeld to Robert Snyder, 3 February 1965, Folder Congo Office 1965 113/121, Box 193, IX-6-3, MCCA.

29 Elmer Neufeld to William Snyder, 10 March 1964, Folder Congo Office 1964 II 111/128, Box 190, IX-6-3, MCCA.

30 Elmer Neufeld to William Snyder, 10 April 1965, Folder Congo Office 1965 113/121, Box 193, IX-6-3, MCCA; Jim Kliewer to Elmer Neufeld, 28 May 1965, Folder Congo Office 1965 113/121, Box 193, IX-6-3, MCCA.

31 Archie Graber to Co-workers, February 1966, Folder CPRA 1966 115/124, Box 197, IX-6-3, MCCA.

32 For examples of ANC destruction of livestock and fields, see C. Davis, *Death in Abeyance: Illness and Therapy Among the Tabwa of Central Africa* (Edinburgh: Edinburgh University Press, 2000), 32; Verhaegen, *Mulele*, 75, 215–16.

33 Interview, Alvin Dahl, 17 May 2017.

5. The CPRA brought food and supplies to camps set up by the Congolese government for people displaced by the government campaign to defeat Pierre Mulele's rebels in Kwilu province. This relatively happy scene from 1966 fit with CPRA aid workers' hopes for reconciliation, but survivors of these camps recall hunger and abuses by Congolese soldiers. (MCCA)

offered protection for MCC aid workers from refugees themselves. With only one or two North American MCC volunteers with an equally small number of Congolese assistants, the relief teams lacked the ability to maintain distribution in an orderly way.[34] 'Food distribution led to riotous situations,' Dahl recalled as he remembered being thankful for having the ANC troops around to keep people in line and to even help carry food off of the trucks.[35]

MCC drivers also delivered food to refugee camps established in rural areas by the ANC military. MCC oral and written narratives about these camps differ significantly from the memories of Congolese survivors collected by Emery Kalema. At least for people who recalled living in these camps, ANC troops abused displaced people who were suspected of being rebel

34 Ibid.
35 Ibid.

sympathisers.[36] Other refugees remembered people dying of hunger at the camps.[37] While Mennonite written accounts of these camps acknowledged how some refugees died of starvation, North American relief workers also viewed the camps as a place of reconciliation. Archie Graber wrote about his visit to one camp in a rural area in 1966. In an essay entitled 'Danger of Getting Used to It', Graber's account verified oral accounts of starvation at the camps without passing blame on the ANC. A man at the camp asked Graber to come to a hut to see a corpse. 'This man like so many others who were in hiding too long. Should we not sympathise with the lad? Or are we becoming used to it,' wondered Graber.[38] He concluded that the real tragedy of the news the next morning that at least seven people had died from hunger was that they had not all converted to Christ.[39]

CPRA staff engaged with refugees, but not surprisingly, hardly anyone dared criticise the military. Some refugees claimed they were loyal to the government. Many refugees had fled the town of Mukedi to Kikwit in early 1965. Some told missionaries and CPRA volunteers that Nzamba, the local Pende chief of Mukedi, had tried to fight off rebels from the Mbunda ethnic community.[40] When Nzamba sent a girl to tell the rebels he would not surrender to them, they left her decapitated head on a stake to intimidate government loyalists. Whether or not the reports were accurate, they did serve as a way of trying to convince aid workers (and indirectly the Congolese military) that some regions deserved aid and could be trusted by government soldiers.

Some communities were not so fortunate. Alvin Dahl remembered how he tried to find a village he had previously visited to bring a new round of food and tools.[41] ANC troops had entered the town and accused people of giving MCC food to rebels. The army then slaughtered the people in the town in retaliation. Though Dahl knew only of this single case, he admitted that it was difficult for him to be sure how the ANC treated civilians. His limited knowledge of the Kwilu lingua franca of Kituba along with the gruelling task

---

36   Kalemba, "Violence and Memory," 73–130.

37   Ibid., 60–72.

38   Archie Graber, "Danger of Getting Used to It," (Unpublished manuscript, 1966), Folder Congo Office 1966 115/123, Box 197, IX-6-3, MCCA.

39   Ibid.

40   The following is taken from John Kliewer to Elmer Neufeld, 28 May 1965, Folder Congo Office 1965 113/121, Box 193, IX-6-3, MCCA; Jim Bertsche to Elmer Neufeld, 6 May 1965, Folder Congo Inland Mission 1965 113/120, Box 193, IX-6-3, MCCA.

41   Telephone interview, Alvin Dahl, 17 May 2017.

of hauling and handing out supplies made it hard to draw much information from refugees. Naturally, if displaced people saw ANC soldiers with relief trucks, they would have been highly unlikely to publically disapprove of the behaviour of the Congolese army.

MCC workers expressed mixed views of their relationship with the Congolese military. Archie Graber reported to his Mennonite colleagues how some CNL rebels agreed to surrender to obtain food. After a tense night where Graber heard voices speaking in the forest around his truck, the rebels came forward.[42] For Graber, this was an example of Christian reconciliation brought through MCC's work. Not all MCC staff kept quiet about the ANC as a potential threat to civilians and prisoners. Elmer Neufeld noted that civilians feared both the rebels.[43] Mennonite medical volunteers Ralph and Ruth Milhous in the city of Tshikapa in Kasai province were disgusted that ANC soldiers had stoned and bayoneted APL prisoners from Kwilu 'as an example for the people'.[44] Even Graber felt unnerved that ANC soldiers manned machine guns around one refugee camp.[45] Yet these anxieties did not deter Mennonite cooperation with the Congolese army. In northeastern DRC, CPRA aid workers proved more willing to openly partner with the ANC than their Mennonite counterparts.

Saving the Simba's victims: the CPRA in eastern DRC, 1965–1967

Mercenaries and Congolese troops captured towns in the northeastern province of Orientale beginning in the spring of 1965. Although the rebels gradually lost their grip over small urban centres, they continued to move through rural regions for the next two years. Some rebels eventually made their way into the Sudan. By early 1966, regular ANC forces took over much of the mopping up operations. Due to the war, rural people in much of northeastern DRC had no access to medicine, reliable sources of food, or clothes from 1964 until in some cases as late as early 1967.

---

42 Archie Graber to Co-Workers, 17 September 1966, Folder Zaire 1965–1966, Box 22, Record Group 8, CWS/PHS.

43 Elmer Neufeld to William Snyder, 10 April 1965, Folder Congo Office 1965 113/121, Box 193, IX-6-3, MCCA.

44 Ralph and Ruth Milhous, Activity Report, 1 March 1964, Folder Congo Activity Reports 1964 111/125, Box 190, IX-6-3, MCCA.

45 Graber, "Danger of Getting Used to It."

The CPRA relied on a small group of missionaries and CWS staff members to supervise food distribution over the vast province. The food crisis reached the point that evangelical missionaries no longer raised their previous objections to the CPRA for its ties to the World Council of Churches. Instead, they gave out food and supplies to internally displaced Congolese people at their missions. Bill Gilvear, a Scottish missionary from the Unevangelised Fields Mission, agreed to direct relief operations from Kisangani. MCC volunteer Don Kurtz helped deliver food further to the east, from the Orientale town of Isiro to Bukavu in Kivu province. African Inland Mission missionaries also drove trucks and distributed food. Although some missionaries considered placing Congolese in charge of this work, expatriates still remained in leadership roles. In a meeting in Kisangani in September 1965, CPRA staff objected to a proposal backed by Catholic Relief Services to allow a local committee of Congolese church leaders and officials to oversee relief.[46] McVeigh contended that there was 'no local interest in it', though he only mentioned expatriate doctors and aid workers' fears of corruption to explain why Congolese should not control relief.[47]

CPRA personnel considered their work to be a way of rescuing Congolese from the clutches of Simba rebels. Helen Roseveare, a missionary doctor who assisted CPRA, agreed to organise the distribution of food and medicine in the Orientale town of Wamba in June 1966. 'I began hearing of the pathetic flight of the refugees in Wamba, liberated after 20 months of rebel occupation,' she wrote in her report.[48] There, she worked with over 50 Congolese to hand out medicine, clothes, and food sent via the Congolese army. More than 25,000 people came to receive the aid over the span of five days. Like David Grenfell's operation for Angolan refugees, Roseveare also handed out ration cards. Once they had given away all their supplies, she wrote, 'We felt like crying – from exhaustion, yes; from the pathos knowing we had only scratched the surface of overwhelming need, yes; this little way, to show forth His Love to those in such desperate need.'[49] Civilians were objects of charity

46 Malcolm McVeigh, Report of Trip to Stanleyville, September 4–10, 1965, 10 September 1965, Folder FPC 6 Congo Protestant Relief Agency FY 66, Box 4, US-AID Program Files Congo 1961–1967, Record Group 286, Records of the US Agency for International Development, NARA II.

47 Ibid.

48 The following information is drawn from Helen Roseveare, "Relief Distribution at Wamba," (Unpublished manuscript, 1966), Folder FPC 6 Congo Protestant Relief Agency FY 1966, Box 4, USAID Program Files Congo 1961–1967, Record Group 286, Records of the US Agency for International Development, NARA II.

49 Ibid.

rather than possible insurgents. People fled into rural areas and had to keep moving to escape wandering APL forces. Those caught by rebels lost all they owned, from bicycles and umbrellas to 'the shirts of their backs.'[50] Similar events played out in Aungba, Watsa, and other mission stations.

Just as in the Kwilu, CPRA aid workers – mainly Protestant missionaries – only commenced relief work once they received permission from the army. Even with the approval of ANC officers, CPRA workers occasionally became targets of the APL. Bill Gilvear, a Scottish Protestant missionary, evaded APL soldiers on a road north of Kisangani who opened fire on his truck thanks to his failed breaks, which made it impossible to stop.[51] ANC soldiers justified their presence with missionary relief trucks on the grounds of security. 'A large truck – with a white man in the cab – was a prize indeed [for APL soldiers]. Because of this the [CPRA] demanded that Bill be accompanied by an armed escort,' wrote Gilvear's biographer.[52]

Evangelical volunteers with the CPRA tended to have very good relations with ANC officers, particularly Yossa Malasi, the leader of ANC forces in northeastern DRC. Researchers and mercenary accounts have neglected Yossa's pivotal role in the war against the APL in Oriental province, as they did with the parts played by most mid-level ANC officers. CPRA personnel, by contrast, recognised Yossa's importance. Colin Buckley approved that Yossa thanked the CPRA for 'caring for the needy'.[53] Another CPRA worker wrote, 'The local military commander, Colonel Yossa, is very sympathetic to our relief work.'[54] During the 1967 revolt of a group of Katangese gendarmes along with European and South African mercenaries, Yossa provided security for Jerry Wilkerson, a CPRA aid worker in Isiro.[55] Yossa tried to repair roads south of Isiro towards Gao and Wamba to allow CPRA trucks better access to

---

50 Ruby Pinkerton, "Hunger," (unpublished manuscript, no date [1966]), Folder Zaire 1965–1966, Box 22, Record Group 8, CWS/PHS.

51 S. Brown, *Rough Diamond: The Life Story of Bill Gilvear* (Geanies House: Christian Focus, 1997), 211.

52 Ibid., 205.

53 Colin Buckley to Malcolm McVeigh, 13 February 1967, Folder Zaire 1967–1968, Box 22, Record Group 8, CWS/PHS.

54 Jerry Wilkerson, Field Report April 10 – May 1967, Folder Zaire 1967–1968, Box 22, Record Group 8, CWS/PHS.

55 Lawrence Spears to Jan S.F. van Hoogstraten, 5 August 1967, Folder Zaire 1967–1968, Box 22, Record Group 8, CWS/PHS.

displaced people.[56] A French mercenary officer assisted CPRA relief north of Kisangani on the road to the town of Panga, which remained partially under APL control until February 1967.[57] Such good ties to commanders helped to prevent possible trouble with ANC troops themselves. On occasion, mishaps did occur. A government airplane strafed in error a CPRA distribution centre in Mambuti in January 1967, leaving four dead.[58] 'It was a little ironic to have an American grenade launcher pointed at our faces,' CPRA aid worker Jerry Wilkerson remarked about a roadblock stop in the east-central Congolese town of Wamba before ANC officers cleared the CPRA truck to move along.[59] A CPRA volunteer requested an ANC general to ensure his officers in the far eastern region of Baraka did not interfere with relief distribution.[60]

CPRA staff assisted ANC forces to convince displaced people to come out of hiding. Some displaced communities sent emissaries to the CPRA to ask for help. An old man, 'a mere skeleton,' pleaded in Kisangani in 1965 that 'one hundred people like me die every day where I was in the forest.'[61] Others refused to do so without a good deal of negotiation. Local newspapers in Bukavu claimed a rebel commander had rejected an offer of food in no uncertain terms: 'They'll feed you American food, fatten you up, and then the Americans will eat you!'[62] If this was merely a rumour, it was certainly heard elsewhere. Missionary Ruby Pinkerton blamed the reluctance of people in rural Orientale province to receive aid for the national army

56 Colin Buckley to Malcolm McVeigh, 1 July 1967, Folder Zaire 1967–1968, Box 22, Record Group 8, CWS/PHS.

57 Malcolm McVeigh to Jan S.F. van Hoogstraten, 13 June 1967, Folder Zaire 1967–1968, Box 22, Record Group 8, CWS/PHS.

58 Colin Buckley to Malcolm McVeigh, 15 January 1967, Folder FPC 6 Congo Protestant Relief Agency FY 1967, Box 4, USAID Program Files Congo 1961–1967, Record Group 286, Records of the US Agency for International Development, NARA II.

59 Jerry Wilkerson, Field Report April 10 – May 1967, Folder Zaire 1967–1968, Box 22, Record Group 8, CWS/PHS.

60 Don Kurtz to Malcolm McVeigh, 3 June 1967, Folder Zaire 1967–1968, Box 22, Record Group 8, CWS/PHS.

61 Malcolm McVeigh, Report of Trip to Stanleyville, September 4–10, 1965, 10 September 1965, Folder FPC 6 Congo Protestant Relief Agency FY 1966, Box 4, USAID Program Files Congo 1961–1967, Record Group 286, Records of the US Agency for International Development, NARA II.

62 Don Kurtz to Jan S.F. van Hoogstraten, 12 February 1966, Folder FPC 6 VolAgs, Programming CY 1966 (formerly Title III), Box 4, USAID Program Files Congo 1961–1967, Record Group 286, Records of the US Agency for International Development, NARA II.

on 'Simba stories' that white mercenaries intended to either kill or enslave them.[63] While Pinkerton viewed the emergence of starving people from their hidden refuge as an opportunity for evangelisation, to the Congolese government, accepting relief was also a tacit sign of acceptance of its authority. Displaced people who did turn themselves in risked the wrath of the ANC. '[Some people] say [the Congolese army] are starving the rebels (and all the others I suppose too) out ... One of the tragedies is that rebels have no way to give up even if they want to. If they surrender but are identified as former rebels, they are immediately shot. Under those conditions not many surrender,' Malcolm McVeigh reported.[64]

Suspected rebels still sought out assistance from the CPRA. Some APL prisoners told Bill Gilvear of their desire to convert to Christ. While the Scottish missionary gave thanks to God for their change of heart, they could also have been using Gilvear to save themselves through a foreign aid worker.[65] Pinkerton viewed a crowed of at least one hundred displaced persons in the Maitulu region of Oriental province in October 1966, 'staggering along the road towards us, some leading on sticks, most clothed in loin clothes or grass skirts, all emaciated to the place' where their 'protruding bones gave the appearance of mummies come to life.'[66] These people had been forced to walk over 70 miles after being accused by neighbouring groups of 'calling in the Simbas to destroy their land.'[67]

Relief supplies could become entangled in local conflicts or end up in the hands of traders. In May 1966, Kurtz brought supplies to Kalemie, a city located in northern Katanga province.[68] There, soldiers handed out CPRA relief supplies. He discovered that market women sold supplies of cornmeal given out for free at a Catholic mission. A man sold used clothes he claimed he had bought in Lubumbashi to the south, but Kurtz suspected it came from MCC bundles of clothes based on the packaging.[69] A few months later, a joint

---

63 Pinkerton, "Hunger."

64 Malcolm McVeigh, Report of Trip to Stanleyville, September 4–10, 1965, 10 September 1965, Folder FPC 6 Congo Protestant Relief Agency FY 66, Box 4, US-AID Program Files Congo 1961–1967, Record Group 286, Records of the US Agency for International Development, NARA II.

65 Brown, *Rough Diamond*, 213–14, 220.

66 Pinkerton, "Hunger."

67 Ibid.

68 Don Kurtz to John Gaeddert, 25 May 1966, Congo (Zaire) 1967–1968 Folder 119/59, Box 203, IX-6-3, MCCA.

69 Ibid.

CPRA/USAID/Catholic Relief Services inspection team tried to settle a dispute between missionaries and Congolese churches. Conservative Baptist missionaries clashed with a dissident church that had broken away in 1960.[70] The Congolese independent Baptist church in Goma tried to take over CPRA food distribution from the missionaries with the endorsement of local authorities. The inspectors took the side of the missionaries and warned they would shut off aid if anyone tried to divert food away from the expatriates.[71] In the northeast Congolese town of Mahagi, evangelical Protestant missionaries griped about a Catholic priest who was said to favour Catholics in obtaining food relief.[72]

The Congolese military provoked the ire of the CPRA. Although Kurtz did not openly condemn ANC operations, he did not share evangelical missionaries' more unqualified support for the Congolese army. Describing the region of Mutwanga bordering on Uganda in February 1967, Kurtz wrote: 'Up till now, the area has suffered constantly from military occupation [since a 1957 anti-colonial revolt] ... With the unsettling influence of ten years occupation by various forces came a persecution both personally and economically: women were constantly stolen and/or raped, and food was always demanded by the military, especially meat. Now there are only a few chickens and pigs left in the area, and no cows at all.'[73] Interviewed in 2016, Kurtz recalled with trepidation how mercenaries had left the corpse of a dead APL fighter on the outskirts of Bukavu as a warning for passersby.[74] Yet his personal doubts appear to never led him to openly challenge the military.

Besides the army, local political authorities and businessmen also profited from CPRA relief. Don Kurtz grumbled about Jiwa, an Indian businessman 'who is about crooked as they come,' but who agreed to help transport supplies into the northeastern DRC.[75] While details about transportation entrepreneurs like Jiwa are scarce, undoubtedly relief supplies could generate revenue. They could also be appropriated by local officials. At Mahagi, a local customs

70 See Nelson, *Christian Missionizing.*

71 Sarah Jane Littlefield to Joseph Mintzes, 7 June 1966, Folder PRM 7-2 UNDP FY 67, Box 1, USAID Program Files Congo 1961–1967, Record Group 286, Records of the US Agency for International Development, NARA II.

72 Ibid.

73 Don Kurtz, Report of Trip January 27 – February 7, 1967, Folder Zaire 1967– 1968, Box 22, Record Group 8, CWS/PHS.

74 Telephone interview, Don Kurtz, 10 March 2016.

75 Don Kurtz to Malcolm McVeigh, 23 March 1967, Folder Zaire 1967–1968, Box 22, Record Group 8, CWS/PHS.

official took for himself CPRA supplies such as peanut oil.[76] Some local chiefs chose to use relief as a means of rebuilding communities (and perhaps also the opportunity to distribute CPRA supplies as patronage). CPRA material aid director Malcolm McVeigh visited the village of Moku (near Watsa in Oriental province). There, a local chief agreed to collect three tons of plantain roots to be then given to people in the community via a CPRA truck.[77]

The CPRA response to the mercenary mutiny of the summer of 1967 ultimately reinforced the power of Mobutu Sese Seko's regime at a time when the new dictatorship faced a serious challenge from his own army. The US State Department worked with CPRA quite closely to provide material aid to sites of conflict between ANC units loyal to the government and the rebels. USAID agreed to send C-130 US Air Force planes to deliver food and supplies to CPRA staff as a 'psychological gesture'.[78] CPRA staff helped to coordinate food deliveries and transport from Kinshasa to Kisangani and Bukavu.[79] Though the CPRA was officially an independent humanitarian organisation, it again collaborated with the Congolese and US governments to repair the damage caused by armed rebellion.

Curing pain with protein:
CPRA rehabilitation projects in the aftermath of the revolt

How could areas once occupied by rebels recover? This question troubled CPRA aid workers as well as their colleagues in other aid organisations. As early as 1965, a joint committee of aid organisations declared, 'Practical plans for rehabilitation of the stricken areas remain fragmentary, and for some areas, non-existent.'[80] One common solution was to increase the amount of protein in Congolese diets. A draft of a press release from the US embassy repeated a common opinion that rebels alone were responsible for the 'disruption of

76   Don Kurtz, Report of Trip January 27 – February 7, 1967, Folder Zaire 1967–1968, Box 22, Record Group 8, CWS/PHS.

77   Malcolm McVeigh, Report of Field Trip June 6–28 1967, Folder Zaire 1967–1968, Box 22, Record Group 8, CWS/PHS.

78   Don Kurtz to Malcolm McVeigh, 24 June 1967, Folder Zaire 1967–1968, Box 22, Record Group 8, CWS/PHS.

79   Malcolm McVeigh, Report of Field Trip June 6–28 1967, Folder Zaire 1967–1968, Box 22, Record Group 8, CWS/PHS.

80   Minutes, Restricted Inter-Agency Committee on Food Shortages, 9 December 1965, Folder FPC 2 Disaster Relief Inter-Agency Committee CY 65 and 66, Box 1, USAID Program Files Congo 1961–1967, Record Group 286, Records of the US Agency for International Development, NARA II.

Congolese agriculture' leading to 'the marked decrease in the protein content in the diet of thousands of people'.[81] A local relief operation in the Ngweshe region in Kivu province noted how the war had cut rural villages off from supplies of milk and fish. People were lucky to eat meat once or twice a month.[82] As a skilled farmer, Archie Graber was appalled by the loss of livestock in Kwilu villages. 'Rebels and soldiers have killed most of the chickens, sheep, goats, and cattle. One company man lost more than 6000 head. Nearly all small private herds have been killed. Now it is almost impossible to find,' he warned Mennonite colleagues in 1966.[83]

Augmenting protein turned the question of rehabilitation into a technical issue to be solved by Western agricultural knowledge rather than taking on the political causes of malnutrition. Jennifer Tappan has noted a similar process in Uganda in the 1960s.[84] Such an approach resembled to some degree how the South African government under apartheid claimed the blame for poor diets lay in African culture rather than economic inequalities.[85] It also fitted with the dominant model of modernisation theory with its goal of encouraging an economic take-off via Western technological advances. For Mennonites like Archie Graber, agricultural innovations to assist recovery in the Kwilu reflected his North American Mennonite background. First, Graber shared the ideal of self-sufficient rural communities that had so strongly guided Canadian and US Mennonites in the late 19th and early 20th century.[86] Although North American Mennonites were increasingly leaving isolated rural farm life behind by the 1960s, Mennonite aid workers and missioners saw prosperous and stable agricultural communities as a solution for Congolese people

81 USINFO PRIORITY FOR IPS, no date [1965], Folder FPC 2 Title II, Kivu and Kwilu Food and Asst., FY 1964–1966, Box 1, USAID Program Files Congo 1961–1967, Record Group 286, Records of the US Agency for International Development, NARA II.

82 "Annexe C: Le Bwaki (Kwashiorkor) dans le Ngweshe," (Unpublished manuscript, 1966), 3–4, Folder FPC 2 Title II, Kivu and Kwilu Food and Asst., FY 1964–1966, Box 1, USAID Program Files Congo 1961–1967, Record Group 286, Records of the US Agency for International Development, NARA II.

83 Archie Graber to Co-workers, 17 August 1966, Folder CPR 1966 115/124, Box 197, IX-6-3, MCCA.

84 J. Tappan, *The Riddle of Malnutrition: The Long Arc of Biomedical and Public Health Interventions in Uganda* (Athens, OH: Ohio University Press, 2017).

85 D. Wylie, *Starving on a Full Stomach: Hunger and the Triumph of Cultural Racism in South Africa* (Charlottesville: University of Virginia Press, 2001).

86 P. Bush, *Two Kingdoms, Two Loyalties: Mennonite Pacifism in Modern America* (Baltimore: Johns Hopkins University Press, 1998), 129–52.

devastated by civil war and colonialisation. North American Mennonite workers in the mid-1960s in the Congo saw themselves as a means of bridging cultural divides outside of formal politics.

In 1966, Graber and his assistant Alvin Dahl developed an idea to bring more meat into Kwilu diets. Their inspiration came from a common Western image of the Congo: its natural riches. Dahl looked at grasslands and thought they would be perfect to raise cattle.[87] Graber concurred. He proposed to the Mennonite mission boards and the Mennonite Central Committee a project to buy cattle for Kwliu communities to establish herds. It became known as the Programme Protestante Agricole (PPA). The project's goals were to assist Christians rebuild their lives from the damage caused by the revolt and to 'help [Christians] help themselves', even as Graber knew most people could not afford to buy cattle.[88] In a short description tellingly entitled 'The Nest Has Been Stirred, They Must Fly,' Graber expressed his hope tools and better livestock raising would allow Kwilu communities to recover.[89] 'All of Congo is pretty hungry for meat, but we can only give [rations] to the most needy', Graber added as he discussed winding down rations.[90]

From the end of 1966 to 1968, the PPA expanded on its initial projects of chicken and cattle production. Dahl and Graber purchased cattle for use by village cooperatives. Each herd was to have five Christian shareholders who in return for their investment would receive a calf of their own, while the adult cattle still belonged to the project. Shareholders had to either watch over the livestock or hire at least one herdsman. Each herd would be placed at a different Protestant mission station where rebels had wiped out the cattle.[91] Along with promoting cattle, Graber also supervised the distribution of chicks and supplies. CPRA supplied Rhode Island Red chicks, heavier than Congolese varieties, to Kwilu farmers. Oxfam and the US Protestant organisation Heifer International donated funds to purchase chicks and cattle.[92]

---

87 Interview, Alvin Dahl, 17 May 2017.

88 Archie Graber to Co-workers, 17 August 1966, Folder Congo Protestant Relief Agency 1966, 115/124, Box 197, IX-6-3, MCCA.

89 Archie Graber, "The Nest Has Been Stirred, They Must Fly," (Unpublished manuscript, 1966), Folder 115/123 Congo Office 1966, Box 197, IX-6-3, MCCA.

90 Ibid.

91 Archie Graber to Co-workers, 17 August 1966, Folder Congo Protestant Relief Agency 1966, 115/124, Box 197, IX-6-3, MCCA.

92 Malcolm McVeigh to J.H. Klassen, 15 July 1967, Folder Zaire 1967–1968, Record Group 8, Box 22, CWS/PHS.

Congolese churches had no direct role in how the PPA operated in its early years. At least in regards to development projects run by missionary organisations in the DRC in the 1960s, the PPA appears to be typical in that foreign staff controlled the logistics and the goals of the programme. Graber also was relatively free to determine how his projects were run, in similar fashion to his earlier relief efforts in South Kasai. Likewise, MCC and the Mennonite churches left Graber with the task of evaluating what constituted success for the project. This personalised approach to aid made long-term planning vague at best.

Though there was no clear way for donors to evaluate if Graber's plans could become self-sufficient over time, MCC and Mennonite Brethren staff were optimistic about the future of the PPA. John Gaeddert, MCC director for the Congo, asserted in 1966: 'This programme will require supervision over a period of years to be assured that supplements, fences, grazing land, [and] medical attention are given.'[93] MCC and the Mennonite Brethren convinced agriculture professor Clarence Hiebert to evaluate Graber's project. Hiebert endorsed the Kwilu development plans for the 'tremendous' grazing land and what he considered to be evidence of Congolese support for the plan. 'Archie Graber indicated already more deposits had been received from Congolese than he could provide cattle for,' Hiebert noted.[94] The professor's conversations with Congolese – whose identities and social class were not identified in the report – pointed to concerns about ways to make revenue for churches, from sawmills to market garden and cash crop farming.[95] This conflation of poor farmers with church leaders would also be a problem later for the PPA.

The project attracted many Congolese, yet Mennonite expatriate CPRA staff discovered that Africans had their own ideas about the benefits of the PPA. Congolese farmers flocked to the cattle project: 'By the end of 1970 the demand for [PAP] cattle was such that it would have taken eleven years to meet requests received by the then-existing herd of 140 cows. A further herd of 170 cows and 10 bulls [was] purchased with USAID counterpart funds.'[96] Peter Kroeker, who later directed the PPA in the mid-1970s before pursuing

93 John Gaeddert to Vern Preheim, 14 November 1966, Folder Congo Office 1966 115/123, Box 197, IX-6-3, MCCA.

94 Clarence Hiebert, A Report on the Feasibility of Agricultural Service to Congolese in Connection with a Ministry to the Congo Mennonite Brethren, p. 2, February 1967, Folder Congo IX-12 (#3), Box 3, MCCA.

95 Ibid.

96 Alvin Dahl, Programme Protestante Agricole: Descriptive Report 1970, Folder Congo MCC 1969–1971, IX-12-6, MCCA.

a doctorate in anthropology, returned to the former Kwilu province in 1976 to understand how Congolese envisioned the PPA.[97] He found cooperative members accused managers of stealing and butchering cattle without the permission of other members. Managers forged the names of individual members on documents authorising cattle sales and most likely kept the profits for themselves. Villages disputed ownership rights over cattle. Some local village leaders enrolled other family members in a cooperative to solidify their control over the entire herd, even as these family members often were unaware their names had been used.[98]

Oxfam required veterinarians to check on the cattle, but Mennonite veterinarians complained about poor resources, a lack of direction, and the unwillingness of Congolese to correctly feed and take care of their livestock. Ned Kaufman, a veterinarian assigned to the PPA in 1968, bemoaned the financial and logistical difficulties of his work. He also found the cattle project was nowhere near the force for community development he had hoped: 'There are no (I have yet to meet one) Congolese livestock farmers. There are investors (one who commits money for a financial return) and farmhands (a hired laborer on a farm), but there are no farmers (a person who cultivates land or raises livestock).'[99] African workers accused Kauffman of racism when he 'pushed [them] to be efficient'.[100]

One solution to these challenges was to expand the project. When Peter Kroeker became the project director in 1973,[101] based on his previous career running industrial farms in his native Manitoba, he decided to expand chicken production through an industrial feed mill paid for by a large grant from the Canadian government. After roughly two years of relative success in 1974 and 1975, Kroeker's emphasis on increasing the scale of the PPA was undone by internal and external factors. The rapid downturn of the Congolese economy, the global recession, rampant corruption, the declining state of roads, high inflation, and poor management by Congolese staff all gradually sapped away

97 P. Kroeker, "Change and Continuity as Illustrated in the Introduction of Cattle in Zaire," (PhD thesis, University of Kansas, 1978).

98 Ibid., 115–46.

99 Ned Kauffman, August 1971 Activity Report, Folder Congo Activity Reports 1971 127/93, Box 215, IX-6-3, MCCA.

100 Ned Kauffman, April 1971 Activity Report, Folder Congo Activity Reports 1971 127/93, Box 215, IX-6-3. MCCA.

101 On the later history of the PPA, see J. Rich, "A Mennonite Development Project Betwixt Ambition and Confusion in the Democratic Republic of Congo," Unpublished presentation at the Global Anabaptism Workshop, Goshen College, June 2017.

at the PPA. After MCC decided to finally end its financial backing for the PPA at the end of the 1979s, the CPRA failed to find new sources of funding and the programme finally closed down in 1984.

It is clear that the depiction of Kwilu people as passive victims of the rebellion had greatly shaped the later evolution of the PPA. CPRA staff in the 1960s thought their benevolence and their technical knowledge would be the panacea to triumph over the dearth caused by the war. Merrill Ewert saw how the government created obstacles for development that no technical approach could solve. He remembered how he and his Congolese partner Tshimaka organised a night meeting at a village held to identify barriers to development in the early 1970s. Ewert convinced people to speak of their problems and one man stood up and started to pound the heel of his foot into the ground. The man then declared, 'We all know who is the real problem. Mobutu!'[102] Others joined in denouncing the brutality and corruption of the government. The meeting ended, and Tshimaka mused that perhaps bringing the rural people guns to fight the government might make more sense than asking them about their problems.[103] Nothing came of this suggestion. PPA staff and rural people alike knew all too well the Congolese government was ready to crush dissent. Critiques of the authoritarian and violent nature of Congolese rule – and the US foreign policy that ensured its survival – could not be a part of CPRA rehabilitation efforts that came out of the mid-1960s.

Conclusion

The 1963–7 civil wars in the DRC had horrendous consequences for Congolese civilians. Humanitarian aid workers and government officials kept little track of the thousands who succumbed to famine, arbitrary killings, and disease. Food and medical aid became valuable tools for the Congolese government in its war against the APL. A range of reasons explain the failure of the APL to succeed in conquering the DRC: US covert interventions, poor leadership, a lack of aid from its erstwhile Communist and Arab nationalist allies abroad, and abuses against civilians. Another factor that deserves attention is the role of humanitarian relief. Congolese state efforts to assist refugees were limited at best so aid programmes stepped into the breach. CPRA and MCC staff willingly followed the direction of the Congolese military. Though humanitarian workers had practical reasons to ask for ANC protection, this

102 Interview, Merrill Ewert, 13 March 2017.

103 Ibid.

collaboration between the ANC and Protestant aid organisations gave the Congolese military a valuable tool.

Determining the military value of effectiveness of humanitarian relief cannot be judged with precision, but it is logical to conclude that the influx of supplies helped the government. Though the APL and the ANC both abused civilians, displaced people could only benefit from humanitarian aid in government-controlled areas. Furthermore, aid workers did not empathise with the APL, in contrast to Biafra and South Vietnam, where representatives of humanitarian agencies increasingly sided with rebels rather than official governments.[104] MCC and CPRA staff knew full well the cruelty of the ANC. Yet, they kept quiet. Likewise, US State Department staff bemoaned corruption and the arbitrary violence of Mobutu's government even in the late 1960s and early 1970s, but such complaints remained an internal matter.[105]

Unlike in South Kasai, CPRA workers closely collaborated with government authorities in the mid-1960s. Even if the ferocity of counterinsurgency offended the pacifist values of Mennonites, they also had no choice but to acquiesce to the military if they wanted to help civilians. By depicting civilians as passive victims of violence, CPRA personnel may have ignored the nuances of how Congolese people responded to aid, but they also may have saved some rebels who surrendered in the process. Protestant aid workers sought to depoliticise their work despite their complicity with the Congolese state. They deemed their work to be acts of mercy for innocent victims. Such attitudes shaped development projects designed to ensure a return to stability in regions hard-hit by the revolt. Focusing on protein sources allowed aid workers to avoid openly criticising Mobutu's regime and to treat the aftermath of the rebellion as a technical problem to be solved by North American ingenuity. The CPRA certainly healed wounds in the name of national unity, but it did so in a way that failed to question how the Congolese government was guilty of inflicting harm on civilians with impunity. As Emery Kalema has shown, the Congolese state's muzzling of the pain of civilians in Kwilu corresponded to the callousness of authoritarian rule in the colonial era and in later decades after independence.

104 On Vietnam and aid workers, see S. Flipse, "The Latest Casualty of War: Catholic Relief Services, Humanitarianism, and the War in Vietnam, 1967–1968," *Peace and Change* 27:2 (2002), 245–70; Elkind, *Aid under Fire*. On aid workers supporting Biafran independence, see Oko Omaka, *Humanitarian Crisis*; Moses and Heerten, *Postcolonial Conflict*.

105 Bechtolsheimer, "Breakfast."

5

Operation Doctor: The Rise and Fall of a Protestant Short-Term Medical Volunteer Programme

In September 1962, the United Methodist Church magazine *World Outlook* published an article about Operation Doctor, a short-term medical mission project overseen by the Congolese Protestant Relief Agency. Dr James Jay, a doctor from Indianapolis who volunteered at the Kimpese mission hospital, had returned full of a 'missionary zeal that would fire the imagination of even the most doubtful skeptic'.[1] Hundreds of Belgian as well as US missionary doctors had fled the Democratic Republic of Congo in 1960. The article assured readers, 'Thousands of Congolese, emaciated with malnutrition and stricken with an assortment of rare jungle diseases, plus others long ago brought under control in the United States, threw themselves on the mercy of a handful of mission hospitals and already overworked doctors.'[2] Such images of a newly independent Congo in desperate need of American saviours were commonplace in the US press in the early 1960s, just as the State Department and the Central Intelligence Agency sought to block Soviet influence and install a pro-Western government. Jay articulated the celebration of economic development in Africa as a means of showing the good will of Americans: 'This is the assistance the church and the United States needs to bring, not atomic weapons and guns.'[3]

Jay's enthusiastic description of his volunteer work expresses the hopes of ecumenical Protestants in Operation Doctor in the early 1960s. The Congo crises, much as the Nigerian civil war of 1967 to 1970, created new prospects for humanitarian medical interventions. Operation Doctor joined other organisations in filling the void left by the departed Belgians and the impoverished Congolese government. With the fate of North American Protestant missions in the DRC unclear in the early 1960s, Operation Doctor's approach

---

1   R. Gildea, "Congo's Operation Doctor." *World Outlook* (September 1962), 1.

2   Ibid., 1.

3   Ibid., 3.

appeared to be a possible alternative to the colonial-era model of medical services offered by individual denominations. Operation Doctor demonstrated a practical, altruistic model of ecumenical ideals faced with the challenges of African decolonisation.

Operation Doctor's chaotic origins in 1960 led to a small but steady supply of North American medical professionals from 1961 to 1964. The Church World Service (CWS), the main benefactor of the programme, had envisioned Operation Doctor as a five-year project that would close down once the DRC's state medical services were ready. However, the Simba revolts disrupted Operation Doctor's ability to convince professionals to come to the Congo. Although a small number of medical professionals joined from 1964 to 1966, the CWS effectively terminated Operation Doctor by ending its financial support and curtailing recruitment by 1967. Other conflicts attracted the attention of US volunteers and US donors, particularly the Biafra and Vietnam wars.

As it tried to fill the vacuum caused by the sudden end of the Belgian paternalist colonial medical system, Operation Doctor was an experimental project that tried to separate itself from the baggage of colonialism and the Cold War. In contrast to much of the historical work on colonial medical missionaries that highlights how biomedicine reaffirmed colonial racial and gendered hierarchies, the CPRA's medical programme had very little control over institutions, donors, and medical practice. Mission boards and government authorities permitted the CPRA to send volunteers rather than directly control hospitals and clinics. Since the CWS was by far the main financial sponsor of Operation Doctor, the CPRA could not effectively run its medical programme without the permission of its main patron. The CPRA also lacked the personnel to supervise the actions of volunteers in the field.

Recruits considered Operation Doctor to be a politically impartial movement against suffering. Operation Doctor drew support from donors and participants through its generalised presentations of Congolese in need, rather than by highlighting the threat of Communist subversion. Liisa Malkki has observed how generic narratives of suffering obscure the political context of particular setting for humanitarian action.[4] Press coverage of Operation Doctor featured images of benevolent (and almost always white) medical staff working with sick Africans. In contrast to David Grenfell's openly partisan position for the FNLA (Frente Nacional de Libertação de Angola), Operation Doctor maintained itself as an apolitical aid operation.

---

4   Malkki, *Need to Help.*

The short-term medical missionary team became ubiquitous as a form of ministry from North America to other countries from the 1990s, but the historical development of this phenomenon still remains obscure. Melani McAlister and David Hollinger have respectively analysed foreign service programmes and short-term missions that emerged from evangelical and ecumenical Protestant churches.[5] Both mainline and evangelical Protestants believed that importing American technology and culture could radically improve other societies, much as the Peace Corps did.[6] Operation Doctor, in keeping with its ecumenical Protestant foundation, focused on technical expertise much more than on converting Congolese, even if individual volunteers may have identified themselves as evangelicals. Furthermore, Operation Doctor's membership indicates grassroots short-term medical missions formed in the 1960s, even before such missions drew more national attention in the following decade. The careers of CPRA short-term medical missionaries demonstrate the project was part of a broader Protestant medical outreach to African, Caribbean, and Asian countries in the 1950s and 1960s. The programme also allowed volunteers to focus on their own individual experiences as medical staff, consumers, and tourists, just as McAlister notes how evangelical short-term missions constituted 'a sanctified kind of travel' which participants hoped would transform 'their own hearts and minds'.[7]

Interviews and written sources demonstrate how participants wrestled with how to fit short-term service with their broader plans. Physicians with successful practices had the financial resources to step back from their professional careers. Participants who had only recently graduated had the freedom to join Operation Doctor and then complete their internships after returning from the DRC. A group of a dozen or so medical professionals in Indianapolis made agreements with their employers to rotate their mission work in the DRC. These calculations included challenges to prevailing views on gender and family. A number of married couples had children during their participation in the Congo, while single female volunteers challenged racialised stereotypes of the dangers white women faced in the DRC.

Operation Doctor also marks a significant departure from better-known examples of shifting public health after the end of colonial rule. The limited research on public health in African countries following independence indicates Western doctors from the colonial era continued to serve in medical

---

5   Hollinger, *Protestants Abroad*, 252–65; McAlister, *Kingdom*, 195–212.

6   E.C. Hoffman, *All You Need Is Love: The Peace Corps and the Spirit of the 1960s* (Cambridge, MA: Harvard University Press, 2000).

7   McAlister, *Kingdom*, 197.

institutions in the 1960s. Many other African governments showcased medicine as a form of nation building in the 1960s and a means of establishing a
developmentalist state.[8] This was not the case in the DRC. Contrasted with
the massive commitment to public health in South and East Asian countries in
the 1950s and 1960s, the Congolese state's efforts were particularly unimpres-
sive.[9] Prolonged political conflicts ensured the Congolese government would
not commit many resources to medical institutions until Mobutu Sese Seko
had solidified his power. Medical NGOs operated with little governmental
oversight in the DRC in the 1960s. This was particularly the case outside
of urban hospitals and clinics. Franklin Baer, a director of Protestant public
health programmes in the 1980s, noted: 'Responsibility for rural health fell
increasingly to mission hospitals who were setting up their own dispensaries.
This resulted by 1970 in a motely of services. Within a given geographical
area one might find state, Catholic, Protestant and private dispensaries each
with an independent administration.'[10] In this environment, projects such as
Operation Doctor emerged, prefiguring the host of foreign medical missions
and NGOs which entered the DRC in droves in the 1990s.

The twilight of Operation Doctor coincided with the uneven emergence of
government-run public health programmes. Congolese officials did sponsor
medical education at home and abroad, and by 1964, some of these graduates began to work in hospitals outside of Kinshasa. The new authoritarian
order under Mobutu imposed itself on medical practice by the early 1970s
by partially resurrecting the alliance between state authority and medical
missionaries that had largely come undone in the first decade of Congolese
independence. The Zairian government recruited foreign doctors, established
ambitious plans with USAID funding for improving rural public health, and
used medical information as a means of enforcing state authority. The gradual

8   For examples, see P.W. Geissler, "Parasite Lost: Remembering Modern Times
     with Kenyan Government Scientists," in P.W. Geissler, and C. Molyeneux (eds)
     *Evidence, Ethos, and Experiment: The Anthropology and History of Medical Research
     in Africa* (New York: Berghahn, 2011), 297–332; T. Giles-Vernick and J. Webb, Jr.,
     (eds) *Global Health in Africa* (Athens, OH: Ohio University Press, 2013).

9   S. Amrith, *Decolonizing International Health: India and Southeast Asia, 1930–1965.*
     New York: Palgrave, 2006; L. Bu and K.C. Yip (eds), *Public Health and Nation-
     al Reconstruction in Post-War Asia: International Influences, Local Transformations*
     (New York: Routledge, 2015).

10   Franklin Baer, "SANRU: Lessons Learned (1981–1991)," (Unpublished manu-
     script, 1992), 6. Available at sanru.org/documents/sanru-lessons-learned.pdf (Ac-
     cessed 3 March 2020).

collapse of Mobutu's regime and the onset of new civil wars in the 1990s opened the door to a new era of foreign medical volunteer projects.

With the majority of missionary doctors evacuated at independence, mission boards could no longer be sure that their medical work could continue. Operation Doctor was an ecumenical response to this period of uncertainty. Most US and Canadian missions in the DRC never entirely abandoned their medical work, but once the disruption of the civil wars had begun to fade away by 1967, the justification for maintaining an interdenominational volunteer programme outside of any particular mission structure also lost support. Bolstering Congolese capacity in primary care took precedence over short-term volunteer staffing. Donors like the CWS focused more on other crises and became frustrated with continued Congolese Protestant demands for financial aid (as will be discussed at length in chapter 7). The era of ad hoc improvisation exemplified by Operation Doctor came to an end. Though the CPRA continued to be engaged in public health, the loose organisation and foreign-run model of Operation Doctor appears only to have made a return to the Congo during the collapse of centralised state authority after 1990.

Healing the Congo: An overview of Operation Doctor

The onset of Congolese independence set off a major health crisis. Belgian officials had celebrated government and missionary healthcare as virtuous examples of Belgian paternalist rule. Medical authority worked hand in hand with colonial efforts to control African mobility, encourage population growth, and promote the formation of a healthy African workforce for Belgian companies.[11] Though the Belgian government had invested significantly in public health particularly after World War II, the colonial government had done nothing to train Congolese physicians. Not a single Congolese doctor worked in the entire country at independence. After Congolese troops revolted against Belgian officers a mere week after Congolese independence on 30 June 1960, private as well as government doctors fled the country. Most American Protestant medical missionaries also joined the exodus of health professionals

---

11 M. Lyons, "Public Health in Colonial Africa: The Belgian Congo," In D. Porter (ed.) *The History of Public Health and the Modern State* (Amsterdam: Rodopi, 1994), 356–84. For an overview of public health from the perspective of a Belgian health official, see M. Kivits, "Hygiene et santé publique," in *Livre blanc: Apport scientifique de la Belgique au développement de l'Afrique*, vol. 2 (Brussels: Academie Royale des Sciences d'Outre-mer, 1963), 899–916.

in July 1960. This came even as Congolese president Joseph Kasavubu pleaded with American Baptist missionaries to send physicians to the DRC.[12]

Bill Rule and Glen Tuttle, two of the original CPRA team who returned to the DRC in the summer of 1960, put together the medical mission programme. Glen Tuttle was particularly prepared to organise Operation Doctor. From early in his career in the colonial era, Tuttle had promoted training Africans to take on medical procedures normally taken on by trained doctors, including hernia surgeries and cesarean sections.[13] In 1953, he became the first director of the Institut Médical Evangélique (IME), a hospital located in the town of Kimpese in Bas-Congo province staffed with doctors and nurses from over a dozen different mission boards. As an interdenominational project, IME was a precursor of the CPRA and an example of how Protestant missionaries sought to claim a role in medical work in the DRC. Rule, a Presbyterian missionary doctor, collaborated with the Congolese ministry of health and mission boards to place doctors and nurses.

In October and November 1960, Bill Rule met with officials of most of the Congolese provincial ministers of health along with the health ministry of the Autonomous State of South Kasai.[14] In Mbandaka, World Health Organisation doctors and the head provincial health officer reported that at least a dozen government hospitals had no doctors.[15] A World Health Organisation doctor and a Congolese hospital director reported there were only four doctors in Kasai province.[16] Compared to Equateur province's grand total of three doctors in government service, the northeast Orientale province had thirty-eight doctors mainly working in Kisangani, the largest city in the province.[17] William Rule also negotiated in December 1960 and January 1961

---

12 J.L. Spragg, American Baptist Foreign Missionary Society, to Chester Jump, 22 July 1960, Box 14, Record Group 8, Folder Congo Emergency June–July 1960, CWS/PHS.

13 Keith, *First Wars*, 68.

14 The following is drawn from Notes on Bill Rule's Trip to the Provincial Capitals (CPRA Medical Relief), *Congo Protestant Relief Agency* 7 (29 November 1960), 2-4, Folder 5 Congo Protestant Relief Agency News Sheets, Box 137, Post-War Baptist International Mission, American Baptist Foreign Mission Society, ABH-SA.

15 Ibid., 2–3.

16 Rule III, *Milestones*, 143.

17 Notes on Bill Rule's Trip to the Provincial Capitals (CPRA Medical Relief), *Congo Protestant Relief Agency* 7 (29 November 1960): 2-4, Folder 5 Congo Protestant Relief Agency News Sheets, Box 137, Post-War Baptist International Mission, American Baptist Foreign Mission Society, ABHSA; Rule III, *Milestones*, 148.

with Congolese officials to ensure approval of volunteer doctors, even if they did not know French or have experience in tropical medicine. Rule stitched together through a long series of meetings an emergency programme of doctors using airplanes to visit rural hospitals. Cleophas Kamitatu, the influential leader of the Parti Solidaire Africain, endorsed Rule's plans along with a number of provincial officials in different provinces.[18]

CPRA staff in the USA soon found donors willing to send supplies. CPRA member Roland Metzger secured agreements with the United Nations mission in DRC and the World Health Organisation in August 1960.[19] The International Medical Association (IMA), a charity that distributed medicine donated by various companies, agreed to send drugs to the Congolese office of CPRA. Evangelical hostility to internationalism did not preclude aid to the medical programme. However, finding doctors willing to join Operation Doctor proved more trying than obtaining material aid.

Recruitment and motives of Operation Doctor volunteers

After the CIA helped orchestrate military officer Joseph-Désiré Mobutu's coup against Lumumba in September 1960, which placed a new pro-Western government in power, the CPRA began to recruit new doctors to come to the DRC by contacting mission boards and medical schools. Recruitment relied on word of mouth, individual connections with missionaries in the Congo, Protestant magazines, and interdenominational organisations. Over a dozen informants claimed they first heard about Operation Doctor through the Christian Medical Society, an interdenominational organisation that drew members from ecumenical Protestant churches as well as evangelical denominations. Christian Medical Society director Raymond Knighton joined future surgeon director C. Everett Koop in a visit to Kinshasa in 1961. He also had recruitment brochures sent to over 2000 of its members.[20] American missionaries convinced Charles Proudfit and Wendell Kingsolver (father of author Barbara Kingsolver) to join Operation Doctor.[21] Still others had relatives who were missionaries in the DRC.[22]

---

18   Rule III, *Milestones*, 153–6, 159–60.

19   George Carpenter, CWS, to William Du Val, World Council of Churches, 25 August 1960, Folder Congo Emergency August 1960, Box 14, Record Group 8, CWS/PHS.

20   Bob Miller to William Snyder and Orie Miller, 6 January 1961, Folder 105/139 Congo Office 1961, IX-6-3, Box 181, MCCA.

21   W. Kingsolver, "The Congo," *YouTube*, 18 February 2018, Accessible at: www.youtube.com/watch?v=aisg6ABcP7U (Accessed 28 October 2019).

22   Interview, Arthur and Peggy Gerdes, 3 November 2016.

Harold Raines, the United Methodist bishop of Indianapolis, aggressively recruited doctors. Over a dozen doctors and nurses came to Operation Doctor through his efforts. Since many of the doctors worked at hospitals, it was easier for them to set up rotations of three-month terms. Richard Nay, originally convinced to go the Congo by Raines, helped recruit several more doctors and medical students on his own.[23] These personal connections explain why Indiana had by far the largest number of recruits at 25, more than any other state or province. Although the United Methodist Church in the US firmly backed the Katangese secession, Raines appears to have kept open partisanship to a minimum. The CPRA avoided endorsing the Katangese state. Methodist volunteers worked at the remote Katangese Methodist mission at Kapanga, the capital of the Ruund kingdom far from the fighting in other parts in Katanga.

The programme had its greatest success in recruitment between late 1961 and 1963. The CPRA only managed to get its first two new medical volunteers after its founders at the end of 1960, leprosy expert Oliver Hasselblad and New Orleans obstetrician E. Dorothea Nix. Applications only significantly picked up in the summer of 1961. Between November 1961 and December 1963, over 20 Operation Doctors per month served as volunteers. This coincides with the collapse of the Lumumbist counter government based in Kisangani and the secession movements in South Kasai and Katanga. The relative calm of this period did not convince family members and friends of volunteers that going to the Congo could be safe, though. Buford Washington, an eye doctor and among the handful of African American Operation Doctor members, told guests at a CPRA luncheon in New York of how others reacted to his decision to go to the DRC: 'This was during the time when the newspapers were having a heyday writing about all the atrocities, and everyone was telling me, "You have to be crazy even to consider going."'[24] Once the Simba revolts began in earnest by early 1964, applications dropped precipitously.

CPRA staff in New York, with representatives of mission boards, reviewed applications from individual doctors. Unfortunately, relatively few applications for volunteer positions have survived. CPRA executive committee members were more concerned with technical competence and psychological stability than judging the faith lives of volunteers as long as they identified as Protestants. Harold Brewster, a Methodist missionary doctor who served on CPRA's medical applicant committee, noted that CPRA's early demands for proof of

23 Interview, Lois Smith Markham, 19 June 2018.

24 *Congo Protestant Relief Agency News Sheet* 43 (28 February 1963), Folder 6 Congo Protestant Relief Agency News Sheets, Box 137, Post-War Baptist International Mission, American Baptist Foreign Mission Society, ABHSA.

the religious views, psychological character, and medical expertise of candidates was too cumbersome. 'To expect that these doctors would produce the same kind of statement of faith and missionary motivations which candidates are required to have who are volunteering for full time missionary service, I think, is unrealistic,' he noted in March 1961.[25]

CPRA staff and their collaborators in the DRC, particularly at the IME hospital, worried particularly about candidates who lacked in their view the necessary flexibility and basic knowledge of Africa to work in the field. David Wilson, the head of IME, opposed approving an x-ray specialist in 1966. 'His statement of belief is such as to make us feel that he might find it difficult to fit into our community ... He seems to have no understanding of Africa and its present problems. Although I appreciate his dependence upon Christ, to say "I haven't read or cared about the world" is about as impractical as his statement that "if you just smile that will breach any language barrier".'[26] Particularly after applications for the programme plummeted following the revolts of 1964, CPRA staff tried with limited success to convince mission hospital directors to accept volunteers whose personalities might not make them ideal candidates.[27]

CPRA secretary Helen Bjertness tried to persuade David Wilson to take two candidates he did not want at IME, Elsa Bell and Robert Grant. Bell's references drew on stereotypes about women to raise questions with Wilson: 'The physical, political and social strain of a situation like ours make it very unwise to accept someone who is described as being "somewhat over-emotional, argumentative, easily offended, frequently worried and anxious".'[28] Bjertness argued that the candidates' alleged inflexibility owed much to their gendered and racial identities: '[Bell] has personality difficulties which are in part due to her feeling, perhaps justified, perhaps not, of having to fight against a man's world in attaining her professional goals ... Mr. Smith has some of the same tendencies, and for somewhat the same reasons. Any sensitive individual

---

25 Harold Brewster to Roland Metzger, 3 March 1961, Folder CPRA Screening Committee, Box 14, Record Group 8, CWS/PHS.

26 David Wilson to Helen Bjertness, 13 June 1966, Folder Congo Protestant Relief Agency (CPRA), 1964–1967, Box 14, Record Group 8, CWS/PHS.

27 Though no statistics on applicant numbers can be determined from available records, CPRA secretary Helen Bjertness reported a decline in applications between 1964 and 1966. Helen Bjertness to David Wilson, 22 September 1966, Folder Congo Protestant Relief Agency (CPRA), 1964–1967, Box 14, Record Group 8, CWS/PHS.

28 David Wilson to Helen Bjertness, 8 September 1966, Folder Congo Protestant Relief Agency (CPRA), 1964–1967, Box 14, Record Group 8, CWS/PHS.

living in the United States today cannot help but be aware of the situation that might make an American Negro defensive, argumentative, and over-emotional.'[29] Such statements might explain why only a relatively small number of single women and African-Americans participated in Operation Doctor.

Individual doctors often presented their choice to come to DRC as a religious calling. Antonio Feliciano, a Filipino surgeon who was the sole volunteer to come from outside of North America and Europe, asserted: 'I have realised why a person would come to this part of the world to serve Jesus Christ and God ... We have come to realise why others come and stay. It is the feeling of being needed and helping our fellow humanity,' he wrote in 1961.[30] Robert Wesche observed in a similar vein, 'As I left New York City for four months service in the Congo I tried to decide why I was going. The one thing that did drive me on was that I was impressed that this was the will of God.'[31] Some viewed a visit as a test to see if they wanted to become full-time medical missionaries in the future.[32] Despite his involvement in a Baptist church, volunteer William Kunkel was described by his son as an atheist who simply wanted to help others.[33] His skepticism apparently remained quiet enough not to attract attention.

CPRA staff were concerned about behaviour that they deemed to be signs of instability, even if candidates demonstrated their commitment to Christian belief. The case of Margaret Ogilvie particularly vexed CPRA staff. Ogilvie had originally worked with the Unevangelised Field Mission (UFM) fundamentalist mission in northeastern Congo. After she spoke in tongues for the first time in 1963, the UFM forced her to resign since the mission rejected Pentecostal beliefs.[34] Ogilvie's candidacy led to some controversy at the CPRA when she applied in 1965. Her references did her no favours: 'She only has one major problem and that is her definiteness of opinion which does not leave room for other possibilities, i.e., she has stated many times that missions

29 Helen Bjertness to David Wilson, 22 September 1966, Folder Congo Protestant Relief Agency (CPRA), 1964–1967, Box 14, Record Group 8, CWS/PHS.

30 *Congo Protestant Relief Agency Newsletter* 15 (August 1961), 1, Folder 5 Congo Protestant Relief Agency News Sheets, Box 137, Post-War Baptist International Mission, American Baptist Foreign Mission Society, ABHSA.

31 *Congo Protestant Relief Agency Newsletter* 17 (January 1962), 1, Folder 5 Congo Protestant Relief Agency News Sheets, Box 137, Post-War Baptist International Mission, American Baptist Foreign Mission Society, ABHSA.

32 Interview, Clayton Peters, 23 January 2016.

33 Interview, Paul Kunkel, 26 January 2016.

34 Margaret Ogilvie to Helen Bjertness, 7 January 1965, Folder CPRA Screening Committee, Box 14, Record Group 8, CWS/PHS.

should not be in education but should get into village evangelism exclusively. Frankly, I am amazed she has applied to CPRA for she has told us she will not be going into medical work in the future as evangelism is her calling now.'[35] Another praised her strong character and impeccable skills, but added she was 'intolerant of a man's "superiority complex" but I don't think these things would reduce her effectiveness.'[36] Male candidates rarely encountered such scrutiny. Despite these objections, the CPRA screening still accepted her.

Ogilvie's particular background and motivations were somewhat unusual among the approximately 78 individuals who participated in Operation Doctor between 1960 and 1966. Interviews with surviving Operation Doctor participants reveal a complex set of motivations. For Mennonites, Operation Doctor served as an alternative to military service. Elizabeth Shelly, a physician who worked with her husband in Kwilu province, initially responded to the question of what brought her to Congo: 'Ask my husband!' She and Walter Shelly were both Mennonite physicians, and her husband decided to declare himself a conscientious objector from mandatory US military service.[37] Ray Milhous chose to fulfill their two years of volunteer work in lieu of military service as a conscientious objector. The Mennonite Central Committee offered Ray Milhous and his wife Ruth (a nurse) two choices where he could go as a volunteer doctor: Labrador or the DRC. Remembering why he turned down a Canadian rural post, Milhous laughed as he recalled, 'The reason why we weren't participating [in the military] was not because we were afraid to go to a war zone. We were doing it on principles that no one should be fighting ... Going to the Congo was more consistent with our beliefs [than going to Canada].'[38]

Operation Doctor also allowed individuals to test whether or not they wanted to make missionary work their career. Some volunteers had family members or other connections to missionaries. Arthur Gerdes had an older sister who had become a Mennonite Brethren medical missionary in the DRC in 1955.[39] 'I wasn't really certain of what I wanted to do in the long term

---

35 Jean Raddon reference, Margaret Ogilvie Operation Doctor application, 27 January 1965, Folder CPRA Screening Committee, Box 14, Record Group 8, CWS/ PHS.

36 Mrs A. Larson reference, Margaret Ogilvie Operation Doctor application, 25 January 1965, , Folder CPRA Screening Committee, Box 14, Record Group 8, CWS/ PHS.

37 Interview, Elizabeth Shelly, 13 January 2016.

38 Interview, Ray and Ruth Milhous, 8 January 2016.

39 Interview, Arthur and Peggy Gerdes, 3 November 2016.

[and I felt] a little restless about mission work,' he later recalled.[40] Clayton Peters, a Mennonite dentist, had a brother who was a youth volunteer in the DRC shortly before independence. 'Our two years in the Congo were not as an alternative work instead of going to the military. It was not that. We volunteered to see if we wanted [to be missionaries] for life,' Peters said.[41] Jim Stough was the son of a parents stationed at Africa Inland Mission posts in northeastern Congo. His mother died from an infection after repeated cases of tonsillitis. The day before his mother passed way, Stough promised her on her deathbed that he would become a doctor. His father pressured him to become a missionary. As Stough put it, 'My father used to put guilt trips on me. He was a good travel agent. He liked to dispense a lot of guilt trips.'[42] A return to the DRC with Operation Doctor allowed Stough to consider following his father's dream without committing completely to it. Only about ten volunteers became full-time missionaries once their time in Operation Doctor ended.

A small number of recruits actually had been missionaries. Prior to independence, Mark Poole was a doctor at the Presbyterian mission at Bulape, the capital of the Kuba kingdom in Kasai province. To train medical assistants so they could maintain the hospital, Poole agreed to go back for four months in 1961.[43] Besides Poole and Witt, no others beyond the original CPRA founders had previously been medical missionaries in the DRC. The project also did not attract doctors who already had been missionaries elsewhere. The only exception was orthopedic surgeon Edward Payne. He had already worked in Ethiopia with the Sudan Inland Mission and sat on several missionary boards prior to volunteering for the Congo.[44]

In keeping with the rise of ecumenicalism among mainline Protestants, no single denomination made up a majority of volunteers. Methodists and Mennonites made up more than forty per cent of the total number of volunteers. Mainline Protestant churches such as the United Church of Canada, the American Baptists, and the Disciples of Christ comprised another third of Operation Doctor members. What is more noticeable are the churches that were not represented at all. Only a few members identified with an evangelical church. Some denominations such as the Africa Inland Mission

40 Ibid.

41 Interview, Clayton Peters, 23 January 2016.

42 Interview, James Stough, 26 February 2016.

43 Mark Poole, "Reflections Based on CPRA Diary of 1961 Assignment to Congo and Other Reminiscences," (Unpublished manuscript, 1967), Amelia Poole Sudderth Archives, Waco, Texas. I thank Ms. Sudderth for providing this manuscript to me.

44 "Obituaries: Dr Edward B. Payne," *Arizona Republic* (28 January 1976), 14.

refused at first to take Operation Doctor members because the CPRA accepted funds from the World Council of Churches (WCC), a *bête noire* of conservative Protestants. Jim Stough grew up in the theologically conservative Evangelical Free Church. Even so, the Africa Inland Mission refused to take him because of the CPRA/WCC connection.[45] Since conservative evangelical missions predominated in eastern DRC, very few Operation Doctor members went there.

No matter what denomination participants belonged to, a common theme among volunteers was a sense that work in the DRC would fulfill a vital need in ways that never could compare with the more mundane demands of practice in North America. Despite (or perhaps because of) the technological successes of North American biomedicine in the 1940s and 1950s, volunteers believed the DRC was more fulfilling than the tedium of their regular working lives. William Kunkel stated that his time in Congo was more meaningful than in America because it did not involve the 'profit motive that destroys so much of the spirit of medicine.'[46] Nicholas Siksay, a Canadian doctor, echoed this sentiment in his application: 'Although we do not consider that we could, for all time, leave this Western way of life, we do feel … in a setting such as the Congo offers, that we would be more useful in that short time than we could ever hope to be in the whole of our lives here in Canada. We sincerely look forward to the opportunity, and – in truth – life experience in the Congo.'[47] Volunteer doctor David Fluck wrote of his Operation Doctor colleague William Kunkel, 'He felt [his service] was perhaps due to a guilty conscience like many Americans have at the present time, knowing that they live in such a bountiful and comfortable land while much of the world is hungry, unhoused, and ill'.[48]

Although most volunteers did not have close ties to other participants in Operation Doctor, the Indianapolis group of doctors developed a sense of camaraderie based on this common encounter with the Congo. Beverly Maxam recalled how he and other doctors had made an agreement. Volunteers who

45 Interview, Jim Stough, 26 February 2016.

46 *Congo Protestant Relief Agency News Sheet* 17 (January 1962): 2, Folder 5 Congo Protestant Relief Agency News Sheets, Box 137, Post-War Baptist International Mission, American Baptist Foreign Mission Society, ABHSA.

47 Quoted in Helen Bjertness to CPRA Screening Committee, 29 June 1965, CPRA Screening Committee, Box 14, Record Group 8, CWS/PHS. Siksay's entire application was not preserved.

48 *Congo Protestant Relief Agency News Sheet* 19 (May 1962), Folder 5 Congo Protestant Relief Agency News Sheets, Box 137, Post-War Baptist International Mission, American Baptist Foreign Mission Society, ABHSA.

had already gone over 'wouldn't talk about what they did or what happened while they were there. I had no experiences to try to anticipate what was going to happen … We'd have our own experience. When we'd get back together, well, there was lots of talking between us.'[49] A search for authentic individual experiences, not just out of selfless sacrifice, thus became an attraction for the programme. This juxtaposition between the banalities of comfort and the individual value of service in poor African countries, along with the possibilities of building a sense of personal community for those volunteers who went over as a group, did not directly reference Christian belief.

As heartfelt and seemingly apolitical as such statements might have been, they reflected a common sense among some participants that Congolese were utterly unprepared for independence. Roger Youmans, a doctor stationed at Sona Bata in Bas-Congo province, recalled a range of images of political disaster, warfare, and rape. 'The Congolese people were both helpless and pathetic. I turned away in anguish and tried to push those images out of my mind, but I couldn't … The reports and images haunted me and I kept thinking about what I could do in one of those abandoned hospitals,' Youmans wrote.[50] After returning from a two-month stint at the Gemena hospital in Equateur province, Eugene Damstra informed a journalist in 1964: 'There is a saying in Congo: "Now that we have our independence, when will you take it back?" … These people just weren't ready for independence. They will do anything for a little authority, but they have few doctors, lawyers, trained men to help the country.'[51]

Some CPRA volunteers incorrectly believed that the Belgians had completely abandoned Congolese hospitals. William Rule III's memoirs include references to many doctors who had stayed in the DRC, predominantly in urban centres, even as few stayed behind in rural posts.[52] Yet the narrative of a country entirely bereft of physicians still had adherents. 'The [DRC] had just gained its independence from Belgium and nearly all the Belgian doctors departed, involuntarily, I believe,' wrote volunteer Ernest Carlson.[53] Elizabeth Shelly asserted, '[The Congolese] had kicked [the Belgians] all out. The

---

49 Interview, Beverly Maxam, 1 February 2016.

50 R. Youmans, *When Bull Elephants Collide: An American Surgeon's Chronicle of Congo* (Tarentum, PA: Word Association Publishers, 2006), 4.

51 R. Morrow, "Local Doctor Never Met Carson – But Knew Him," *Dayton Daily News*, 29 November 1964, 23.

52 Rule III, *Milestones*, 143–65.

53 E. Carlson, *Autobiography* ([No place of publication]: Self-published, no date [c. 1996]), chapter XII, 4.

Belgians hadn't gotten any Zairian doctors.'[54] Several other former volunteers echoed similar views.[55] Such images of the DRC as a region in need of Western intervention was nothing new, but this particular point allowed volunteers to distance themselves from a direct connection with the colonial past.

Operation Doctor's membership was significantly different from participants of volunteer programmes such as the Peace Corps and VISTA. The average age of a volunteer was nearly 40, although a significant number of members (31 out of 78) were born after 1930. 4 volunteers out of 78 were people of colour, in keeping with the vast white middle- and upper-class majority of North American doctors. Out of 23 female participants, only 6 were unmarried. Besides the time needed to complete medical school, the challenges of beginning a career after graduation complicated the ability of younger doctors and nurses to join. These obstacles also threatened to undermine the ideal of male doctors supporting their families. Roger Youmans noted, 'There were many obstacles in the way of my going to Congo at all ... We did not have the money to support me in Congo and my wife here in America, nor did we have the money to transport the family to return.'[56] Another volunteer noted how his work slowed down his career: 'I'd been in practice for a little more than two years [before leaving for the DRC], and those of you who have practiced know it takes at least that long when you're starting from scratch.'[57]

Middle-aged and elderly doctors, by contrast, had the financial means to take an extended amount of time away from their practice. For older volunteers, committing to Operation Doctor demonstrated their ability to step away from their careers. Sydney Cable convinced a colleague to temporarily take over his successful practice, even though his oldest son Ritchard resented his father's decision to leave for months with his mother expecting the fifth child in the family.[58] Retirees, naturally, had even more flexibility. Floyd Woodward

---

54 Interview, Elizabeth Shelly, 13 January 2016.

55 Interview, Carol Swarts, 21 March 2016; Interview, Lois Smith Markham, 19 June 2018.

56 *Congo Protestant Relief Agency News Sheet* 27 (6 September 1962), Folder 5 Congo Protestant Relief Agency News Sheets, Box 137, Post-War Baptist International Mission, American Baptist Foreign Mission Society, ABHSA.

57 *Congo Protestant Relief Agency News Sheet* 43 (28 February 1963), Folder 6 Congo Protestant Relief Agency News Sheets, Box 137, Post-War Baptist International Mission, American Baptist Foreign Mission Society, ABHSA.

58 Interview, Ritchard Cable, 19 February 2016.

(b. 1892), a late convert to Christianity, agreed to go after reading about the project in a Methodist magazine.[59]

Perhaps the most remarkable example of an established physician who used the CPRA to continue a personal commitment to service was V. McKinley Wiles, a Barbadan immigrant who had become a nationally respected urologist. Wiles, one of the three African-American volunteers, had operated on the legendary singer Paul Robeson and had even testified to the House Un-American Activities Committee about the extraordinary stresses his most famous patient bore.[60] He was the sole Operation Doctor volunteer who had already gone to the DRC independently as well as to Nigeria to assist in hospitals after independence.[61] After his time in the DRC, Wiles went to Mississippi in 1963 and reported on the wretched state of public health for African Americans there.[62]

Only six participants in Operation Doctor were single women. For young female participants, Congo service allowed them to combine a personal sense of exploration with a broader commitment to aid and mission work. Lois Smith Markham, a medical technician straight out of university, went to the DRC heeding her mother's strong interest in travel and adventure.[63] Markham's sense of African volunteer work as a means of self-discovery was shared by Carol Swarts. Originally from a small farming town in Nebraska, Swarts took pride in managing to achieve her childhood dream of becoming a doctor: 'Always wanted to be a physician, which was pretty unique back then. How many times was I told be a nurse.'[64] When CPRA founders Warren and Gretchen Berggren asked Swarts to help in the Congo, she interrupted her internship to join Operation Doctor.

Though the membership of Operation Doctor demonstrated how much white men dominated the medical profession in the 1950s and early 1960s, CPRA medical volunteers did differ significantly in terms of origins, their relationship to mission work, and their careers. CPRA evaluators did not pay close attention to individual religious convictions in their search for candidates as mission boards normally would have done for medical missionaries. Rather than emphasise denominational divisions, the programme put into practice the

59 Helen Bjertness to CPRA Screening Committee, 22 October 1962, Folder CPRA Screening Committee, Box 14, Record Group 8, CWS/PHS.

60 Horne, 2016, 159.

61 "Travelogue," *Jet* (8 January 1959), 40.

62 V.M. Wiles, "Medical Mission to Mississippi," *Freedomways* 5 (1965), 314–17.

63 Interview, Lois Ann Markham, 19 June 2018.

64 Interview, Carol Swarts, 21 March 2016.

ecumenical attitudes that flourished in mainline churches in North America at mid-century. Admittedly, this willingness to ignore denominational differences among Protestants came more from necessity than any clear principles.

Congolese public health, donor cutbacks, and the end of Operation Doctor, 1964–1971

In 1966, the World Council of Church sent the US physician William Nute to conduct a survey of Protestant hospitals in the DRC. He concluded his report with a somewhat sobering warning that 'it should be emphasised that the church is not the state … It cannot take merely the existence of need as sufficient justification for committing itself to programmes which are beyond its strength to carry out adequately'.[65] Particularly concerned that mission boards had overextended themselves to maintaining hospitals from the colonial era, Nute added: 'The analogy of a lifeboat comes to mind. The man at the tiller must make an agonizing choice between jumping overboard to rescue one or two, or remaining in the lifeboat which can ultimately be the means of saving a great many more. It is in the very agony [of] these choices that the true meaning of Christian commitment may be seen.'[66]

Nute's survey described a constellation of hospitals. Big centres such as IME, the American Baptist hospital at Vanga, and the Nyankunde evangelical Protestant hospital in northeastern Congo operated with a large number of expatriate medical professionals. The prognosis at smaller hospitals was less rosy. The Disciples of Christ hospital in Lotumbe in Equateur province, for example, had no clear budget and no credible records on how many patients it treated. 'The doctor is away on various duties from a third to a half of the time, and the fees are too high for the local people to pay … The doctor is an airplane pilot, mechanic, and purchasing agent in addition to answering professional calls to other stations,' observed Nute.[67] Yet other mission hospitals still had no permanent physician on staff since 1960. The Baptist Missionary Society, unable to recruit doctors as in the colonial period, downgraded a number of hospitals into dispensaries without doctors.[68]

---

65   William Nute Jr., "Report on Christian Medical Work in the Congo, September 14 – October 22, 1966," (Unpublished manuscript, 1966), 45, Record Group 8, Box 69, Folder 1 Surveys: Africa, East Africa, Cameroon, Congo, Ethiopia, CWS/PHS.

66   Ibid., 45.

67   Ibid., 13.

68   Ibid., 9.

The collapse of the colonial medical system that engendered Operation Doctor in 1960 no longer excluded Congolese from leadership roles. Nute estimated twenty Congolese had graduated from government medical schools and 225 medical assistants had enrolled in an accelerated medical education programme in France between 1960 and 1966.[69] While these numbers were hardly adequate, one must recall there were no Congolese physicians at independence. Roughly two-thirds of all Congolese physicians worked in Kinshasa, while expatriates predominated at rural medical institutions.[70] Africans had also taken up administrative positions.

Nute's solutions to the adversity (and diversity) of these institutions did not include short-term medical volunteers. While he wanted expatriates to teach at a new Protestant medical school and to collaborate with government universities, he did not recommend the continuation of Operation Doctor.[71] Ideally, Protestant churches would help form the Congolese medical professionals of the future rather than encourage continued dependence on mission boards: 'The Congo cannot be expected to rely indefinitely on expatriate physicians, nor accept permanently the situation in which its own nationals are confined to subordinate positions in the health professions.'[72] The cost of expatriate physicians was high. Relying on short-term doctors also made long-term planning difficult, as demonstrated at the Baptist hospital of Nsona Mpangu: '[Short-term doctors] are reluctant to create issues which they may not be there to see through, or urgent upgrading of equipment.'[73]

Operation Doctor's decline after 1963 was not merely due to new priorities to develop a cadre of Congolese medical professionals. However chaotic the landscape of Congolese medical facilities was, the system was no longer in danger of total collapse. Church World Service staff had originally envisioned that Operation Doctor would only last from 1960 to 1965. If Operation Doctor was a humanitarian enterprise, CWS staff members assumed eventually the DRC would no longer need emergency medical assistance. The majority of volunteers worked in DRC in 1962 and 1963, and the United Nations victory over the Katanga secession and the gradual end of fighting in Kasai province by 1963 suggested the worst of the crisis was over. However, the onset of the leftist rebellion against the Kinshasa-based government in late 1963 led to unprecedented hardship. Violence by government troops, South African and

69 Ibid., 6–7.
70 Ibid., 3.
71 Ibid., 38–9.
72 Ibid., 38.
73 Ibid., 20.

European mercenaries bankrolled by the US Central Intelligence Agency, and the rebels themselves devastated civilians and displaced at least half a million people. These revolts clearly indicated that the DRC still was in a state of emergency in 1964.

Operation Doctor's fortunes waned considerably after the Simba revolts. Paul Carlson, a former CPRA volunteer who became a full-time medical missionary, lost his life to rebels shooting at civilians during the Belgian recapture of Kisangani in November 1964. Though Carlson became the most famous participant from Operation Doctor, his martyrdom did not inspire many other volunteers to join the project. Only a handful of Operation Doctor participants stayed on from the end of 1964. Almost all of them took up positions at IME in Kimpese rather than at poorly-staffed rural hospitals elsewhere. Although a few new recruits went to the DRC in 1965, there were only two volunteers left in the country three years later. Former Operation Doctor participants tried to raise awareness of the programme and even considered extending it to other countries, but neither the CWS nor other institutions committed to these plans.[74] The final volunteer, radiologist Audrey Kimber, worked as a radiologist at Kimpese from 1968 until 1971.[75]

Another reason for the slow end of Operation Doctor were individual mission boards. Instead of backing short-term medical missions, North American and British denominations invested in their Congolese partners' churches. William Rule III left the CPRA in 1961 and soon directed a new Presbyterian training hospital near the city of Kananga, the Institut Medical Chretien du Kasai.[76] The Vanga hospital became the centrepiece of American Baptist involvement in public health under the able command of Dan Fountain, a medical missionary.[77] The Mennonite Central Committee decided to send medical volunteers independently of Operation Doctor, on the grounds the CPRA no longer had the funds to contribute.[78] Mission boards could focus on their own individual programmes as the threat of a complete evacuation had subsided by 1967.

74 Minutes, CPRA in America Executive Committee, 15 February 1965, Folder 75/7 Congo Protestant Relief Agency, OMP.

75 Institut Médical Evangélique, Annual Reports 1968–1969, 1969–1970, 1970–1971, Folder Institut Evangélique Kimpese, Zaire, Box 425.5.030, WCCA.

76 Rule III, *Milestones*, 181–218.

77 D. Fountain, *Health For All: The Vanga Story* (Pasadena, CA: William Carey, 2014).

78 On MCC concerns about the CPRA's finances for Operation Doctor, see Elmer Neufeld to Robert Miller, Folder Congo Office II 111/129, Box 190, 6 February 1964, IX-6-3, MCCA; Elmer Neufeld to Robert Miller, 14 September 1964, Folder Congo Office 1964 I, Box 190, IX-6-03, MCCA.

By the late 1960s, the CPRA also was turning away from stop-gap measures such as Operation Doctor. Congo Protestant Council chairman Jean Bokeleale and CPRA director Samuel Bukasa wanted to create development projects to raise income for the national churches. Outside of continued medical donations from North America and Western Europe, the CPRA became less involved in public health in the early 1970s. It would later again become a key stakeholder in rural healthcare with the ambitious SANRU (Santé Rurale) project (largely funded by USAID) in 1981. It is unclear if the improvisations of Operation Doctor had any influence on later CPRA engagements in public health. Despite its ephemerality, Operation Doctor was a piece of broad engagement by North American doctors in short-term medical service abroad in the 1960s and 1970s.

Lastly, the CWS had become preoccupied with more pressing humanitarian emergencies. The escalation of US military involvement in Vietnam became a central focus of CWS work after 1964.[79] North American Protestants were also increasingly focusing their attention on the widely publicised famine in Biafra by the late 1960s. CWS staff reported financial problems to their CPRA colleagues in 1965. With the famine and refugee crises of the Simba revolts receding by 1966, other countries took priority over the DRC. The CPRA New York office continued to meet and occasionally review applicants to Operation Doctor into at least 1968. However, applicants by this point needed to find other sources of funding.

Mobutu's regime had became more engaged with public healthcare by the early 1970s as a means of promoting national unity.[80] Despite the official cultural nationalist ideology of authenticity, the Zairian state still relied extensively on expatriate medical personnel. Bill Close, a volunteer doctor with the conservative evangelical group Moral Re-Armament, became Mobutu's personal physician and formed his own North American volunteer physician project to staff hospitals from 1970 to roughly 1976.[81] CPRA volunteer Roger Youmans joined this new effort after learning Mobutu had put more than one million dollars behind the project.[82] Missionary doctors continued to provide care at over 400 Congolese clinics and hospitals in 1974 and forty-seven per

79 Gill, *Embattled*.

80 US Government, Department of Health, Education, and Welfare, Office of International Health, Division of Program Analysis, *Syncrisis: The Dynamics of Health: An Analytic Series on the Interactions of Health and Socioeconomic Development. Vol. XIV Zaire*, Washington, DC, 1975, 86–106.

81 Youmans, *Elephants*, 195–289.

82 Ibid., 199–200.

cent of all physicians came from outside the DRC.[83] According to a 1975 US government survey of Congolese public health, Protestant hospitals still operated with a 'lack of direction from government authorities'.[84] But, officials harnessed Protestant hospitals in ways reminiscent of the Belgian colonial state. For example, medical missionary Patricia Evans recalled how Congolese troops took over the IME hospital during a cholera epidemic in the early 1970s. Army planes flew in vaccines. After the military contingent misread the IME staff's vaccine cards and thought their vaccinations were obsolete, soldiers nearly arrested expatriate medical personnel – including the medical director of the hospital, former CPRA volunteer Jim Evans.[85] In Mobutu's Zaire, the government had again taken the upper hand over NGOs and missionaries, ending the more freewheeling era of the early 1960s.

Although few volunteers living in the early 21st century recalled keeping close ties to anyone they had known during their Operation Doctor days, some continued to assist Congolese public health in other ways. Sydney Cable, Wendell Kingsolver, and William Kunkel hosted Congolese health practitioners who received additional training at US hospitals.[86] Albert Knighton financially supported a Congolese student studying medicine at a Canadian university.[87] Richard Nay participated in fundraising activities for the Protestant medical school in Kisangani and agreed to teach there from 1968 to 1971.[88] A few chose to visit their old posts after their retirement. Karin and Bill Arkinstall discovered their surgical instruments at Kibunzi hospital were still in the same place they left them in 1966.[89] Jim Stough, angry that Congolese had neglected the cistern built by missionaries to collect water at Tandala hospital in Equateur province, decided to repair it himself in 2007, more than half a century after he worked there.[90] While its impact may have been fleeting, the Operation Doctor programme did leave traces behind in the history of Congolese public health.

83 US Government, *Syncrisis*, 167–70.

84 Ibid., 108.

85 Interview, Patricia Evans, 15 August 2018.

86 Interview, Paul Kunkel, 26 January 2016; Interview, Ritchard Cable, 19 February 2016; Kingsolver, "The Congo."

87 Personal communication, Jane Oshinowo, 23 July 2018.

88 "Congo's Medical Needs Topic of 'Operation Doctor' Meeting," *Indianapolis Star* (9 May 1970), 12.

89 Interview, Bill and Karin Arkinstall, 18 March 2016.

90 Interview, James Stough, 26 February 2016.

Conclusion

Operation Doctor illuminates the improvisational nature of humanitarian assistance to the DRC in the 1960s. Just as in the cases of CPRA relief to internally displaced persons and foreign refugees, the medical programme was a loosely run project that filled a vacuum left by the collapse of Belgian medical care and the failure of the nascent Congolese state to concern itself with public health. North American ecumenical Protestant medical professionals joined World Health Organisation and Red Cross doctors in providing short-term service. Like these organisations, Operation Doctor participants sought to depoliticise the problems of public health through presenting their work as a Christian response to need. Following David Hollinger, the project can also be seen as part of an extensive period of self-interrogation by North American ecumenical Protestants about their duties towards poor and marginalised people. Cold War rhetoric of fighting Communism did not drive members to join the project. Yet this chapter also suggests that claims about the conservative nature of ecumenical laity in contrast with more liberal and internationalist church leadership in mainline Protestant churches in the 1960s may not be a safe generalisation to rely on.[91]

Operation Doctor in some ways was a transitional programme between the dominance of long-term medical missionaries with the secular and evangelical short-term medical missions of later decades. The CPRA decided to play down theological issues in favour of technical skill. Though faith inspired many participants to join, their motives also reflected the same interest to gain individual life experience that pulled other volunteers into secular organisations such as the Peace Corps in the 1960s. While it is hard to determine how much Operation Doctor directly shaped later short-term medical missions, it is clear that the CPRA medical programme belonged to a broad trend of short-term medical projects in the 1960s and 1970s that doctors and nurses joined. Professionalism took precedence over evangelisation, in contrast to the plethora of explicitly evangelical mission trips later in the 20th century.

The composition of the Operation Doctor project both reflects dominant trends within North American medicine in the mid-20th century and denotes how short-term projects had room for individuals who normally would not have gone abroad to practice medicine. Its largely white, male, married, and middle-aged membership certainly fit the typical profile of doctors in Canada and the US in the 1950s and 1960s. At the same time, CPRA staff were willing to take on very young medical professionals, single women, and a very small number of African Americans. This was again not a deliberate decision

91 Hollinger, *Cloven Tongues.*

to be inclusive so much as a scramble to find competent volunteers, yet the programme thus allowed room for doctors and nurses who did not fit the typical demographics for medical professionals in the early 1960s.

Finally, the growth and eventual decline of Operation Doctor corresponds to the shifting fortunes of Congolese politics and the infrastructure of public health. In 1960 and early 1961, the chaotic evacuations of medical professionals allowed the CPRA to intervene, even if the organisation at first lacked the capability to engage medical professionals. The highest numbers of volunteers came between the fall of 1961 and the end of 1963, a period in which the US-backed Congolese government managed to overcome its major enemies. The civil wars from late 1963 to 1966 disrupted Operation Doctor and Congolese public healthcare. Once Mobutu's authoritarian regime defeated the revolts, mission boards again turned to support their own projects rather than continue Operation Doctor. By the early 1970s, the DRC's public health policies fell more in line with other African governments than in the chaotic early years of independence.

6

Protestant Volunteers and Medical Practice in the Congo in the 1960s

Jim Stough could never forget his first day as a CPRA volunteer doctor in 1962.[1] He had agreed to serve with his wife for two years at Tandala, a rural mission hospital in Equateur province. His first patient was a woman trying with difficulty to deliver her child. Preparing to conduct a cesarean section, Stough performed spinal anesthesia, but had done so too high on the spinal column. He said to his nurses, 'Her diaphragm is paralyzed. We got to hook her up to the anesthesia machine.' Their answer was a reminder he was far from his practice in Illinois: 'Well, we don't have an anesthesia machine.' Stough then told them to infibulate the patient and use a bag valve mask to manually respirate her. There were no masks at the station. 'If I can't sustain her breathing, she's going to die,' Stough said. The nurses agreed. To add to Stough's consternation, he and his nurses were not alone. A crowd had formed to watch the new doctor through the operating room's windows. The woman's husband sat at the foot of the operating table as his wife died, even as the baby survived. Stough left the room and told his wife, 'This isn't for me. We're leaving as soon as we can get out of here.' Instead, someone called him back to perform surgery on a patient with an incarcerated strangulated hernia. He returned to duty.

Stough's improvisations illustrate the challenges for Congolese and volunteers in the Operation Doctor programme. North American doctors had come from what historian James Burham has called the 'golden age' of medicine in the 1950s and early 1960s. Technological breakthroughs helped ensure public confidence in medical professionals, who increasingly worked within a bureaucratic public health structure that emphasised specialisation. If medical care under Belgian rule articulated colonial anxieties, independence had left the position of medical missionaries – particularly volunteers – imbued with insecurities: technical, political, and psychological.

We do not know what the Congolese spectators thought of Stough's vain scramble to keep his patient alive. Yet it is clear the authority of missionaries under Belgian rule could no longer be taken for granted. The paternal

1   The following is drawn from Interview, James Stough, 26 February 2016.

missionary order backed by the colonial state had frayed. Individual volunteers could be threatened by government soldiers and rebels. Volunteers usually lacked the linguistic and cultural competence to effectively communicate with Congolese stakeholders. Even so, Congolese effectively shaped their relationships with medical volunteers in ways that were considerably more egalitarian than one might expect from a public healthcare system that formed in the colonial period. Local communities protected Operation Doctor staff from political threats, since Protestant medical institutions could not count on support from Congolese political leaders.

Volunteer service could reinforce rather than undermine their sense of cultural superiority, even if they objected to what they deemed to be the overly colonialist attitudes of older missionaries. Some volunteers recalled their work in DRC as a mixture of individual successes against a backdrop of deprivation and failure. Especially for doctors at isolated hospitals, where a lack of supplies as well as plentiful adversities plagued their efforts, they found themselves taking on the role of general, independent practitioners that had largely come to an end in North America decades earlier. However, they could also consider themselves allies of a downtrodden Congo.

To reconstruct the choices and the limitations of Operation Doctor volunteers, I use a series of sources that each come with their own problems for interpretation. Only some volunteers wrote reports to mission boards or CPRA staff members. These accounts rarely discuss particular patients or difficulties, although there are some notable exceptions. Interviews with former volunteers and their family members greatly expand on the limited documentation in the archival record. While some family members remembered being in the DRC, others had to rely on stories told by their parents. Catherine Siksay-Smith, daughter of the Canadian volunteer Nicholas Siksay (1939–2000), also raised another challenge: 'He protected his daughters from much "difficult" information to protect us, and I am sure [his] experience [in Congo] falls under that category.'[2] Still others had fragmented memories, such as watching their parents show photographic slides taken in the Congo.[3]

Volunteers' views of Congolese reflected tensions common among North American liberal Protestants regarding race and Africa in the mid-20th century. Volunteers generally did not share the view held by US officials about the cultural and intellectual inferiority of most Africans in the early 1960s, but their work did often assume sharp cultural and even biological differences

2   Catherine Siksay-Smith to Jeremy Rich, personal communication, 24 January 2016.

3   Interview, Paul Kunkel, 26 January 2016.

between Americans and Africans. Only some volunteers learned French or African languages, so their ability to speak directly to Congolese medical workers and patients was limited. Doctors and nurses tended to have little knowledge of most Congolese outside of nurses, domestic servants, and clergy. The dislocations that shook the DRC after independence influenced their views regarding Congolese culture. Volunteers had relatively little understanding of Congolese views on health, so they made broad generalisations rather than be effectively informed by local knowledge.

Despite all of these problems, these interviews also contain a great deal of value about the dilemmas of public health in the Congo crises. Operation Doctor volunteers' accounts of healthcare reveal how Congolese people tried to overcome the near-collapse of Western medicine in the early 1960s. Vignettes about European patients also articulated anxieties about maintaining racial hierarchies after independence. The cohort of volunteers reveal a new dimension to previous research on North Americans working in development and humanitarian projects. The religious dimension of aid work separated Operation Doctor workers from more secular-minded internationalist volunteer programmes such as the Peace Corps.

This chapter will particularly evaluate how Operation Doctors became embroiled in political unrest. Though few Operation Doctor volunteers appear to have many qualms about the US government's role in Congolese politics, they received little attention from US embassy staff. Scattered in largely rural locations, Operation Doctor nurses and doctors relied on the missionary and Congolese communities that hosted them. A central theme of most Operation Doctor informants was their powerlessness in the face of soldiers, political conflict, and a lack of supplies. At the same time, Congolese people clearly looked at Operation Doctor participants as valuable resources both as healers and sources of patronage.

Where soldiers outrank doctors: Operation Doctor volunteers, fractured sovereignty, and armed conflict, 1960–1965

Armed Congolese men frequently took a prominent position in volunteer narratives. Paul Carlson, an Operation Doctor volunteer who later became a medical missionary, was killed by Simba rebels as Belgian paratroopers recaptured the city of Kisangani (then Stanleyville) in 1964.[4] Though Western media publicised this case as proof of the ruthless savagery of the Simba

---

4   L. Carlson Bridges, *Monganga Paul: The Congo Ministry and Martyrdom of Paul Carlson, M.D.* (New York: Harper and Row, 1966).

rebellion, Operation Doctor participants remembered how Armée Nationale Congolaise (ANC) government soldiers were dangerous and unpredictable in their own right. Mark Poole, a Presbyterian missionary surgeon who worked at the Bulape mission hospital in the Kuba kingdom in northern Kasai for over two decades prior to independence in 1960, came back in August 1961 to train his medical staff to work more independently.

Within a week of returning to the DRC, Poole began to traverse the conflicts between ANC troops, United Nations peacekeeping forces, Lulua militias seeking to drive out Luba people from the northern Kasai, and the Katangese secession led by Moïse Tshombe. When a United Nations officer offered to give Poole a ride, the doctor refused. 'I preferred to go separately and not be associated in the minds of the natives, as being closely associated with the UN, because no doubt the [UN] will soon be pulling out, and though most of their actions good and they're helpful, we don't want ... to be considered part of the UN.'[5] As a result, ANC soldiers stopped Poole at checkpoints to see if he was carrying weapons.[6] This early encounter with soldiers went relatively well.

Unluckily for Poole, other soldiers were far less friendly. Poole was a trained pilot as well as a physician. Mutinous soldiers opened fire on his plane as he crossed over territory disputed by the South Kasai government [ASSK] and Lulua militias in September 1962.[7] A month later, Poole's plane colours ended up making him a target, since the Katangese air force also used red and white for their plane markings.[8] Some government troops in the Kasai believed American missionaries were spying for Katanga, and it was no secret that some US missionaries (particularly Methodists) preferred Moïse Tshombe to any leader in the official Congolese government. After being tailed by a UN pilot on the morning of 1 November 1961, Poole landed his plane in Kananga. Drunk mutinous government soldiers seized the European and American population in the city. Soldiers marched Poole at gunpoint with an Austrian UN doctor. The Austrian had foolishly kept a Katangese franc as a keepsake, and managed to sneak the bill to Poole, who tore it up in his pocket rather than be accused of being one of Tshombe's agents.[9] After troops found a radio transmitter where Poole was staying, he and the rest of the missionaries were nearly killed before a provincial official managed to intervene. Poole flew

5   Poole, "Reflections," 6.
6   Ibid., 6.
7   Ibid., 13.
8   Ibid., 20.
9   Ibid., 21.

towards Luebo, but fortunately decided to return to Bulape instead at the last minute. It turned out government troops in Kananga had radioed their counterparts at Luebo to open fire on Poole's plane if it landed.[10]

Several days later, government troops arrived at Bulape and found Poole's hunting rifle and the hospital radio transmitter. They broke the transmitter and started to drag Poole to Mweka, a village roughly 35 kilometers away. Shortly after Poole and his captors started to move, a large group of people from the town of Banzuba surrounded the twenty-eight soldiers. This group had already killed four government soldiers, most likely to protect themselves. Poole later learned the townspeople had agreed to intervene to save the doctor: 'they determined that if I was beaten up or anything drastic was done, that they would kill all of the soldiers.'[11] Intimidated, the ANC troops took Poole back to Bulape, and then stole his car. The next day, some soldiers reentered Bulape, but after some tense moments, convinced Poole to treat their venereal infections.[12]

This willingness to defend doctors sometimes extended to government soldiers themselves. At the Bambuya dispensary, Poole found himself in a dispute regarding the Congolese clinic director. Some members of one ethnic group demanded the resignation of the director since he belonged to a rival community. Poole, unable to resolve the argument, was bailed out by the timely arrival of two ANC deserters. Poole had known one of the soldiers as a boy. The mutinous soldiers turned their rifles on the group at the meeting and showed off their power: '[A] soldier gave them a lecture stating that of course the doctor was there before the Belgians arrived, which made me then over 100 years old, and he said, "Do you agree?" And of course with a rifle on 'em, they agreed. Next, he said, "You know, you'd all be dead if the doctor wasn't here, do you agree?" And nodding to them with a rifle, they agreed.'[13]

Other doctors also became uneasy mediators. The CPRA assigned Ray and Ruth Milhous to work at a hospital in Tshikapa in 1962, a city in the south Kasai province known as a centre of diamond mining. Tshikapa was located on the Kasai River, which marked the de facto border between Lulua, Luba, Pende, and Chokwe rival militias. The city stayed under government control during Kalonji's rule in South Kasai. Though ANC troops definitively defeated Kalonji's South Kasai government in October 1962, the Milhouses became embroiled in bitter disputes between Luba politician Joseph Ngalula,

10 Ibid., 22–3.
11 Ibid., 24.
12 Ibid., 25.
13 Ibid., 28.

the first appointed governor of the newly created Unité Kasaienne province, and his critics. Lulua groups claimed Ngalula had snubbed Lulua people in favour of other ethnic groups, and Kalonji loyalists considered Ngalula (who had been Kalonji's prime minister) a traitor who had sold out the Luba to the Congolese government.

Lulua militias attacked government troops in November 1962 and forced the Milhouses to move from Tshikapa across the river to the smaller Mennonite missionary hospital at Kalonda.[14] At Kalonda, there were no laboratory equipment or x-ray machines available. 'We had to work from the seat of our pants,' Ray Milhous observed.[15] The Kalonda side was made up of Lulua people who were hostile to any Luba patients. When a Lulua woman gave birth in Tshikapa to triplets on Ruth's birthday in December 1962, she could not return home for fear of being attacked by Luba people in the city. A missionary nurse sheltered the woman and her children, but she demanded to return to Kalonda. Ray Milhous drove her past government checkpoints across the river to Tshikapa and then hosted her and her triplets at the house.[16] 'We saved those peoples' lives,' Ray Milhous recalled. United Nations troops guarded the Milhouses in Kalonda. They had less success protecting Lulua patients in Tshikapa. After the Milhouses were briefly evacuated, Luba militiamen killed some Lulua patients too ill to escape.[17]

The Simba revolts also placed some CPRA doctors in harm's way. Unlike the CPRA relief programmes discussed in chapter 4, Operation Doctor volunteers did not view themselves as partners with the Congolese military. Armée Populaire de la Libération (APL) rebel troops found Siksay while he worked at a Methodist hospital at Wembo Nyama in August 1964 and held him until government troops recaptured the east-central Congolese mission station almost three months later.[18] APL forces allowed Siksay to continue his medical work and he never felt seriously threatened by his captors.[19]

---

14 Ray and Ruth Milhous, Activity Report, November 1962, Folder Activity Reports 1963, 107/109, IX-6-3.104, Box 184, MCCA; Interview, Ray and Ruth Milhous, 16 January 2016.

15 Interview, Ray and Ruth Milhous, 16 January 2016.

16 Ibid.

17 Ray and Ruth Milhous, Activity Report, September 1962, Folder Activity Reports 1963, 107/109, IX-6-3.104, Box 184, MCCA.

18 *Congo Protestant Relief Agency News Sheet* 88 (September 1964); *Congo Protestant Relief Agency News Sheet* 90 (October 1964), Folder 6 Congo Protestant Relief Agency, Box 137, BIM Post-War, ABHSA.

19 "Rebels Looted Hospital, Congo Doctor Reports," *Los Angeles Times* (25 November 1964), 10.

Mennonite volunteers Arnold and Lorene Nickel endured two encounters which left them more fearful of the Congolese army than the APL. They initially went to a Protestant missionary in Mukedi run by the American Mennonite Brethren Mission. Mukedi, located in the Kwilu province, became a target of Pierre Mulele's guerilla movement. In early January 1964, Nickel put a cast on the arm of a Belgian Roman Catholic priest. A day later, he learned some of Mulele's soldiers had killed his missionary patient.[20] Mulele's forces seized the town shortly after the Nickels fled and ransacked the hospital. Mennonite Central Committee (MCC) Congo director Elmer Neufeld soon placed the Nickels at the small town of Bolobo, located 150 miles north of Kinshasa on the Congo River. Neufeld had thought this western Congolese post would be far away from rebel forces.

Neufeld was wrong. A small group of Congolese rebels crossed over from the Republic of Congo and briefly captured Bolobo in the summer of 1964, at the height of APL rebel military successes. After APL forces arrived at dawn, government forces immediately fled. 'The fact was brought out that [the people] had not been satisfied with the army or the government till [sic] now and that [the rebels] had something better to offer them … Indeed the soldiers were most polite and kind and were trying to win favour with all,' Lorene Nickel wrote.[21] A rebel doctor trained in China was expected to come to the hospital and the Nickels heard rumours about a technician who was to offer free medicine to the townspeople. The rebels only stayed in Bolobo several days, and Nickel remembered treating a few of them before they withdrew. ANC reinforcements arrived and briefly held the Nickels and the rest of the hospital staff prone on the ground.

The return of the ANC deeply troubled Nickel. He recounted in 2016 that government control 'was very difficult … There was no negotiating with [the government troops], and they treated the people cruelly. When I tried to intervene, I was told clearly to mind my own business.'[22] Nickel wrote to MCC Congo director Neufeld, '[The rebels'] success or failure doesn't enter here since the results for the hospital will remain the same.'[23] The Nickels' determination to assist anyone regardless of political affiliation was tested

---

20 Interview, Arnold Nickel, 19 January 2016.

21 Arnold Nickel to Elmer Neufeld, no date [August 1964], Congo Inland Mission 1964 111/127, IX-6-3.104, Box 190, MCCA.

22 Interview, Arnold Nickel, 19 January 2016.

23 Arnold Nickel to Elmer Neufeld, no date [August 1964], Congo Inland Mission 1964 111/127, IX-6-3.104, Box 190, MCCA. This is a different letter than referenced earlier.

again on 23 January 1965, a year after their evacuation from Mukedi. Rebels again occupied Bolobo. Though the rebels allowed Nickel to work freely, so many people had fled into the surrounding countryside that he had almost no patients.[24] ANC forces fought their way back to the mission. After government troops had retaken Bolobo, Nickel and other missionaries and foreign medical staff boarded a boat and prepared to go to Kinshasa. A government patrol boat quickly stopped their vessel and demanded that Nickel return to the hospital to treat a wounded European businessman. 'If I had deserted the Congolese at that mission station, I certainly was not going back to treat someone just because they were a European,' Nickel stated.[25] Despite threats from a Congolese official, Nickel was eventually allowed to go to the Congolese capital.[26]

The Nickels' experiences demonstrate the insecurity of humanitarian workers in the Congo crises. Contrary to the image of kidnapped missionaries under the grip of sadistic Congolese rebels, the Nickels presented themselves as caught between two dangerous and unpredictable sides. The intoxicated ANC soldiers that 'rescued' the Canadian CPRA volunteers seemed more dangerous than the rebels. As a Mennonite pacifist, Arnold Nickel did not view himself as a supporter of the government. Both APL and ANC forces considered a Western doctor as a valuable resource.

Clayton Peters, a Mennonite dentist volunteer, became an unlikely witness to the 1963–1965 civil wars. In early 1965, MCC Congo director Elmer Neufeld heard rumors that some of the South African and European mercenaries hired by the Congolese government were looking for medical excuses to leave the country. Neufeld had Peters go to Kisangani to treat mercenaries and to hopefully provide them with a rationale to leave the Congo. Peters had a surprise. The mercenaries did not want dental examinations. Instead, they wanted penicillin to cure the gonorrhea that they had apparently acquired through sexual relationships with local women.[27] 'They were sleeping with the local ladies,' Peters said, minimising the sexual violence committed by white soldiers. On the other hand, Peters was horrified to listen to an interrogation by ANC troops of a rebel. A Congolese pastor translated for Peters, and so the dentist learned the prisoner was being forced to tell his captors where his fellow soldiers and his family were hiding.

24   Interview, Arnold Nickel, 19 January 2016.

25   Ibid.

26   Ibid.

27   Interview, Clayton Peters, 23 January 2016.

These vignettes reveal how medical volunteers were vulnerable in the violence that pervaded the Congo in the early 1960s. Volunteers depended on their mission boards, the loosely organised CPRA, and Congolese people around them. Each of the cases discussed here reveals how competing parties wanted access to Western biomedicine. Less dramatic examples of everyday negotiations between medical volunteers and Congolese reveal how Congolese patients, medical assistants, and civilians also sought to turn to the precious asset of Western biomedicine.

Constructing the Congolese patient

Operation Doctor medical personnel found themselves working in a nexus of medical practices established over the course of the colonial period. It was easy for them to exaggerate how colonial Congolese biomedicine was effective and stable compared to their chaotic situation after independence, much as medical personnel believed in the post-colonial decline of public health in Papua New Guinea.[28] Unlike their colonial predecessors, though, they were not required to have any background in tropical medicine. Unless they worked at a hospital with other physicians, volunteers who had begun their careers during the rise of medical specialisation in North America in the 1950s and 1960s took on all cases that came their way.

However, their version of biomedical practice stood at odds with the increasing reliance of diagnostic tests and labs in North America. To use medical anthropologist Alice Streets' insights on medical practice in rural Papua New Guinea, volunteers had to treat patients with 'a single spectrum of sick' in which alternative biomedical practices to keep patients alive took precedence over clearly identifying specific diseases.[29] Although Kimpese had working labs and some of the basic equipment North American doctors took for granted, other rural hospitals did not. At Daniel Riihimaki's post at a rural hospital in Equateur province in 1962, there was a lab for malarial tests and a broken x-ray machine. Riihimaki managed to fix the machine, but then ran out of film.[30] As Robert Mertz put it, 'There wasn't much to work with. You were back in the old days when you worked with your hands and you listened

---

28 A. Street, *Biomedicine in an Unstable Place: Infrastructure and Personhood in a Papua New Guinean Hospital* (University Park: Pennsylvania State University Press, 2014), 85.

29 Ibid., 111.

30 Interview, Daniel Riihimaki, 28 January 2016.

with a stethoscope ... If you were in the habit of relying on laboratory work, you'd be out of luck over there ... You have to be an expert in everything.'[31]

Medical supplies constituted another difficulty. Anesthesia in the Congo relied heavily on ether. With the advent of halothane and other new anesthetics by the early 1960s, ether had begun to fall out of favour in North American hospitals. Some hospitals were well-stocked through mission boards and the CPRA. Others, like Kapanga, did not always have even antibiotics. Beverly Maxam lamented how little he could do for tuberculosis patients other than to put them in a separate ward, since he had no medicine to treat them.[32] Even IME, the most respected Protestant hospital in the whole country, had shortages at times.[33]

CPRA medical personnel also had to adjust to a public setting for their work. Even at larger hospitals, family members fed patients and stayed on hospital grounds. Sometimes spouses stayed in the operating room as surgery was performed. This lack of privacy, radically different from North American medical practice, troubled some volunteers less than others. Daniel Riihimaki opened the abdomen of one patient and discovered parasitic worms: 'People would gather around and watch things going on ... I took a big handful [of the worms] and a big roar went up from the crowd.'[34] Paul Carlson took a dislike to spectators at Wasolo hospital in Equateur province. A missionary colleague took action to discourage onlookers by planting cacti in front of the operating room's windows.[35]

Improvisation became the foundation for medical practice. In similar fashion to rural hospitals in Papua New Guinea in the early 21st century, CPRA doctors had to treat patients without recourse to lab work. While this often led to risky decisions, informants took pride in their individual successes without the safety net of specialists and technological aids of North American hospitals. Treating a girl burned in a gasoline spill, Daniel Riihimaki had to graft skin on her face and to remove infected skin, a very painful process. To avoid using general anesthesia every time, Riihimaki found a recipe for mixing olive oil and ether as a local anesthetic in an English textbook.[36] Other volunteer doctors also relied on textbooks on stands next

---

31 R. Mertz, "Congo Doctor," *Tampa Bay Times* (3 December 1961), 120.

32 Interview, Beverly Maxam, 1 February 2016.

33 Mertz, "Congo Doctor," 120.

34 Interview, Daniel Riihimaki, 28 January 2016.

35 Carlson Bridges, *Monganga*, 81.

36 Interview, Daniel Riihimaki, 28 January 2016.

to the operating table. Perhaps this was testimony to advances in Western medicine, but it also showed the limits of volunteer skills.[37]

Just as colonial doctors thought Congolese could withstand pain that would be lethal to Europeans, some CPRA volunteers believed their patients could survive conditions fatal to North American patients. 'The Congolese people seem to have tremendous ability to overcome infection and surgical shock … So many badly infected wounds, neglected wounds, even neglected meningitis problems seem to recover in many cases which would be considered a miracle at home,' wrote one volunteer.[38] Another described how a man with a strangulated hernia walked 50 miles to Kapanga hospital: 'Yes, he is living and doing fine. It would have killed any American, though.'[39] In one case, Jim Stough met a woman with a knobby mass in her abdomen. The woman claimed she was not pregnant. Stough discovered she had a fetus die after a ruptured uterus that had calcified in her abdomen. She claimed she thought she might be pregnant a year before, but in her words, 'The baby never stood up,' which meant she never had any contractions. 'Now, any woman who had ruptured her uterus in this country [with a dead fetus in her abdomen] would have died on the spot. She just kept hoeing her peanuts and kept right on going,' marvelled Stough.[40] Yet doctors also believed poverty rather biological difference could explain Congolese health issues. Ernest Carlson advised one patient to eat more meat since she had a low hemoglobin count, a result of malaria common in central Africa. People in the ward let loose a 'ripple of laughter,' and a Congolese nurse explained, 'They are laughing, for it is very rare for people to afford meat in their diet.'[41]

Although medical researchers and historians have become convinced that HIV infections had emerged in the Congo basin by the 1920s and had increased in the early 1960s, it should come as little surprise that Operation Doctor volunteers did not take notice of unusual illnesses associated with AIDS.[42]

37 Interview, Jim Stough, 26 February 2016; Interview, Patricia Evans, 15 August 2018.

38 *Congo Protestant Relief Agency News Sheet* 39 (10 January 1963), 3, Folder 5 Congo Protestant Relief Agency, Box 137, BIM Post-War, ABHSA.

39 *Congo Protestant Relief Agency News Sheet* 71 (November 1963), 2, Folder 5 Congo Protestant Relief Agency, Box 137, BIM Post-War, ABHSA.

40 Interview, Jim Stough, 26 February 2016.

41 Carlson, *Autobiography*, Chapter XII, 2.

42 On the gradual spread of AIDS in the DRC from the 1920s to the early 1960s, see J. Pépin, *The Origins of AIDS* (New York: Cambridge University Press, 2011); T. Giles-Vernick, G. Lachenal, C.D. Gondola, and W. Schneider, "Social History,

Beyond the simple fact that AIDS had yet to be identified, volunteer doctors generally had little background in tropical medicine, had very limited access to laboratories, and were further hampered by their assumptions about patients. A number of volunteers who later treated HIV-infected patients in the US did not recall any similar symptoms in the Congo.[43] Patricia Evans, the wife of Operation Doctor volunteer James Evans, worked with her husband at IME and the American Baptist hospital in Vanga in the 1970s. 'I think [AIDS] was probably there [in Congo], but in terms of the kinds of pneumonias and tumors related to AIDS, we might have seen those and not realised what it was.'[44] One volunteer may have come across the illness. Kenneth Comer described one mysterious condition as 'Slim's disease' during his time in Kapanga hospital in late 1963 and early 1964. For reasons that baffled Comer and his uncle, some young men rapidly lost weight and sometimes died, sometimes with symptoms of large amounts of fluid in the abdomen.[45] Whether or not this was due to HIV is conjecture, but Comer was later convinced the illness might have been AIDS. David Fluck, a CPRA volunteer and a pathologist, conducted a postmortem on a middle-aged Congolese woman in 1962 with symptoms commonly associated with AIDS. When Belgian doctor Jean Sonnet had begun to research possible AIDS cases from the Congo in the early 1980s, he contacted Fluck. The former volunteer agreed with the Belgian researcher that the patient must have had AIDS.[46] An Operation Doctor volunteer thus had conducted an autopsy on a woman most likely infected with HIV.

Reproductive health was a central issue for Congolese seeking care from volunteers. North American medical personnel inserted themselves into the debris of pro-natalist programmes under Belgian rule. Confronted with rural migration to urban areas and high rates of venereal diseases, Belgian doctors and Protestant missionaries alike promoted policies designed to increase population. One of the results of these colonial policies was the widespread use of caesarean sections. Nancy Rose Hunt's nuanced discussion of the introduction of cesarean sections at the Yakusu mission hospital near Kisangani indicates how Congolese patients and midwives often objected to the practice for the

---

Biology, and the Emergence of HIV in Colonial Africa," *Journal of African History* 54:1 (2013), 11–30.

43 Interview, Elizabeth Shelly, 13 January 2016; Interview, Carol Swarts, 21 March 2016.

44 Interview, Patricia Evans, 15 August 2018.

45 Interview, Kenneth Comer, 4 October 2016.

46 E. Hooper, *The River: A Journey to the Source of HIV and AIDS* (Boston: Little, Brown, and Company, 1999), 260.

dangers it posed to women.[47] Volunteer doctors did not recall opposition to caesarean deliveries, but rather how often they performed this procedure. William Arkinstall performed no less than 7 caesarean sections in one day while working at Kimpese in 1966.[48]

Why did women encounter so much adversity in giving birth? Some volunteers referenced high rates of cephalopelvic disproportion in which women's pelvises were too narrow to allow for unobstructed deliveries.[49] Recent research does confirm that some Congolese women do suffer from this condition.[50] However, medical practice also endangered women's health. Volunteer Carol Berggren had been taught that once a woman had a cesarean section, then the same procedure had to be done for subsequent births.[51] Arthur Gerdes, stationed at several hospitals, attributed life-threatening ruptured placentas in part to the fact women often had previously undergone cesarean sections: 'The surgical incisions hadn't healed well. There was a weakness in the muscle. With prolonged labour … the uterus ruptured.'[52] A recent study corroborates Gerdes' observation by arguing poor medical care in caesarian operations was a major cause of fistulas in eastern DRC.[53]

Still another difficulty that imperiled the lives of Congolese women was simply reaching a rural hospital. Carol Berggren described what she saw as the three delays that endangered women in prolonged labour. At the village level, family members and indigenous healers did not always recognise symptoms of obstructed labour. The next obstacle came from transport, which was a major problem given the deteriorating roads and warfare in the early 1960s in DRC. One example was an incident told by Linda Macilvaine, the daughter of volunteer Richard Nay. She remembered being confused by the sight of a crawling animal headed toward the Kapanga hospital in 1961. It was a woman with leprosy who had crawled with her sick baby from a town some miles

---

47 N. Hunt, *A Colonial Lexicon: Of Birth Ritual, Medicalisation, and Mobility in the Congo* (Durham, NC: Duke University Press, 1999), 196–236.

48 Interview, William Arkinstall, 18 March 2016.

49 Interview, Carol Berggren, 19 March 2016

50 H. Liselele, M. Boulvain, K. Tshibangu, and S. Meuris, "Maternal Height and External Pelvimetry to Predict Cephalopelvic Disproportion in Nulliparous African Women: A Cohort Study," *British Journal of Gynecology* 107:8 (2000), 947–52.

51 Interview, Carol Berggren, 19 March 2016.

52 Interview, Arthur and Peggy Gerdes, 3 November 2016.

53 S. Sjøveian, "Gynecological Fistula in the DR Congo," (MS thesis, University of Oslo, 2009), 12–13.

away.[54] Transportation problems also impeded outlying clinics from quickly sending seriously ill patients to hospitals staffed by CPRA doctors.[55] Even once patients finally arrived, poorly-staffed and equipped hospitals placed women at risk.[56]

Treating Congolese women for reproductive health led Operation Doctor personnel to question gender roles in Congolese society, echoing similar views from the colonial era. Their comments also reflected what they believed to be the proper role of Congolese women: to be objects of male desire and to be eligible for marriage. Several doctors felt conflicted about performing hysterectomies, since women unable to conceive would be abandoned by spouses and family members.[57] Doctors sometimes removed physical abnormalities such as elongated toes at the behest of female patients fearing they would not find a spouse.[58] William Reed, a doctor and an occasional lecturer at Indiana University, wrote: 'Female children are regarded highly as income producers.'[59] Another doctor celebrated delivering the baby of an 11-year-old mother and then joked, 'If a couple do not have a baby in two years, the husband sends the wife back to the father, gets his money back and buys another. Simple, eh?'[60] Kenneth Comer told his nephew after performing a cesarean section, 'She won't be wearing a bikini.'[61]

Volunteers wrestled with their own technical limitations as well as their disdain for Congolese social norms. In one case, Bill Arkinstall had a patient with a ruptured placenta, causing her to bleed heavily into her abdomen. Arkinstall had a Swedish nurse put the leaking blood into a bottle, suctioned it up, and then put the blood back into her intravenously.[62] Not every improvisation fared as well. Arnold Nickel said he found himself confronted with cases that greatly exceeded his abilities. After failing to control bleeding from

---

54 Personal communication, Nancy Macilvaine, 7 August 2018.

55 *Congo Protestant Relief Agency News Sheet* 65 (September 1963), 2, Folder 5 Congo Protestant Relief Agency, Box 137, BIM Post-War, ABHSA; Interview, Arthur and Peggy Gerdes, 3 November 2016.

56 Interview, Carol Berggren, 19 March 2016.

57 Youmans, *Elephants*, 56; Personnel communication, Charles Proudfit Jr., 14 June 2018.

58 Interview, Kenneth Comer, 4 October 2018.

59 *Congo Protestant Relief Agency News Sheet* 69 (November 1963): 1, Folder 5 Congo Protestant Relief Agency, Box 137, BIM Post-War, ABHSA.

60 *Congo Protestant Relief Agency News Sheet* 75 (February 1964), 3, Folder 6 Congo Protestant Relief Agency, Box 137, BIM Post-War, ABHSA.

61 Interview, Kenneth Comer, 4 October 2018.

62 Interview, William and Karin Arkinstall, 18 March 2016.

a woman's ruptured uterus, Nickel took the patient to a World Health Organisation (WHO) doctor at a nearby hospital for a second surgical procedure that did not succeed: 'That was one of the most traumatic surgical failures on my part.'[63] Other participants had the same regrets.[64]

Despite the mixed track record of Operation Doctor volunteers, the participants themselves believed Congolese trusted in their expertise. At the rural hospital of Kibunzi left bereft of a full-time doctor since 1960, the local Congolese pastor announced the arrival of Filipino doctor Antonio Feliciano as a gift from God: 'It seems they have been praying for a doctor to arrive.'[65] One reason was for ensuring deliveries: 'On my first day, I performed a Caesarean section on a mother who has had four stillbirths. The baby was dying and would have died if we had not done the Caesarean … It seems that every wife would like to have a baby and come to be operated on.'[66] Feliciano toured villages in Bas-Congo to conduct surgery and was lauded with loud cheers and gifts of eggs, bananas, and chickens.[67] Volunteers were generally as touched by Feliciano by expressions of thanks by Congolese, even if they often did not understand much about the details. After Beverly Maxam had removed an external (enterocutaneous) fistula, the family came to him with white powder (probably kaolin) on their faces. They then rubbed their faces on Maxam's feet.[68]

Volunteers juxtaposed their warm memories of Congolese patients with their disdain for Congolese cultural practices and their discomfort with aspects of their own society. While such contractionary feelings were at the heart of colonial missionary evangelisation, volunteers also expressed their concerns about changes in North American medicine. Doctors and nurses became anxious about the increasingly vocal role of patients as healthcare consumers in Canada and the US by the early 1960s.[69] By contrast, Operation Doctor

---

63 Interview, Arnold Nickel, 18 January 2016.

64 Interview, Elizabeth Shelly, 13 January 2016; Interview, William and Karin Arkinstall, 18 March 2016.

65 Roland Metzger, 3 August 1961, Folder 5 Congo Protestant Relief Agency, Box 137, BIM Post-War, ABHSA.

66 Ibid.

67 594 *Congo Protestant Relief Agency News Sheet* 16 (October 1961), Folder 5 Congo Protestant Relief Agency, Box 137, BIM Post-War, ABHSA.

68 Interview, Beverly Maxam, 1 February 2016.

69 N. Tomes, *Remaking the American Patient: How Madison Avenue and Modern Medicine Turned Patients into Consumers* (Chapel Hill, NC: University of North Carolina Press, 2016).

participants presented Congolese as grateful and obedient. Janelle Goetcheus dedicated much of her life to assisting the homeless of Washington, DC. She recalled her Congolese patients: 'I saw tremendous poverty in Zaire, but I still saw hope among the people. Here [in Washington] I see no hope. I just see so much despair.'[70] Other volunteers considered North Americans to be spoiled and selfish. Arnold Nickel remembered being angered by what he saw as his overly pampered Canadian clients. 'I had saved one life every day when I was [in the Congo] in some form or another because of basic intervention. When I got back to Canada and saw the consumer type medicine ... I was very disheartened.'[71]

Volunteers simultaneously praised the kindness of Congolese people and disparaged what they deemed to be their primitive understandings of health. Paul Hodel, a Mennonite doctor from Indiana, summer up his conclusions after two years of service: 'We were impressed with the tremendous advantage we as westerners had in our cultural heritage ... These cultural aspects of Congolese culture with which we had to deal with most adaptively tended be in the areas of personal responsibility (honesty, initiative, dependability), general lack of educational background...and material poverty.'[72] CPRA nurse Natalia Similie asserted, 'Something these people have yet to discover is that fire burns and a bullet forcibly introduced into a body makes a hole and will hurt ... Parents <u>will</u> leave a three [or] four year old alone at home with fire going, and then are surprised at the result. Grown-ups also are as bad about themselves.'[73]

Some doctors took a different approach. Without endorsing the effectiveness of indigenous healing, they acknowledged its importance to people. Berggren empathised with efforts by local healers to place herbs in the birth canal to induce delivery.[74] She also wished she had known more about Congolese health practices. For example, a patient complained that he had not dreamed for a long time, which to him meant he was ill. Berggren did not know how to respond to his anxieties, which she felt were genuine.[75] In Bas-Congo province, Bill

---

70 G. Esler, *The United States of Anger: People and the American Dream* (London: Michael Joseph, 1997), 101.

71 Interview, Arnold Nickel, 18 January 2016.

72 *Congo Protestant Relief Agency News Sheet* 92 (November 1964), 2, Folder 6 Congo Protestant Relief Agency, Box 137, BIM Post-War, ABHSA.

73 *Congo Protestant Relief Agency News Sheet* 104 (December 1965), 2, Folder 6 Congo Protestant Relief Agency, Box 137, BIM Post-War, ABHSA.

74 Interview, Carol Berggren, 19 March 2016.

75 Ibid.

Arkinstall collaborated with anthropologist John Janzen to better understand indigenous perspectives on healing.[76] Even more skeptical volunteers learned to respect aspects of Congolese health practices. The mother of Stough's deceased first patient came to the hospital to take the baby.[77] Stough doubted her claim that she could nurse the baby thanks to eating some herbs. To prove her point, she shot milk from her breast into his eye.

Volunteers imagined themselves to belong to a Christian and American response to African need, no matter what their views on Congolese culture. Witnessing and trying to care mattered more than individual successes or failures. 'In the long run the attitudes which these people take towards America and Americans may be more important than the individual care given,' Wendell Kingsolver wrote in 1963.[78] Beverly Maxam summed up the feeling of many participants: 'There was so little you could do. The only thing you could do was to let them know you're there to help. Not to convert, but just to be there. They responded to your attention, your kindness, your interest in them.'[79]

This idealised vision of respectful, appreciative Congolese patients was hardly wishful thinking. Congolese leaders relied on Operation Doctor volunteers, particularly Congolese president Joseph Kasavubu. Kasavubu regularly received treatment from CPRA co-founder Glen Tuttle.[80] African-American volunteer Buford Washington also treated Kasavubu, particularly for his longstanding issues with hypertension.[81] In Katanga province, the Ruund monarchy also relied on CPRA. In 1964, Beverly Maxam did a prostatectomy on David Tshombe, the reigning Mwaant Yaav (king) and the brother of Katangan leader Moïse Tshombe.[82] Maxam used a short-wave radio to have a urologist from Indianapolis guide him through the surgery. The Mwaant Yaav thanked Maxam by presenting the doctor with a leopard killed by his hunters.[83] Besides their technical skill, these doctors were early examples of how Congolese leaders relied on expatriate physicians. CPRA volunteers fit into

---

76 See Janzen and Arkinstall, *Quest.*

77 Interview, James Stough, 26 February 2016.

78 *Congo Protestant Relief Agency News Sheet* 65 (September 1963), Folder 5 Congo Protestant Relief Agency, Box 137, BLM Post-War, ABHSA.

79 Interview, Beverly Maxam, 1 February 2016.

80 D.A. Tuttle, *A Tribute to Glen and Jeannette Tuttle: Medical Missionaries to the Congo* (Bloomington, IN: Xlibris, 2009), 214.

81 Interview, Angela Thames, 18 May 2016.

82 Interview, Beverly Maxam, 1 February 2016.

83 Ibid.

a long tradition of how central African political leaders recruited individuals with specialised knowledge.[84]

A comment by a CPRA nurse from 1965 suggests how Congolese were not always so easy to control: 'The Congolese <u>love</u> to be operated on and will even tell you where and how the operation should be done.'[85] Congolese patients were not always as docile as doctors generally believed. Family members of patients sometimes took patients home before doctors agreed to discharge them, to the point Jim Stough created an alarm system with glass bottles designed to make a noise if a patient was moved at night.[86] Indigenous communities cajoled volunteers to take on roles that tacitly accepted aspects of local beliefs about health. Medical volunteer John Fine gave a man in Kwilu province Vicks vapor rub, which convinced his Congolese interlocutor that the rub could cure cuts. Fine tried to dissuade the patient, but his Congolese interpreter warned the American that the patient was an important clan leader who should not be insulted. Even when the man winced after putting it on his lips, he still took a scoop home.[87] Arthur Gerdes became frustrated with a woman he was trying to diagnose, since she would not admit she had gone to indigenous healers. He pretended his broken x-ray machine could serve as a lie detector: 'Mama, we got that machine over there in the dark room that can look into your heart.'[88] Gerdes' maneuver may have compelled his patient to answer, but it also corresponded to the ways medical missionaries took advantage of how Congolese considered them to be healers with access to mystical knowledge. This also meant volunteers could be blamed for harming others. After Beverly Maxam took a photograph of a boy who subsequently succumbed to smallpox, some family members accused the doctor of being responsible for the child's death.[89]

At times, Congolese managed to persuade volunteers to act in ways that engaged with their own understandings of health. Autopsies, for example, allowed Congolese to use volunteers' expertise to challenge beliefs about supernatural powers. At Tandala hospital in Equateur province, a village chief

84   J. Guyer and S.E. Belinga, "Wealth in People as Wealth in Knowledge: Accumulation and Composition in Equatorial Africa," *Journal of African History* 36:1 (1995), 91–120.

85   *Congo Protestant Relief Agency News Sheet* 104 (December 1965): 1, Folder 6 Congo Protestant Relief Agency, Box 137, BIM Post-War, ABHSA.

86   Interview, James Stough, 26 February 2016.

87   J.C. Fine, *The Hunger Road* (New York: Atheneum, 1988), 59–60.

88   Interview, Arthur and Peggy Gerdes, 3 November 2016.

89   Interview, Beverly Maxam, 1 February 2016.

convinced Carol Swarts to perform an autopsy on a boy to show he had died from natural causes. She discovered parasitic worms: 'I could back up the village chief that [the boy] was not cursed by somebody in the village, so they didn't have to go through the trouble of finding who was guilty.'[90] Swarts thus put her expertise at the service of the chief. This chief may have been the same leader who authorised Jim Stough to conduct another autopsy at Tandala roughly two years later.[91] Bill Arkinstall agreed to cut open a dead crocodile in Kibunzi to see if a missing child was inside it. The boy's uncle had killed the animal. Since the uncle was embroiled in a dispute with the boy's family, some speculated he had used mystical force to send the crocodile after the boy, whose corpse Arkinstall found after opening the animal up.[92] Though Arkinstall did not himself agree with the rumours surrounding the tragic death, he inadvertently became a participant in the discussion. Likewise, volunteers became part of the transition from expatriate to African-led public health.

Medical volunteers, Congolese health workers, and missionaries in an era of transition, 1960–1966

Describing why she want to stay on at the Kwilu-Ngongo hospital, CPRA nurse Muriel Bizi remembered how Angolan midwives had called her in to help: "'Oh we need you here, we've been praying that you'd come back well to us." Since the Belgian nurse has come, several of the [Congolese] nurses have come to me saying, "Don't be discouraged, at least you are a buffer for us."'[93] The turbulence of the early 1960s opened up new opportunities for Congolese to take leadership roles. Volunteers held an ambiguous position regarding these changes. Like Bizi, some volunteers believed they should share their knowledge to allow Congolese to take control of their healthcare. Other volunteers were less committed to – or at least less familiar with – maintaining white authority over medical practice. CPRA medical staff felt more uneasy with the Africanisation of hospital administrators. To volunteers, rather than being junior partners, administrators were equals – if not in some cases the supervisors – of Operation Doctor participants.

---

90 Interview, Carol Swarts, 21 March 2016.

91 "Austin's Globetrotting Doctor Tours Far East," *Chicago News* (22 April 1964), 16.

92 Interview, Bill and Karin Arkinstall, 18 March 2016.

93 Muriel Stevens to Roy Webster, 27 May 1963, Folder 30 Correspondence Stevens, Congo 1963, Board of World Mission, Associate Secretary for Zaire, Box 2, Accession Number 83.031C, UCCA.

Volunteers praised the Congolese nurses and midwives who helped them. Paul Carlson praised his head nurse: 'Wanzi was always Paul's right-hand man in surgery. He had a deep respect for Paul, and Paul was just as grateful for Wanzi's faithfulness and loyalty.'[94] Roger Youmans wrote, 'I could see the futility of what I was doing, but I also could see that the hopelessness and suffering was mitigated by the labors of the nurses I worked with daily.'[95] Youmans admitted his Congolese nurses had much better skills in treatment than he did. The American doctor performed his first cesarean section, a very familiar procedure for his nurses.[96] Nurses could speak to African patients, whereas Youmans did not know either French or Kikongo. One spectator joked in broken English after hearing Youmans trying to formulate questions, 'Doctor talk question. No hear answer.'[97] Nurses were already able to diagnose illnesses and perform numerous tasks done by physicians in North America. When Ray Milhous dislocated his shoulder, an injury that doctors dealt with in the US, a medical assistant treated it successfully.[98] Another volunteer told family and friends he simply followed the instructions of nurses most of the time, since their competence vastly exceeded his own.[99]

Operation Doctor volunteers made sure to teach nurses to take on tasks they had not done in the colonial period, in keeping with broader ideas about moving beyond the colonial legacy. Mark Poole trained his former medical assistant of two decades so he could operate without any help in the future.[100] After about a year, Jim Stough told his chief medical assistant: 'You take the lead now. I will assist.' For the remaining year, Stough let the assistant lead in routine surgical procedures, knowing the nurse would have to run the operating room once the American volunteer left. In 2007, Stough returned to Tandala and met his old partner, who showed him the hospital log. Stough's former assistant had meticulously logged over 10,000 surgeries he had performed since 1964.

This model of technology transfer, in keeping with developmentalist theories of the 1960s, relied a great deal on the optimism of volunteers. Operation Doctor personnel expressed their faith in Congolese medical staff. One volunteer declared, 'The Congolese nurses and station leaders were so pleased

---

94 Carlson Bridges, *Monganga*, 79.

95 Youmans, *Elephants*, 51.

96 Ibid., 31.

97 Ibid., 31.

98 Interview, Ray and Ruth Milhous, 8 January 2016.

99 Interview, Patricia Evans, 15 August 2018.

100 Poole, "Reflections," 32.

to have us help ... These people seem to thirst so much for knowledge ...
Now after Independence, the church has such a potential to train, in Christian
spirit, the future leaders of Congo!'[101] Another took pride in helping train some
newly graduated nurses: 'The more I work with these Congo young people, the
more hopeful I am for the future of this young nation.'[102]

Such positive sentiments tended to be less frequent in regards to financial
matters. Ray and Ruth Milhous became upset that Congolese hospital staff
stole money from their hospital: 'We found the nurses took a share for themselves [of fees]. Sadly, the Christians seem to be as dishonest as others.'[103] Jim
Stough denounced his Congolese hospital administrator to African church
leaders, albeit in somewhat garbled Lingala. When Stough tried to say the
man should go to jail, the Congolese pastors hearing the accusation gasped.
Inadvertently, Stough had said the man should be sent straight to Hell.[104] One
probable motivation came from low pay and the lack of consistent financial
support from the government. At Sona Bata hospital in Bas-Congo in 1961,
nurses received roughly half of what their counterparts at government hospitals earned.[105] Despite such criticisms, however, volunteers remained relatively
hopeful for the future of public health in the DRC. Roger Youmans, for example, greatly respected the Congolese director at Sona Bata.[106]

Few Operation Doctors went as far as William Arkinstall to change medical procedures at a mission hospital. He and his wife Karin left the Institut
Médical Evangélique hospital in Bas-Congo (IME) to work at the isolated
hospital of Kibunzi, where he was expected to oversee a leprosarium. Although
other volunteers also had to manage leper colonies, Arkinstall was the only
one who decided to close one down. 'They put all these people in the leprosarium because of the fear. So, there was no need for it to be there. We were
able to get all of them to go home to go back to the villages,' he said in 2016.[107]
How Congolese afflicted with the illness may have responded to the change
is unclear. Arkinstall had more leeway to make changes because Kibunzi had

101 *Congo Protestant Relief Agency News Sheet* 39 (10 January 1963): 1, Folder 5 Congo
Protestant Relief Agency, Box 137, BIM Post-War, ABHSA.

102 *Congo Protestant Relief Agency News Sheet* 75 (February 1964), 1, Folder 6 Congo
Protestant Relief Agency, Box 137, BIM Post-War, ABHSA.

103 Ray and Ruth Milhous to Mother and Daddy, 1 November 1962, RRMP.

104 Interview, James Stough, 26 February 2016.

105 Youmans, *Elephants*, 41.

106 Ibid., 32.

107 Interview, Bill and Karin Arkinstall, 18 March 2016.

no permanent missionary after 1960. At Kapanga in Katanga province, the leprosarium stayed open.[108]

Missionaries kept relatively quiet about their own concerns about volunteers, but a few sources indicate how volunteers tried the patience of the missionaries. The CPRA itself had no direct way to supervise volunteers. Margaret Ogilvie, the Pentecostal nurse who the screening committee approved with reservations in 1965, wore out her welcome at IME by the time she left four years later. The IME director accused her of believing 'she alone has the real Christian faith' and of being 'a very sick woman – mentally', but she had stayed far longer than she would have if she had had to answer to a particular mission board.[109] CPRA secretary Helen Bjertness wrote about a volunteer who apparently had alienated his missionary posts during his initial stay in the DRC: 'When the hospital administrator in the Congo heard about this, he wrote ... "Under no circumstances should Dr. __ be permitted to return" ... The hospital administrator hadn't mentioned it to us at the time because Dr. ___'s term had been completed.'[110] Only one CPRA volunteer was singled out by name. John Fine, a young law student with some limited medical training, came to Kimpese for several months in the summer of 1965. David Wilson at IME refused to take Fine back on the grounds he allegedly left behind unpaid debts, cheated a taxi driver, pretended to be a medical doctor, and encouraged Mennonite Central Committee volunteers to complain about missionaries.[111]

Volunteers criticised other missionaries for a variety of reasons. A few felt mission efforts to evangelise took away from focusing on education and social advancement.[112] Others had more petty gripes. Rather than follow a ban on tobacco use on mission grounds, some volunteers managed to hide out and smoke.[113] Ray and Ruth Milhous expressed their concern about the paternalism of Mennonite missionaries to Mennonite Central Committee director Elmer Neufeld, who repeatedly objected to such behaviour as a relic

---

108 Interview, Beverly Maxam, 1 February 2016.

109 Frank Anderson to Perry Smith, 31 October 1969, Folder Zaire 1969, Box 8, Record Group 22, CWS/PHS.

110 Helen Bjertness to David Wilson, 29 August 1966, Folder Congo Protestant Relief Agency 1964–1967, Record Group 8, Box 14, CWS/PHS.

111 David Wilson to Helen Bjertness, 28 June 1966, Folder Congo Protestant Relief Agency (CPRA), 1964–1967, Record Group 8, Box 14, CWS/PHS.

112 Interview, Beverly Maxam, 1 February 2016.

113 Interview, Bill and Karin Arkinstall, 18 March 2016; Personal communication, Charles Proudfit Jr., 14 June 2018.

of colonialism. 'We were told [by other missionaries] you shouldn't even voice a criticism of what was going on until you'd been in the field for three years … We were upset about the old-time missionaries, who retained this attitude towards the Congolese, looking down on them,' Ray Milhous said.[114] Though they sympathised with their challenges more over time, they also worried missionaries 'lived too much in a transplanted Western culture'.[115]

Yet the everyday lives of all volunteers reflected continuities with the social order of missions in the colonial period. Though a few volunteers consciously chose not to live on mission grounds, most did so. Volunteers hired cooks and domestic servants just as permanent missionaries did. Relatively few missionaries recalled having close friendships with Congolese outside of the workplace, although their heavy workload made it difficult to do so. As one volunteer put it, 'It was really essential [to have servants] because the conditions were so primitive that I really had to have help to carry on our activities that needed doing … Their pay was very low … It was a job that was really sought after from the Congolese point of view.'[116] When Roger Youmans felt awkward about having a staff of servants for the first time, the wife of the head of the mission told them Congolese were desperate to find work, a testament to the high unemployment rate of the early 1960s.[117]

Muriel Bizi broke conventions on social divisions between Africans and expatriate missionaries. In 1966, she resigned from the CPRA to marry Paul Bizi, a Congolese university student.[118] Out of all the volunteers, she is the only one who had an open intimate relationship with a Congolese national. Originally assigned by the United Church of Canada to Angola in 1961, Bizi was an exception to the studious avoidance of partisanship among CPRA medical volunteers. She formed prayer groups and found jobs for southern Angolan refugees feeling isolated among the vast BisiKongo majority of exiles in Bas-Congo province, distributed fish to newly arrived Angolans, and managed to continue her work as a nurse.[119] Bizi also allowed two girls to

114 Interview, Ray and Ruth Milhous, 8 January 2016.

115 Ray and Ruth Milhous, Report, 1 August 1964, Folder 111/125 Congo Activity Reports 1964, Box 190, IX-6-3, MCCA.

116 Interview, Arnold Nickel, 18 January 2016.

117 Youmans, *Elephants*, 36.

118 Muriel Stevens to Garthe Legge, 28 August 1966, Folder 76a Correspondence Stevens Congo 1963, Board of World Mission, Associate Secretary for Zaire, Box 3, Accession Number 83.031C, UCCA.

119 Muriel Stevens to Friends, 25 May 1963, Folder 30 Correspondence Stevens Congo 1963, Board of World Mission, Associate Secretary for Zaire, Box 2, Accession

live with her so they could attend school along with watching over two boys left orphaned after the death of their mother from malnutrition.[120] No other volunteers placed themselves into African family life like Bizi, but instead ultimately kept their distance. Beverly Maxam, for example, recalled seeing Congolese children and thought, 'They were just like little kids over here. They were wild and feisty and got into trouble. I just wish I could've had some of these kids over and brought them up. Made them Americans, you know. But, that's impossible.'[121] Volunteers may not have entirely fitted into the set relationships of white missionary authority from the colonial period, but with rare exceptions did not break from previous practice.

Conclusion

Operation Doctor showed the enthusiasm of Protestant North American medical professionals to help heal the Congo from the legacy of civil war and colonialism. The project tried to put into practice ecumenical Protestant ideals of international cooperation, even if some of its participants would not have identified themselves as political or theological liberals. Just as Peace Corps participants viewed their service as an opportunity for individual growth in a time of rampant consumerism, Operation Doctor staff saw their time in Congo as a means of exploring practising medicine outside of the confines of the increasingly bureaucratised and profit-driven medical system. Operation Doctor's participants viewed Congolese individually as grateful and receptive, even as they generally viewed Congolese culture as primitive and an obstacle to progress. Volunteers never expressed the kind of cynicism that pervaded US government development circles about Africa in the 1960s.[122] Yet their views about the Congolese needing foreign assistance corresponded with

---

Number 83.031C, UCCA; Muriel Stevens to Roy Webster, 6 October 1964 and 23 October 1964, Folder 39 Correspondence Stevens, Congo 1964, Board of World Mission, Associate Secretary for Zaire, Box 2, Accession Number 83.031C, UCCA.

120 Muriel Stevens to Roy Webster, no date [October 1963], Folder 30 Correspondence Stevens Congo 1963, Board of World Mission, Associate Secretary for Zaire, Box 2, Accession Number 83.031C, UCCA; Muriel Stevens to Roy Webster, 16 December 1964, Folder 39 Correspondence Stevens, Congo 1964, Board of World Mission, Associate Secretary for Zaire, Box 2, Accession Number 83.031C, UCCA.

121 Interview, Beverly Maxam, 1 February 2016.

122 Grubbs, *Secular Missionaries*.

assumptions made by US officials about the role of American technological in promoting social progress.

Practising medicine in the Congo in the wake of decolonisation posed serious challenges to volunteers. They could not rely on access to specialists and technological resources readily available in North America. Instead, they could test their individual skill in areas far outside their ordinary expertise. Though volunteers regretted their lack of skill, they also took pride in what they accomplished. Volunteers generally rejected local healing practices. However, their main opponents were not so much indigenous cultural beliefs as logistical and technical problems.

Volunteers could not count on support from state authorities in the same way as missionaries in the colonial period. Belgian officials clearly favoured Catholic missions over their Protestant rivals, but medical missionaries could at least count on the colonial state to provide security. From APL rebel soldiers to Congolese president Joseph Kasavubu, Congolese stakeholders sought to take advantage of volunteers' skills. The clear preference of some Protestant missionaries for Katanga occasionally placed volunteers at risk. Individual volunteers often found US-backed government forces to be repugnant and dangerous rather than defenders of missions. Since Congolese political leaders did not make public health a priority, volunteers often felt they worked in an environment where the state was relatively absent in regards to healthcare.

Congolese patients and healthcare workers took advantage of the ambiguous position of volunteers. Seeking advancement opportunities denied to them in the colonial era, Congolese medical auxiliaries found volunteers quite willing to provide training. Volunteers relied on Congolese nurses for their technical ability and linguistic competence in daily practice. This transfer of knowledge and authority was not done in a systematic way, but it did hasten the decline of expatriate-directed public health in the DRC over the course of the 1960s and early 1970s. Patients generally were receptive to volunteers' assistance and treatment, particularly with the evacuation of many medical professionals in 1960. Still, some Congolese seeking treatment did not always blindly follow commands, even if there appears to have been no general resistance to Western biomedicine.

7

Changing Dollars into Zaires:
The Challenges of a Humanitarian Aid
NGO in the DRC, 1965–1973

The early years of Mobutu Sese Seko's dictatorship in the Democratic Republic of Congo (DRC) from 1965 to 1973 constituted a period of misplaced optimism for foreign aid. Critics of foreign aid have used the DRC as the model of how state corruption, Cold War politics, and poorly designed donor aid packages led to disaster.[1] After briefly reviewing Mobutu's success in obtaining aid, Carol Lancaster succinctly summarised her findings: 'The implication of this analysis is that foreign aid, when provided to a regime whose legitimacy is weak, can prolong the life of the regime.'[2] Likewise, the squandering of aid by Mobutu's government reinforces James Ferguson's conclusion that aid only reinforced state power, rather than achieve its stated objectives.[3]

This chapter examines how Congolese stakeholders and Western donors debated the terms of their relationship from Mobutu's ascension to power until the Congolese economy fell into decline beginning in 1973. The negotiations of the World Council of Churches (WCC) with the CPRA reveal the complexities of the role of humanitarian aid in the DRC. Church World Service (CWS) and WCC funding show how humanitarian assistance served the US government's goal of ensuring Mobutu remained in power. CWS officials initially viewed their efforts as building a stable DRC, particularly from 1965 to 1968. Over the course of the late 1960s and early 1970s, CWS staff became frustrated with Disciples of Christ pastor Jean Bokeleale, a committed Congolese nationalist. A majority of Congolese representatives of different churches had elected Bokeleale as chairman of the Congo Protestant Council in 1968,

---

1 For example, see D. Moyo, *Dead Aid: Why Aid is Not Working and How There is a Better Way for Africa* (New York: Farrar, Straus and Giroux, 2009), 22–23.

2 C. Lancaster, *Aid to Africa: So Little Done* (Chicago: University of Chicago Press, 1999), 66.

3 J. Ferguson, *The Anti-Politics Machine: Development, Depoliticisation, and Bureaucratic Power in Lesotho* (Minneapolis: University of Minnesota Press, 1994).

which served to promote cooperation between churches. Bokeleale convinced representatives to vote to transform the Congo Protestant Council (CPC) into the Église du Christ au Congo (ECC). This new institution served as an umbrella organisation of different denominations under a single legal framework and constituted the most ambitious example of church union in Africa in the 20th century. While individual churches (now known as communities) could maintain separate theological views and liturgical practices, they henceforth operated under a single bureaucratic structure designed to handle legal disputes, government relations, and oversee development programmes.

The CWS and WCC had doubts about Bokeleale's dreams of making the ECC a key partner in Mobutu's nation building. WCC staff concerned themselves more with the lack of financial accountability in CPRA operations than criticising Bokeleale. CWS Africa department director Jan S.F. van Hoogstraten found Bokeleale intolerable for his refusal to accept CWS dictates on how donor funds should be used. Congolese state refusals to pay for shipping of CPRA supplies, fears of embezzlement, and personality conflicts led the CWS to reduce funding for the CPRA. Though these findings correspond well to literature on US government ties to Mobutu in the same period, they also show how disputes between private donor agencies and Congolese NGO leaders also could lead to cutbacks in aid.

The transition from humanitarian relief to development aspirations in African countries in the 1960s and early 1970s remains little understood, particularly if one considers NGOs rather than state actors. Karen Jenkins' brief overview of Christian NGOs offers little historical evidence between the end of colonial rule and the 1990s.[4] In the few works on civilian operations by the United Nations, authors have generally contented themselves with broad overviews and technical exchanges rather than actually considering the delimmas and impact of aid programmes on the ground.[5] Though a rich literature has developed on aid from the 1990s onward in the DRC by Linda Seay and

---

4   K. Jenkins, "The Christian Church as an NGO in Africa: Supporting Post-Independence Era State Legitimacy or Promoting Change?" in E. Sandburg (ed.) *The Changing Politics of Non-Governmental Organisations and African States*, (Westport, CT: Praeger, 1994), 82–99.

5   For a range of works on the United Nations in the DRC in the 1960s, see E. Lefever, *Uncertain Mandate: Politics of the U.N. Congo Operation* (Baltimore: Johns Hopkins University Press, 1967; Kent, *America*; S. Williams, *Who Killed Hammarskjöld? The UN, the Cold War, and White Supremacy in Africa* (New York: Oxford University Press, 2011).

Theodore Trefon among others, this literature has little about aid programmes before the collapse of the Mobutu regime.[6]

With strong assistance from the US government, Mobutu's regime reformed its currency in 1967 and set the value of the new currency at 1 zaire to two US dollars. Changing US aid dollars to the new zaire currency was more than just a matter of accounting for aid agencies, as Congolese church leaders sought to sell on the black market US currency sent to fund projects. Donor/Congolese financial relationships entangled ethical concerns, Western paternalism, cultural nationalism, and the contours of transnational relationships between African and Western churches. This is new terrain for the study of aid in the early independence era.

Furthermore, aid workers encountered a changing environment for Congolese state and civil society partners. Congolese officials and church leaders were determined to control and supervise how foreign aid agencies operated in their country by the late 1960s. Although Western observers have long mocked Mobutu's cultural nationalist ideology of authenticity as a hypocritical sham, Congolese church leaders such as Jean Bokeleale used cultural nationalism to justify their unwillingness to heed donors. Foreign aid workers in the CWS felt at odds with their assertive Congolese partners, even though their assistance had helped the Congolese government recover from civil wars.

By taking the focus away from a single-minded focus on Mobutu's theatrics, this chapter is a significant contribution to the historiography of Mobutu's rule. For too long, the critiques of Mobutu's crippling policies have overshadowed other actors. Aid has primary been discussed in regards to Mobutu's expensive and large failures, such as the ill-fated Zairian space programme or the Inga dam.[7] Though scholars such as Götz Bechtolsheimer and Sean Kelly have paid close attention to the ways Mobutu used his position as the leader of a Western client state and his Third Worldist aspirations to obtain foreign aid, the role of humanitarian assistance in the DRC before the onset of

6   For some works on aid programmes in the DRC since the early 1990s, see L. Seay, "Authority at Twilight: Civil Society, Social Services, and the State in the Eastern Democratic Republic of Congo" (PhD thesis, University of Texas – Austin, 2009); Autesserre, *Trouble*; T. Trefon, *Congo Masquerade: The Political Culture of Aid Inefficiency and Reform Failure* (London: Zed, 2011).

7   T. Turner and C. Young, *The Rise and Decline of the Zairian State* (Madison, WI: University of Wisconsin Press, 1985), 298–300; B. Verhaegen, "Les safaris technologiques au Zaïre, 1970–1980," *Politique Africaine* 18 (1985), 71–87; J.C. Willaume, *Zaïre, L'épopée d'Inga: Chronique d'une predation industrielle* (Paris: L'Harmattan, 1986).

new international conflicts in the 1990s is not well understood. In donor correspondence on aid in the late 1960s and early 1970s, Mobutu is a distant and shadowy figure rather than the omnipresent dictator portrayed so skillfully by Colette Braeckman and Michela Wrong.[8]

Instead, go-betweens such as Bokeleale and Minister of Social Affairs Sophie Lihau-Kanza were the main figures that frustrated CWS officials. The CWS' bureaucratic squabbles may not tilitate readers as much as Mobutu's colossal failures, but these everyday negotiations indicate how Congolese and American partners operated with little clear influence from Mobutu himself. At this level, DRC government policies in the late 1960s and early 1970s already appeared to be rife with problems, despite the upbeat views of top US officials. CWS staff members chose ultimately to cut funds – even though they blamed the failures of the programmes on their Congolese partners rather than take into account their own role or broader political and economic issues.

Another value to concentrating on the CWS' varied fortunes in Mobutu's Zaire is to better understand how humanitarian aid adjusted to Cold War politics. The CWS and WCC stayed silent about Mobutu's authoritarian policies and showed no interest in either democracy or human rights. While these organisations fit well with US policy goals of shoring up Mobutu's rule, CWS workers felt slighted by US officials who seemingly did little to solve conflicts about aid and programmes. US diplomatic staff in the DRC and the Congolese state actually did not do much to assist the CPRA. Much as Severine Autesserre and Theodore Trefon contended in ther review of the failures of foreign aid, foreign governments often neglected the concerns of aid agencies.[9]

This chapter will focus on the changing relationship between the CWS and Congolese partners. One reason for this choice lies in the nature of the sources, which draw mainly from CWS and WCC written correspondence. These sources from the late 1960s and early 1970s rarely focused on refugees and recipients of aid actually engaged with foreign aid workers. Instead, CWS internal correspondence on the DRC mainly dealt with Congolese church leaders. Though CWS members identified themselves generally as liberals, they privately belittled their Congolese associates. Without an examination of archives from Congolese institutions, how Bokeleale and other Congolese viewed their negotiations with CWS remains unclear. The very fact that the overwhelming amount of correspondence reviewed here is in English, a

---

8   C. Braeckman, *Le dinasoure, le Zaïre de Mobutu* (Paris: Fayard, 1992); M. Wrong, *In The Footsteps of Mr. Kurtz: Living on the Brink of Disaster in Mobutu's Congo* (New York: HarperCollins, 2001).

9   Autesserre, *Trouble*; Trefon, *Masquerade*.

language few Congolese knew, testifies to the skewed nature of the sources. It is unclear if any Congolese government archival materials that could contain information on the CWS has survived. Fieldwork in areas where CWS-funded projects took place might provide valauble perspectives on foreign aid programmes, since there is little sense of how aid recipients responded to aid projects in the CWS correspondence. A thorough overview of USAID policies in this period is beyond the scope of this study. More generally, there is no way of knowing how typical the CWS case might be without more research on humanitarian and development organisations in the DRC. Despite its limitations, this provisional foray broadens and sharpens discussion of the role of aid in the aftermath of civil wars in the early independence era and international aid in the early years of Congolese independence.

Healing the wounds of the Congo crises, 1965–1967

When Mobutu's troops removed the old government from power on 23 November 1965, CWS and donors made no immediate public response. Ecumenical Protestant aid workers and missionaries questioned their relationships to the US and South Vietnamese regimes, the case that has drawn the most scholarship on the link between US policy and private NGOs.[10] The same can not be said for the Congo. With the Congolese parliament locked in a quagmire between president Joseph Kasa-Vubu and prime minister Moïse Tshombe before the coup, Mennonite Central Committee (MCC) director John Gaeddert expressed what was likely a common feeling among aid workers: 'No one is really able to understand or to interpret Congo politics, let alone predict it.'[11] A week after the military took power, Gaeddert admitted he could not make any sense of what would happen next.[12] CWS staff had already hoped someone could finally bring the country together. CWS material relief director James Paton had wondered in 1964 if Moïse Tshombe would finally settle the country down, even though he felt little personal sympathy for Tshombe.[13]

---

10 On this issue, see J. Nichols, *The Uneasy Alliance: Religion, Refugee Work, and US Foreign Policy* (New York: Oxford University Press, 1988); D. Leaman, "Politicized Service and Teamwork Tensions: Mennonite Central Committee in Vietnam, 1966–1969," *Mennonite Quarterly Review* 71 (1997), 544–70; Gill, *Embattled*.

11 John Gaeddert, Annual Report, 16 November 1965, Folder 113/121 Congo Office 1965, Box 193, IX-6-3, MCCA.

12 John Gaeddert to Vern Preheim, 7 December 1965, Folder 115/123 Congo Office 1966, Box 197, IX-6-3, MCCA.

13 Interview, James Paton, 14 August 2018.

By early 1966, CPRA staff had officially endorsed the new regime. Hans Schaffert, still the CPRA director, made clear to donors and other missionaries that his organisation would be an ally to the Congolese government. He wrote in the Protestant missionary magazine *Congo Mission News*, 'We can understand why [president Mobutu] has called the whole nation to "roll up its sleeves" and to all the people to give themselves up with all their force to the reconstruction of the country … [The CPRA], as representatives of the church of Christ, is grateful to be able to participate in the reconstruction of the country.'[14] The CPRA director listed the work of Protestant relief in eastern Congo, among Angolan refugees, and in Orientale province. Protestant agencies and aid workers had no choice but to endorse Mobutu's new regime. After years of chaos, one can hardly blame European and North American aid workers for hoping Mobutu would bring about stability where others had failed.

After his coup, Mobutu claimed that only he could restore order. However, the DRC suffered from continued unrest. Fighting between Pierre Mulele's guerillas in the western Kwilu province and government troops left villages bereft of livestock, possessions, and fields in 1964 and 1965. In the northeast Ituri region, Simba nationalist rebels remained in control over rural areas until 1966. European and Katangese mercenaries who had fought Simba rebels from 1964 to 1966 turned on troops loyal to Mobutu in July 1967. These mercenary troops ultimately fled to Rwanda after seizing the eastern Congolese city of Bukavu for several months.[15]

The mercenary revolt in eastern Congo beginning in July 1967 further illustrates the close links between CPRA programmes and the Congolese government. Ex-Katangese mercenary troops took over Bukavu under the command of European officers in the summer of 1967. In the previous three years, these urban centres had suffered from food shortages, the destruction of buildings and infrastructure, and epidemics during and after the Simba revolts.[16] CPRA staff managed to help coordinate relief efforts after the mercenaries withdrew. CPRA material aid director Malcolm McVeigh toured Kisangani, one of the centres of the mercenary revolt, only a few days after the mercenary forces had left the city in July 1967. McVeigh took a US Air

---

14 H. Schaffert, "Pastor Schaffert Reports." *Congo Mission News* 211 (January–March 1966) 5.

15 M. Honorin, *La fin des mercenaires: Bukavu, novembre 1967* (Paris: Robert Laffont, 1968).

16 The East Congo of the Congo Protestant Relief Agency and Christian World Service Involvement (no date – c. spring 1967), Folder Zaire 1967–1968, Box 22, Record Group 8, CWS/PHS.

Force C-130 Hercules airplane to the city with 16 tons of food and several US diplomats, a sign of the close relationship between the US government presence in the Congo with CPRA. US diplomatic staff viewed aid as a key means of restoring order, to the point the US embassy instructed CPRA and Catholic Relief Services to deliver food to Bukavu shortly after the munity as 'psychological distributions' – a telling statement of how humanitarian aid served US policy interests.[17] Congolese government troops as well as rebels pillaged stores and left almost nothing behind, and food prices skyrocketed as a result.[18] Much as in Bukavu, Congolese CPRA staff filled the gaps left behind after the evacuation of foreign staff workers.

By 1968, CRPA staff believed that the political situation in much of the Congo had improved. Malcolm McVeigh took pride in noting how CPRA could move away from emergency aid distribution towards economic development. He predicted that CPRA aid would no longer be needed for Angolan refugees in Bas-Congo by 1969, and noted how CPRA programmes in Kwilu had already replaced emergency aid with agricultural projects. 'If the political situation remains stable, we can look for a gradual improvement in the general economic situation. The economic potential of the country is enormous and certainly should permit the Congo to care for its people and institutions,' McVeigh noted.[19] Just as US officials viewed Mobutu as crucial to maintaining stability, McVeigh and other CPRA staff did not discuss potential problems with the new regime. This resembled all too well the glowing assessments of Mobutu's performance in the late 1960s by US diplomats such as ambassador Sheldon Vance, who worked to silence criticism of corruption and financial mismanagement from the lower ranks of State Department and USAID personnel in the DRC.[20]

With the end of violent revolts, the CPRA and Congolese church leaders turned to rehabilitation and economic development by the end of the 1960s. These programmes did not resemble expensive and gigantic state-sponsored programmes such as the Inga dam. CWS certainly lacked the funds at the disposal of the US, Belgium, and the World Bank, and CPRA projects were much smaller in scope. While CPRA projects themselves initially did not

---

17   Donald Kurtz to Malcolm McVeigh, 24 July 1967, Folder Zaire 1967–1968, Box 22, Record Group 8, CWS/PHS. State Department correspondence also notes this connection, as referenced by Bechtolsheimer, "Breakfast," 78–79.

18   Ibid.

19   Malcolm McVeigh, "Additional Information FY 1969," 1 January 1968, Folder Zaire 1967–1968, Box 22, Record Group 8, CWS/PHS.

20   Turner and Young, *Decline*, 214, 217–18.

provoke concern with donors, CPC chairman Jean Bokeleale's grand schemes for developing new ways to raise funds for churches had mixed reactions among Western donors.

CPRA projects and Congolese independence, 1965–1972

As the era of emergency aid was coming to an end, CWS and CPRA staff members had to reconsider their goals. Critiques of paternalism surviving from colonial times concerned CWS and CPRA staff. For Protestant churches and their aid affiliates, the issue of Congolese leadership ran parallel with the views of American officials about Mobutu. Most Protestant missionaries had done relatively little to promote African leadership of churches and their financial resources until 1960.[21] The majority of US Protestant denominations agreed to surrender formal control of mission-founded churches to Congolese pastors between 1960 and 1968. Most Congolese Protestant leaders grew to see church union as a way of asserting the value of a Congolese conception of Christianity, a better means of ensuring benefits from the DRC government, and an end to being treated as junior partners by foreign missionaries.[22] Some Congolese Catholics raised critiques of Western condescension as well.[23] Bokeleale's ambition to lead a united single Protestant church in the DRC rested in no small part on his access to funds from foreign donors, although scholarship on Protestants in the Mobutu years only acknowledges this in passing.[24] Charges that missionaries treated Congolese Protestants like the Belgians treated colonial subjects fueled the creation of a single Protestant church in March 1970, the ECC. Mobutu turned against the Catholic hierarchy after Cardinal Joseph-Albert Malula in 1969 made clear he opposed Mobutu's policies. Congolese Protestants saw opportunities in building an alliance with Mobutu to settle internal church disputes, and to gain access to state patronage. And, as Jean-François Bayart has noted, victors in struggles over financial funds inside churches can afford to use their wealth to solidify their power.[25]

21 Makowitz, *Cross and Sword*.

22 K. Adelman, "The Influence of Religion on National Integration in Zaire" (PhD thesis, Georgetown University, 1975); Kabongo-Mbaya, *Église*.

23 For Congolese Catholic critiques of missionary attitudes, see V. Mulago, "Christianisme et culture: apport africain à la théologie," in G. Baeta (ed.) *Christianity in Tropical Africa* (Oxford: Oxford University Press, 1968), 308–32.

24 Kabongo-Mbaya, *Église*, 375–6, 397.

25 J.F. Bayart, "Les Eglise chrétiennes et la politique du ventre: le partage du gateau ecclesial." *Politique Africaine* 35 (1989), 68–76.

6. Jean Bokeleale with Methodist Thomas Roughface at a World Council of Churches meeting in Tulsa, Oklahoma, USA in 1969. Bokeleale was determined to wrest control of aid projects from expatiate aid workers in favour of Congolese leaders, much to the chagrin of donor agencies like the Church World Service. (WCCA/B8627–45)

Congolese members of the ECC were fully aware that only foreign aid allowed CPRA to operate, and CWS staff had little confidence in Congolese pastors in regards to finances. The CWS espoused decolonisation, as attested by aid programmes in Algeria after independence from France in 1962 and assistance to Mozambican refugees in Tanzania.[26] Even so, this did not mean they viewed their Congolese partners as their equals. Malcolm McVeigh, a CWS staff member assigned to administer CPRA from 1965 to 1967, recalled in an interview how he felt the CPC finance committee wanted to steal money from CPRA. He tried to make sure he attended their meetings to make sure they did not succeed.[27] These doubts about the honesty and rationality of Congolese partners coalesced around Jean Bokeleale. Rather than critique the role of the Congolese state or their own agenda as aid workers, CWS staff considered Congolese individuals to be to blame for the adversities that plagued the CPRA.

Bokeleale's denounciation of missionary criticism led to attacks from some missionaries and from CWS staff. Conservative Baptist mission board member Milton Baker and Congolese Methodist bishop John Welsey Shungu directed a failed effort to form a dissident and more theologically conservative federation of churches from 1970 to 1972. One US missionary portrayed the ECC as an authoritarian and meddlesome threat to evangelicals.[28] CWS staff also had negative views about Bokeleale's alleged recklnessness. Bokeleale had a poor relationship with Perry Smith, the CWS worker who had replaced Malcolm McVeigh as the director of material aid for CPRA in 1968. Smith noted to van Hoogstraten how Bokeleale did nothing to resolve CPRA's financial problems with the Congolese government and questioned the value of CPRA's programmes.[29]

Bokeleale's election to lead the CPC in 1968 came just as three major difficulties plagued the CWS-funded CPRA. One came from a decision by the US government. A conflict over Congolese government aid to CPRA greatly complicated the CPC's struggle to control CWS funding. In 1968, the US government mandated that governments that received aid from USAID had to pay ten per cent of shipping costs. Why the Johnson administration had made this decision in the last months of its mandate is unclear, but the results

26 J. Rosenthal, "From 'Migrants' to 'Refugees': Identity, Aid, and Decolonisation in Ngara District, Tanzania," *Journal of African History* 56:2 (2015), 261–79.

27 Interview, Malcolm and Marion McVeigh, Whiting, New Jersey, 6 October 2012.

28 Oldberg, "History," 353–75.

29 Perry Smith to Jan S.F. van Hoogstraten, 20 January 1969, Folder Zaire 1969, Box 22, Record Group 8, CWS/PHS.

were catastrophic for CPRA. The Congolese government refused to abide by the demand of the US government, and then refused to fund the transport of CPRA supplies from the port of Matadi into the rest of the country after August 1968.[30] CPRA had a contract with the state-owned OTRACO company (Office des transports au Congo) to handle the transport of supplies, but the Congolese government would not resume transporting CPRA supplies. Donald Brown, the head of the US Agency for International Development (USAID) in the Congo, tried to convince minister of social affairs Sophie Lihau-Kanza and minister of finance Victor Nendaka to resume its payments to OTRACO in January 1969.[31] Outgoing US Ambassador to the Congo Robert McBride met with Mobutu and noted CWS anxieties about the problems, but Mobutu said he was unaware of the situation.[32] Though the CWS considered the Congolese government and men like Bokeleale as the prime culprits, it was a US State Department policy change that prompted retaliation by the Congolese government.

Two other problems troubled CWS staff. CPRA was running at a growing deficit by 1968, and that shortfall kept growing for years afterwards. Another dispute came from how the CWS sent funds to the CPRA. Mobutu's 1967 monetary reforms pegged the value of the new zaire currency at 1 zaire to 2 dollars. Black marketeers bought and sold US dollars for much higher rates. Since CWS sent dollars to Kinshasa, Congolese pastors wanted to sell the dollars illegally to raise more money. Smith, clearly frustrated, asked his CWS superior J.F. van Hoogstraten for 5000 dollars to be ideally placed in a new CWS bank account in Belgium. This would allow for CWS money to be exchanged directly into zaires without Bokeleale using the black market.[33] Meanwhile, other donors wanted to know how van Hoogstraten wanted to deal with the CPC. Reginald Helfferich, director of the United Methodist Church Board of World Mission, asked van Hoogstraten if he was going to set up an independent bank account rather than go through Bokeleale.[34] Hoogstraten noted on the letter that 'donors should push the CPC to change their

---

30 Perry Smith to Jan S.F. van Hoogstraten, 16 January 1969, Folder Zaire 1969, Box 22, Record Group 8, CWS/PHS.

31 Donald Brown to Sophie Lihau-Kanza and Victor Nendaka, Folder Zaire 1969, 16 January 1969, Box 22, Record Group 8, CWS/PHS.

32 Perry Smith to Jan S.F. van Hoogstraten, 20 January 1969, Folder Zaire 1969, Box 22, Record Group 8, CWS/PHS.

33 Perry Smith to Jan S.F. van Hoogstraten, 17 February 1969, Folder Zaire 1969, Box 22, Record Group 8, CWS/PHS.

34 Reginald Helfferich to Jan S.F. van Hoogstraten, 5 March 1969, Folder Zaire 1969, Box 22, Record Group 8, CWS/PHS.

patterns.'[35] At the same time, van Hoogstraten had decided to halt most CWS funds for CPRA to pressure the CPC and (indirectly) the Congolese regime.[36]

These tensions point out the strains in the relationship between the US government and CPRA. Given how much CPRA helped Mobutu's government, it would seem that their alliance would be quite firm. Yet the transport crisis had led Perry Smith to think the embassy 'is not giving [the problem] their fullest attention.' He complained that he had been pressured by USAID to quickly furnish them reports on CPRA for McBride's meeting with Mobutu over the issue, yet USAID did not take up the issue.[37] Several months later, Smith expressed dismay about USAID staff member Neboysha Brashich for haranguing Smith about CPRA's oversight of mentioning US government aid in their annual 1968 report. Brashich had berated Smith, since 'the United States was not officially allowed to publicise and it was up to the voluntary agencies to acknowledge the fact that the US was the major supplier of our foodstuffs.'[38] To Smith, Brashich treated CPRA and CWS as subordinates to USAID.[39]

CWS doubts about Bokeleale only widened in 1969. Efforts by USAID manager Donald Brown in June 1969 to resolve the problems between Bokeleale, CPRA, and USAID did not quickly resolve the situation.[40] Samuel Bukasa, Smith's Congolese supervisor and the head of CPRA who answered to Bokeleale at the CPC, joined Bukasa in an overview of CPRA's financial woes. Bokeleale responded by asking why CPRA still needed food supplies. The CPC president then asked 'why the US was insisting on the Congo government paying 10% of the ocean freight when the US government is spending millions on its aid to Biafra.'[41] The CWS had devoted much to the cause of Biafran refugees, and Bokeleale felt the DRC's own problems were neglected. After two hours, the meeting concluded with Smith and Brown both feeling unsure what Bokeleale would do to work with CWS and the

35 Ibid.

36 Jan S.F. van Hoogstraten to Perry Smith, 23 March 1969, Folder Zaire 1969, Box 22, Record Group 8, CWS/PHS.

37 Perry Smith to Jan S.F. van Hoogstraten, 17 January 1969, Folder Zaire 1969, Box 22, Record Group 8, CWS/PHS.

38 Perry Smith to Jan S.F. van Hoogstraten, 27 March 1969, Folder Zaire 1969, Box 22, Record Group 8, CWS/PHS.

39 Ibid.

40 The following is drawn from Perry Smith to Jan S.F. van Hoogstraten, 20 June 1969, Folder Zaire 1969, Box 22, Record Group 8, CWS/PHS.

41 Ibid.

US government. Brown told Smith, 'I've done all I can to help. It is up to the Congolese [i.e. Rev. Bokeleale] to fight their own battle.'[42] While Smith presented these statements as more proof of Bokeleale's inability to work with others, they also demonstrated Bokeleale's nationalist views regarding aid. By calling out US double standards and openly questioning the value of US government food assistance, Bokeleale had made clear that he was not going to accept being treated as an unequal partner. CPRA reports also expressed this concern about wealth inequalities between Western countries and the Congo. 'The means of the human community are at the disposition of only 20% of the world population which is mostly concentrated in the Northern hemisphere, while those remaining constantly struggle against an oppressive poverty which weights them down,' stated the 1968 annual CPRA report.[43] Bokeleale's forthright views show how Congolese in civil society demanded control over aid programmes.

Bukasa had the unenviable task of mediating between Bokeleale, the Congolese government, USAID, and CWS. For example, Bukasa refused to allow Smith to send minister Lihau-Kanza reports on how the shipping crisis impeded their programmes on the grounds this move would be too 'political.'[44] Bukasa wrote a history of the shipping problems and noted how CPRA had consequently lost millions of dollars in aid.[45] His scrambling to appease other parties in these complicated disputes became particularly hard by September 1969. When Bokeleale learned that Smith now transferred CWS funds in Congolese currency rather than dollars, he demanded Bukasa not accept the money since it could no longer be exchanged on the black market.[46] Bukasa's role as a middleman demonstrate how different actors within Congolese civil society could engage with donor aid agencies at cross purposes. Neither Bukasa's efforts to alleviate problems nor Bokeleale's defence of ECC autonomy can be ascribed simply to Mobutu's policies.

Minister Lihau-Kanza's criticism of the USAID shipping policy and Bokeleale's intransigence went over poorly with van Hoogstraten. In a letter

42   Ibid.

43   Congo Protestant Relief Agency Annual Report 1968, Folder Zaire 1969, Record Group 8, Box 22, Folder Zaire 1969, CWS/PHS.

44   Perry Smith to Jan S.F. van Hoogstraten, 9 September 1969, Folder Zaire 1969, Record Group 8, Box 22, CWS/PHS.

45   Samuel Bukasa, Les causes de l'arrêt de l'aide materielle de l'entr'aide protestante, 1 October 1969, Folder Zaire 1969, Box 22, Record Group 8, CWS/PHS.

46   Perry Smith to Jan S.F. van Hoogstraten, 4 October 1969, Folder Zaire 1969, Box 22, Record Group 8, CWS/PHS.

to Smith, van Hoogstraten noted how Congolese people had missed out on roughly $3 million of supplies since the shipping quarrels started in August 1968.[47] He warned that CWS would withdraw if it was not wanted. When Smith requested money for Bukasa to visit agricultural co-operatives in Cameroon a month after Bokeleale questioned the value of CWS assistance, van Hoogstraten balked. 'How far do we have to constantly bail out the basic CPC/CPRA administration which apparently is partially representative for the local churches, but does not get supported by them,' fulminated the CWS agent.[48] This points out a basic problem with church-affiliated aid partnerships: national federations of churches did not always have much ability to ensure individual congregations could actualy contribute.

Van Hoogstraten decided to resolve the disputes with Bokeleale in a visit to Kinshasa in October 1969, and his failures displayed the lack of trust between Congolese and CWS partners in aid.[49] '[Bokeleale] subjected me, far beyond expectations, to a series of invectives and insults for a period of 2 ½ hours … Although in my years of "experience" in Africa with some African church leaders, I was forewarned, it nevertheless took some effort not be sucked into a series of counter arguments,' van Hoogstraten told his CWS superiors Nancy Nicalo and James McCracken.[50] One might wonder how Bokeleale himself would describe being lectured to by a CWS representative. Despite Bukasa's efforts to try to make sure that the profits made in currency exchanges went to CPRA projects, apparently the CPC's Finance Committee and Bokeleale had chosen to use the money for salaries and staff cars. Bokeleale decided to no longer accept any CWS money in zaires unless the money could be sold on the black market. Van Hoogstraten and Smith tried to change Bokeleale's mind, which led to a long tirade of 'rude remarks, innuendoes, [and] anti-white absurdities' by Bokeleale in which he accused Smith and his CWS predecessor, Malcolm McVeigh, of stealing money that should have gone to CPRA. The CPC argued that he had the right to use CPRA funds as he and the all-Congolese Finance Committee saw fit, and that the CWS had no right to set limits on how CWS money was dispersed.

---

47 Jan S.F. van Hoogstraten to Perry Smith, 23 July 1969, Folder Zaire 1969, Box 22, Record Group 8, CWS/PHS.

48 Jan S.F. van Hoogstraten to Perry Smith, 20 August 1969, Folder Zaire 1969, Box 22, Record Group 8, CWS/PHS.

49 Jan S.F. van Hoogstraten to James McCracken and Nancy Nicalo, 11 November 1969, Folder Zaire 1969, Box 22, Record Group 8, CWS/PHS.

50 Ibid.

Bokeleale also wanted more money from the CWS. The CPC finance committee had pressured Perry Smith to solicit funds for Bukasa's salary. Bokeleale told van Hoogstraten that the finance committee had lay people and politicians in its ranks, and van Hoogstraten thought they had used Smith to obtain too much money for Bukasa.[51] Bokeleale blasted van Hoogstraten and Smith at their meeting, and even accused Smith of stealing CPRA money.[52] The CWS African department director decried how the CPC kept no financial records and allowed foreign donor money for CPRA to be treated as a 'grab-bag' by other CPC staff to be spent on anything they liked.[53] Van Hoogstraten also derided the World Council of Churches, which was 'on vacation or asleep and the CPC/CPRA deficit bookkeeping continues into fuller astronomical figures'.[54] Such declarations obscure the basic fact that Bokeleale felt entitled as a Congolese church leader to hold the reins over aid projects in the country, while van Hoogstraten had no confidence in him – much as Western politicans viewed Patrice Lumumba as too erratic to be allowed to lead his country in 1960 and 1961.

Van Hoogstraten advised CWS director James McCracken to refuse to allow for black market money exchanges and to make sure that CWS funds were only sent to CPRA in zaires. No one in CPC could be trusted, and 'poor Bukasa is the patsy but he is the best of all [the Congolese]'.[55] One positive development was that USAID agreed to drop the ten per cent of shipping fees demand on the Congolese government, and that new ambassador Sheldon Vance convinced Lihau-Kanza to start releasing funds so CPRA goods might finally be sent out of Matadi.[56] However, van Hoogstraten refused to authorise food shipments paid or donated to CWS in 1970 until CPC and CPRA changed their positions.[57] Thus, scaling back aid for the CWS had nothing to do with improved conditions in the DRC, but rather Van Hoogstraten and Smith's frustration with Bokeleale. The CWS staff never

---

51 Jan S.F. van Hoogstraten to James McCracken, 7 November 1969, Folder Zaire 1969, Box 22, Record Group 8, CWS/PHS.

52 Jan S.F. van Hoogstraten to James McCracken and Nancy Nicalo, 11 November 1969, Record Group 8, Box 22, Folder Zaire 1969, CWS/PHS.

53 Ibid.

54 Ibid.

55 Jan S.F. van Hoogstraten to James McCracken, 7 November 1969, Record Group 8, Box 22, Folder 1969, CWS/PHS.

56 Ibid.

57 Jan S.F. van Hoogstraten to Melvin Myers, 17 June 1970, Folder Zaire 1970, Box 22, Record Group 8, CWS/PHS.

questioned the wisdom of the US-backed monetary reforms that had prepared the way for the black market. Again, Congolese greed was responsible for the problems in their view.

These quarrels reveal much about the very different understandings of how aid should operate in the DRC between Bokeleale and the CWS. Bokeleale considered himself the senior partner in his dealings with the CWS. The arbitrary decision to artificially bolster the zaire currency's value against the dollar promoted by the US government and the International Monetary Fund did not actually reflect the market value of the dollar in the DRC. The CWS considered Bokeleale's recognition of the failure of the new monetary reforms to be unethical, while Bokeleale considered it insulting that he had to seek approval for how donor funds should be used. Instead of recognising Bokeleale's criticism of the condescension of CWS and CPRA as valid, van Hoogstraten's comments painted Bokeleale as irrational and racist. These disagreements continued into the early 1970s.

CWS conflicts over CPRA, 1970–1972

In March 1970, a majority of CPC assembly delegates representing various Protestant denominations voted to form a single Protestant church, the Église du Christ au Congo (ECC).[58] Each denomination would henceforth be a 'community' within the ECC, and the ECC could also help determine what churches deserved official recognition by the Congolese state and which would not. Bokeleale, now president of the ECC, used rhetoric that emphasised Congolese unity and a need to break free of missionary domination. These views ran parallel to Mobutu's new ideology of African authenticity, which only his cultural nationalist regime could restore among Congolese by challenging colonialist legacies of African inferiority. While the Congolese government increasingly targeted the Catholic Archbishop of Kinshasa Joseph-Albert Malula hierarchy as a rival, the ECC had a much friendlier relationship with the Congolese state.[59]

---

58 The best source on the early history of the ECC remains Kabongo-Mbaya, *Église*. See also Nelson, *Missionizing*.

59 On the disputes between the Roman Catholic Church and Mobutu, see K. Adelman, "The Church-State Conflict in Zaire, 1969–1974." *African Studies Review* 18:1 (1975), 102–16; L. Ngomo Okitembo, *L'engagement politique de l'Eglise catholique au Zaïre, 1960–1992* (Paris: L'Harmattan, 1998); C. Makiobo, *Eglise catholique et mutations socio-politiques au Congo-Zaïre: La contestation du régime Mobutu* (Paris: L'Harmattan, 2004); J.B. Mukanya Kaninda-Muana, *Eglise catholique et pouvoir au Congo-Zaïre: Enjeux, options et négociations du changement*

The establishment of the ECC did not improve Congolese Protestant relations with the CWS. Over the course of 1970 and 1971, CWS and ECC staff continued to lock horns. Van Hoogstraten noted his concerns to Dan Owen, who had replaced the beleaguered Perry Smith in the summer of 1970 as CPRA's head of material aid. After stating that CWS was facing financial hardship and would have to make funding decisions based more on need than older historical relationships, van Hoogstraten added: 'Our CPC brethren, especially Mr. Bokeleale, will have a hard time in seeing it in this way, especially as you heard him say that we should double, nay triple our contributions to the Congo now that "they" are in charge.'[60] Apparently, Bokeleale had told Owen that the CWS wanted to intimidate Congolese by restricting black market currency exchanges, and that the ECC would not stand either the CWS or the World Council of Churches giving 'neo-colonialist' orders about financial matters.[61] Although the Congolese government finally released money to pay for shipping CPRA supplies from Matadi to the rest of the country by late 1970, difficulties remained. The Congolese government had never made a permanent accord with CPRA to import supplies without paying customs, and customs officials began to demand payment and imposed their own regulations (apparently not always based on actual law) once shipments began to come in again.[62]

1971 proved to be a particularly dramatic year for CPRA. CWS made the decision to end the shipments of US government food donations in July of that year.[63] Besides the hostility of the ECC, other factors included a budget crisis in CWS, the Congolese government's claims of a renewed economy, and more serious problems elsewhere in Africa. Just as CWS limited funding for CPRA, the organisation ran into a nearly $60,000 deficit for its warehouse expenses, even as CWS only furnished $25,000.[64] With CWS no longer providing all the funds for the warehouse, ECC had to use funds allocated to

social à Kinshasa, 1945–1997 (Paris: L'Harmattan, 2007). On relations between the DRC government and Protestants, see Kabongo-Mbaya, *Église.*

60 Jan S.F. van Hoogstraten to Dan Owen, 17 September 1970, Folder Zaire 1970, Box 22, Record Group 8, CWS/PHS.

61 Jan S.F. van Hoogstraten to Dan Owen, 18 December 1970, Folder Zaire 1970, Box 22, Record Group 8, CWS/PHS.

62 Jan S.F. van Hoogstraten to Melvin Myers, 19 September 1970, Folder Zaire 1970, Box 22, Record Group 8, CWS/PHS.

63 Jan S.F. van Hoogstraten to Dan Owen, 18 January 1971, Folder Zaire 1971, Box 22, Record Group 8, CWS/PHS.

64 Jean Bokeleale, Operational Expenses for the Kinshasa warehouse, ECC Project 11/71, Folder Zaire 1971, Box 22, Record Group 8, CWS/PHS.

other programmes to cover the cost.[65] CPRA started charging programmes who received CPRA aid fees to raise money and become more self-sufficient – a shock to these aid organisations who did not expect to pay tribute to Bokeleale.[66] In November 1971, the World Council of Churches held a meeting of representatives of aid donors and ECC representatives, which included van Hoogstraten and Bokeleale. Without CWS funds, CPRA's deficit had come close to reaching $100,000.[67] The Swiss Protestant aid agency Hilfswerk der Evangelischen Kirchen der Schweiz (HEKS), German Protestant charities, the World Council of Churches, and CWS agreed to pay the deficit on the understanding that HEKS and WCC would work with ECC and CPRA to prevent another financial crisis in the future. Much as US officials repeatedly chose to keep funding Mobutu's government despite its manifold financial problems after the early 1970s, donor aid agencies agreed to continue supplying CPRA with funds. Though certainly research is needed on the ECC's development programmes, it is clear that ECC ambitions to expand its social role in the DRC exceeded its ability to pay for it, much as Mobutu's dream of becoming an intellectual and political model for Africa led to colossally misguided projects.

Over the course of 1972, CWS decided to cut all ties to CPRA. Shipping problems from Matadi to the rest of the country made the delivery of US government donated food difficult and slow. Since Lihau-Kanza continued to inadequately fund the cost of transport within DRC for CWS supplies, the cost was very high. Bokeleale's plan of charging a fee for shipping CWS supplies was not acceptable. The best CWS would offer was to send supplies to various missionary boards through CPRA.[68] Van Hoogstraten wanted to stay clear of the Zaire Protestant Relief Agency, CPRA's new name after Mobutu's decision to make Zaire the new name of the country. He considered partnering with Catholic Relief Services, making a separate agreement between the CWS and the Zairian government, and maintaining a separate CWS office not connected to CPRA.[69]

---

65 "Congo Protestant Relief Agency 1971," 10, Folder Zaire 1971, Box 22, Record Group 8, CWS/PHS.

66 Ibid., 12.

67 Alan Brash, Aide-Memoire, Meeting at the Ecumenical Centre, Geneva, to consider question in Congo (Zaire) related to CPA and office building, 20 November 1971, Folder Zaire 1971, Box 22, Record Group 8, CWS/PHS.

68 Jan S.F. van Hoogstraten to Africa Committee NCCC, 25 January 1972, Folder Zaire 1972, Box 22, Record Group 8, CWS/PHS.

69 Jan S.F. van Hoogstraten to James McCracken, 14 February 1972, Folder Zaire 1972, Box 22, Record Group 8, CWS/PHS.

Donor agencies disagreed on the best path to take regarding aiding CPRA. CWS's decisions proved much less supportive of CPRA than the World Council of Churches. Van Hoogstraten noted, 'It is clear that the days of a major CWS input [in DRC] are over,' but he wanted to have CWS aid missionary boards still running programmes in DRC. CWS even might consider aid for CPRA, as long as CPRA reconsidered its finances and its expensive Kinshasa warehouse.[70] The WCC took a more respectful approach to CPRA. WCC staff member Alan Brash opposed the idea of an independent CWS presence, as it would be 'washing your hands of the local church structure.'[71] Meanwhile, the WCC continued to send money to CPRA, even as strife between ECC and dissident US missionary and Congolese church leaders had emerged in 1971 and 1972. The net result was summed up in a pithy van Hoogstraten memo in 1972: 'CCPW [a church affiliated aid programme] has dropped Zaire. ACTS [a church affiliated aid programme] too. German [Protestant aid agencies] passive. I hit the roof – moral issue of WCC et al. leading Bokeleale and company to dream and then nil.'[72]

Yet van Hoogstraten suddenly made a decision to authorise aid to CPRA, despite his skepticism regarding the ECC. Steven Miller, still working as the assistant material aid director for CPRA, agreed to ship materials paid by CWS on behalf of different mission boards.[73] Interim material aid director H.N. Schöll and Bukasa thanked van Hoogstraten for releasing $13,000 for CPRA.[74] Van Hoogstraten's superior, CWS director James McCracken, expressed his surprise: 'How come you are starting shipments after all the stop, cease, etc?'[75] Van Hoogstraten admitted this would not be easy to explain, but noted how '[CWS] would stand to lose little.'[76] Van Hoogstraten believed that

70   Jan S.F. van Hoogstraten to Alan Brash, World Council of Churches, 4 April 1972, Folder Zaire 1972, Box 22, Record Group 8, CWS/PHS.

71   Alan Brash to Jan S.F. van Hoogstraten, 13 April 1972, Folder Zaire 1972, Box 22, Record Group 8, CWS/PHS.

72   Jan S.F. van Hoogstraten, 3 August 1972, Folder Zaire 1972, Box 22, Record Group 8, CWS/PHS.

73   Steven Miller to Jan S.F. van Hoogstraten, 25 July 1972, Folder Zaire 1972, Box 22, Record Group 8, CWS/PHS.

74   Hans Martin Schöll and Samuel Bukasa to Jan S.F. van Hoogstraten, 25 July 1972, Folder Zaire 1972, Box 22, Record Group 8, CWS/PHS.

75   Note by James McCracken on Jan S.F. van Hoogstraten to H.N. Schöll and Samuel Bukasa, 14 August 1972, Folder Zaire 1972, Box 22, Record Group 8, CWS/PHS.

76   Jan S.F. van Hoogstraten to James McCracken, 20 August 1972, Folder Zaire 1972, Box 22, Record Group 8, CWS/PHS.

Miller had been asked to reconcile with CWS, and that Bukasa and Schnöll seemed reasonable – and perhaps a buffer to Bokeleale. At the same time, various mission boards wanted CWS to recommence aid to their projects via CPRA. CWS would only ship supplies if asked to do so by CPRA or the US mission boards. Another reason for the change of heart may have been the flood of refugees fleeing from the ongoing genocide in Burundi into the eastern DRC.[77]

Soon after van Hoogstraten's turnaround, the unreliability of the Congolese government struck a sour note yet again. It had apparently signed off on an agreement to not collect customs duties on CPRA aid shipments in April 1965, but officials decided to ignore this accord.[78] In 1972, Mobutu's government approved a similar duty-free exoneration for CPRA shipments. Even with this new government agreement, some customs officials still tried to force CPRA staff to pay duties on imported goods.[79] Storage fees in Kinshasa for goods awaiting duty-free clearance were very high.[80] CWS funding and CPRA programmes fitted well into the Zairian government's ostensible goals of national economic recovery and development. The US government had furnished aid to CPRA for over a decade to help pro-Western governments overcome the social and economic consequences of the violent conflicts in the DRC. CPC and ECC authorities relied on CWS for money and technical expertise. All of these reasons for mutual collaboration still ran aground on the chaotic nature of daily governance in Mobutu's Zaire.

CWS staff members' goal to foster self-sufficiency led to quarrels with Jean Bokeleale. Both CWS and Bokeleale had similar goals to emphasise the role of religious institutions in economic development. However, Jan van Hoogstraten's determination to impose rules on how CPRA should use foreign donor money turned CWS against the ECC's Congolese leader. Mobutu's notorious ideological authenticity campaign expressed a cultural nationalism that also deeply influenced Congolese Protestant figures. Van Hoogstraten's voluminous correspondence attests to the ways he held individual Congolese accountable rather than considering how his determination to control funds appeared to Congolese partners as patronising. Bokeleale's stubbornness in

---

77 Jan S.F. van Hoogstraten to Milton Engebretson, 21 August 1972, Folder Zaire 1972, Box 22, Record Group 8, CWS/PHS.

78 H. Schaffert, "Report," *Congo Mission News* 210 (October–December 1965), 26.

79 Hans Martin Schöll Jan S.F. van Hoogstraten, 25 September 1972, Folder Zaire 1972, Box 22, Record Group 8, CWS/PHS.

80 Steven Miller to Glen Eschtruth, 28 September 1972, Folder Zaire 1972, Box 22, Record Group 8, CWS/PHS.

standing up to CWS complicated what might seem to be a simple alliance between US and Congolese aid and religious organisations. Finally, it is telling that van Hoogstraten decided to wearily endorse CPRA aid requests even without lasting reforms. His decision to heed CRPA's need also shows an early example of what Zoë Marriage noted in regards to faltering Congolese NGOs three decades later: 'Lobbying [international] donors freed [Congolese] NGOs of the responsibility for what may have been seen as under-performance on their part.'[81] The same words equally applied to Mobutu's foreign aid requests throughout his reign.

The World Council of Churches and the CPRA, 1968–1975

Bokeleale's relationship with the World Council of Churches was far less antagonistic than with WCC in the 1970s, but it had its own challenges, particularly after the global recession in 1973. Even as the CWS had diminished its role in the ECC's ambitious forays into development, the WCC initially funded CPRA projects, administrative costs, and even the purchase of an apartment complex to generate income for the church in the late 1960s and early 1970s. The evangelical fight against church union served Bokeleale in good stead with the WCC. Clinton Marsh from the All-Africa Council of Churches asked the WCC to consider backing Bokeleale: 'You remember how we rejoiced when the "Young Turks" overthrew the old regime [at the CPC] and elected [Bokeleale] secretary ... Much of this will come to naught, unless we can support Bokeleale with the budget with which he can start.'[82] To try to loosen the tightening purse strings in Geneva, the Congolese church leader referenced the Congo crises. 'Our Christians lost everything during the troubles and it is still hard for them to be able to succeed in honorably supporting their family, the churches and the Congo Protestant Council.'[83] Bokeleale raised the legacy of the Congo crises to justify continued funding from 'our overseas brothers and sisters' in Europe: 'You know the problems of Zaire caused by the destruction during the first years of independence and it

---

81 Z. Marriage, *Not Breaking the Rules, Not Playing the Game: International Assistance to Countries at War* (London: Hurst, 2006), 110.

82 Clinton Marsh to Jean Fischer, 9 January 1969, Folder 71/4 ECZ, Box 425.05.028, WCCA.

83 Jean Bokeleale to the Church of Norway, 15 April 1969, Folder 71/4 ECZ, Box 425.05.028, WCCA.

will take a long time before Christians in the villages and the large centres alike come to the place of supporting the ECC General Secretariat.'[84]

However, the CPRA's mounting deficits had set off concerns within the WCC by 1972. During a series of discussions in late 1972, WCC African secretary Frédéric Randriamamonjy took partial responisibility for the escalating expenses of the CPRA by arguing that the WCC called for churches to take up the cause of national development. The ECC embodied the WCC's ideals of ecumenicalism and social responsibility, but neither the WCC nor the ECC could afford to fund these ambitions.[85] Randriamamony feared too many WCC-funded programmes in the Congo served a 'bureaucratic elite' rather than the poor. Ultimately, he felt that expenses could only be kept in line by mandating the ECC submit a list of individual projects rather than continue to pay out funds in the name of Christian solidarity with no accountability.[86]

In May 1973, the WCC held a consultation in Kinshasa with Bokeleale and the ECC. This meeting included representatives from the CWS, US Protestant mission boards, and European donor agencies. The Zairian state sent no less a personage than Remy Bisengimana, Mobutu's most influential cabinet member in the early 1970s.[87] While the final recommendations of the conference were hardly remarkable in its calls for better management of funds and more accountability, the report designated more than half of outside support to income-generating projects.[88] The principle of income-producing programmes created its own set of difficulties, as will be discussed in Chapter 8. The consultation also marked the end of an era in regards to WCC funding. The global economic crisis of 1973 meant that the WCC could not longer afford to be as generous to the CPRA. When the WCC, confronted with budget shortfalls, placed a moratorium on funds destined to the DRC in late 1975, Bokeleale vainly pleaded with Randriamamondjy to furnish more aid,

---

84 Itofo Bokeleale to Frédéric Randriamamonjy, 23 November 1972, Folder 71/4 ECZ, Box 425.05.028, WCCA.

85 Frédéric Randriamamonjy, Les problèmes de l'ECZ comme problèmes du COE, (unpublished manuscript, 25 September 1972), 2, Folder 74/1 Fonct. du Sec. Général ECZ, Box 435.5.029, WCCA.

86 Ibid, 2–3.

87 "Consultation on the participation of the Church of Christ in Zaire (CCZ) in the development of Zaire (Kinshasa, May 2–5, 1973)," (unpublished manuscript, no date [1973]), 1–2, Folder 71/4 ECZ, Box 425.05.028, WCCA.

88 Ibid., 5.

noting the annual $30,000 allotment from the WCC was only worth a third of its value a decade earlier.[89]

Ultimately, Bokeleale's quest for funds for the CPRA were not abandoned despite reduced ties with the CWS and WCC. Instead, he managed to find still other backers. German church organisations became a lynchpin of the ECC's development efforts from the mid-1970s onward. The Mennonite Central Committee agreed to send volunteers to manage the CPRA's supply chains after the CWS pulled out of the Congo. USAID became a major partner in reforming rural primary healthcare beginning in 1981. Though the evolution of the CPRA after the early 1970s lies outside the scope of this study, the unwillingness of the ECC to consider structural reforms proved to have major consequences. WCC staff may have been more understanding of Congolese Protestant determination with development than the CWS, but neither organisation could force Bokeleale to back away from his plans or assert his control over the management of the CPRA.

Conclusion

The Democratic Republic of Congo under Mobutu is a classic example of how foreign aid was largely based on US efforts to contain Communism, rather than concerns regarding the viability or effectiveness of aid programmes. On the surface, US Protestant aid funding for programmes in the DRC cor-responded well with US policies designed to bolster Mobutu's regime. The CPRA ran programmes for civilians in areas devastated by fighting between Congolese government and rebel troops. Just as in South Vietnam until the late 1960s, US Protestants involved in aid programmes in the Congo never expressed doubt regarding the close collaboration between themselves and the US government. Likewise, few CPRA or CWS staff expressed doubts regarding Mobutu, even as he was later vilified for using foreign aid to enrich himself at the expense of the Congolese people.

However, a close examination of the interaction between Congolese church leaders, CWS staff, US officials, and the Congolese state reveals a more complex picture. US officials might have provided CWS and CPRA with transport and food, but they tended not to do much to support CPRA in its troubles with unclear Congolese laws and Jean Bokeleale. The Congo-lese government also penalised CPRA as a bargaining chip in disputes over how much Mobutu's regime should help offset the cost of shipping aid. The IMF- and US-imposed currency reforms made black market trading more

89 Ifoto Bokeleale to Frédéric Randriamamonjy, 18 November 1975, Folder 71/4 ECZ, Box 425.05.028, WCCA.

attractive, but CWS staff viewed CPC and ECC efforts to use this to their advantage to be signs of poor judgement. The Congolese administration punished CWS by refusing to fund the transport of supplies for CPRA in retaliation for USAID demands for the Congolese government to pay for part of aid shipping costs. Even so, the CWS considered Bokeleale and Congolese ministers to somehow be responsible for the subsequent complications. Mobutu's role in influencing the CWS was very limited at best. Aid organisations might not always place Cold War considerations at the top of their agenda in dealings with African NGOs.

US aid organisation staff and Congolese religious leaders understood their mutual relationship in very different ways. Jan S.F. van Hoogstraten wished to restrict how CWS money could be used. In contrast, WCC personnel who felt common cause with Bokeleale's goals, even if they also recognised the CPRA could not sustain so many expensive plans. Congolese aid workers might have some role in shaping policy, but donors and foreign aid workers were expected to have the upper hand. Van Hoogstraten's decision to cut CPRA off from money and food shipments undermined his claims of respecting Congolese partners as equals. Bokeleale contended that foreigners had no right to dictate how money should be spent. Bokeleale's decision to sell CWS dollars on the black market also reveals how he recognised how new financial policies set by Mobutu (with US backing) could earn profits for the CPRA. The legacy of missionary paternalism clearly rankled Bokeleale in his dealings with CWS. It is striking that Bokeleale demanded more foreign money in the name of Congolese national self-determination. This mirrored Mobutu's own grandiose projects to make the DRC an example of African modernity and development. And, the improbable ability of the ECC to convince CWS to renew funding resembled Western countries' willingness to rescue Mobutu's government in the 1970s and 1980s.

How typical was the CWS' actions compared to other private aid agencies in DRC or elsewhere in Africa in the 1960s? The lack of research on humanitarian aid and private NGOs make this question hard to answer. Caritas and Catholic Relief Services both had programmes in the DRC in the 1960s, but their archives are closed to researchers. WCC's distance from US policy goals and missionary concerns might explain why the WCC did not endorse the CWS' stringent approach to Congolese partners. Private aid donors did communicate with one another, and this suggests multiple programmes needed to be examined before one could try to make general conclusions about the role and impact of private humanitarian assistance.

What can historians of development in early independent Africa learn from this case? Battles between foreign donors and African organisations could lead to major problems even in cases where donors and indigenous associations had close political ties and common goals. Bokeleale's critiques of condescending Western missionaries could not be simply dismissed out of hand, especially as Western churches and aid agencies claimed to recognise their African colleagues as worthy of mutual respect, even as CWS staff still had doubts about the competence of African partners. While Cold War politics might seem to dictate how aid was distributed and managed, the specific actions and views of various parties brought together by aid could shape and even override the influence of global political interest.

8

The Centre for Community Development

The late 1960s marked a new era for the Democratic Republic of Congo and the CPRA. General Mobutu Sese Seko toppled the government of Moïse Tshombe and Joseph Kasavubu in November 1965 in the name of restoring order and economic growth. The escalating Vietnam war drove up US demand for copper and other mineral resources that abound in the DRC. As copper prices rose, so did the revenue of the Congolese state. The humanitarian crises of the first five years of Congolese independence gradually improved, particularly after Mobutu pitilessly disposed of political rivals. The rhetoric of crisis, so engraved in CPRA projects in the first of half of the 1960s, no longer accurately corresponded with conditions on the ground.

This chapter is a case study of a CPRA emergency relief programme that transformed into an African-led development effort: the Centre for Community Development (CEDECO). This case shows how blurred the separation was between humanitarian relief and development programmes in the DRC in the 1960s. The evolution of this project reveals the shift from emergency assistance to new goals: self-sufficiency and eliciting the perspectives of Angolan refugees and Congolese. Unlike many of Mobutu's programmes, CEDECO relied on low-cost and low-tech solutions. As CEDECO's name indicates, the project was an example of small-scale community development, an ideal of some Western development personnel.

Community development offered an alluring ideal of harmonious rural communities working with foreign experts to adapt Western technical innovations to their own needs. Its proponents rejected costly development projects that drove Cold War modernisation programmes. Yet community development had its own blind spots. Daniel Immerwahr has noted: 'What community development overlooked was power: power within communities and power relationships between communities and the larger society around them.'[1] CEDECO staff made no effort to transform local power relations. Not surprisingly, Congolese officials voiced their approval of CEDECO's projects, since it did not threaten the government's grip on power. The CEDECO

---

1   D. Immerwahr, *Thinking Small: The United States and the Lure of Community Development* (Cambridge, MA: Harvard University Press, 2015), 178.

case suggests that the Congolese state could ignore agriculture by permitting NGOs to take on this burden themselves. Community development's emphasis on building peaceful relationships through technology transfer thus resonated with Congolese and North American stakeholders.

Although Immerwahr only considered secular programmes, Protestant missionaries had their own motivations in endorsing community development. British and Canadian missionaries, banished from Angola for their criticism of Portuguese oppression, viewed Angolan refugees in the Congo as victims of colonialism who needed to become self-supporting in exile. CEDECO was thus a peaceful form of activism and a means of finding a new place for missionaries outside the old hierarchical confines of North American patrons and African clients. With little oversight from Congolese officials and initially from Congolese churches, CEDECO staff could thus develop a wide range of projects that fell under the vague mandate of community development.

Although missionaries initially had almost total freedom in directing CEDECO, Congolese churches began to demand more control over CEDECO after 1970. Mobutu's dictatorship cynically employed cultural nationalism to stamp out opposition and to justify the mass confiscation of foreign-owned property, but it would be a serious mistake to ignore how Congolese and Angolan intellectuals outside of government made use of the rhetoric of decolonisation to pressure Western donors and missionaries. Once Angolan and Congolese men took over CEDECO, expatriate staff condemned how the new leaders used the organisation for their own personal benefit. However, neither donors such as the United Church of Canada nor individual aid workers were willing to simply jettison CEDECO.

The African leadership of CEDECO often appear in Western aid correspondence as incompetent and morally dubious figures, but this case should not be seen as simply proof of the inherent inability of Angolans and Congolese to run projects begun by North Americans. Individual Angolans' and Congolese expectations of modernity, to use James Ferguson's term, had a chance to be met after the end of Belgian paternalism and the years of crisis in the 1960s through ideals of development.[2] CEDECO appeared to allow these goals of economic self-sufficiency and personal advancement, at least as long as foreign aid could offset the sparse economic opportunities in Bas-Congo. Bob White and Ch.-Didier Gondola have noted how Congolese men sought to redefine themselves as big men in gangs and in musical

---

2   J. Ferguson, *Expectations of Modernity: Myths and Meanings of Urban Life on the Zambia Copperbelt* (Berkeley: University of California Press, 1999).

groups.[3] Foreign aid projects also furnished some men with the assets and the intellectual resources to establish themselves as patrons instead of mere clients of foreign aid.

The CEDECO example adds nuances to the lengthy literature on development and humanitarianism in the DRC. Critics of Mobutu's regime have lampooned his colossal failures funded by Western governments and the World Bank, particularly the Inga Shaba dam. Billions of dollars furnished by Mobutu's allies in Washington and Paris allowed Mobutu's inner circle to embezzle state funds in keeping with their leader. Despite the government's repeated calls for improved agriculture, the Zairian state generally invested little in farming. With the global recession and rampant corruption both sapping away at the Congolese economy from 1973 onward, the optimism and ambitions of the Congolese state in Mobutu's first years rapidly faded. This broad and often accusatory literature highlights US and Western collusion in Mobutu's kleptocracy.

One problem with this approach – and the ways the paternalism of NGOs has been repeatedly condemned since the early 1990s – is how it can obscure internal debates within aid organisations and how Congolese stakeholders could make claims for themselves. David Mosse has observed how viewing development projects solely through the lens of collaboration and resistance obscures the role of cooperation and shifting negotiations between aid workers and their intended collaborators.[4] The Congolese state aggressively co-opted and attacked members of civil society like university students and the Catholic church. However, CEDECO shows how community development could inspire a different orientation for NGOs. Rather than openly attacking the Congolese government or simply following its commands, CEDECO staff worked parallel to the state. Aid workers, in turn, did not see themselves as tools of US foreign policy, but instead as part of a transnational Christian community that brought wealthy and poor together. This uneasy alliance fits David Mosse's contention that 'development interventions are not driven by policy but by the exigencies of organisations and the need to maintain relationships'.[5] In striking contrast to the demand for quantitative evidence to prove a development project had succeeded that was so dominant in later decades,

3   Bob White, *Rumba Rules: The Politics of Dance Music in Mobutu's Zaire* (Durham, NC: Duke University Press, 2008); C.D. Gondola, *Tropical Cowboys: Westerns, Violence, and Masculinity in Kinshasa* (Bloomington: Indiana University Press, 2015).

4   D. Mosse, *Cultivating Development: An Ethnography of Aid Policy and Practice* (London: Pluto, 2005), 7–8.

5   Ibid., 16.

mission boards and the World Council of Churches supported CEDECO as a 'good project' in the late 1960s because it represented hope for Protestants in rebuilding the DRC and assisting Angolans.

I draw in this chapter on the insights of Gregory Mann, who has traced how Western NGOs began to take on attributes of the developmentalist state previously promised by African regimes in the Sahel (particularly Mali and Niger).[6] Yet the chronology of Mann's Sahelian protagonists was substantially different from the DRC. The drought crisis of the early 1970s had exposed the financial and political weaknesses of Sahelian states, opening the door for NGOs to take on duties reserved in the previous decade by African governments themselves. By contrast, the crises of decolonisation in the DRC and the rhetoric of state collapse had created room for a range of NGOs to become political actors in the DRC. Mobutu's claims in the late 1960s of restoring an orderly African cultural foundation allowed space for African members and partners of NGOs to take the upper hand in debates with Westerners on who should control the property and the agenda of development programmes. Here, the end of the era of emergencies allowed Congolese and Angolan actors to grasp hold of NGOs instead of becoming dependent on them.

CEDECO and the ideals of rehabilitation, 1964–1967

As hundreds of thousands of Angolans risked death to escape the Portuguese military between 1961 and 1965, Western aid organisations feared that these refugees would become dependent on foreign-funded relief. The League of Red Cross Societies (LRCS) and the United Nations High Commission for Refugees (UNHCR) initially committed themselves to supplying food to Angolan refugees in 1961. However, foreign Red Cross personnel became convinced that Angolans preferred aid to establishing fields on Congolese soil. 'A prolongation of the general relief programme for Angola refugees beyond the first harvest cannot be justified,' contended a visiting American Red Cross representative.[7] UNHCR official Vladimir Temnomeroff argued in late 1961, '[The Angolan refugees] look apathetic ... the refugees don't believe that the Red Cross will stop the distribution; they don't wish to plant because they will go back when all is quiet in Angola.'[8] By February 1962,

---

6   Mann, *Empires to NGOs*, 207–208.

7   R.T. Schaeffer to Henrik Beer, Memorandum, 21 November 1961, Folder F11, S1, Angolan Refugees 15/GEN/ANG [1], Box 250, Series 1 Classified Subject Files 1951–1970, UNHCRA.

8   Vladimir Temnomeroff to UNHCR director, 20 November 1961, Folder F11, S1, Angolan Refugees 15/GEN/ANG [1], Box 250, Series 1 Classified Subject Files

the LRCS and the UNCHR had cut off food distribution in the name of promoting self-sufficiency. These secular organisations pointed out that most Angolans belonged to the same BisiKongo ethnic group that predominated in Bas-Congo province and contended Angolans simply needed to work harder to establish themselves. They also blamed the FNLA (Frente Nacional de Libertação de Angola) rebel organisation for duping refugees by encouraging them not to return to Angola, even as the Portuguese military dropped napalm on northern Angolan villages and routinely slaughtered civilians seeking to flee colonial rule. For the LRCS and UNHCR, cutting aid was also a means of avoiding an expensive long-term commitment to Angolan refugees for both cash-strapped agencies.

The Congo Protestant Relief Agency also committed itself to creating a self-supporting Angolan refugee community in Bas-Congo, but its personnel had a far more personal attachment to Angolan refugees. British, Canadian, and US missionaries expelled from Angola for their sympathy with the anti-colonial FNLA volunteered to aid Angolan refugees. As discussed in chapter 3, British and North American missionaries had committed themselves to join the Angolan fight for independence. Protestant missionaries wanted to promote agricultural and artisanal careers for Angolans, but soon understood they could not do so at the expense of Congolese. Congolese officials complained to UNHCR personnel that Angolan refugees created new competition for jobs in Bas-Congo province. While UNHCR and LRCS only agreed to assist Angolan refugees, the CPRA could develop projects that did not distinguish between Angolans and Congolese.

CPRA plans to encourage economic growth in Bas-Congo differed significantly in some ways from the US government and the World Bank in the late 1960s, but US government and missionary projects shared confidence about reshaping the DRC after Mobutu Sese Seko took power in November 1965. Trusting in Mobutu's leadership and anxious to promote investment, the US government supported Mobutu's efforts to favour US business interests against Belgian companies. While missionaries lacked the means to favour industrialisation, they too imagined how the DRC might become a stable and prosperous country after the end of years of unrest.

CEDECO first began in 1964 and 1965. With CPRA staff unwilling to furnish food and clothing to Angolan refugees for longer than twelve months, missionaries called for job training and improved agriculture. Just as the exodus of Belgian doctors at independence in 1960 opened a new field for North American Protestant medical intervention, decolonisation also provided the

---

1951–1970, UNHCRA.

fledgling project with the infrastructure to operate. Adolfs Klaupiks, director of relief for the Baptist World Alliance, agreed to fund vocational training programmes for refugees in 1964.[9] David Grenfell managed to find a former cement company building abandoned by Belgian owners in Thysville to serve as the initial school.[10] When this site was deemed unviable, CPRA staff found a farm abandoned by *colons* in the Bas-Congo town of Kimpese as the new site for the organisation.[11]

US, British, and Canadian missionaries who had previously served in Angola prior to the 1961 revolt against Portuguese rule led CEDECO. Protestant missionaries identified with the revolt, particularly since much of the FNLA leadership came from Protestant backgrounds.[12] Warren Jackson, a US United Methodist missionary prohibited by the Portuguese government from returning to Angola, became the director of the carpentry training project.[13] Lynn Stairs, an experienced Canadian Baptist missionary, joined Jackson in developing programmes in machine repair, carpentry, and tailoring.[14] A central figure emerged to direct CEDECO's agricultural extension: Allen Knight, a Canadian Baptist missionary who had worked in Angola from 1946 to 1961. Knight agreed in 1965 to direct CEDECO's agricultural efforts. Eschewing the expense of tractors and the industrial farming model that had come to dominate in Canada and the US, Knight argued that community development could only succeed through low-technological and low-cost methods. 'It is not necessary to spend $100,000 in order to make the first steps in village improvement,' stated the annual 1969 report.[15]

CEDECO officially relocated to its permanent headquarters in the town of Kimpese in 1966. Kimpese was a crucial part of Congolese Protestant networks, since it was already home to the interdenominational Institut Médical

---

9   David Grenfell, "The Work Amongst the Angolan Refugees of the Lower Congo, Annual Report 1964," (unpublished manuscript, January 1964), 5, Folder 40 Notes D. Grenfell, Baptist Missionary Society 1964, Box 2, Associate Director Congo, UCCA.

10   Ibid., 5.

11   Juel Norby to Alan Knight, no date [1965], Knight Family CEDECO papers [henceforth KFP]. I sincerely thank Gerald Knight, Alan Knight's son, for providing me access to these documents.

12   Burlingham, "Image of God."

13   "Three Missionaries Return: Only Three Left in Angola," *Together* (April 1963), 5; Grenfell, Work Amongst the Angolan Refugees, 5.

14   Grenfell, Work Amongst the Angolan Refugees, 5.

15   Report of the Community Development Centre Kimpese General Report for the School Year 1968–1969, p. 1, Folder 147 Report CEDECO, Board of World Mission Congo 1969, Box 4, UCCA.

Évangélique (IME) hospital. Given that Congolese Baptist and other Protestant churches had close ties to the interdenominational centres already active in Kimpese, the new location for CEDECO served as a key centre in a network of religious institutions as well as being centrally located along a major road in Bas-Congo province.

The centre's school had on average roughly seventy students per year in the trades and agricultural programmes. Students could bring wives and children to stay on campus. The nearby IME hospital agreed to provide medical care for students. Although a majority of students belonged to Congolese Protestant churches, Catholics and members of the independent African Kimbanguist church could also enroll. Angolans and Congolese at the school could stay for up to three years. Besides the formal training, the school also provided services such as vaccinations for chickens and training sessions for farmers in various Bas-Congo towns.

Knight's approach to community development, like many other Protestant missionaries who had served in Angola, was strongly opposed to colonialism. When he worked in Angola prior to 1961, Knight decided that self-sufficiency was vital for Angolans. He successfully introduced soybean cultivation to increase protein consumption at his mission station at Dondi, inspired by a visit to the Tuskegee Institute founded by Booker T. Washington.[16] Knight denounced Catholic missionaries and the Portuguese state for doing practically nothing to encourage better farming methods and 'respect for God's earth'. Like the 'Southern US', he argued Europeans had simply assumed Congolese did not care about ameliorating farming, rather than comprehend that Congolese were simply unaware of technical advances.[17] Technological modernisation would disprove racist stereotypes. 'This is not the lazy continent that our geography books told us about many years ago. Give people a motivation for work, get the malaria parasite removed from their bloodstreams … teach them some scientific agriculture and how to feed their children good protein food and watch them good,' Knight wrote in 1965.[18]

While Knight viewed his work as empowering for Africans, he also considered North American farming methods to be far superior to indigenous agricultural practices in Bas-Congo. In 1968, CEDECO's newsletter featured

---

16　A. Knight, *Memoirs* ([No place of publication]: self-published, 2002), 35–6.

17　Allen Knight, "Some Thoughts on Expansion of the Community Development Program in the Lower Congo under CEDECO, Kimpese," *CEDECO Communiqué* (February 1968), 6, Folder 114 Board of World Mission Congo 1968 Congo Communiqué, UCCA.

18　Allen Knight to Juel Nordby, 31 October 1965, KFP.

an essay that condemned how grass burning in the dry season to prepare fields and up and down ridging on hills would lead to '75% of the top soil [being] lost within a period of five years'.[19] CEDECO's task was to convince Angolan and Congolese farmers to agree to abide by the project's recommendations. Students in the farming programme in the 1966–1967 academic year prepared gardens divided between regular soil and soil treated with chemical fertilisers.[20] This model of top–down technology transfer assumed that trained expertise could effectively identify problems without considering the value of local knowledge. 'Simple rules which for us are everyday living for us, often take long and patient teaching before being accepted by the Congolese … So many of the population suffer from intestinal disease but how few will take the trouble of boil their drinking water,' a CEDECO newsletter suggested in December 1968.[21] Within this line of reasoning, modernisation was a matter of convincing Angolans and Congolese of the value of CEDECO's innovations, rather than potentially entering into a dialogue by which Angolans and Congolese would identify problems to be solved. 'Where the old methods have been employed for generations the new teaching will take a long time and much patience before it is accepted easily,' a CEDECO newsletter article announced in November 1968.[22] This comment reveals the lack of understanding of the historical context of the Bas-Congo economy, as CEDECO staff simply imagined that farming had not changed in the colonial period.

Another aspect of Knight's approach that repackaged older missionary ideals of transforming African societies dealt with technology and gender roles. Knight often noted how low-cost and locally made machines would liberate women from numerous time-intensive tasks. Peanut strippers made with nails and boards, for example, allowed women to shell peanuts ten times faster than by hand.[23] A bike wheel could be made into a furrow opener that reduced women's labour weeding from sixteen hours to merely one.[24] While few women enrolled in CEDECO classes between 1964 and 1973, CEDECO correspondence contended women were impressed by the results of chemical

19 Ibid., 28.

20 Report of the Community Development Centre Kimpese 1967, Folder 18 Zaire 1967–1968, Box 22 Africa Department, Record Group 8, CWS/PHS.

21 *CEDECO Communiqué* (December 1968), Folder 114 Board of World Mission Congo 1968 Congo Communiqué, UCCA.

22 *CEDECO Communiqué* (November 1968), Folder 114 Board of World Mission Congo 1968 Congo Communiqué, UCCA.

23 Knight, *Memoirs*, 61–2.

24 Ibid., 66.

fertiliser and wanted to learn more about the project.[25] Just as Protestant missionaries had long decried the unwillingness of men in Central Africa to take on more tasks in farming, CEDECO echoed long-standing concerns about younger men who had little interest in agriculture. More than half of the first year of the all-male students in the CEDECO agriculture programme did not continue to farm after their finished their training.[26] 'CEDECO would suggest that there is little interest or enthusiasm for agriculture as a career among the 18 to 25 year age group, whether Congo or Angolan, but with regard to more mature men, it is certain they will continue in farming,' Knight observed in 1968.[27]

Congolese farmers and CEDECO, 1966–1973

Some farmers in Bas-Congo willingly adopted some of Knight's technology as well as the ideal of village cooperatives, notwithstanding how male CEDECO graduates did not always become farmers. Originally, CEDECO staff believed their work promoted spiritual progress as well as social advancement. The first issue of CEDECO's monthly newsletter in 1968 featured an article on Zula, a CEDECO graduate who had returned to his home town to farm. In keeping with the missionary goals of CEDECO, Zula was praised as '[a witness] in a village which is suffering from conflicting religious ideas,' such as rival Kimbanguist, prophetic, and Catholic church communities along with a 'witch doctor's house' protected by 'charms and circles and white crosses chalked on the ground'.[28] CEDECO staff noted with pleasure how schoolboys built chicken coops following the CEDECO model and that Zula's cooperative had established fields treated with fertiliser.[29] Zula's success was not merely a matter of his training. He also happened to be the son of the local

---

25 CEDECO General Report for the School Year 1969–1970, p. 4, Folder 172 Board of World Mission Congo 1970 CEDECO Constitution, Minutes, Papers, Box 5, UCCA; *CEDECO Communiqué* (January 1970), Folder 173 Board of World Mission Congo 1970 CEDECO Communiqué, Box 5, UCCA.

26 Report on the Community Development Centre Kimpese 1967, Folder Zaire 1967–1968, Box 22, Record Group 8, CWS/PHS.

27 Allen Knight, "Some Thoughts on Expansion of the Community Development Program in the Lower Congo under CEDECO, Kimpese," *CEDECO Communiqué* (February 1968), 6, Folder 114 Board of World Mission Congo 1968 Congo Communiqué, UCCA.

28 *CEDECO Communiqué* (February 1968), 1, Folder 114 Board of World Mission Congo 1968 Congo Communiqué, UCCA.

29 Ibid.

village chief.[30] This idealised view fitted with how secular US proponents of community development imagined the village to be a single unit.[31]

By 1970, CEDECO expatriate staff had become less naïve about the obstacles to cooperatives and using CEDECO graduates to transmit agricultural innovations. One basic question was whether or not agricultural graduates should continue to receive material assistance from the project. Knight worried that frequent visits to graduates by CEDECO personnel would 'lead villagers to believes that these projects [led by graduates] are part of CEDECO administration and finance … Such an attitude can be fatal to village participation. Everything is being done to let graduates know that the projects are their own.'[32] Even though the worst of the economic problems that beset Bas-Congo in the early 1960s appear to have diminished by 1970, farmers still remained relatively poor.

CEDECO graduates had several major handicaps. Angolan refugees and young Congolese men could not easily obtain land from older BisiKongo clan leaders.[33] While some graduates simply gave up and moved to Kinshasa, others formed cooperative organisations that generally lacked funds and effective leadership.[34] One CEDECO graduate had formed an active cooperative willing to grow sugar cane as a cash crop, but the town's remote location impeded progress.[35] Less than half of the 1966 graduates were still involved in farming a year later.[36] A survey conducted in 1970 did show that the majority of CEDECO agricultural graduates did work [presumably as farmers], but not surprisingly, a far higher percentage of CEDECO trades alumni had found work as mechanics, carpenters, and tailors.[37]

30 Ibid.

31 Immerwahr, *Thinking Small*.

32 CEDECO General Report for the School Year 1969–1970, 10, Folder 172 Board of World Mission Congo 1970 CEDECO Constitution, Minutes, Papers, Box 5, UCCA; *CEDECO Communiqué* (January 1970), Folder 173 Board of World Mission Congo 1970 CEDECO Communiqué, Box 5, UCCA.

33 Centre du Développement Communitaire Kimpese Rapport Général durant l'année scolaire 1970–1971, 9, Folder 192 Board of World Mission Congo 1971 Report CEDECO, Box 6, UCCA.

34 Ibid., 9.

35 Ibid., 9–10.

36 Allen Knight, Report of the Community Development Center Kimpese 1967, 4, Folder Zaire 1967–1968, Box 22, Record Group 8, CWS/PHS.

37 Centre du Développement Communitaire Kimpese Rapport Général durant l'année scolaire 1970–1971, Folder 192 Board of World Mission Congo 1971 Report CEDECO, Box 6, UCCA.

Some of CEDECO's offerings did not attract support from Congolese farmers. 'Our staff has often wondered why it has taken so long for new ideas to be introduced and become accepted by the villagers. Surely a peanut sheller which accomplishes in an hour what takes 3 to 4 days with human fingers would be an instant success … but, such is not the case.'[38] Less than a mile from CEDECO's headquarters, farmers continued to plant up and down hillsides rather than use contoured ridging.[39] Ian Pitkethly, a British agricultural missionary, observed that up and down contour farming allowed farmers 'to use their hoes uphill so they don't have to bend so far to make the impression with the hoe and turn the soil over.'[40] Mutombo Mpanya, a Congolese consultant supported by the Mennonite Central Committee, contended that programmes like CEDECO failed to understand cultural reasons why Congolese farmers did not accept new innovations.[41] For example, Mpanya contended that the unpopularity of the taste of soya undermined CEDECO efforts to encourage people to plant and eat soy crops for protein.[42] Environmental factors also impeded progress for CEDECO projects. In 1968 and 1972, low rainfall forced farmers to plant late and led to small harvests.[43]

Some did form cooperatives and embraced the kind of inventions promoted by CEDECO. Mechanics and some tailors who completed their studies at CEDECO did well in Kinshasa and Matadi.[44] Raising poultry with vaccination provided by CEDECO gained popularity with farmers seeking

38 CEDECO Communiqué (September–October 1972), World Council of Churches, February 1973, Folder 72/5 Agricultural and Community Centre CEDECO, Kimpese (File 1), Box 425.5.030 WCC/CIVWARS Africa Desk Projects, differed, withdrawn or covered in the years 1973/1974, WCCA.

39 Ibid.

40 For a short biography on Pitkethly, see "Gordon Ian Pitkethly 1930–2013 Agricultural Missionary, a Tribute," *Operation Agri Outreach Abroad* no. 1 (2014), 8, Accessible at www.operationagri.org.uk/wpcontent/uploads/2016/09/Outreach_Abroad_2014_01.pdf (Accessed 26 October 2019)

41 M. Mpanya, The Decision to Adopt or Reject New Technologies: A Case Study of Agricultural Development Projects in Zaire," Working Paper 51, Helen Kellogg Institute for International Studies, University of Notre Dame, 1985.

42 Ibid., 13–15.

43 CEDECO Communiqué (September–October 1972), World Council of Churches, February 1973, Folder 72/5 Agricultural and Community Centre CEDECO, Kimpese (File 1), Box 425.5.030 WCC/CIVWARS Africa Desk Projects, differed, withdrawn or covered in the years 1973/1974, WCCA.

44 Centre du Développement Communitaire Kimpese Rapport Général durant l'année scolaire 1970–1971, 9, Folder 192 Board of World Mission Congo 1971 Report CEDECO, Box 6, UCCA.

to increase their profits.[45] The Kiombia village cooperative was perhaps the most successful out of any cooperative related to CEDECO. Part of its success came from its location – Kiombia was only eight kilometers from the Matadi-Kinshasa railroad.[46] Two CEDECO graduates encouraged other villagers to set up an irrigation system and to rent a CEDECO tractor.[47]

The Congolese government gave its own endorsement of CEDECO, although it did not furnish much tangible support. Mobutu Sese Seko's regime did relatively little to promote agriculture in the late 1960s and 1970s, despite the Congolese leader's claims that farming was one of his top priorities.[48] CEDECO's apolitical approach and the willingness of Protestant leaders to praise Mobutu made the programme appear to be a good fit with the developmentalist aims of the DRC government. A newspaper article from the early 1970s celebrated CEDECO for its efforts of 'improving the lives of our peasant masses at every level'.[49] Although a Congolese state agricultural expert briefly aided a single cooperative run by CEDECO graduates, other CEDECO correspondence almost never references any government support beyond admiration for CEDECO's achievements.[50]

Trouble for CEDECO came from its relationship to the Congolese Protestant churches who had endorsed the project. Until the early 1970s, relatively few Congolese Protestant clergy had taken an active role in the organisation other than sending individuals appointed by a church to enroll in the CEDECO school. Newly independent churches such as the Église

---

45 *CEDECO Communiqué* (September–October 1972), World Council of Churches, February 1973, Folder 72/5 Agricultural and Community Centre CEDECO, Kimpese (File 1), Box 425.5.030 WCC/CIVWARS Africa Desk Projects, differed, withdrawn or covered in the years 1973/1974, WCCA.

46 Eduardo Marques, Donné au Rencontre à Moanda CEDECO, (Unpublished manuscript, 1970), 6–7, Folder 172 Board of World Mission Congo 1970 CEDECO Constitution, Minutes, Papers, Box 5, UCCA.

47 Ibid., 6–7.

48 Turner and Young, *Decline*, 310–15; J.P. Peemans, "Accumulation and Underdevelopment in Zaire: General Aspects in Relation to the Evolution of the Agrarian Crisis," in G. Nzongola-Ntalaja (ed.) *The Crisis in Zaire: Myths and Realities* (Trenton, NJ: Africa World Press, 1986), 67–84.

49 Centre de développement communautaire de Kimpese une realisation de grande envergure au service des masses paysannes, *Bas Zaire* (no date [1974?]), Folder 173 Board of World Mission Congo 1970 CEDECO Communique, Box 5, UCCA.

50 Centre du Développement Communautaire Kimpese Rapport Général durant l'année scolaire 1970–1971, 15, Folder 192 Board of World Mission Congo 1971 Report CEDECO, Box 6, UCCA.

Baptiste du Bas-Fleuve (EBBF) lacked the financial resources to engage in agricultural projects. However, some churches viewed CEDECO graduates as an instrument to develop revenue through farming. Dan Beveridge, a Canadian agricultural expert who worked for CEDECO in 1971, noted: 'Two church projects run by [CEDECO] grads are not really community development but they demonstrate the concept of c.d. prevalent in church circles here: obtain a piece of land from a clan (free if possible) with somebody like a CEDECO grad as supervisor ... with all the profits, if any, go into the church cash box ... with no concept of working with non-church members'.[51] Beveridge added that Allen Knight had little faith in Congolese Protestant church leaders embracing community development.[52] Generally, CEDECO graduates worked on their own as entrepreneurs rather than ally themselves with churches.[53]

Although Protestant churches in Bas-Congo had not considered CEDECO to be important, the same could not be said for the Église du Christ au Congo, the single legal Protestant bureaucratic organisation designed to oversee Protestant churches throughout the country in 1970. CEDECO became subordinate to the ECC's national office for development in Kinshasa. Previously, CEDECO had been loosely directed by the Congo Protestant Relief Agency, but ECC staff in Kinshasa had allowed the Kimpese programme to operate autonomously. Samuel Bukasa, the official head of the CPRA from 1966 to 1972, became determined by 1970 to place Congolese in charge of relief and development programmes founded by Protestant missionaries. This new directive to Africanise the leadership of CEDECO set off a long deliberation among expatriate staff, Congolese and Angolan development workers, and international donors over who should lead development programmes. As Mobutu's government increasingly promoted Congolese control over foreign-owned businesses as an expression of Congolese national sovereignty, African personnel and international donors followed suit by demanding that CEDECO no longer be controlled by missionaries.

51 Dan Beveridge to Garth Legge, 24 January 1971, Folder 181 Board of World Mission Congo 1970 Correspondence Beveridge, missionary, Box 6, UCCA.

52 Ibid.

53 Ibid.

Africanisation and the politics of development, 1970–1974

From the standpoint of CEDECO's international donors as well as Samuel Bukasa, the shift to African leadership was vital. Jan S.F. van Hoogstraten, the African department director of Church World Service, blamed missionaries for not settling 'bickering' within CEDECO.[54] He recommended a UN aid worker as a possible replacement, but added: 'Some of the present Cedeco personnel are little kings in their own domain, have too many 'mission' ideas, refuse to make certain departments self-supporting by selling at reasonable going-rate prices, etc.' Congolese church leaders and staff at the World Council of Churches (WCC) in Geneva also believed that Africanisation was a necessity. Liberian Anglican priest Burgess Carr, the Africa Secretary for the WCC, had heard the programme 'was a bit of a white elephant' in part because it had eleven expatriate staff members training only eighty students. Carr recommended leadership should be moved out of the hands of missionaries.[55] Samuel Bukasa and his superior Jean Bokeleale both contended foreign missionaries had to accept Congolese authority, particularly after US evangelical missionaries tried and failed to resist Bokeleale's creation of a single Protestant church in 1971 and 1972. Bukasa became determined that church development programmes should be self-sufficient financially and be clearly led by Africans.

It was one thing to ask missionaries to accept that they would no longer lead; it was another to actually find a competent administrator. One possibility was André Tunamau, a Congolese CEDECO agent who greatly impressed Dan Beveridge as a capable leader.[56] However, Bukasa selected another man to become the head of CEDECO, Eduardo Marques, after Tunamau died in a car crash.[57] How Bukasa became familiar with Marques is unclear, but Marques had the education to effectively direct an agricultural programme. An Angolan educated by Protestant missionaries, Marques had fled into exile

---

54   Jan S.F. van Hoogstraten to James McCracken, Nancy Nicalo, and John Nuilenburg, 12 November 1969, Folder 1969, Folder Zaire 1969, Box 22, Record Group 8, CWS/PHS.

55   Burgess Carr, World Council of Churches, to Mrs. Gutschmidt, Evangelischen Zentralstelle für die Entwicklingshilfe, 15 June 1970, Folder 72/5 Agricultural and Community Centre CEDECO, Kimpese (File 1), Box 425.5.030 WCC/CIVWARS, WCCA.

56   Interview, Dan Beveridge, 18 October 2017.

57   Ibid.

in 1961 and studied agriculture in Ghana and Great Britain.[58] On 1 August 1971, Marques replaced Allen Knight as the director of CEDECO, though Knight stayed on as a technical consultant. Marques' tenure as the head of CEDECO lasted roughly three years.

At least on paper, Marques adopted a cultural nationalist approach that corresponded well with Mobutu Sese Seko's rhetoric of recovering African authenticity. In his annual report, Marques extolled the struggle of black Africans seeking to recover their dignity from the oppression of colonialism. 'A policy of economic education is now in place at CEDECO: to replace the colonial economic structure of exploitation and subservience by a policy based on rationalisation and the development of management responding to the needs of society,' proclaimed the 1971 CEDECO report, in striking contrast to the rhetoric of Christian reconciliation of CEDECO correspondence prior to Marques' commencement.[59] Just as musicians and pastors drew inspiration from the same cultural nationalist rhetoric that Mobutu promoted, so did Congolese and Angolans taking up leadership positions.

A divide emerged between Marques and the remaining expatriates. At least from the standpoint of some, the blame lay with missionaries. Peter Bachelor, a British missionary who had become a well-known consultant on agriculture after his Faith and Farm project in Nigeria became renowned, condemned how African and expatriate staff at CEDECO did not even pray together and warned how retaining Knight as an adviser could undermine (even unintentionally) Marques.[60] Knight expressed his misgivings about Marques to Mennonite Central Committee volunteer Doyle Hartman and Peace Corps volunteer Roy Siebert.[61] The United Church of Canada assigned Canadian agricultural specialist Dan Beveridge in 1971 to advise CEDECO in 1971. He and his wife Angelique soon found fault with Marques.

58 Eduardo Marques curriculum vitae, 18 July 1969, Folder Congo-K CEDECO 1969, Box 425.5.030 WCC/CIVWARS Africa Desk Projects, differed, withdrawn or covered in the years 1973/1974, WCCA.

59 Centre du Développement Communitaire Kimpese Rapport Général durant l'année scolaire 1970–1971, Folder 192 Board of World Mission Congo 1971 Report CEDECO, Box 6, UCCA

60 P. G. Batchelor, Supplementary and Confidential Note, (no date [1971?]) and *CEDECO Communiqué* (September–October 1972), World Council of Churches, February 1973, Folder 72/5 Agricultural and Community Centre CEDECO, Kimpese (File 1), Box 425.5.030, WCCA.

61 Interview, Doyle Hartman, 10 October 2019; Interview, Roy Siebert, 14 October 2019.

While Marques' approach corresponded to the new push for self-sufficiency and African independence on paper, the Beveridges depicted a polarised and barely functional project. Only a few months after arriving, Angelique ruefully remarked, 'It is funny because this place is suppose[d] to be a Community Development Center but they have no time to discuss anything on development ... [Oxfam Congo director David Matchnik] says he does not know the objective of CEDECO and I am sort of agreeing with him. I am sure even the staff really do not have a clear cut idea of what CEDECO is trying to do except for the very vague statement "to help the village people become self sufficient".'[62] She added that villagers seemed to become dependent over time on CEDECO rather than working on their own.[63]

Whatever the Beveridge's doubts about CEDECO's vague mission, they had even less tolerance for Marques. In a letter to United Church of Canada mission board staff member Garth Legge, Angelique described Marques as 'incompetent technically', 'very authoritarian', and described how the CEDECO director had crashed his car – a donation from the United Church of Canada – after drinking alcohol.[64] To her, Marques' high monthly salary of 160 zaires ($320) and his use of CEDECO resources was striking given how expatriates and African staff struggled to get by on less.[65] When Marques condemned British agricultural missionary Ian Pitkethly as 'a colonialist', Angelique suggested the complains came from the unwillingness of Congolese men to accept 'a rigid routine' because it went against 'their concept of work'.[66] Expatriates could do little to challenge Marques, grumbled Dan Beveridge, 'because [Marques] was a yes man or stooge of [CPRA director Samuel] Bukasa'.[67] The director placed his relatives into CEDECO's overcrowded school even as he dismissed a destitute paraplegic man from enrolling because he did not have a mere 5 zaires to enroll.[68] 'What are we

62 Angelique Beveridge to Garth Legge, 29 January 1971, Folder 199 Board of World Mission Congo 1971 Correspondence: Beveridge, missionaries, Box 6, UCCA.

63 Ibid.

64 Angelique Beveridge to Garth Legge, 5 July 1971, Folder 199 Board of World Mission Congo 1971 Correspondence: Beveridge, missionaries, Box 6, UCCA.

65 Ibid.

66 Angelique Beveridge to Garth Legge, 4 August 1971, Folder 199 Board of World Mission Congo 1971 Correspondence: Beveridge, missionaries, Box 6, UCCA.

67 Dan Beveridge to Garth Legge, 9 August 1971, Folder 199 Board of World Mission Congo 1971 Correspondence: Beveridge, missionaries, Box 6, UCCA.

68 Angelique Beveridge to Garth Legge, 22 September 1971, Folder 199 Board of World Mission Congo 1971 Correspondence: Beveridge, missionaries, Box 6, UCCA.

here for then? To watch the poor get poorer, the leaders get more and more rich? This is exactly what we are doing now,' Angelique Beveridge replied to Garth Legge's suggestion she should be empathetic with African leadership styles.[69] The Beveridges resigned in December 1971 and returned to Canada several months later.

CEDECO's vague ideals of technical expertise and African leadership set off a series of debates over how the organisation should be run. Bukasa, committed to raising funds for a single Protestant church and having Congolese Protestants join in the larger nation-building programme of Mobutu's government, relied on Marques to direct expatriates in CEDECO. At least from the vantage point of the Beveridges, Marques lacked the administrative competence to effectively lead the organisation, even as international donors complained missionaries had yet to accept that they could no longer lead Congolese development programmes. Even if Marques had proven to be a brilliant director, though, CEDECO had not been designed to make a profit. The biggest winner in the CEDECO project was Marques. CEDECO offered opportunities for a few young men to receive foreign funds and to set up their own patronage networks. This pattern closely followed a larger process by which intellectuals could find work within Mobutu's numerous foreign-backed development programmes. Self-sufficiency as an idea could be remade as a justification for poor administration of funds and for an unwillingness to accept missionary recommendations.

Dodging collapse: CEDECO in the 1970s and 1980s

By 1972, some international donors had begun to distance themselves from CEDECO. Hans Schaffert, a former CPRA director and an official at the Hilfwerk der evangelischen Kirchen in Schweiz (HEKS), complained that CEDECO never sent his office adequate reports and so HEKS would not provide further aid.[70] The discovery in 1973 that HEKS' donation of 146,000 Swiss francs to CEDECO could not be accounted for did not help matters.[71]

---

69 Ibid.

70 Hans Schaffert to Jean-Géza Béguin, World Council of Churches, February 1973, Folder 72/5 Agricultural and Community Centre CEDECO, Kimpese (File 1), Box 425.5.030 WCC/CIVWARS Africa Desk Projects, differed, withdrawn or covered in the years 1973/1974, WCCA.

71 Hans Schaffert to Hans-Martin Schöll, Folder 72/5 Agricultural and Community Centre CEDECO, Kimpese (File 1), 14 May 1973; Itofo Bokeleale to Hans Schaffert, HEKS, 11 June 1973, Folder 72/5 Agricultural and Community Centre CEDECO, Kimpese (File 1), Box 425.5.030, WCCA.

The World Council of Churches delayed funding in 1971 until CEDECO staff provided evidence of its activities.[72] CPRA director Hans-Martin Schöll, who replaced Bukasa as CPRA director after the Congolese director became terminally ill with cancer, turned down a WCC recommendation to hire an economist for on the grounds the ECC could not afford to pay for the new employee.[73]

The global recession brought about in part by the hike in global oil prices in 1973 struck the DRC and international donors badly, just as CEDECO was already running aground due to its inability to control finances. Allen Knight had written to Dan Beveridge, 'When I asked [Marques] for 900 zaires [$1,800] to buy the second carload of corn (to feed the 1000+ chickens) the truth came out that there was not that much credit available. [ECC] is putting up their big buildings in Kinshasa and all the cash from World Council of Churches, etc., is going into that project.'[74] CEDECO had already become weighed down with a deficit of over 12,000 zaires ($24,000) by 1973. ECC chairman Jean Bokeleale pleaded with his backers at the World Council of Churches for more funds to save CEDECO; if WCC would not intervene, Bokeleale declared he had no choice but to permanently close the organisation. 'We are burdened with mismanagement and, I don't know, perhaps our incompetence in management as well, but I really fear for a young church where one is never sure if funds will continue to be available or predict the miracle of good management where the funds aren't available', lamented Bokeleale.[75] Pascal de Pury, a development expert with the WCC, advised Bokeleale to shut down CEDECO and begin anew solely as a poultry and feed production centre.[76] 'Marques was not a good manager and never will be,' warned Pury, and he countered Bokeleale that without good financial administration, it wouldn't matter even if there was enough money available

---

72 Frédéric Randriamamonjy to Jean Bokeleale, 29 November 1971, Folder 72/5 Agricultural and Community Centre CEDECO, Kimpese (File 1), Box 425.5.030, WCCA.

73 Hans-Martin Schöll to Jean-Géza Beguin, 28 November 1972, Folder 72/5 Agricultural and Community Centre CEDECO, Kimpese (File 1), Box 425.5.030, WCCA.

74 Dan Berveridge to Garthe Legge, 13 October 1972, Folder 216 Board of World Mission Zaire 1972 Correspondence: Beveridge, missionaries, Box 6, UCCA.

75 Itofo Bokeleale to D. Marx, Brot dür die Welt, 27 June 1973, Folder 74/3 PPA ESPI CEDECO, Box 425.5.031, WCCA.

76 Pascal de Pury to Itofo Bokeleale, 5 July 1973, Folder 74/3 PPA ESPI CEDECO, Box 425.5.031, WCCA.

for CEDECO.[77] The ECC head discovered he lacked the funds to pay workers what they were legally owed if they were laid off, but still refused to accept Pury's demand for a European economist to run CEDECO for reasons he 'did not want to put on paper'.[78]

At Kimpese, the delay in foreign funds in 1972 and the beginning of a national recession set off trouble. Just before Peace Corps volunteer Roy Siebert arrived in 1973, CEDECO had run out of money to pay some employees. Disgruntled workers struck by tearing out crops in CEDECO fields in retaliation for not receiving their salaries.[79] CEDECO had run up so much debt with the local Catholic mission that Catholic priests rebuffed Siebert's requests to buy supplies on credit.[80] After working about six months at CEDECO in late 1973 and early 1974, MCC volunteer Doyle Hartman requested a transfer because the programme seemed to be so dysfunctional.[81] In late 1973 or early 1974, ECC authorities dismissed Marques. Allen Knight returned from an extended furlough in Canada to Kimpese and discovered the ECC leadership had dismissed the 'dishonest, racist Angolan' for embezzlement of over $5,000 of CEDECO funds and replaced him. CPRA director Hans-Martin Schöll soon replaced Marques with Pierre Maloka, a Congolese economics graduate of the University of Chicago, who held the position from 1973 to 1977.[82]

Despite the string of financial problems and donor complaints regarding Congolese personnel, the organisation continued to survive for the next two decades. The scattered WCC records on CEDECO jumped from the apparently closure of CEDECO in the summer of 1973 to the following year, when the WCC as well as Oxfam, the German NGO Brot für die Welt and the Disciples of Christ mission board agreed to keep the programme afloat.[83] Maloka firmly believed in economic competition, in keeping with his Chicago economics training. Maloka knew ECC leader Jean Bokeleale well: 'I

77 Ibid.

78 Itofo Bokeleale to Pascal de Pury, 4 July 1973 and Itofo Bokeleale to Pascal de Pury, 25 July 1973, Folder 74/3 PPA ESPI CEDECO, Box 425.5.031, WCCA.

79 Interview, Roy Siebert, 14 October 2019.

80 Ibid.

81 Interview, Doyle Hartman, 10 October 2019.

82 Allen Knight to Friends, 18 May 1974, KFP.

83 Jacqueline van den Akker, World Council of Churches, 29 August 1974; Zemke to Hans-Martin Schöll, 20 September 1974; Hans-Martin Schöll to Mme Zemke, Brot für die Welt, 10 October 1974; Robert Nelson to Itofo Bokeleale, 21 November 1975, Folder 74/3 Zaire Covered, Box 425.5.031, WCCA.

was his economic advisor,' he recalled in a 2017 interview.[84] The new director promoted competition within CEDECO in order to increase profits, arguing that missionaries had been too concerned with cooperation and had neglected the need of agricultural projects to become financially self-sufficient.[85]

His openly commercial approach paid dividends. According to Allen Knight, CEDECO had the biggest hatchery in the entire country by 1977, producing over 100,000 chicks per year and sending them throughout the country by plane.[86] Rather than folding, CEDECO actually expanded as new centres formed in other parts of the country such as the city of Mbuji-Mayi in Kasai Occidental province. CEDECO continued to use North American expatriates as technical experts from the US Peace Corps, the Disciples of Christ mission board, and the United Church of Canada. New foreign donors as well as the United Church of Canada remained committed to supporting the project. In 1980, the US government's Agency for International Development awarded CEDECO a grant of $100,000 for 'appropriate agricultural technology'.[87] Although it is uncertain why international donors selected CEDECO, it managed to retain its favourable reputation.

Congolese farmer Jean-Baptiste Mbula replaced Pierre Maloka in 1977. Unlike Marques and Maloka, Mbula had advanced within CEDECO to become director. He had begun his career raising chickens in the CEDECO school.[88] Gerald Knight, the son of CEDECO's early leader Allen Knight, decided to return in 1987 to Kimpese under the auspices of the United Church of Canada.[89] After a power struggle involving ECC leaders in Kinshasa and Congolese Protestant churches in Bas-Congo, the ECC backed Knight's recommendation to dismiss Mbula for mismanagement. As so many other foreign aid workers had already done, Knight became convinced CEDECO could successfully improve agriculture. However, soldiers frustrated with the lack of payments from Mobutu's government in the early 1990s pillaged

84 Interview, Pierre Maloka, 29 December 2017.

85 Ibid.

86 The Community Development Project Under the Church of Christ in Zaire, Live Love Project Program, United Church of Canada, no date [c. 1978/1979], KFP.

87 US Government, Peace Corps, Office of Program Development., Frederick Conway and James Fickes, "An Assessment of the Potential for Peace Corps–USAID–ost Country Cooperation in Social Forestry Projects Zaire," (March 1981), 15, Available at: pdf.usaid.gov/pdf_docs/PNAAS202.pdf (Accessed 2 March 2020)

88 Interview, Gerald Knight, 16 November 2016.

89 Ibid.

CEDECO's school and farms, forcing the project to close for several years before reopening.

CEDECO's evolution after 1973 reflect broader trends in Congolese development much more than the project's original intent to assist refugees, although it still remained a favourite project of foreign donors. Expatriates like Allen Knight remained active in the project for the remainder of the 1970s, though the older generation of missionaries retired from the scene by 1980. Even when the crushing defeat of the FNLA in the opening of Angola's long civil war in 1975 sent many refugees back into the DRC, CEDECO remained largely concerned with agricultural innovation rather than returning to relief. The organisation managed to operate with much success in the mid-1970s, a time when other Protestant development projects had already begun to fall apart, but the common problems of leaders willing to use the organisation for their personal benefit and the worsening state of basic infrastructure made community development's lofty ideals difficult to achieve. Strikingly, Maloka's openly capitalist approach foreshadowed the re-orientation of Congolese development projects due to the World Bank's structural adjustment and the rise of neo-liberal economics in the 1980s.

Conclusion

The evolution of CEDECO demonstrates how the crises of the 1960s inspired foreign aid organisations to engage in development projects. Canadian and US missionaries originally envisioned CEDECO as a means to liberate Angolan people from the victimisation of Portuguese colonial rule and to ensure refugees did not remain permanently dependent on aid for their survival. However, this initial aim soon encompassed Congolese people as well, whose economic conditions were nearly as hard as the Angolans. In keeping with the model of technical transfer that so dominated Western development thought, Allen Knight and other expatriates sought to convince farmers to embrace low-cost technological innovations and farming methods. The idea that CEDECO was meant to generate income was not under consideration in the late 1960s. As former CEDECO livestock specialist Willard Warnock recalled, 'The only profit we made was selling chickens to missionaries.'[90] Foreign aid from mission boards thus drew on ideals of charity, not making revenue.

The wave of African cultural nationalism in the DRC in the late 1960s and early 1970s undercut the assumption that Western experts could guide modernisation in ways that would make Africans better able to support themselves. Just as Jean Bokeleale condemned the Church World Service for trying to tell

90 Interview, Willard Warnock, 1 December 2017.

Congolese Protestants how to spend donor funds, Eduardo Marques impose his authority on expatriate personnel. Congolese church leaders wanted to overcome their poor financial situation by finding ways to produce profits. For a project like CEDECO, originally designed to aid destitute refugees, it was difficult to turn towards a more openly capitalist model with agendas set by Africans. Another problem for the goal of self-sufficiency came from the global economic recession beginning in 1973. Donors became less willing to finance programmes as funds became harder to obtain. Though other Protestant church programmes foundered along with much of the rest of the Congolese economic in the mid-1970s, CEDECO managed to thrive for some years in part because of its embrace of competition instead of the older missionary ethic of cooperation.

CEDECO is a revealing example of the transition of the CPRA from emergency relief to development projects in the late 1960s and early 1970s. Like most of the CPRA projects between 1960 and 1965, missionaries created and ran CEDECO until the 1970s without much consultation with Angolan and Congolese stakeholders. Mission boards committed to assistance with little assessment of the effectiveness of projects. With the worst of the humanitarian emergencies coming to an end by 1967, CEDECO shifted to promoting agricultural development and job skills. Though the rationale of CEDECO changed, its dependence on foreign funds did not. Mission boards and the WCC would not cut their ties with Congolese church institutions even after increasing concerns over the ethics of Congolese and African leaders. Donors like the World Council of Churches remained committed to CEDECO (and more broadly the CPRA) out of a sense of solidarity with African churches that proved more important than tangible results. Though Christian transnational bonds held together donors with CEDECO, missionaries and donors struggled to deal with the practical problem that Congolese Protestant leaders' lofty aspirations for financial expansion exceeded their own economic resources.

In keeping with other CPRA projects, missionary records dealing with CEDECO tend to muffle the perspectives of the very Angolans and Congolese the project sought to empower. Despite the rosy tone of CEDECO newsletters of the joy of Congolese farmers embracing new technology, it is hard to know how farmers and tradespeople viewed the organisation's efforts. No researchers ever sought to place the idealistic agenda of CEDECO expatriates in the context of local hierarchies of power. Likewise, the role of the Congolese state is hard to discern from CEDECO records. Missionaries could imagine themselves as working outside the confines of an authoritarian state to serve Congolese people. Mobutu's regime, rarely willing to commit to practical support for agriculture beyond rhetorical flourishes about the importance of farming, conveniently allowed international donors to promote programmes like CEDECO rather than provide much state investment. This is reminiscent of how the Belgian colonial government left education largely in the hands of the missionaries, in no small part to avoid having the colonial state taking on the cost of education. Although this chapter can make no claims about the lasting value of CEDECO for Congolese and Angolans, it is clear that the vague premises of community development in restoring harmony within rural communities was attractive to missionaries, mission boards, and African intellectuals at the end of the crises of the 1960s.

Conclusion

This book has offered an alternative approach to the current historiography of the Congo crises. For all of the strengths of the scholarship on the battles for political power in the DRC in the first decade of independence, this state-centred approach has obscured a great deal. Perhaps the greatest lacuna in the literature is how civilians outside of the elite experienced (and sometimes participated in) the violent contests for power in the 1960s. Although CPRA records only offer a limited glimpse into the varied ways Congolese negotiated their survival in this difficult terrain, they do indicate the magnitude of suffering people endured. Hundreds of thousands of Angolans resettled in the DRC and large numbers of Congolese fled their homes. Yet these massive displacements have yet to be seriously examined, outside of exceptions such as this study or the growing scholarship on ethnic identity and politics in the Great Lakes region.[1] Undoubtedly, memories of the 1960s have continued to inform later political struggles. For example, the current Kamina Nsapu revolt in Kasasi province has historical roots in the Lulua/Luba conflict of the 1960s. Though CPRA records often muffled the concerns of Congolese partners, their records do provide sources that can further contribute to understanding the choices of Angolan and Congolese people in this turbulent era.

I deliberately chose not to write a book that placed US foreign policy in the foreground. There is no doubt the CPRA must have indirectly assisted the goal of US officials in establishing a reliable, anti-Communist ally in Kinshasa by furnishing aid. This corresponds to the larger development of US humanitarian NGOs in the 1950s and early 1960s.[2] Yet it is impossible to quantify how effective CPRA's work was in ensuring the victory of Congolese clients of the US government. Rather than try to take on the fruitless task of calculating how successfully the CPRA served the State Department, it seemed to me better to consider the evolution of the CPRA as a humanitarian NGO that tied together Western Protestant churches and donors with Congolese

---

1 G. Mathys, "Bringing History Back In: Past, Present, and Conflict in Rwanda and the Democratic Republic of Congo." *Journal of African History* 58:3 (2017), 465–87.

2 Nichols, *Uneasy Alliance.*

stakeholders. These Christian transnational relationships were not just the products of colonial expansion and the Cold War, but had their own dynamics which were not defined only by state policies.

The evolution of the Congo Protestant Relief Agency reflects the changing understandings of Western humanitarianism in the 1960s. As we have seen, Western Protestant aid workers considered their interventions as a personal moral duty, an opportunity to heal an African country from the violence of decolonisation, and acts of Christian witness to the Congolese people. With some exceptions, aid workers also shared the assumptions of many proponents of development in Africa during the Cold War, particularly in their optimism about the introduction of Western technology and the implicit belief that Africans should model their societies on the models of Canada and the United States. CPRA staff also considered themselves as parts of a project to make the Congo into a strong, Christian nation. Political independence was a chance to build partnerships with Congolese churches and the Congolese government. Though aid workers endorsed aspects of racial and cultural hierarchies that had guided missionaries in the colonial period, they also understood they had to listen to their Congolese partners.

The chaotic politics of the Congo in the early 1960s also shaped the politics of Protestant aid. The CPRA's ad hoc nature meant individual aid workers took widely different attitudes towards political engagement. While the ASSK programme distanced itself from any particular Congolese political faction, David Grenfell helped to maintain the FNLA's control over refugees. CPRA humanitarian aid became a tool of the Congolese government's counterinsurgency campaign against leftist rebels. Though Congolese medical officials approved of Operation Doctor, medical volunteers worked in environments where state authority was a distant presence. The US government was a major supplier of food aid to the CPRA. Yet US embassy officials did not interfere with CPRA activities for the most part, even though the CPRA's goals fitted in well with US foreign policy in establishing a reliable anti-Communist ally in Kinshasa.

The rise of Mobutu Sese Seko's dictatorship in the late 1960s is very familiar to observers of the Cold War in Africa, but the changing role of the CPRA broadens our understanding of how Congolese elites wanted to overcome the disorder of the Congo crises. Cultural nationalism, though wielded with brazen cynicism by Mobutu, attracted Congolese Protestant church leaders and development programme staff. Missionaries knew that Congolese Protestant institutions were no longer under their control, even if they were sometimes quite disappointed by the agenda of Jean Bokeleale. The late 1960s marked a new era in terms of donor engagements in the DRC, as they no longer viewed the country as an emergency and they now had to adjust to Congolese leadership. The World Council of Churches' internationalist and ecumenical positions made its partnership with Congolese churches easier than the more condescending position of Jan van Hoogstraten at the CWS.

Critiques of the overly quantitative and technocratic models of development work from the 1980s rarely probe how this culture came about. The CPRA case suggests changes in development and humanitarian practice may have come in response to the freewheeling era of the 1960s and 1970s. CEDECO staff did not initially question the possibility of continued dependence; they did not consider Angolans and Congolese perspectives on aid; and did not adjust to the ways African stakeholders reshaped the organisation's goals. Donors and CPRA managers placed their trust in expatriate project directors like Archie Graber and Allen Knight rather than require evidence of success. Particularly with the global recession of the 1970s and the deterioration of the Congolese economy, the CWS and WCC showed their frustration with the boundless ambitions of Congo Protestant leaders.

How did Protestant aid programmes influence the politics of development and humanitarianism in the DRC? Theodore Trefon has argued convincingly that Congolese elites have long taken advantage of aid programmes to enrich themselves without implementing effective reforms.[3] In the early 1960s, state authorities only had limited control over the CPRA's activities. After Mobutu took power, the Congolese state and elite church leaders expected aid donors to accept that Congolese authorities would ultimately decide how funds were to be spent. Congolese elites justified their control over foreign aid on the grounds of national sovereignty and their rejection of colonialism. While the CWS largely withdrew from the DRC rather than accept these demands, other Protestant mission boards and foreign NGOs accepted the new order in which expatriate aid workers could operate autonomously of Congolese institutions. The establishment of authoritarian rule ensured that NGOs had to toe the line set by the Congolese government. Once Mobutu's regime weakened in the early 1990s, room again emerged for Protestant and other NGOs to operate with fewer restraints from the government.

The evolution of the CPRA furnishes an example of the changing nature of missionary work in Africa after the end of colonisation. While political independence might have come in 1960, Congolese pastors still had little formal control over property and finances. Missionaries and aid workers divided over the pace of Africanisation, but they did not question that they would increasingly provide technical and advisory support rather than continue to

3   Trefon, *Masquerade*.

lead church institutions. The ideal of assisting Congolese nation building remained a constant, even if donors and aid workers questioned the expansion of Protestant development under Bokeleale. The church union movement took advantage of the frustration of Congolese pastors who felt missionaries had held power for too long as well as the last-ditch effort by evangelical missionaries to create a rival to the Église du Christ au Congo. Ecumenical missionaries and aid workers ultimately accepted Congolese church leaders by the early 1970s.

The CPRA was one of the last triumphs of North American ecumenical Protestant international cooperation prior to the cultural upheavals of the 1960s. The radical critiques of activists like Ivan Illich that rejected Western aid did not arise among CPRA workers. Rather than doubt their alliance with the US government, CPRA staff believed they could work autonomously to help Congolese while still receiving support from Washington. Even if some CPRA donors such as the Mennonite Central Committee had private doubts about US policy, they did not openly raise them. Furthermore, Congolese rivals to the pro-Western governments failed to convince a majority of ecumenical North American and British Protestant organisations to support them, whether the leftist Simbas or the conservative Katangese government. This is strikingly different from the case of Vietnam, where South Vietnamese critics of the war and Communists gained favour with some North American Protestants.

Protestant NGOs increasingly gained ground in the DRC in the 1990s, when the grand ambitions of the Zairian state and the ECC had come undone. In some ways, this new era of NGOs and donor backers resembles the early 1960s. With structural adjustment and the Congolese political elite's embezzlement of state funds, the Congolese state's declining commitment to social services created room for NGOs to take on a larger role in society. The Congo became synonymous with African suffering during the civil wars from 1997 to 2003. Again, depoliticised images of refugees and gruesome violence inspired North American and European organisations to raise funds and set up programmes, ready to try to heal a wounded nation.[4]

However, the international framework of donor agencies had considerably changed. Fears of destabilisation have replaced Communism as a main driver for Canadian and US involvement in the DRC. Secular Western donors, rather than missionaries, were now at the forefront in furnishing aid. Evangelical missions, often operated by individuals rather than by mission boards, had

4   W. Soderland, D. Briggs, T.P. Najem, and B. Roberts, B. *Africa's Deadliest Conflict: Media Coverage of the Humanitarian Disaster in the Congo and the United Nations Response 1997–2008* (Waterloo, ON: Wilfred Laurier University Press, 2012).

become predominant in mission work. Short-term medical missions, largely staffed by evangelicals, had become commonplace through arrangements made with individual Congolese churches. In this new environment, concerns about colonialism no longer informed Western NGO interventions in the Congo, even as NGO staff members sometimes expressed more doubts about the capacity of Congolese than their predecessors in the 1960s.[5] Aid workers still had to negotiate the complex local, regional, and national conflicts in which they became unwilling participants.[6] Humanitarian workers aspired to political neutrality, but just as in the early years of Congolese independence, Congolese stakeholders viewed aid workers as allies or as potential obstacles.[7]

This study offers no particular lessons in terms of policies, yet it is vital that those who want to assist the Congolese people consider the historical trajectory of development and humanitarian altruism. Too often, those engaged with aid are unaware of how earlier generations of aid workers wrestled with similar problems. Even if the political and economic context has changed, fears of dependence, assertions of sovereignty, and awkward negotiations with African officials have shaped humanitarianism in Africa since independence. They continue to do so, albeit in ways no longer shaped by the Cold War or the immediate end of colonial rule.[8] Paradaigms of professionalism, auditing, and peacebuilding have considerably changed and missionaries no longer hold centre stage in humanitarian action. Yet there are continuities: faith-based organisations like WorldVision and the Lutheran World Federation operation in numerous African countries. Aid workers still face danger, as shown by the

---

5   Koddenbrock, *Practice*.

6   J. Pottier, "Roadblock Ethnography: Negotiating Humanitarian Access in Ituri, Eastern DR Congo, 1999–2004," *Africa* 76(2) (2006) 151–79.

7   D. Dijkzeul and C.I. Wakenge, "Doing Good, But Looking Bad? Local Perceptions of Two Humanitarian Organisations in Eastern Democratic Republic of Congo," *Disasters* 34:4 (2010), 1139–70.

8   For several examples of literature probing the political difficulties of humanitarian aid in contemporary Africa, see E. Bornstein and P. Redfield (eds), *Forces of Compassion: Humanitarianism Between Ethics and Politics* (Santa Fe: School for Advanced Research Press, 2011); A. Donini, *The Golden Fleece: Manipulation and Independence in Humanitarian Action* (Boulder, CO: Kumarian, 2012); V. Heins, K. Koddenbrock, and C. Unrau (eds), *Humanitarianism and Challenges of Cooperation* (New York: Routledge, 2016); B. Jansen, "The Humanitatian Protectorate of South Sudan? Understanding Insecuity for Humanitarians in a Political Economy of Aid," *Journal of Modern African Studies* 55:3 (2017), 349–70; M. Hasian Jr., *Communicating During Humanitarian Medical Crises: The Consequences of Silence or "Témoignage"* (Lanham, MD: Lexington, 2019).

killings of UN experts Zaida Catalan and Matthew Sharp in Kasai province in 2017.[9] While it may be easy for donors and aid personnel to imagine the history of humanitatian work in Africam in simplistic terms, the Congolese have now had over half a century of encounters with aid and development that influence how and why they partner with foreign aid. Whether or not foreign aid projects engage and heed African concerns will continue to be a vexing question for years to come.

9 M. Bearak, "Courageous but Not Reckless: The Tragedy of an American U.N. Worker Slain in Congo," *Washington Post* (29 March 2017). Available at: www. washingtonpost.com/news/worldviews/wp/2017/03/29/courageous-but-not-reckless-the-tragedy-of-an-american-u-n-worker-slain-in-congo/?utm_term=.518c7fc6999d (Accessed 25 October 2019)

Bibliography

Archival Sources

Amelia Poole Sudderth Archives, Waco, Texas.

Mark Poole, Reflections Based on CPRA Diary of 1961 Assignment to Congo and Other Reminiscences (Unpublished manuscript, 1967)

American Baptist Historical Society Archives. Mercer University, Atlanta, GA.

Folder 5 Congo Protestant Relief Agency News Sheets, Box 137, Post-War Baptist International Mission, American Baptist Foreign Mission Society
Folder 6 Congo Protestant Relief Agency News Sheets, Box 137, Post-War Baptist International Mission, American Baptist Foreign Mission Society
Folder 20 Mission Conference on Future Programme in the Congo Republic, Box 138 Post-War Baptist International Mission

Archives du Comité International de la Croix Rouge. Geneva, Switzerland.

Folder Généralités 12.4.1961 – 1.8.1975, B AG 234 013-001.01
Folder Condition de detention dans la République démocratique du Congo, B AG 225 229-008
Folder Réfugiés Balubas à Elisabethville 05.10.1961 – 27.02.1963, B AG 234 229-002

Jeremy Rich Archives. Scranton, Pennsylvania.

Robert Bontrager Papers

Mennonite Church USA Archives. Elkhart, Indiana.

Africa Inter-Mennonite Mission Records
Folder 7 Archie and Irma (Beilter) Graber, 1959-1961, Box 70, Gerber to Graber, 1936-1986
Folder 8 Archie and Irma (Beilter) Graber, 1962-1965, Box 70, Gerber to Graber, 1936-1986
Pax Collection, 1944-2005, HM1/927
Allen Horst Diary

Mennonite Central Committee Archives. Akron, Pennsylvania.

Folder Congo 1960-1 104/138, Box 181, IX-6-3
Folder Congo Office 1961 105/138, Box 181, IX-6-03
Folder Congo Office 1961 105/139, IX-6-3, Box 181

Folder MCC Correspondence 1961 - Congo (Zaire) 1960-1961 108/138, Box 181, IX-6-03
Folder Snyder William T. Commissioner Trip to Congo, Folder 109/23, Box 186, IX-6-3.102
Folder Activity Reports 1963 107/109, Box 184, IX-6-3.104
Folder Congo Activity Reports 1964 111/125, Box 190, IX-6-3
Folder Congo Office I 1964 111/128, Box 190, IX-6-3
Folder Congo Office II 1964 111/129, Box 190, IX-6-3
Folder Congo Inland Mission 1965 113/120, Box 193, IX-6-3
Folder Congo Office 1965 113/121, Box 193, IX-6-3
Folder 113/121 Congo Office 1965, Box 193, IX-6-03
Folder CPRA 1966 115/124, Box 197, IX-6-3
Folder Congo Office 1966 115/123, Box 197, IX-6-3
Folder Congo (Zaire) 1967-1968 119/59, Box 203, IX-6-3
Folder Congo Activity Reports 1971 127/93, Box 215, IX-6-3
Folder Zaire Office I 1974 138/23, Box 230, IX-6-3
Folder Zaire Office II 1974 138/24, Box 230, IX-6-3
Folder Congo, IX-12 (#3)
Folder Congo MCC 1969-1971, IX-12-6

Mennonite Historical Society. Goshen, Indiana.

Orie Miller Papers
Folder 75/4 Congo Protestant Relief Agency
Folder 75/5a Congo Protestant Relief Agency
Folder 75/5b Congo Protestant Relief Agency
Folder 75/6 Congo Protestant Relief Agency
Folder 75/7 Congo Protestant Relief Agency

National Archives and Record Administration II. College Park, Maryland.

Record Group 59 Department of State Central Policy Files, 1967-1969
Folder 23-9 THE CONGO 1/1/68, Box 2537 POL 23-9 THE CONGO 11/1/67 to POL 23-9 1/1/69
Record Group 286, Records of the US Agency for International Development, USAID Program Files Congo 1961-1967
Folder FPC 2 Disaster Relief Inter-Agency Committee, Disaster Relief Inter-Agency Committee CY 1965 and 1966, Box 1
Folder PFC 2 Title II, Kivu and Kwilu Food and Asst., FY 1964-66, Box 1
Folder FPC 6 VolAgs, Programming CYs 1961, 1962, 1963, 1964 (formerly Title III), Box 1
Folder FPC 2 Kivu and Kwilu Food and Asst. FY 1964-66, Box 1
Folder PRM 7-2 UNDP FY 1967, Box 1
Folder FPC 6 VolAgs Programming CY 1967, Box 3
Folder FPC 6 Congo Protestant Relief Agency FY 1965, Box 4
Folder FPC 6 Congo Protestant Relief Agency FY 1966, Box 4
Folder FPC 6 Congo Protestant Relief Agency (CPRA) FY 1967, Box 4
Folder VolAgs Programming CY 1966 (formerly Title III), Box 4

Presbyterian Historical Society. Philadelphia, PA.

Record Group 8, Church World Service Records
Folder Congo Emergency July 1960, Box 14
Folder Congo Emergency August 1960, Box 14
Folder Congo Emergency, September 1960 -1962, Box 14
Folder Congo Protestant Relief Agency (CPRA) 1960-1963, Box 14
Folder Congo Protestant Relief Agency (CPRA), 1964-1967, Box 14
Folder CPRA Screening Committee, Box 14
Folder CPRA of America, Box 14
Folder Zaire 1965-1966, Box 22 Africa Department
Folder Zaire 1966-1967, Box 22 Africa Department
Folder Zaire 1967-1968, Box 22, Africa Department
Folder Zaire 1969, Box 22, Africa Department
Folder Zaire 1970, Box 22, Africa Department
Folder Zaire 1971, Box 22, Africa Department
Folder Zaire 1971, Box 22, Africa Department
Folder Surveys: Africa, East Africa, Cameroon, Congo, Ethiopia, Box 69
Record Group 454, Carroll Stegall Papers
Rocke Family Papers, Sevierville, Pennsylvania.
Glenn Rocke Papers

United Church of Canada Archives. Toronto, Canada.

UCC Board of World Mission Associate Secretary for Zaire, Accession no. 83.031C
Folder 6 United Church of Canada Board of Overseas Missions, Congo 1961 Corre-
    spondence: Congo Protestant Relief, Box 1
Folder 9 United Church of Canada Board of Overseas Missions Congo 1961 Ormiston
    Reports on Angolan Refugees, Box 1
Folder 16 United Church of Canada Board of World Mission Congo 1962 Reports on
    Angolan Refugee Situation, Box 1
Folder 31 United Church of Canada Board of World Mission Congo 1963 Baptist
    Mission News Notes D. Grenfell, Box 2
Folder 30 Correspondence Stevens, Congo 1963, Board of World Mission, Associate
    Secretary for Zaire, Box 2
Folder 39 Correspondence Stevens Congo 1964, Board of World Mission, Associate
    Secretary for Zaire, Box 2
Folder 40 United Church of Canada Board of World Mission Congo 1964 Baptist
    Mission News Notes D. Grenfell, Box 2
Folder 58 United Church of Canada Board of World Mission, Box 3 Congo 1965 Floyd
    Honey's Visit to Congo, Box 3
Folder 72 United Church of Canada Board of World Mission Congo 1966 Notes:
    Grenfell, BMS, Box 3
Folder 95 Congo 1967 Board of World Mission Rev. D, Grenfell, Box 4
Folder 172 Board of World Mission Congo 1970 CEDECO Constitution, Minutes,
    Papers, Box 5
Folder 173 Board of World Mission Congo 1970 CEDECO Communique, Box 5

Folder 181 Board of World Mission Congo 1970 Correspondence Beveridge, mission-
    ary, Box 6

United Nations High Commission for Refugees Archives. Geneva, Switzerland.

Folder 15/GEN/ANG [1] Angolan Refugees, Box 250, Fonds 11
Folder 15/GEN/ANG [3] Angolan Refugees, F11, S1, Box 250, Fonds 11
Folder 15/GEN/ANG [4] Angolan Refugees, F11, S1, Box 250, Fonds 11
Folder 51 15/78 Situation in the Congo, Box 272, Fonds 11

World Council of Churches Archives. Geneva, Switzerland.

Folder 71/4 ECZ, Box 425.05.028
Folder Congo 1958-1962, Africa Documents Congo 1958-1962, Box 425.3.272
Folder Institut Evangélique Kimpese, Zaire, Box 425.5.030
Folder Congo-K CEDECO 1969, Box 425.5.030
Folder 72/5 Agricultural and Community Centre CEDECO, Kimpese (File 1), Box
    425.5.030
Folder 74/3 PPA ESPI CEDECO, Box 425.5.031
Folder 74/3 Zaire Covered, Box 425.5.031
Folder 74/1 Fonct. du Sec. Général ECZ, Box 435.5.029

Interviews.

All interviews were by telephone except where otherwise noted.

Malcolm McVeigh. Whiting, New Jersey, 12 October 2012.
Ray and Ruth Milhous. 8 January 2016.
Elizabeth Shelly. 13 January 2016.
Arnold Nickel. 18 January 2016.
Clayton Peters. 23 January 2016.
Paul Kunkel. 26 January 2016.
Daniel Riihimaki. 28 January 2016.
Beverly Maxam. 1 February 2016.
Amelia Poole Sudderth. 4 February 2016.
George Fluck. 6 February 2016.
Ritchard Cable. 19 February 2016.
James Stough. 26 February 2016.
Don Kurtz. 10 March 2016.
Karen and William Arkinstall. 18 March 2016.
Carol Berggren. 19 March 2016.
Carol Swarts. 21 March 2016.
Angela Thames. 18 May 2016.
Suzanne and Timothy Lind. 22 July 2016.
Arthur and Peggy Gerdes. 3 November 2016.
Gerald Knight. 16 November 2016.

Abe Suderman. 18 November 2016.
Daniel Beveridge. 1 March 2017.
Merrill Ewert. 13 March 2017.
Alvin Dahl. 17 May 2017.
Dan Beveridge, 18 October 2017
Willard Wornock. 1 December 2017.
Pierre and Fran Maloka. 29 December 2017.
Allen Horst. 13 June 2018.
Lois Smith Markham. 19 June 2018.
James Paton. 14 August 2018.
Patricia Evans. 15 August 2018.
Kenneth Comer. 4 October 2018.
Doyle Hartman. 10 October 2019.
Roy Siebert. 14 October 2019.

Published Works

Adelman, K. "The Church–State Conflict in Zaire, 1969–1974." *African Studies Review* 18:1 (1975), 102–16.

Adelman, K. "The Influence of Religion on National Integration in Zaire." PhD thesis, Georgetown University, 1975.

Arizona Republic. "Obituaries: Dr. Edward B. Payne." 28 January 1976, 14.

Amrith, S. *Decolonizing International Health: India and Southeast Asia, 1930–1965.* New York: Palgrave, 2006.

Association for Diplomatic Studies and Training. "Democratic Republic of the Congo (Zaire) Country Reader." 2018. Available at: adst.org/wp-content/uploads/2018/02/Democratic-Republic-of-the-Congo-Zaire.pdf (Accessed 27 October 2019).

Autesserre, S. *The Trouble with the Congo: Local Violence and the Failure of International Peacebuilding.* New York: Cambridge University Press, 2010.

Baer, F. "SANRU: Lessons Learned (1981–1991)." Unpublished manuscript, 1992. Available at: sanru.org/documents/sanru-lessons-learned.pdf (Accessed 3 March 2020).

Barnett, M. *Empire of Humanity: A History of Humanitarianism.* Ithaca: Cornell University Press, 2011.

Bayart, J.-F. "Les Eglise chrétiennes et la politique du ventre: le partage du gateau ecclesial." *Politique Africaine* 35 (1989), 68–76.

Bearak, M. "Courageous but Not Reckless: The Tragedy of an American U.N. Worker Slain in Congo." *Washington Post.* 29 March 2017. Available at: www.washingtonpost.com/news/worldviews/wp/2017/03/29/courageous-but-not-reckless-the-tragedy-of-an-american-u-n-worker-slain-in-congo/?utm_term=.518c7fc6999d (Accessed 25 October 2019)

Bechtolsheimer, G. "Breakfast with Mobutu: The United States and the Cold War, 1966–1981." PhD thesis, London School of Economics, 2012.

Bertsche, J. *CIM/AIMM: A Story of Vision, Commitment, and Grace.* Elkhart, IN: Fairway Press, 1998.

Bita Lihun Nzunfu, A. *Missions catholiques et protestantes face au colonialisme et aux aspirations du people autotchone à l'autonomie et à l'indépendance politique au Congo Belge (1908–1960)*. Rome: Gregorian Pontifical University, 2013.

Black, M. *A Cause for Our Times: Oxfam – The First Fifty Years*. Oxford: Oxfam, 2012.

Bornstein, E. and P. Redfield (eds) *Forces of Compassion: Humanitarianism Between Ethics and Politics*. Santa Fe: School for Advanced Research Press, 2011.

Borri, M. *Nous…ces affreux*. Paris: Galic, 1962.

Braeckman, C. *Le dinasoure, le Zaïre de Mobutu*. Paris: Fayard, 1992.

Braeckman, E. *Histoire du protestantisme au Congo*. Brussels: Editions de la Librairie des Eclaireurs Unionistes, 1961.

Brinkman, I. *A War for the People: Civilians, Mobility, and Legitimacy in South-east Angola during the MPLA's War for Independence*. Cologne: Rüdiger Köppe Verlag, 2005.

_____. "Refugees on Routes: Congo/Zaire and the War in Northern Angola (1961–1974)," in B. Heintze and A.V. Oppen (eds) *Angola on the Move: Transport Routes, Communications and History*, 198–220. Frankfurt: Verlag Otto Lembeck, 2008.

Brown, S. *Rough Diamond: The Life Story of Bill Gilvear*. Geanies House: Christian Focus, 1997.

Bu, L. and K.C. Yip. *Public Health and National Reconstruction in Post-War Asia: International Influences, Local Transformations*. New York: Routledge, 2015.

Burlingham, K. "In the Image of God: A Global History of the North American Congregational Mission Movement in Angola, 1879–1975." PhD dissertation, University of Rutgers–New Brunswick, 2011.

Burnham, J. "America's Golden Age of Medicine: What Happened to It?" *Science* 215 (1982), 19 March, 1474–9.

_____. *Health Care in America: A History*. 2nd ed. Baltimore: Johns Hopkins University Press, 2015.

Burstin, E. "The Congo." In H.C. Brooks and Y. el-Ayouty, (eds) *An African Dilemma: Refugees South of the Sahara*, 173–190. Westport, CT: Negro Universities Press, 1970.

Bush, P. *Two Kingdoms, Two Loyalties: Mennonite Pacifism in Modern America*. Baltimore: Johns Hopkins University Press, 1998.

Butterfield, S. *US Development Aid – An Historic First*. Westport: Praeger, 2004.

Byam, P. "New Wine in a Very Old Bottle: Canadian Protestant Missionaries as Facilitators of Development in Central Angola, 1886–1961." PhD thesis, University of Ottawa, 1997.

Carlson, E. *Autobiography*. [No place of publication]: Self-published, no date [c. 1996]. Available at www.scribd.com/document/35481577o/Ernest-Carlson-s-Autobiography. (Accessed 28 October 2019)

Carlson Bridges, L. *Monganga Paul: The Congo Ministry and Martyrdom of Paul Carlson, M.D.* New York: Harper and Row, 1966.

Carpenter, G. "Collapse in the Congo: The Price of Paternalism." *Christianity Today* (19 September 1960), 129–32.

Chicago News. "Austin's Globetrotting Doctor Tours Far East." 22 April 1964, 16.

Coquery-Vidrovitch, C. (ed.). *Rébellions-Révolutions au Zaïre, 1963–1965*. 2 vols. Paris: L'Harmattan, 1987.

Crawford, J. *Protestant Missions in Congo, 1878–1969*. Kinshasa: Librarie Evangelique du Congo, 1969.

David, J. "WFP's Immediate Response Account – Saving Lives in the Kasai Region of DRC." *World Food Program Insight*. 8 March 2018. Available at: insight.wfp. org/wfps-immediate-response-account-saving-lives-in-the-kasai-region-of-drc-b029bdb4e5af?_ga=2.200457256.743967345.1559868501-300330291.1559868501 (Accessed 25 October 2019).

Davis, C. *Death in Abeyance: Illness and Therapy Among the Tabwa of Central Africa*. Edinburgh: Edinburgh University Press, 2000.

Dayal, R. *Mission for Hammarskjold: The Congo Crisis*. Princeton: Princeton University Press, 1976.

Deans, W. *Muffled Drumbeats in the Congo*. Chicago: Moody Bible Institute, 1961.

Desgrandchamps, M.-L. "Organising the Unpredictable: The Nigeria–Biafra War and its Impact on the ICRC." *International Review of the Red Cross* 94:888 (2012), 1409–52.

Dijkzeul, D. and C.I. Wakenge. "Doing Good, But Looking Bad? Local Perceptions of Two Humanitarian Organisations in Eastern Democratic Republic of Congo." *Disasters* 34:4 (2010), 1139–70.

Donini, A. *The Golden Fleece: Manipulation and Independence in Humanitarian Action*. Boulder, CO: Kumarian, 2012.

Dow, P. "Accidental Diplomats: The Influence of American Evangelical Missionaries on US Relations with the Congo during the Early Cold War Period." In B. Sewell and M. Ryan (eds) *Foreign Policy at the Periphery: The Shifting Margins of US International Relations since World War II*, 172–205. Lexington: University Press of Kentucky, 2016.

Dunn, K. *Imaging the Congo: The International Relations of Identity*. New York: Palgrave, 2003.

Ekbladh, D. *The Great American Mission: Modernisation and the Construction of an American World Order*. Princeton: Princeton University Press, 2009.

Elkind, J. *Aid Under Fire: Nation Building and the Vietnam War*. Lexington, KY: University Press of Kentucky, 2016.

Engerman, D., N. Gilman, M. Haeffele, and M. Latham (eds) *Staging Growth: Modernisation, Development, and the Global Cold War*. Amherst: University of Massachusetts Press, 2003.

Esler, G. *The United States of Anger: People and the American Dream*. London: Michael Joseph, 1997.

Fabian, J. *Out of Our Minds: Reason and Madness in the Exploration of Central Africa*. Berkeley: University of California Press, 2000.

Ferguson, J. *The Anti-Politics Machine: Development, Depoliticisation, and Bureaucratic Power in Lesotho*. Minneapolis: University of Minnesota Press, 1994.

_____. *Expectations of Modernity: Myths and Meanings of Urban Life on the Zambia Copperbelt*. Berkeley: University of California Press, 1999.

Fass, H. "Congo Miabi Famine." 26 January 1961. Associated Press. Accessible at: www.apimages.com/metadata/Index/Watchf-AP-I-COG-APHSL32122-Congo-Mia-bi-Famine/70dc8cd9fb4041c2bc0046d74728fa72/12/0 (Accessed 27 October 2019).

Fine, J.C. *The Hunger Road*. New York: Atheneum, 1988.

Flauhault, D., J. Geerts, R. Lasserre, and A. Van der Heyden. "Quelques aspects épidé-miologiques et cliniques de l'épidémie de variole à Léopoldville (septembre 1961 – mai 1962)." *Bulletin of the World Health Organisation* 29:1 (1963), 117–125.

Flipse, S. "The Latest Casualty of War: Catholic Relief Services, Humanitarianism, and the War in Vietnam, 1967–1968." *Peace and Change* 27:2 (2002), 245–70.

Fountain, D. *Health For All: The Vanga Story.* Pasadena, CA: William Carey, 2014.

Fountain, P. and L. Meitzner-Yoder. "Quietist Techno-Politics: Agricultural Development and Mennonite Mission in Indonesia." In C. Scheer, P. Fountain, and R.M. Feener. (eds) *The Mission of Development: Religion and Techno-Politics in Asia,* 213–242. Leiden: Brill, 2018.

Fox, R.C. Claire and W. De Craemer. *The Emerging Physician: A Sociological Approach to the Development of a Congolese Medical Professional.* Stanford: Hoover Institution Press, 1968.

Gann, J. *Counterinsurgency in Africa: The Portuguese Way of War, 1961–1974.* Westport: Greenwood, 1997.

Garrard, D. "The Protestant Church in Congo: The Mobutu Years and Their Impact." *Journal of Religion in Africa* 43:2 (2013): 131–66.

Gatrell, P. *Free World?: The Campaign to Save the World's Refugees, 1956–1963.* New York: Cambridge University Press, 2011.

Geissler, P.W. "Parasite Lost: Remembering Modern Times with Kenyan Government Scientists." In P.W. Geissler, and C. Molyeneux (eds) *Evidence, Ethos, and Experiment: The Anthropology and History of Medical Research in Africa,* 297–332. New York: Berghahn, 2011.

Gerard, E. and B. Kuklick. *Death in the Congo: Murdering Patrice Lumumba.* Cambridge, MA: Harvard University Press, 2015.

Gérard-Libois, J. *The Katangese Secession.* Madison: University of Wisconsin Press, 1966.

Gibbs, D. *The Political Economy of Third World Intervention: Mines, Money, and US Policy in the Congo Crisis.* Chicago: University of Chicago Press, 1991.

Gildea, R. "Congo's Operation Doctor." *World Outlook* (September 1962), 1–3.

Giles-Vernick, T., G. Lachenal, C.D. Gondola, and W. Schneider. "Social History, Biology, and the Emergence of HIV in Colonial Africa." *Journal of African History* 54:1 (2013), 11–30.

Giles-Vernick, T. and J. Webb, Jr. (eds) *Global Health in Africa.* Athens, OH: Ohio University Press, 2013.

Gilman, N. *Mandarins of the Future: Modernisation Theory in Cold War America.* Baltimore: Johns Hopkins University Press, 2007.

Gill, J. *Embattled Ecumenism: The National Conference of Christian Churches, the Vietnam War, and the Trials of the Protestant Left.* DeKalb, IL: Northern Illinois University Press, 2011.

Glasman, J. "Seeing Like a Refugee Agency: A Short History of UNHCR Classifications in Central Africa (1961–2015)." *Journal of Refugee Studies* 30:2 (2017), 337–62.

Gleijeses, P. "Flee! The White Giants Are Coming!: The United States, the Mercenaries, and the Congo, 1964–65." *Diplomatic History* 18:2 (1994), 207–37.

____. *Conflicting Missions: Havana, Washington, and Africa, 1959–1976.* Chapel Hill: University of North Carolina Press, 2002.

Gondola, C.D. *Tropical Cowboys: Westerns, Violence, and Masculinity in Kinshasa.* Bloomington: Indiana University Press, 2015.

Grenfell, J. "Refugees in the Republic of Zaire (Congo-Kinshasa)." In L. Holborn, (ed.), *Refugees: A Problem of Our Time – The Work of the United Nations High Commissioner for Refugees. Vol. 2*, 1045–115. Metuchen, NJ: Scarecrow Press, 1975.

Grubbs, L. *Secular Missionaries: American and African Development in the 1960s.* Amherst: University of Massachusetts, 2009.

Guyer, J., and S.E. Belinga. "Wealth in People as Wealth in Knowledge: Accumulation and Composition in Equatorial Africa." *Journal of African History* 36:1 (1995), 91–120.

Halvorson, B. *Conversionary Sites: Transforming Medical and Global Christianity from Madagascar to Minnesota.* University Park: Pennsylvania State University Press, 2018.

Hasian Jr., M. *Communicating During Humanitarian Medical Crises: The Consequences of Silence or "Témoignage".* Lanham, MD: Lexington, 2019.

Haug, H. (ed.) *Humanity for All: The International Red Cross and Red Crescent Movement.* Berne: Paul Haupt Publishers, 1993.

Hayes, M. *Captive of the Simbas.* New York: Harper and Row, 1966.

Heins, V., K. Koddenbrock, and C. Unrau (eds). *Humanitarianism and Challenges of Cooperation.* New York: Routledge, 2016.

Hess, G. "Waging the Cold War in the Third World: The Foundations and the Challenges of Development." In L. Friedman, and M. McGarvie, (eds) *Charity, Philanthropy, and Civility in American History*, 319–340. New York: Cambridge University Press, 2003.

Heimer, F.–W. *Decolonisation Conflict in Angola, 1974–1976.* Geneva: Institut Universitaires de Hautes Études Internationales, 1979.

Higgins, R. *United Nations Peacekeeping, 1946–1967: Documents and Commentary. Vol. 3.* Oxford: Oxford University Press, 1980.

Hoare, M. *Congo Mercenary.* New York: Bantam, 1967.

Hoffman, E.C. *All You Need Is Love: The Peace Corps and the Spirit of the 1960s.* Cambridge, MA: Harvard University Press, 2000.

Hollinger, D. *After Cloven Tongues of Fire: Protestant Liberalism in Modern American History.* Princeton: Princeton University Press, 2013.

____. *Protestants Abroad: How Missionaries Tried to Change the World but Changed America.* Princeton: Princeton University Press, 2017.

Hollinger-Janzen, R., N. Myers, and J. Bertsche (eds) *The Jesus Tribe: Grace Stories from Congo's Mennonites 1912–2012: A Project of Africa Inter-Mennonite Mission.* Elkhart: Institute of Mennonite Studies, 2012.

Honorin, M. *La fin des mercenaires: Bukavu, novembre 1967.* Paris: Robert Laffont, 1968.

Hooper, E. *The River: A Journey to the Source of HIV and AIDS.* Boston: Little, Brown, and Company, 1999.

Horne, G. *Paul Robeson: The Artist as Revolutionary.* London: Pluto, 2016.

House, A. *The U.N. in the Congo: The Political and Civilian Efforts.* Washington, DC: University Press of America, 1978.

Houser, G. *No One Can Stop The Rain: Glimpses of Africa's Liberation Struggle.* New York: Pilgrim Press, 1989.

Hoyt, M. *Captive in the Congo: A Consul's Return to the Heart of Darkness*. Annapolis, MD: Naval Institute Press, 2000.

Hudson, A. *Congo Unravelled: Military Operations from Independence to the Mercenary Revolt, 1960–1968*. Solihull, UK: Helion, 2012.

Hunt, N.R. *A Colonial Lexicon: Of Birth Ritual, Medicalisation, and Mobility in the Congo*. Durham, NC: Duke University Press, 1999.

_____. *A Nervous State: Violence, Remedies, and Reverie in Colonial Congo*. Durham, NC: Duke University Press, 2016.

Immerwahr, D. *Thinking Small: The United States and the Lure of Community Development*. Cambridge, MA: Harvard University Press, 2015.

Indianapolis Star. "Congo's Medical Needs Topic of 'Operation Doctor' Meeting." *Indianapolis Star*, 9 May 1970, 12.

International Committee of the Red Cross. *SOS Congo*. 1960. Available at avarchives. icrc.org/Film/5534 (Accessed 27 October 2019).

Jansen, B. "The Humanitatian Protectorate of South Sudan? Understanding Insecruity for Humanitarians in a Political Economy of Aid." *Journal of Modern African Studies* 55:3 (2017), 349–70.

Janzen, J. and W. Arkinstall. *The Quest for Therapy: Medical Pluralism in Local Zaire*. Berkeley: University of California Press, 1978.

Janzen, J. and L. Graber. *Crossing the Loange*. Newton, KS: Mennonite Press, 2015.

Jenkins, K. "The Christian Church as an NGO in Africa: Supporting Post-Independence Era State Legitimacy or Promoting Change?" In E. Sandburg (ed.) *The Changing Politics of Non-Governmental Organisations and African States*, 82–99. Westport, CT: Praeger, 1994.

Jennings, M. *Surrogates of the State: NGOs, Development and Ujamaa in Tanzania*. Bloomfield, CT: Kumarian Press, 2008.

Jet. "Travelogue." 8 January 1959, 40.

Jewsiewicki, B. "The Formation of the Political Culture of Ethnicity in the Belgian Congo, 1920–1959." In L. Vail, (ed.), *The Creation of Tribalism in Southern Africa*, 320–49. Berkeley: University of California Press, 1991.

Johnson, J. *The Battle for Algeria: Sovereignty, Health Care, and Humanitarianism*. Philadelphia: University of Pennsylvania Press, 2015.

Johnson, T. and M. Larson. *When Congo Bursts at Its Seams*. Chicago: Moody Bible Institute, 1961.

Juengst, D. "Cultural Dynamics at Luebo: An Ethnography of Religious Agents of Change in Zaire." PhD thesis, University of Florida, 1975.

Kabemba, C. "The Democratic Republic of Congo: The Land of Humanitarian Interventions." In B. Everill and J. Kaplan, (eds) *The History and Practice of Humanitarian Intervention and Aid in Africa*, 140–57. New York: Palgrave Macmillan, 2013.

Kabongo Malu, E. *Épurations ethniques en RD Congo (1991–1995): La question Luba-Kasaï*. Paris: L'Harmattan, 1995.

Kabongo-Mbaya, P. *L'Église du Christ au Zaïre: Formation et adaptation d'un protestantisme en situation de dictature*. Paris: Karthala, 1992.

Kalanda, M. *Baluba et Lulua, une ethnie à la recherche d'un nouvel équilibre*. Brussels: Remarques Congolaises, 1959.

Kalb, M. *The Congo Cables: The Cold War in Africa from Eisenhower to Kennedy.* New York: MacMillan, 1982.

Kalema, E. "Violence and Memory: The Mulele 'Rebellion' in Post-Colonial D.R. Congo." PhD thesis, University of the Witwatersrand, 2017.

Kalonji, A. *Congo 1960: La secession du sud-Kasaï. La verité du Mulopwe.* Paris: L'Harmattan, 2005.

Kalt, M. *Tiermondismus in der Schweiz der 1960er und 1970er Jahre.* New York: Peter Lang, 2010.

Kasongo, M. *History of the Methodist Church in the Central Congo.* Lanham, MD: University Press of America, 1998.

Kauffman, C. "Politics, Programs, and Protests: Catholic Relief Services in Vietnam, 1954–1975." *Catholic Historical Review* 91:2 (2005), 223–50.

Keidel, L. *War to Be One.* Grand Rapids, MI: Zondervan, 1977.

Keith, J. *The First Wars Are The Worst.* Mississauga, ON: Canadian Baptist Ministries, 1998.

Kelly, S. *America's Tyrant: The CIA and Mobutu of Zaire.* Lanham, MD: University Press of America, 1993.

Kennedy, P. *Black Livingstone: A True Tale of Adventure in the Nineteenth-Century Congo.* New York: Viking, 2002.

Kennes, E. and M. Larmer, *The Katangese Gendarmes and War in Central Africa: Fighting Their Way Home.* Bloomington, IN: Indiana University Press, 2016.

Kent, J. *America, the UN, and Decolonisation: Cold War Conflict in the Congo.* New York: Routledge, 2010.

Kestergat, J. *Congo Congo.* Paris: Table Ronde, 1965.

Kingsolver, B. *The Poisonwood Bible.* New York: HarperCollins, 1998.

Kingsolver, W. "The Congo." *YouTube,* 18 February 2018. Accessible at: www.youtube.com/watch?v=aisg6ABcP7U (Accessed 28 October 2019).

Kirkwood, D. *Mission in Mid-Continent, Zaire: One Hundred Years of American Baptist Commitment in Zaire, 1884–1984.* Valley Forge, PA: International Ministries ABC/USA, 1984.

Kivits, M. "Hygiene et santé publique." In *Livre blanc: Apport scientifique de la Belgique au développement de l'Afrique.* Vol. 2, 899–916. Brussels: Academie Royale des Sciences d'Outre-mer, 1963.

Klose, F. *Human Rights in the Shadow of Colonial Violence. The Wars of Independence in Kenya and Algeria.* Translated by D. Geyer. Philadelphia: University of Pennsylvania Press, 2012.

Knight, A. *Memoirs.* [No place of publication]: self-published, 2002.

Koddenbrock, K. *The Practice of Humanitarian Intervention: Aid Workers and Institutions in the Democratic Republic of Congo.* New York: Routledge, 2016.

Kotz, N. *Judgement Days: Lyndon Baines Johnson, Martin Luther King Jr., and the Laws that Changed America.* New York: Houghton Mifflin, 2005.

Kreider, R. and R.W. Goossen. *Hungry, Thirsty, A Stranger: The MCC Experience.* Scottsdale, PA: Herald Press, 1988.

Kroeker, P. "Change and Continuity as Illustrated in the Introduction of Cattle in Zaire." PhD thesis, University of Kansas, 1978.

Kumin, J. "Orderly Departure from Vietnam: Cold War Anomaly or Humanitarian Innovation?" *Refugee Survey Quarterly* 27:1 (2008), 104–17.

Lagergren, D. *Mission and State in the Congo: A Study of the Relations between Protestant Missions and the Congo Independent State Authorities with Special Reference to the Equator District 1885–1903*. Uppsala: Studia Missionalia Upsaliensia, 1970.

Lal., P. "Decolonisation and the Gendered Politics of Developmental Labor in Southeastern Africa." In S. Macekura and E. Manela (eds) *The Development Century: A Global History*, 173–94. New York: Cambridge University Press, 2018.

Lantzer, J. *Mainline Christianity: The Past and Future of America's Majority Faith*. New York: New York University Press, 2012.

Lancaster, C. *Aid to Africa: So Little Done*. Chicago: University of Chicago Press, 1999.

Lanza, N. "Le Comité international de la Croix-Rouge et le soulèvement des Mau-Mau au Kenya, 1952–1959." *Relations Internationales* 133:1 (2008), 91–110.

Latham, M. *The Right Kind of Revolution: Modernisation, Development, and U.S. Foreign Policy From the Cold War to the Present*. Ithaca: Cornell University Press, 2011.

Leaman, D. "Politicized Service and Teamwork Tensions: Mennonite Central Committee in Vietnam, 1966–1969." *Mennonite Quarterly Review* 71 (1997), 544–70.

Lefever, E. *Uncertain Mandate: Politics of the U.N. Congo Operation*. Baltimore: Johns Hopkins University Press, 1967.

Lemarchand, R. *Political Awakening in the Congo: The Politics of Fragmentation*. Berkeley: University of California Press, 1964.

Libata, M.-B. "Regroupement des Balubas et ses conséquences géopolitiques dans la périphérie de Luluabourg (1891–1960)." *Annales Aequatoria* 8 (1987), 99–129.

Life. "Harvest of Anarchy in the Congo." 17 February 1961, 22–7.

Liselele, H., M. Boulvain, K. Tshibangu, and S. Meuris. "Maternal Height and External Pelvimetry to Predict Cephalopelvic Disproportion in Nulliparous African Women: A Cohort Study." *British Journal of Gynecology* 107:8 (2000), 947–52.

Lodge, H.C. "Telegram from the Mission at the United Nations to the Department of State." 26 August 1960." *Foreign Relations of the United States, 1958–1960*. Vol. XIV Africa, 444–6.

Loffman, R. "An Obscured Revolution? USAID, the North Shaba Project, and the Zaïrian Administration, 1976–1986." *Canadian Journal of African Studies* 48:3 (2014), 425–44.

———. "Belgian Rule and its Afterlives: Colonialism, Developmentalism, and Mobutism in the Tanganyika District, Southeastern DR-Congo, 1885–1985." *International Labor and Working Class History* 92 (2017), 47–68.

Los Angeles Times. "5-Ton Food Shipment to Starving Congo." 21 February 1961, 8.

Los Angeles Times. "Rebels Looted Hospital, Congo Doctor Reports." 25 November 1964, 10.

Lowenstein, F. "An Epidemic of Kwashiorkor in the South Kasai, Congo." *Bulletin of the World Health Organisation* 27:6 (1962), 751–8.

Luadia-Luadia, N. "Les Luluwa et le commerce Luso-Africain (1870–1895)." *Etudes d'histoire africaine* 7 (1974), 55–104.

Lushiku Lumana, M.B. *Les Baluba du Kasaï et la crise congolaise (1959–1965)*. Lubumbashi: [no publisher], 1985.

Lyons, M. "Public Health in Colonial Africa: The Belgian Congo." In D. Porter (ed.) *The History of Public Health and the Modern State*, 356–84. Amsterdam: Rodopi, 1994.

Mahoney, R. *JFK: Ordeal in Africa*. New York: Oxford University Press, 1983.

Mabeko Tali, J.-M. *Dissidências e poder de estado: O MPLA perante si próprio (1962–1977)*. 2 vols. Luanda: Editorial Nzila, 2001.

Makiobo, C. *Eglise catholique et mutations socio-politiques au Congo-Zaïre: La contestation du régime Mobutu*. Paris: L'Harmattan, 2004.

Makumunwa Kiantandu, M. "A Study of the Contribution of American Presbyterians to the Formation of the Church of Christ in Zaire, with Special Reference to Indigenisation, 1891–1960." ThD thesis, Union Theological Seminary in Virginia, 1978.

Malkki, L. *The Need to Help: The Domestic Arts of International Humanitarianism*. Durham, NC: Duke University Press, 2015.

Manji, F. and O'Coill, C. "The Missionary Position: NGOs and Development in Africa." *International Affairs* 78:3 (2002), 567–83.

Mann, G. *Native Sons: West African Veterans and France in the Twentieth Century*. Durham, NC: Duke University Press, 2006.

____. *From Empires to NGOs in the West African Sahel: The Road to Nongovernmentality*. New York: Cambridge University Press, 2015.

Marcum, J. *The Angolan Revolution. Volume II: Exile Politics and Guerilla Warfare, 1962–1976*. Cambridge, MA: Massachusetts Institute of Technology Press, 1978.

Markowitz, M. *Cross and Sword: The Political Role of Christian Missions in the Belgian Congo, 1908–1960*. Stanford: Hoover Institution Press, 1973.

Marriage, Z. *Not Breaking the Rules, Not Playing the Game: International Assistance to Countries at War*. London: Hurst, 2006.

Martens, D. "A History of European Penetration and African Reaction in the Kasai Region of Zaire, 1880–1908." PhD thesis, Simon Fraser University, 1980.

Mathys, G. "Bringing History Back In: Past, Present, and Conflict in Rwanda and the Democratic Republic of Congo." *Journal of African History* 58:3 (2017), 465–87.

Mbikay, M. *Entre le rêve et le souvenir*. Bloomington, IN: Lulu, 2013.

McAlister, M. "The Body in Crisis: Congo and the Transformations of Evangelical Internationalism, 1960–1965." In A. Preston and D. Rossinow (eds) *Outside In: The Transnational Circuitry of US History*, 123–52. New York: Oxford University Press, 2016.

____. *Kingdom of God Has No Borders: A Global History of American Evangelicals*. New York: Oxford University Press, 2018.

McCleary, R. *Global Compassion: Private Voluntary Organisations and U.S, Foreign Policy since 1939*. New York: Oxford University Press, 2009.

McVety, A. *Enlightened Aid: U.S. Development as Foreign Policy in Ethiopia*. New York: Oxford University Press, 2012.

Meier, L. *Swiss Science, African Decolonisation and the Rise of Global Health*. Basel: Schwabe Verlag, 2014.

Mertz, R. "Congo Doctor." *Tampa Bay Times* (3 December 1961), 119–20.

Monnier, X. "Au Congo-Kinshasa, la guerre des visas aura bien lieu." *Le Monde*, 8 July 2016. Available at: www.lemonde.fr/afrique/article/2016/07/08/au-congo-kinshasa-la-guerre-des-visas-aura-bien-lieu_4966630_3212.html (Accessed 25 October 2019).

Morrow, R. "Local Doctor Never Met Carson – But Knew Him." *Dayton Daily News*, 29 November 1964, 23.

Moses, A. and L. Heerten (eds) *Postcolonial Conflict and the Question of Genocide: The Nigeria–Biafra War, 1967–1970*. New York: Routledge, 2017.

Mosse, D. *Cultivating Development: An Ethnography of Aid Policy and Practice*. London: Pluto, 2005.

Mountz, W. "Americanizing Africanisation: The Congo Crisis, 1960–1967." PhD thesis, University of Missouri, 2014.

Moyo, D. *Dead Aid: Why Aid is Not Working and How There is a Better Way for Africa*. New York: Farrar, Straus and Giroux, 2009.

Mpanya, M. "The Decision to Adopt or Reject New Technologies: A Case Study of Agricultural Development Projects in Zaire." Working Paper 51, Helen Kellogg Institute for International Studies, University of Notre Dame, 1985.

Muehlenbeck, P. *Betting on the Africans: John F. Kennedy's Courting of African Nationalist Leaders*. New York: Oxford University Press, 2012.

Mukanya Kaninda-Muana, J.-B. *Eglise catholique et pouvoir au Congo-Zaïre: Enjeux, options et négociations du changement social à Kinshasa, 1945–1997*. Paris: L'Harmattan, 2007.

Mulago, V. "Christianisme et culture: apport africain à la théologie." In G. Baeta (ed.) *Christianity in Tropical Africa*, 308–32. Oxford: Oxford University Press, 1968.

Munongo, B. "Aspects du protestantisme dans le Congo-Zaïre indépendant (1960–1990)." PhD thesis, Université de Lille III, 2000.

Mwamba Mputu, B. *Le Congo-Kasai (1865–1950): De l'exploration allemande à la consécration de Luluabourg*. Paris: L'Harmattan, 2011.

Namikas, L. *Battleground Africa: Cold War in the Congo, 1960–1965*. Stanford: Stanford University Press, 2013.

Ndaliko, C.R. *Necessary Noise: Music, Film, and Charitable Imperialism in the East of Congo*. New York: Oxford University Press, 2016.

Ndaywel é Nziem, I. *Histoire Générale du Congo: De l'héritage ancient à la République Démocratique*. Brussels: De Boeck et Larcier, 1998.

Nelson, J. *Christian Missionizing and Social Transformation: A History of Conflict and Change in Eastern Zaire*. New York: Praeger, 1992.

Nelson, R. *Congo Crisis and Christian Mission*. St. Louis, MO: Bethany Press, 1961.

Ngomo Okitembo, L. *L'engagement politique de l'Eglise catholique au Zaïre, 1960–1992*. Paris: L'Harmattan, 1998.

Nichols, J. *The Uneasy Alliance: Religion, Refugee Work, and US Foreign Policy*. New York: Oxford University Press, 1988.

Nzongola-Ntalaja, G. *Patrice Lumumba*. Athens, OH: Ohio University Press, 2014.

O'Brien, C.C. *To Katanga and Back: A UN Case History*. London: Hutchinson and Co, 1962.

Oko Omaka, A. *The Biafran Humanitarian Crisis: International Human Rights and Joint Church Aid*. Lanham, MD: Rowman and Littlefield, 2016.

Oldberg, N. "A History of the Zaire Mission of the Evangelical Free Church, 1922–1975." MA thesis, Trinity Evangelical Divinity School, 1977.

Omasombo Tshonda, J. (ed.) *Kasaï-Oriental. Un noeud gordien dans l'espace congolais*. Tervuren: Musée Royal de l'Afrique Centrale, 2014.

Onoma, A.K. *Anti-Refugee Violence and African Politics*. New York: Cambridge University Press, 2013.

Operation Agri Outreach Abroad. "Gordon Ian Pitkethly 1930–2013 Agricultural Missionary, a Tribute." No. 1 (2014), 8, Accessible at: www.operationagri.org.uk/wpcontent/uploads/2016/09/Outreach_Abroad_2014_01.pdf (Accessed 26 October 2019).

Packham, E. *Freedom or Anarchy?* Happauge, NY: Nova Science, 1996.

Parker, E. "The Congo: Another China?" *Christian Century*. 2 September 1960, 1081–84.

Paulmann, J. "Conjectures in the History of International Humanitarian Aid during the Twentieth Century." *Humanity* 4:2 (2014). Available at: humanityjournal.org/issue4-2/conjunctures-in-the-history-of-international-humanitarian-aid-during-the-twentieth-century/ (Accessed 25 October 2019)

Pavlakis, D. *British Humanitarianism and the Congo Reform Movement, 1896–1913*. New York: Routledge, 2015.

Pearson, J.L. *The Colonial Politics of Global Health: France and the United Nations in Postwar Africa*. Cambridge, MA: Harvard University Press, 2018.

Peemans, J.P. "Accumulation and Underdevelopment in Zaire: General Aspects in Relation to the Evolution of the Agrarian Crisis." In G. Nzongola-Ntalaja (ed.) *The Crisis in Zaire: Myths and Realities*, 67–84. Trenton, NJ: Africa World Press, 1986.

Pépin, J. *The Origins of AIDS*. New York: Cambridge University Press, 2011.

Perret, F. and F. Bugnion. *De Budapest à Saigon: Histoire du Comité international de la Croix-Rouge 1956–1965*. Geneva: Georg, 2009.

Plummer, B.G. *In Search of Power: African Americans in the Age of Decolonisation, 1956–1974*. New York: Cambridge University Press, 2013.

Poppen, A.V. *Terms of Trade and Trust: the History and Contexts of Pre-Colonial Market Production around the Upper Zambezi and Kasai*. Hamburg: LIT, 1993.

Pottier, J. "Roadblock Ethnography: Negotiating Humanitarian Access in Ituri, Eastern DR Congo, 1999–2004." *Africa* 76:2 (2006), 151–79.

Pingle, Y. "Humanitarianism, Race and Denial: The International Committee of the Red Cross and Kenya's Mau Mau Rebellion, 1952–1960." *History Workshop Journal* 84 (2017), 89–107.

Rangil, T. "The UN and Economic Policy Design and Implementation during the Congo Crisis, 1960–1964." Unpublished paper presented at the Work Bank Workshop, Using History to Inform Development Policy: The Role of Archives, October 2012.

Redekop, C. *The Pax Story: Service in the Name of Christ, 1951–1976*. Telford, PA: Pandora Press, 2001.

Reed, D. *111 Days in Stanleyville*. London: Collins, 1966.

Reid, A. *Congo Drumbeat: History of the First Half Century in the Establishment of the Methodist Church among the Atetela of Central Congo*. New York: World Outlook Press, 1964.

——. *The Roots of Lomomba: Mongo Land*. Hicksville, NY: Exposition Press, 1979.

Rich., J. "A Mennonite Development Project Betwixt Ambition and Confusion in the Democratic Republic of Congo." Unpublished presentation at the Global Anabaptism Workshop, Goshen College, June 2017.

_____. "Manufacturing Sovereignty and Manipulating Humanitarianism: The Diplomatic Resolution of the Congolese Mercenary Crisis, 1967–1968." *Journal of African History* 60:2 (2019), 277–96.

Ridolf von Rohr, S. "L'intervention du CICE au Congo au lendemain de l'indépendance (1 juillet 1960 – 30 juin 1961)." Mémoire de licence, Université de Genève, 2006.

Riley, B. *The Political History of American Food Aid: An Uneasy Benevolence*. New York: Oxford University Press, 2017.

Roberts, J. *My Congo Adventure*. London: Jarrods, 1963.

Rogers, J. "Ye Are All One: Missionaries in the Congo and the Dynamics of Race and Gender, 1890–1925." PhD thesis, Ohio Union Institute and University, 2006.

Rosenthal, J. "From 'Migrants' to 'Refugees': Identity, Aid, and Decolonisation in Ngara District, Tanzania." *Journal of African History* 56:2 (2015), 261–79.

Rule III, W. *Milestones in Mission*. Franklin, TN: Providence House, 1998.

Ruttan, V. *United States Development Assistance Policy: The Domestic Politics of Foreign Economic Aid*. Baltimore: Johns Hopkins University Press, 1996.

Schaffert, H. "Report." *Congo Mission News* 210 (October–December 1965), 26.

_____. "Pastor Schaffert Reports." *Congo Mission News* 211 (January – March 1966), 5–7, 19, 25–27.

Schmidl, E. *Blau Helme – Rotes Kreuz: Das österreichische UN-Sanitätskontingent im Kongo, 1960–1963*. Vienna: Studien Verlag, 1995.

Schmitz, D. *The United States and Right-Wing Dictatorships, 1965–1989*. New York: Cambridge University Press, 2006.

Scott, J. *Seeing Like a State: How Certain Schemes to Improve the Human Condition Have Failed*. New Haven: Yale University Press, 1998.

Seay, L. "Authority at Twilight: Civil Society, Social Services, and the State in the Eastern Democratic Republic of Congo." PhD thesis, University of Texas – Austin, 2009.

Settje, D. *Faith and War: How Christians Debated the Cold and Vietnam Wars*. New York: New York University Press, 2011.

Shaloff, S. *Reform in Leopold's Congo*. Richmond, VA: John Knox Press, 1970.

Sjøveian, S. "Gynecological Fistula in the DR Congo." MS thesis, University of Oslo, 2009.

Soderland, W., E.D. Briggs, T.P. Najem, and B. Roberts. *Africa's Deadliest Conflict: Media Coverage of the Humanitarian Disaster in the Congo and the United Nations Response 1997–2008*. Waterloo, ON: Wilfred Laurier University Press, 2012.

Spooner, K. *Canada, The Congo Crisis, and UN Peacekeeping, 1960–1964*. Vancouver: University of British Columbia Press, 2010.

Stanley, B. *The History of the Baptist Missionary Society 1792–1992*. Edinburgh: T. and T. Clark, 1992.

Stanley, R. *Food For Peace: Hope and Reality of U.S. Food Aid*. New York: Gordon and Breach, 1973.

Staunton, E. "The Case of Biafra: Ireland and the Nigerian Civil War." *Irish Historical Studies* 31:124 (1999), 513–35.

Stenning, R. *Church World Service: Fifty Years of Help and Hope*. New York: Friendship Press, 1996.

Street, A. *Biomedicine in an Unstable Place: Infrastructure and Personhood in a Papua New Guinean Hospital.* University Park: Pennsylvania State University Press, 2014.

Tague, J. "American Humanitarianism and Portugal's African Empire: Institutional and Governmental Interests in Assisting Angolan Refugees in Congo, 1961–1974." *Portuguese Journal of Social Science* 14:3 (2015), 343–59.

_____. *Displaced Mozambicans in Postcolonial Tanzania: Refugee Power, Mobility, Education, and Rural Development.* New York: Routledge, 2019.

Taithe, B. "Humanitarian History?" In R. Mac Ginty and J. Peterson, J. (eds) *The Routledge Companion to Humanitarian Action*, 62–73. New York: Routledge, 2015.

Tappan, J. *The Riddle of Malnutrition: The Long Arc of Biomedical and Public Health Interventions in Uganda* (Athens, OH: Ohio University Press, 2017.

Thompson, A. "Humanitarian Principles Put to the Test: Challenges to Humanitarian Action during Decolonisation." *International Review of the Red Cross* 97 (2016), 45–76.

Tomes, N. *Remaking the American Patient: How Madison Avenue and Modern Medicine Turned Patients into Consumers.* Chapel Hill, NC: University of North Carolina Press, 2016.

Trefon, T. *Congo Masquerade: The Political Culture of Aid Inefficiency and Reform Failure.* London: Zed, 2011.

Trouillot, M.-R. *Silencing the Past: Power and the Production of History.* Boston: Beacon Press, 1995.

Truby, D. *Regime of Gentlemen: Personal Experiences of Congolese Christians During the 1964 Rebellion.* London: Marshall, Morgan, and Scott, 1971.

Tullberg, A. "We are in the Congo Now: Sweden and the Trinity of Peacekeeping during the Congo Crisis 1960–1964." PhD thesis, Lund University, 2012.

Turner, T. and C. Young. *The Rise and Decline of the Zairian State.* Madison, WI: University of Wisconsin Press, 1985.

Tuttle, D. *A Tribute to Glen and Jeannette Tuttle: Medical Missionaries to the Congo.* Bloomington, IN: Xlibris, 2009.

United States Government. Department of Health, Education, and Welfare, Office of International Health, Division of Program Analysis. *Syncrisis: The Dynamics of Health: An Analytic Series on the Interactions of Health and Socioeconomic Development. Vol. XIV Zaire.* Washington, DC, 1975.

United States Government. Peace Corps. Office of Program Development. "An Assessment of the Potential for Peace Corps – USAID – Host Country Cooperation in Social Forestry Projects Zaire." By Frederick Conway and James Fickes. March 1981. Available at: pdf.usaid.gov/pdf_docs/PNAAS202.pdf (Accessed 25 October 2019).

United States Government. Department of State. "348. Memorandum of Conversation." 24 October 1962. *Foreign Relations of the United States. Volume XIII, Western Europe and Canada, 1961–1963*, 946–52.

Van Reybrouck, D. *Congo: The Epic History of A People.* Translated by S. Garrett. New York: HarperCollins, 2014.

Vanderstraeten, L. *Histoire d'une mutinerie: De la Force Publique à l'Armée nationale congolaise.* Brussels: Academie Royale de Belgique, 1993.

Vandewalle, F. *L'Ommegang: Odysée et reconquête de Stanleyville 1964*. Brussels: Le Livre Africain, 1970.

Verhaegen, B. *Rébellions au Congo*. 2 vols. Brussels: CRISP, 1969.

_____. "Les safaris technologiques au Zaïre, 1970–1980." *Politique Africaine* 18 (1985), 71–87.

_____. (ed.) *Mulele et la revolution populaire au Kwilu (République Démocratique du Congo*. Paris: L'Harmattan, 2006.

Villafaña, F. *Cold War in the Congo: The Confrontation of Cuban Military Forces, 1960–1967*. New Brunswick, NJ: Transaction, 2009.

Vinckel, S. "Violence and Everyday Interactions between Katangese and Kasaians: Memory and Elections in Two Katangese Cities." *Africa* 85:1 (2015), 78–102.

Wagner, M. and M. Meisels. *The Righteous of Switzerland: Heroes of the Holocaust*. Jersey City: Ktav, 2000.

Watenpaugh, K.D. *Bread From Stones: The Middle East and the Making of Modern Humanitarianism*. Berkeley: University of California Press, 2015.

Waters, K. "Influencing the Message: The Role of Catholic Missionaries in Media Coverage of the Nigerian Civil War." Catholic Historical Review 90:4 (2004), 697–718.

Weissman, S. *American Foreign Policy in the Congo, 1960–1964*. Ithaca: Cornell University Press, 1974.

Westad, O.A. *The Global Cold War: Third World Interventions and the Making of Our Times*. New York: Cambridge University Press, 2005.

White, B. *Rumba Rules: The Politics of Dance Music in Mobutu's Zaire*. Durham, NC: Duke University Press, 2008.

Wild-Wood, E. *Migration and Christian Identity in Congo (DRC)*. Leiden: Brill, 2008.

Williams, P. "The Disciples of Christ Congo Mission (DCCM), 1897–1932: A Missionary Community in Colonial Central Africa." PhD thesis, University of Chicago Divinity School, 2000.

Wiles, V.M. "Medical Mission to Mississippi." *Freedomways* 5 (1965), 314–17.

Williams, S. *Who Killed Hammarskjöld? The UN, the Cold War, and White Supremacy in Africa*. New York: Oxford University Press, 2011.

Willaume, J.C. *Zaïre, L'épopée d'Inga: Chronique d'une predation industrielle*. Paris: L'Harmattan, 1986.

Witte, L.D. "The Suppression of the Congo Rebellions and the Rise of Mobutu, 1963–5." *International History Review* 39:1 (2016), 107–125.

Witte, L.D. *The Murder of Lumumba*. London: Verso, 2001.

Wrong, M. *In The Footsteps of Mr. Kurtz: Living on the Brink of Disaster in Mobutu's Congo*. New York: HarperCollins, 2001.

Wylie, D. *Starving on a Full Stomach: Hunger and the Triumph of Cultural Racism in South Africa*. Charlottesville: University of Virginia Press, 2001.

Yarom, R. and J. McFie. "Kwashiorkor in the Congo (A Clinical Survey of a Hundred Successive Cases in the Congo." *Journal of Tropical Pediatrics and African Child Health* 9:2 (1963), 56–63.

Youmans, R. *When Bull Elephants Collide: An American Surgeon's Chronicle of Congo*. Tarentum, PA: Word Association Publishers, 2006.

Young, C. "The Zairian Crisis and American Foreign Policy." In G. Bender, J. Coleman, and R. Sklar (eds) *African Crisis Areas and U.S. Foreign Policy*, 209–24. Berkeley: University of California Press, 1985.

Young, C. *Politics in the Congo*. Princeton: Princeton University Press, 1965.

Zeilig, L. *Lumumba: Africa's Lost Leader*. London: Haus, 2015.

Zimmerman, R. *Dollars, Diplomacy, and Dependency: Dilemmas of US Economic Aid*. Boulder: Lynne Rienner, 1993.

Index

255